Farming Practice in British Prehistory

Farming Practice in British Prehistory

EDITED BY ROGER MERCER

Edinburgh
UNIVERSITY PRESS

22 George Square, Edinburgh

First published 1981
This edition 1984

Printed in Great Britain by
Kingprint Ltd, Richmond

British Library Cataloguing
in Publication Data
Farming practice in British prehistory
1. Agriculture—Great Britain—
Origin—Congresses
I. Mercer, Roger
630'.9361 GN805

ISBN 0 85224 501 7

Grateful acknowledgment is made to
Peter Reynolds for kind permission to use,
on the cover, the photograph of
emmer at harvest

Contents

Preface p.vii

Introduction by Roger Mercer p.ix

British Farming Today: a Bird's-Eye View 1
Michael J. Nash

Part One: The Landscape and Crops

Wildscape to Landscape: 'Enclosure' in Prehistoric Britain 9
Peter Fowler

Early Agriculture in Scotland 55
S. P. Halliday, P. J. Hill and J. B. Stevenson

Agricultural Tools: Function and Use 66
Sian Rees

Slash and Burn in the Temperate European Neolithic 85
P. Rowley-Conwy

Deadstock and Livestock 97
Peter Reynolds

Reconstructing Crop Husbandry Practices from Charred Remains of Crops 123
Gordon Hillman

Discussion 163

Part Two: Animal Husbandry

Aspects of Cattle Husbandry 169
A. J. Legge

Livestock Products: Skins and Fleeces 182
Michael J. Ryder

Early Manuring Techniques 210
Alexander J. Fenton
Discussion 218
A Summing-Up by Peter Jewell p. 223
Appendix by Roger Mercer p. 231
List of Contributors p. 238
Index p.239

Preface

This book is based on a symposium held in late November 1980 under the auspices of the Munro Bequest of the University of Edinburgh. The symposium was designed to reflect both the archaeological and anthropological interests of Robert Munro and much that emerged during its course has a more than passing relevance to modern agricultural problems as well as to those of prehistory.

Publication of the first volume of *The Agrarian History of England and Wales* (Cambridge 1981) at last gives scholars of British Prehistory a firm basis upon which to establish their view of this central aspect of the existence of societies of the remoter past. Farming was indeed the foundation on which culture and economy were built in these islands in the last four millennia bc. So important is it for us to understand the extent and potential of this activity, that research in this area is fortunately moving very rapidly indeed. It is the purpose of this book to offer a number of newly forged ideas and approaches to the foundation that the *Agrarian History* provides. These ideas and approaches fall under two heads. First, we record advances in our understanding of the nature of farming practice in prehistory, such as in the interpretation of the field traces, of implement-types, of the raw materials of farming that survive to us and of the methods of good husbandry which these suggest. Two of the contributions are indeed direct *addenda* of material and thought to sections of the *Agrarian History*, by two of the authors contributing to that work (Peter Fowler and Michael Ryder). Second, we explore aspects of the development of techniques, and trajectories of study, that will enable our understanding to advance in the future.

All the contributions reflect both aspects, and all contribute a number of new ideas. As might be expected, much debate was prompted by the speakers, and I have endeavoured to reflect this in shorter papers, requested from some of the principal contributors to that discussion. In the Introduction, I have tried to present a brief review of the evidence for changing farming practice in the British Isles over the four millennia with which we are concerned, as a backcloth against which the more specific interdisciplinary contributions can be seen. Professor Peter Jewell has provided, in a short summing up, an overview of the trends visible within the whole.

I must here offer my best thanks to all the contributors to this volume, for their promptness in delivery, and for their understanding, in the somewhat fraught business of production of the results of such a wide ranging symposium within six or seven months. So rapidly is archaeological information expanding and research proceeding, that the need for its prompt exchange and availability is becoming increasingly important and I must pay especial tribute to Archie Turnbull, Secretary to the University Press, and to his staff, for their generosity with time, skill and patience during this admirably short gestation period. Lastly I must thank the Munro Committee of the University of Edinburgh for the substantial grant that made possible the initial organisation of the symposium.

R. J. Mercer

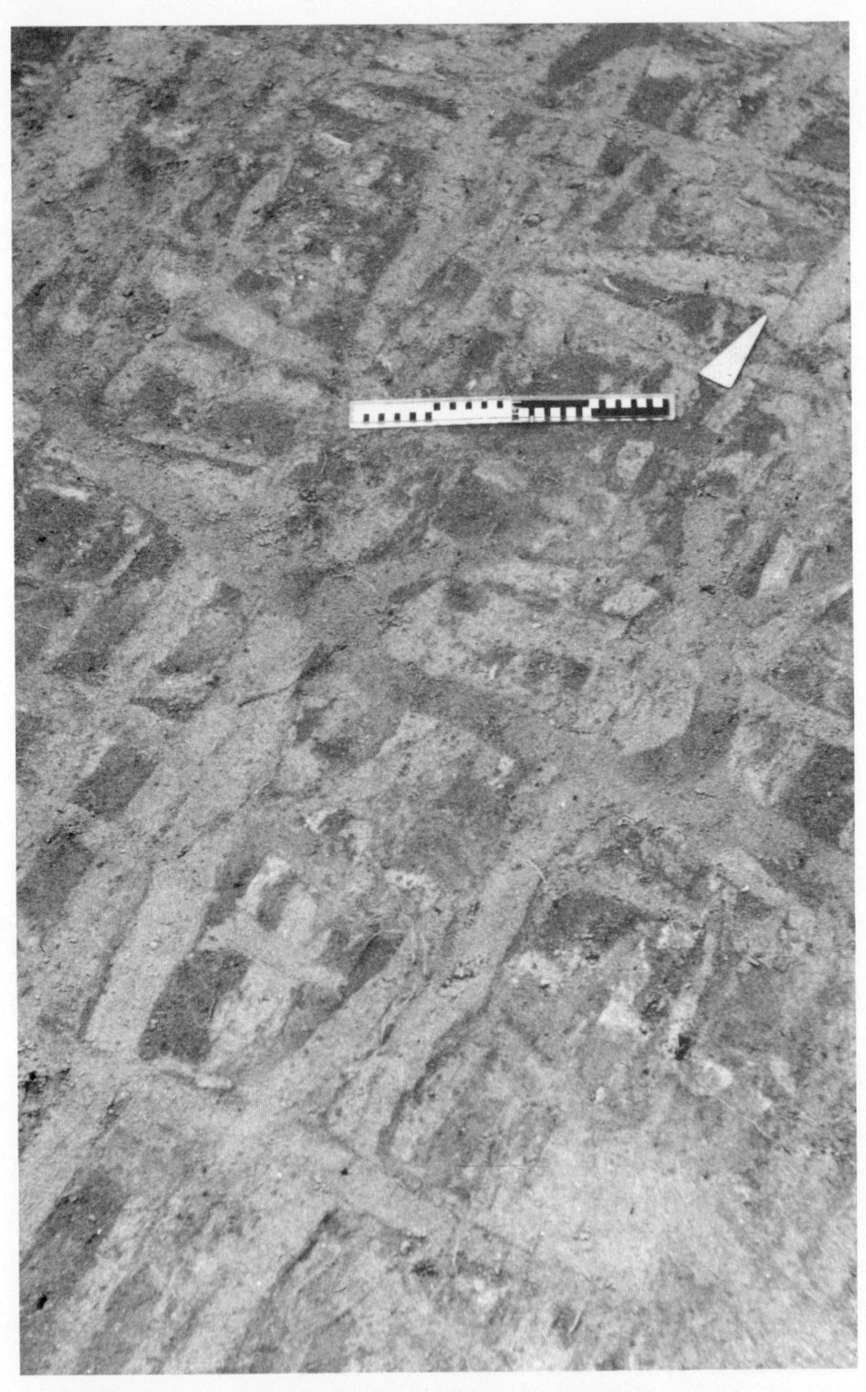

Prehistoric ard-marks retrieved during exploratory excavation
in 1981 of the site of Cnoc Stanger, Sandside Bay, near Thurso, Caithness

Introduction

ROGER MERCER

> The soil can bear all produce, except the olive, the vine and other natives of warmer climates, and it is fertile. Crops are slow to ripen but quick to grow – both facts due to one and the same cause, the extreme moistness of land and sky. (Tacitus, *Agricola,* XII)
> The population is exceedingly large, the ground thickly studded with homesteads, closely resembling those of the Gauls, and the cattle very numerous. . . . The climate is more temperate than in Gaul, the cold being less severe. (Caesar, *De Bello Gallico,* V, 2)

Thus is Southern Britain described, at second and at first hand, in the centuries immediately succeeding and preceding the beginning of the Christian era. The scene portrayed is as recognisable today as at the time of the Roman conquest. It is likely (and is indeed a *leitmotif* of this book) that a visitor to these islands in the middle of the second millennium bc, might have found it equally recognisable. The climatic idiosyncracy of Britain, described so tersely by Tacitus, and all too familiar to us today, has not, however, been constant throughout our history and prehistory. Beyond this bald statement unanimity among experts begins to falter.

ORIGINS OF BRITISH FARMING

In broad terms, the period when we can first perceive developed farming communities, about 3500 bc, appears to have been one of relatively wet climate in Southern England. Such at least is the interpretation suggested by Coles and Hibbert, for the development of timber trackway construction in the Somerset Levels (Coles and Hibbert 1968). An early phase of trackway construction in the Levels, radiocarbon dated 3200–2100 bc, may have been a response to the drying out of earlier reed swamps and the slow development of fen wood. This lessening of average annual rainfall between 2800–2200 bc would seem to be supported by other sites in the south of Britain where there is evidence for the sub-aerial erosion of soil during this period. For example, at Broome Heath, Norfolk (Wainwright 1972), a banked enclosure, constructed about 2200 bc, was built on top of fine wind-blown sand, apparently eroded from a surface bare of vegetation.

The sealed old land surfaces beneath long barrows in both the south and north of Britain have produced soils that had already been cultivated, and indeed had been relinquished to rough pasture by the time of the barrows' construction. The existence of pedestals of pre-barrow soils, now vanished from the southern downland surface, indicates a base of fertility which it would be easy to underestimate, looking at that landscape today. At South Street long barrow, North Wiltshire (Ashbee *et al.* 1979), woodland clearance, possibly on a relatively local scale, was followed by breaking in of the site by use of a 'rip-ard'. The severity of this treatment is indicated by the scores sustained by the chalk bedrock as a result of the passage of the implement. To have created this effect the ard must have been pulled by an ox, and the process was taking place at a date before c.2800 bc, as indicated by radiocarbon dating. The end-product of this process is suggested by a sickle flint located in the buried soil. The Horslip long barrow on Windmill Hill, again in northern Wiltshire (Ashbee *et al.* 1979), reveals a basically similar situation. Here, clearance for arable agriculture had taken place and the land relinquished to a growth of hazel scrub, before the construction of the barrow c.3250 bc – a radiocarbon date derived from antler at the base of the long barrow quarry ditch. On the Yorkshire Wolds, a similar situation is apparently visible – the Willerby Wold long barrow (Manby 1963), constructed about 3000 bc, lay upon extant grassland; while at Kilham (Manby 1976), constructed at a date earlier than c.2880 bc, the initial phase of the barrow was built upon a soil that had undergone arable agriculture in two separate phases, with a period of disuse and some woodland recovery between. The point is again brought out at this site that radical distinctions between the neolithic soils of the area and those present today is to be expected. In the north, the Dalladies long barrow near Fettercairn in Kincardineshire (Piggott 1972) would also appear to have been constructed in an environment of cleared land.

The inference is that, by the time the earliest major funerary monuments were being built in southern and northern Britain, substantial areas of the lighter more tractable soils, particularly on the chalk but probably also on our river gravels and on the unrivalled fertility of the loams and brickearths of south eastern England, had been broken in to arable cultivation. Bordering such clearances were, probably, areas of depleted forest where cattle and pigs were grazed. Clearances of this kind are witnessed in the fossil pollen record over a very wide area of Britain. In Northern Ireland, at Ballynagilly, Co. Tyrone, settlement traces linked with ceramics related to our Middle Neolithic cultures, are found in association with C14 dates as early as c.3675 bc (ApSimon 1976), and activity, matched by disturbance of the pollen sequence in peat bogs, occurs at no great distance.

The study of the impressions of seed grains on pottery and of (generally poorly retrieved) sample remains of carbonised plants available in Britain, was first undertaken by Helbaek (1952), who discerned the cereal crop species present. He argued for a changing balance of crop husbandry over time, from a predominantly emmer (*Triticum dicoccum*) wheat-producing economy in the Middle Neolithic of southern England (largely derived from causewayed enclosure remains), to primarily barley production in the Bronze and Iron Ages – the second and first millennia bc. Dennell (1976) has challenged this view and, on the basis of differential 'point of origin' analyses carried out upon the pottery, notably from the Windmill Hill causewayed enclosure (Smith 1965) – not available to Helbaek – has convincingly shown that, on the lighter soils of the chalk downland, with probably slightly lower average annual rainfall, emmer wheat (with einkorn, *Triticum monococcum*, as an incidental rarity) and naked and hulled barley (*Hordeum vulgare* var. *nudum* and *H. vulgare*) were grown alongside one another. On the heavier soils in the region of north-east Somerset, whence some twenty-two per cent of the pottery from Windmill Hill emanated, the pattern was markedly different, with a very much more pronounced emphasis upon the production of wheat, with barley appearing only as a rather minor element. Such an emphasis is hinted at, by Dennell, for the area around Hembury Fort, Devon – another causewayed enclosure – where similarly heavy soils are encountered. Bearing in mind the tiny samples with which Dennell, *faute de mieux,* is working, the emergence of a picture of local variability, and sensitivity of adaption of husbandry practice to environment is still an attractive one. The attraction of this suggested reconstruction is perhaps also enhanced by its familiarity to the modern eye, and it is therefore important to remember the radical changes in soil structure and distribution that have occurred since the earlier Neolithic – certainly in the chalk uplands.

Ard cultivation, the traces of which are preserved for us only under the most exceptional circumstances, postulates *a priori* the existence of fields, fenced or not, at least on the chalk lands of southern England. Our failure to recognise these (discussed by Bowen 1978) may well be due to attrition brought about by subsequent natural agricultural erosion of the area. It may also be due to a greater flexibility in field layout in the Neolithic, which did not allow the plough to 'sculpt' the landscape in the way that has given such permanent expression to later prehistoric agricultural activity. Nevertheless the very considerable importance of stock raising in this downland economy, alongside arable husbandry (see Legge below), and the evidence for controlled timber exploitation – 'coppicing' (Coles *et al.* 1978) – as well as other requirements for more massive timbers in vast quantities (Mercer 1980), imposed severe limits upon the degree of this flexibility. Certainly 'shifting agriculture' would seem to be unnecessary and indeed uneconomic in the circumstances of prehistoric southern Britain (see Rowley-Conwy below).

In the south west, in the rugged granite lands of West Cornwall, near the Neolithic enclosed village at Carn Brea (Mercer, forthcoming) simple stone clearance heaps are disposed in a relatively random fashion, so that hand digging by hoe was probably the only feasible means of cultivation. In the far west, in County Mayo in Ireland, at a rather later date, irregular stone-walled fields associated with ard marks are associated with a C14 sample which implies a date c.2500 bc (Caulfield 1978).

Evidence from the wider context of the British Isles for this earliest phase of farming depends largely upon the achievements of palaeo-botanists working with sequences of fossil pollen assemblages from waterlogged deposits. A very substantial body of evidence has now accumulated to indicate that, probably by the time an established farming landscape was present on the lighter soil uplands of southern and eastern Britain (see above), there was a widespread occurrence of clearance throughout Britain. Many of these areas were on more 'marginal' land, of poorer soils, where Neolithic clearance was an irreversible process and only partial re-establishment of the forest ever took place. Coastal areas of hospitable aspect, like the south-west coast of Cumbria, were apparently the subject of fairly intensive clearance at this time (between 3400 and 3000 bc). An excellent survey of this aspect is set out by A. G. Smith (in Simmons and Tooley 1981, 152–80).

THE THIRD MILLENNIUM

Whittle has, however, demonstrated (1978) that the initial expansion of farming activity was not to continue unchecked. Between the beginning and the middle of the third millennium bc we are able to observe a considerable pattern of forest regeneration – in East Anglia, north Yorkshire, Ireland, Cumbria and in Scotland. The very intensity and success of the first phase of agricultural expansion may have been the principal cause. Sims (1973) has suggested, in this connection, that between 35 and 80 km^2 of land were cleared and cultivated at Hockham Mere in East Anglia. Certainly, very large tracts of the southern English downland were open, and farmed by this time. By 2500 bc hillwash deposits were accelerating in some parts of the chalk downland (Dimbleby 1976) and the existence of a de-structured *sol lessivé* beneath the bank of the henge at Stanton Harcourt, Oxfordshire, as well as the evidence for soil erosion beneath the bank at Broome Heath, Norfolk, may point to a combination of drying climate and over-exploitation by man.

It is at this point, between 2800 and 2500 bc, that we appear to see the construction of a number of causewayed enclosures on the chalk uplands. At Windmill Hill (Smith 1965) charcoal from the primary silt of one of the enclosure ditches produced a radiocarbon date c.2580 bc, and at Hambledon Hill (Mercer 1980) a range of dates between 2900 and 2600 bc exist for the construction of a massive fortified complex incorporating a great ritual centre similar to Windmill Hill. These sites would appear, generally, to cluster towards the end of the altogether broader chronological span covered by long barrow construction. The evidence from Hambledon and from Crickley Hill, Glos. (Dixon 1979), would indicate that some of these sites were heavily fortified complexes, which at Hambledon (see Legge below) would appear to have been intimately associated with cattle farming (alongside a substantial arable element). The apparent tendency of large tracts of these southern uplands to become grassland by this stage may indicate a general move towards cattle grazing upon old cleared and cultivated land in response, possibly, to climatic development (a lower annual rainfall) and to land impoverishment. Such a shift would lead to some degree to economic crisis due to the lower efficiency of cattle raising as a means of nutrition production and would demand some degree of demographic adjustment. This crisis may be tangibly represented to us by the construction of defensive works like Hambledon and Crickley Hill, and even its dramatic events, hinted at in the visible traces of attack, destruction and burning which mark the end of these sites' existence. *Circa* 2800 bc, then, after some seven hundred radiocarbon years of the development of one agricultural régime, a major contraction apparently confronts us, and the two or three centuries that follow saw massive changes taking place in the British archaeological record. These changes, radical as they are in archaeological terms, in fact merely continued the adjustments already visible in the Hambledon–Windmill Hill phase of the middle Neolithic – a move, in the face perhaps of contracting resources, towards wider based cooperation and the focussing of that cooperation upon, and its direction by, hierarchies. It is possible that the heavy overtones of a ritual nature present on excavated causewayed enclosure sites indicate that this hierarchy was a priestly one.

Once again variety was the essence of the reaction to the crisis throughout Britain. On the chalkland, grazing was maintained throughout the period 2500–1500 bc, with little evidence for forest redevelopment; and upon this grazing must have been based the power of the hierarchies of the region that emerged in the latter half of the third millennium bc. This power enabled these groups to direct their peoples to the vast construction tasks that survive today as the great earthwork structures with their timber and stone embellishments which characterised the area at the turn of the second millennium bc. That cattle were not the only source of wealth in these communities is demonstrated by the recurrent importance of pigs in the bone assemblages at these very enclosures. The woodland which such a porcine population would have found most congenial may well have still existed in a number of valley bottoms, and the clearance of these areas may date from this period. In the Yorkshire Wolds (Bramwell, in Manby 1974), sites of the Later Neolithic display a similar emphasis and it is presumably these sites that, again, provided the economic substructure for the construction of the great enclosures which also dominated this area at this date.

In Ireland, traces of agriculture show a shift (at Ballynagilly) to an economy based upon grazing, before forest regeneration commences c.2600 bc, a regeneration mirrored in many Irish peat stratigraphies.

These changes that we have observed on the chalklands of southern and eastern England, and have seen to occur elsewhere, may have been responsible for the agricultural development of the most northerly and westerly parts of Britain, where boulder clay and developing *machair* deposits were apparently colonised at this time. Radiocarbon dates from Northton on the Isle of Harris (Evans 1971, Simpson 1976) show Neolithic population and a measure of woodland clearance established by a date somewhat before c.2460 bc. In the Northern Isles, a series of dates from the Knap of Howar, Papa Westray, Orkney (Ritchie 1975) is seen to focus around 2500 bc although one earlier and perhaps somewhat anomalous date of 2815 ± 70 bc does occur. Similarly at Skara Brae, Mainland, Orkney (Clarke 1976a, b) the occupation sequence appears to commence c.2500 bc. The evidence from both Northton and Skara Brae (both sites as yet in an incomplete state of assessment) would seem to indicate that this northern environment favoured the breeding of small cattle and sheep (sheep slowly increasing in importance with the passage of time at Skara Brae). A small number of pigs were also kept at Skara Brae (these presumably might well not thrive in the largely open environment) and deer were hunted at both sites. Fishing and shellfish-collecting clearly played an important role in the economy of both. On Shetland, excavation at the Scord of Brouster, near Walls (Whittle 1979) has produced traces of Neolithic houses set within a 'cairnfield' of clearance heaps with pollen evidence of a substantial increase in plantain and other plants of open country about 2700 bc. A field wall set under peat on Shurton Hill near Lerwick has been associated with a radiocarbon date, providing a *terminus post quem* for building the wall, c.2800 bc (Whittington 1978). This expansion of agriculture may lead us to suspect that the crisis that occurred in the focal areas of Early/Middle Neolithic agriculture may have been resolved by a local reduction of population (leaving a still very considerable 'rump' to judge by their monumental achievements), a reduction possibly reflected in contemporary expansion into suitable niches elsewhere. Naturally, such a radical economic and environmental change would involve cultural and social transformations which are not our concern here – but which certainly are registered in the archaeological record at this juncture. If monuments of the calibre of the Quanterness chambered tomb (Renfrew *et al.* 1979) do mark the first horizon of farming penetration of Orkney then clearly, here too, we see hierarchical development taking place as elsewhere at the same juncture.

Climatic developments towards the end of the third millennium bc seem to indicate a period of enhanced precipitation, to judge by the appearance of recurrent horizons of renewed bog growth in western Britain. The laying down of trackways in the Somerset Levels seems to end about 2000 bc, as flooding occurs. The moister prevailing conditions may well have favoured the move across to pastoral farming which we have seen taking place in the south from the middle of the third millennium.

Other agricultural developments pointing in this direction are perhaps evidenced at North Mains, Strathallan, Perthshire where parallel ridges, 2 m apart, presumably spade dug, have been located beneath a great, apparently cenotaphic, round barrow. The date of construction of the barrow is indicated by charcoals located on top of ridging immediately beneath the barrow as c.1850 bc (Barclay forthcoming). Such an agricultural technique, presumably dated soon after 2000 bc may well be linked to increasing precipitation.

By the end of the third millennium bc, then, centres of high population exhibiting an apparent degree of centralised control had been established. Their very considerable resources were based, it would seem, upon an agricultural economy biased towards stock husbandry carried out on grassland established over relict areas of arable land of Early/Middle Neolithic date. Possibly as a product of pressures exerted by this change, a further penetration of agriculture into the most isolated parts of the British Isles, the western coast of Ireland, the Hebrides, Orkney and Shetland appears to have occurred. In many areas, however, where agriculture had been practised prior to 3000/2600 bc, a failure of the available system is seen, with a probable consequent contraction of population (or its movement elsewhere), and a regeneration of forest.

THE SECOND MILLENNIUM

With the opening of the second millennium we apparently enter a period of drier and warmer climate. Again, evidence for wind-blown soils, suggesting the existence of tracts of bare soil open to erosion, are a feature of sites relating to this date (Cornwall 1953), and in the Somerset Levels some drying out seems to have taken place with formation of highly humified peat.

With the onset of this dryer and probably warmer period many more elevated areas of Britain would have become viable for the farmer, and from about 2000 bc onwards we see a remarkable and seemingly very rapid expansion of arable farming into, particularly upland, areas which hitherto had not been subject to such activity. This *floreat* of arable agriculture, as well as pastoral farming, in areas of an elevation up to well over 1000 ft (310 m) effectively blurs the sharp distinction between Lowland and Highland Zones, a concept which was to become of perhaps greater relevance in more recent times. A massive extension of land under cultivation took place at this time but, unlike the preceding expansionary phase of the mid and late fourth millennium bc, the elements of agricultural management now demanded laid-out field systems, which frequently survive today in visible form on the ground, or from the air. Upland areas from Caithness (Mercer 1980), to Cumbria (Higham 1978), to Caernarvonshire (Johnson 1978), to Cornwall (Johnson 1980) exhibit complex and very extensive field system patterns that relate to at present uncertain but certainly prehistoric date. In the Island of Arran, widespread settlement and cognate cultivation can be dated to between 2000 and 1000 bc

(Barber 1979) while on Dartmoor the 'reave' systems indicate a subdivision of the moor, for pastoral purposes, at this time, with fields linked to the reaves in the lower fringes of the moor (Fleming 1978, Collis 1978).

Not merely the more isolated uplands, but also the downland of southern Britain was, over very substantial areas, parcelled out into field systems. This process, however, would appear to be somewhat later and not generally to occur, on present evidence, until after about 1500 bc – at a time when the hegemonies of the later third millennium appear to be finally decaying. When this development did occur, however, it was remarkable for the preconceived and carefully surveyed layout of the fields over wide areas – perhaps indicating that older wide-ranging land tenurial rights still retained significance and influence. Clearance once again was started in those areas where regeneration had largely removed the effects of earlier Neolithic activity; and from other peat bog locations where Neolithic clearance is not so certainly indicated (e.g. Sluggan Moss, Ballylurgan, Co. Antrim; Smith 1975) clearance is apparent at this time. At Belderg Beg, reoccupation of surfaces already subject to peat growth took place and small irregular fields were laid out, associated with C14 dates c.1250 bc (Caulfield 1978) – although the use of ridging here may indicate, at the end of this period, the onset of wetter conditions again (see below).

This relatively massive and sudden expansion must have had a very substantial population base, which had been concentrated in favoured areas, and then widely dispersed into outlying locations during the 'contractional' period of the Later Neolithic. The addition of an 'invasive' element is also a possibility at this time (Case 1977), and indeed such elements may have provided a major stimulus to this reorientation of the economy. In the present context, the major supportive evidence for this interpretation is in my opinion the introduction of a new bovine type that henceforward formed the basis of British cattle rearing: the so-called Celtic shorthorn – *Bos longifrons*.

Dennell (1976), once again, has indicated that views set out by Helbaek (1952) on the basis of cereal remains may be simplistic in their interpretation. Barley grains form eighty-five per cent of the total cereal remains available for this period, and there is little doubt that barley was an important product – not surprisingly, perhaps, in view of the vast tracts of poorer and more elevated land taken into cultivation. However, the selective basis upon which barley cereal impressions are located on certain pottery styles leads him to suspect an inherent bias and to conclude that wheat may be under-represented in the record.

The valleys of southern Britain, also, may well have been subdivided and laid out into a field landscape, and the destruction of barrows in the Upper Thames Valley by cultivation at this period may point in that direction. In other lowland contexts – on the fen edge near Fengate, Peterborough (Pryor 1980) – we find sophisticated and carefully laid out fields (apparently for stock retention, to judge by complex gate arrangements and the attention given to drove access to all parts of the area) – a system exploiting the rich grazing to be had in these mild and wetter circumstances. The careful subdivision of land, however, within this different landscape, whatever its precise significance, again points to the maximisation of land resources, and a population configurate with that. The extremely sophisticated control system for stock exhibited at Fengate might well hint at day-by-day exploitation of these animals for at least part of the year, and milk-orientated cattle farming has been demonstrated for other sites at this period (see Legge forthcoming and below). Sheep, too, appear to become more significant at this stage and the earliest clear evidence for wool production and use is now found (see Ryder below).

Maximisation of resources, however, frequently entails exploitation of marginal and vulnerable resource areas, and it is clear that from the outset this phase of massive expansion stood in such a danger. In a number of areas (for example in the New Forest, Hants, and the North Yorkshire Moors (Dimbleby 1962)), round barrows of about 1500 bc appear to have been built upon an impoverished, destructured soil which may have been the product of the exposure of vulnerable soils to over-rigorous exploitation. To this ever-present threat was also added a further apparent climatic shift, at a date which still remains uncertain but almost certainly late within the latter half of the second millennium bc, to a wetter and probably cooler phase. In much recent archaeological publication this change has been represented as an environmental 'catastrophe', and it is certain that, in the archaeological record, as we approach the turn of the first millennium, many changes are occurring in technology, in weaponry, in settlement development and in agricultural strategy. Once again, archaeologists, faced with apparent discontinuity, have sought refuge in 'invasionist' interpretation (Burgess 1980) and indeed an element of enhanced external influence is apparent (as it was towards the end of the third millennium bc). Indeed the elements noted at the end of the third millennium, a period of similar environmentally induced difficulty, are worthy of note here. Once again we appear to see the emergence of centralising and strongly directive forces within society, but on this later occasion of rather a different complexion. These forces would now appear to have been more secularly based upon an élite which expressed itself and its status in a massively developed armaments industry, a trend never to be absent from the whole course of the subsequent history of these islands. As with the crisis of the mid-third millennium, fortification reappeared as a major phenomenon, as centres of wealth-exchange and expression become more vulnerable to the ambitions of rival élite factions. Agriculture, too, saw far-reaching changes, although the people who practised it may well have known little enough of the stirring events which may have characterised the age. The upland areas, colonised and exploited throughout the second millennium, were either deserted or underwent major changes of agricultural strategy. On Bodmin Moor peat growth seals the field surfaces and house floors of the MBA settlement at Stannon Down (Mercer 1970). On Dartmoor, peat growth developed over the upland reave systems (Fleming 1978), and a somewhat similar major land division located beneath peat at Achnacree, near Oban, Argyll (Barrett *et al.* 1976) went out of use at a date of about 980 bc. However, these changes were not confined to the uplands. On the southern English downland, whole landscapes of the carefully laid out 'Celtic' fields, apparently disused and of no relevance, are at this period crossed in haphazard fashion by linear earthworks enclosing very large areas of ground, which make best sense as enclosures for stock running. Even on the fen edge change is visible, and the Fengate system, operative for a thousand years, went out of use.

THE FIRST MILLENNIUM

We now move into a period of 500 years or more for which we have little evidence. Massive population diminution consequent upon the agricultural debacle, which appears to take place in the archaeological record, has been postulated. It is, however, likely that prime agricultural land on the river gravels and other well drained resilient soils would have continued to support arable farming, adjusted perhaps in its balance, and that large areas of land beyond these *foci*, once arable, would have been grazed for the rich grass yields which such a period of moist climate might well have fostered. The evidence of the ranch boundaries on Salisbury Plain (Bowen 1978) supports this suggestion, as does the continuation of occupation (and thus farming) into the Late Bronze Age on a number of coastal sand dune sites in the north and west. Here, arable farming producing wheat as well as barley would appear to have continued throughout this period, ever since the initial development of the area in the late third millennium bc. The apparent introduction of peas in the late second millennium bc (see Legge forthcoming) and the availability of the 'Celtic' bean (*Vicia faba*) by the beginning of the Iron Age may indicate the presence of other highly nutritious crops which enable the preservation of some demographic equilibrium through the period (indeed one impression of Celtic bean is reported by Hillman (1981, 188) from a Late Neolithic sherd from Ogmore, Glamorganshire). By about 650 bc massive erosion caused the deposition of heavy silts in the Severn and Avon valleys, which Shotton (1978) has argued are the result of large scale cultivation on the slopes of these river valleys. Such activity may herald the equally ill-defined end of the moist climatic interlude. In the Kennet Valley near Reading in Berkshire the excavation of two LBA settlements (Bradley *et al.* 1980) has shed some further light on developments. The evidence is fairly clear for continuous occupation of this area near the river from the later second millennium down to 500 bc. Different sites express different economic emphases but cattle and sheep are present on the sites, and emmer wheat would appear the dominant crop type with hulled barley also present.

That this period is one of agricultural contraction and re-adjustment is, at present, incontestable. Nevertheless, the use of vast areas of previously cultivated land as rough grazing (leaving little tangible archaeological trace) and the successful and perhaps intensified exploitation of favoured areas could have maintained a stable and resilient economy, the existence of whch is demanded by the more archaeologically palpable traces of wealth and surplus displayed by the supported hierarchies of the time. Such a resilience is also more in keeping with the apparently immediate availability of a thriving agricultural economy, as 'settlement archaeology' becomes generally available to us, once again, in the period after 500 bc. It is from the changes clearly visible by this latter juncture that we must project backwards in order to create a picture of the kind of complex adjustment and development that may be concealed from us in the earlier centuries of the first millennium bc.

By the latter part of the first millennium, the definition of Highland and Lowland Zones, agriculturally speaking, has begun to crystallise and has continued to 'harden' ever since. The ultimate degradation of many upland soils from the end of the second millennium bc, to some extent due to earlier farming activity, has to a large extent created a landscape of which our modern conception is the direct descendant. In southern Britain the evidence of plant remains indicates the presence of a whole new range of plant types. The 'Celtic' bean and the pea are present in the archaeological record as well as rye (*Secale*), oats (*Avena*) and breadwheat (*Triticum vulgare*) appearing as apparently new cereal types. Spelt wheat (*Triticum spelta*) largely replaces emmer as the standard cereal and hulled barley (*Hordeum hexastidium*) would appear to supplement the naked variety throughout the latter part of the first millennium. To the writer it would seem as likely that such far-reaching adjustments (in the main to crops more suited to cooler, wetter circumstances) would have been made in the difficult farming environment of the early part of the millennium than in the latter part when conditions, by and large, were improving (although he accepts the burden of argument *ex silentio*). Helbaek (1952) recognised long ago that, in the south, there appeared to be a division between cultivation in the west (Somerset) and in the east (Wiltshire), with barley dominant in the latter and wheat in the former, as Dennell (1976) points out, impressively redolent of the situation three millennia previously.

Throughout the second half of the first millennium, in Lowland Britain, arable farming, still based upon the crook-ard as the principal cultivating tool, appears to have yielded wheat and barley as principal products. As in the Neolithic and Bronze Age, cattle appear to have been the mainstay of animal-rearing economy over Britain as a whole, with sheep and then pigs generally less important. This 'basic' prehistoric economy is, of course, derived from the presence of bone on settlement sites and is thus a matter of human selection. It is indeed likely that cattle will always predominate in such selection as they generally will always form the animal element most closely associated at all stages of development with the homestead. Sheep *carcases,* especially where wool production is the objective, will tend to be next in frequency of association and, finally, in prehistoric terms, pigs. Such a 'basic' assemblage would appear to the writer to be relatively meaningless in terms of the detailed bias of prehistoric animal-rearing economy, and it may be only in departure from this pattern (for instance in the occurrence of pig bone predominance in later third millennium contexts in southern Britain) that significant indications can be sought. In this context it is proper also to raise the problem of site *function* as this may artificially bias the animal-bone component (or indeed the plant component) for reasons that are inaccessible to the archaeologist. One would not expect to encounter a large deposit of pig bone in direct association with a modern synagogue. For similar reasons, at potentially ritual sites, the occurrence of cattle bone in causewayed enclosures or even on a hillfort is perhaps not to be accepted simply at face value.

The cattle of the late first millennium show little change in type or build from those of the second millennium bc. On a number of sites they remain the dominant species in the bone record. The Moulton Park Enclosure, Northampton (Williams 1974), Fisherwick, near the confluence of the rivers Tame and Trent (Smith 1977), where a valley bottom mixed arable/animal economy appears to be based upon cattle, and the southern coastal plain at North Bersted, Sussex (Bedwin and Pitts 1977), where cattle bone dominates on a settlement set within a ditched field system, provide examples. Cattle ranching enclosures are also a feature of the period – the so-called 'banjo enclosures' of the south and a widespread series of animal corral annexes associated with hillforts and other sites in the Highland Zone. Again, in Hampshire, banjo enclosures excavated recently (Monk and Fasham 1980) reveal – despite their palpable cattle corralling function – the mixed arable/pastoral economy that must characterise agriculture at this and earlier periods.

Nevertheless, in the south, some shift in economy is visible. A number of sites in rather different environments show a distinct increase in the importance of and indeed, in some instances, the dominance of sheep. The village settlement at Glastonbury (Bulleid and Gray 1911, 1917) set in the Somerset levels at the foot of the Mendips has very few cattle in a bone assemblage dominated by sheep. In an equally low-level setting, the settlement dating to the period between 500 and 0 bc retrieved by excavation during the development of the Ashville Trading Estate, Abingdon, Oxon (Parrington 1978) produced evidence of an economy biased apparently towards sheep farming. Equal dominance of sheep is to be noted in the bone assemblage from the hillfort at Eldon's Seat, Dorset (Cunliffe 1968) in a downland setting. The enhanced importance of sheep may well indicate that whole areas of downland – the Mendips, the Berkshire

Downs and elsewhere were open grazing areas at this time upon which sheep were run.

In the south western peninsula of England, reoccupation of the peat covered moorlands began and at Kestor, Devon (Fox 1955) a settlement associated with the development of a ploughsoil within a walled field system on top of the earlier peat formation is evident. Despite this arable element, however, it would appear likely that the principal component of farming economy in this area was cattle and sheep husbandry on the abundant local rough grazing. Spindle whorls located on many sites of the period presumably indicate the importance of sheep to the economy. In the last two centuries bc Dartmoor seems to have been relinquished as farming land, perhaps indicating the onset of a further moister climatic phase which may also be responsible for an apparent intensification of stock rearing on the downland of Wessex. Certainly, areas of the Somerset Levels were becoming subject to freshwater flooding by the first century A.D.

In the Welsh highlands and in northern England and Scotland throughout this period, stock rearing, with bias towards sheep or cattle varying from area to area, was consistent in importance. The frequent appearance of spindle whorls on the sites emphasises the importance of sheep. But equally important, the wide-ranging occurrence of quern stones points to the continuing importance of cereal cultivation in fields that, in Scotland at least, are only now beginning to be really understood in their complexity and ubiquity (see Halliday, Hill and Stevenson below).

Upon the establishment of Roman hegemony in these islands, then, we can find no cause for surprise in Caesar's and, later, in Tacitus's description of an intensively farmed landscape, and we may experience little difficulty in extending their descriptions, based upon familiarity with the southern areas facing the European continent, to far wider areas of the country, perhaps violating long-held preconceptions of a Highland Zone of relative impoverishment.

It is the purpose of this book to illustrate both the spread of a farming economy into all areas of this country from an early date, and the very high efficiency and sophistication of which its practitioners were capable, allowing the production of massive food reserves. These can only have been produced to support an equally substantial population, and upon the volume of this population must depend the nature of many of our approaches to the evidence which forms the basis of our understanding of British prehistory.

Table of radiocarbon dates (5568±30 year half-life)

Site	Lab. No.	Date bc	Sample provenance, notes
Achnacree	N-1468	980±80	Base of peat formation over field boundary.
Ballynagilly, Co. Tyrone	UB-197	3675±50	Earliest phase of Neolithic occupation, a pit
	UB-559	3550±85	containing sherds.
	UB-201	3215±50	Somewhat later phase of Middle Neolithic occupation and house structure (burnt plank in wall).
Belderg Beg, Co. Mayo	SI-1470	2270±95	Date from tree 100 years old at death growing directly on cultivated surface.
	SI-1471	1270±85	
	SI-1472	1260±85	Second phase of 'ridged' field cultivation.
	SI-1473	1220±85	
Broome Heath, Ditchingham, Norfolk	BM-679	3474±117	Charcoal from base of fossil soil under bank of enclosure.
	BM-755	2217±78	Charcoal from surface of fossil soil under bank of enclosure.
Dalladies, Kincardineshire	I-6113	3240±105	
	SRR-289	2710±50	
	SRR-290	2585±55	
Hambledon Hill, Dorset	NPL-76	2790±90	Main causewayed enclosure.
	HAR-1802	2610±90	Primary silts.
	HAR-1886	2890±150	
	HAR-3062	2900±100	
	HAR-3058	2750±120	Stepleton enclosure (settlement?)
	HAR-3060	2620±110	
	HAR-2378	2870±80	Outwork (defending 120-acre enclosure)
Horslip, Wilts.	BM-180	3240±150	
Kilham, Yorks.	BM-293	2880±125	Phase IIc at construction.
Knap of Howar, Papa Westray, Orkney	SRR-348	2815±70	House I.
	SRR-344	2501±70	From an identical context to SRR-348.
	SRR-346	2582±70	
	SRR-349	2472±70	Midden predating House I.
	SRR-452	2131±65	Midden deposit within wall core of House I.
	A difficult series. SRR-348 is the earliest radiocarbon date in a cultural context from the Orkney Islands of which the writer is aware. Dates c.2600 bc have also been retrieved from the Quanterness chambered tomb (Renfrew 1979) where Q-1294 2640±75 bc was obtained from Stratum I – a series of thin burn deposits superimposed upon the natural soil within the cairn – and which presumably relates to first use and construction of the site.		
North Mains, Strathallan, Perthshire	GU-1134	1855±100	Date *ante quem* for 'ridging'.
Northton, Isle of Harris	BM-705	2461±79	Date for Neolithic Level II.
	Neolithic Level I – associated with 'a number of plain undecorated sherds' lies beneath Level II, separated from it by 1.20 m of sterile wind-blown sand in a period of apparently rapid deposition. Level I is set upon the boulder clay surface.		

Table of radiocarbon dates—*contd*

Site	Lab. No.	Date bc	Sample provenance, notes
Skara Brae	Birm-637	2480±100	Earliest five dates, the beginning of Clarke's Phase I
	Birm-638	2480±120	
	Birm-639	2450±100	
	Birm-636	2400±130	
	Birm-480	2370±100	Occupation on old ground surface.
Somerset Levels	2800–2100. The earliest Neolithic trackway, on the basis of radiocarbon dating, would appear to be the Sweet Track, Shapwick.		
Sweet Track	Q-968	3274±75	Raised bog peat over upper fringes of track.
	Q-963	3268±75	Hazel peg by track.
	Q-966	3209±76	Hazel plank peg by track.
	Q-1102	3180±100	Peat immediately underlying trackway rails.
	The latest Neolithic trackway would appear to be the Abbots Way.		
Abbots Way	Q-926	2068±80	Wooden peg from track.
	Q-908	2014±60	Peat under track.
	BM-386	1984±111	Alder by track.
South Street	BM-356	2810±130	Charcoal on buried soil surface under mound.
Willerby Wold	BM-187	3010±150	Timber of facade structure.
	BM-188	2950±150	From cremated burial deposit.

BIBLIOGRAPHY

ApSimon, A. M. (1976) Ballynagilly and the beginning and end of the Irish Neolithic, in *Acculturation and Continuity in Atlantic Europe (ed. S. J. de Laet) 15-30.* IVth Atlantic Colloquium.

Ashbee, P., *et al.* (1979) Excavation of three long barrows near Avebury, Wilts. *Proc. Prehist. Soc. XLV*, 207-300.

Barber, J. (1980) *Discovery Excav. Scot.*, 34.

Barclay, G. (forthcoming) The excavation of the barrow and henge monument at North Mains, Strathallan, Perthshire. *Proc. Soc. Antiq. Scot. CXII.*

Barrett, J., P. Hill & J. Stevenson (1976) Second millennium BC banks in the Black Moss of Achnacree : some problems of prehistoric landscape, in *Settlement and Economy in the Third and Second Millennia BC* (eds C. Burgess & R. Miket) 283-8. Brit. Arch. Rep. 33.

Bedwin, O. & M. W. Pitts (1977) The excavation of an Iron Age settlement at North Bersted, Bognor Regis, West Sussex, 1975-76. *Sussex Archaeol. Collect. CXVII*, 293-346.

Bowen, H. C. (1978) 'Celtic' fields and 'ranch' boundaries in Wessex, in *The Effect of Man on the Landscape: the Lowland Zone* (eds S. Limbrey & T. G. Evans) 115-23. CBA Res. Rep. no.21.

Bradley, R., *et al.* (1980) Two Late Bronze Age settlements on the Kennet Gravels : excavations at Aldermaston Wharf and Knight's Farm, Burghfield, Berkshire. *Proc. Prehist. Soc. XLVI*, 217-96.

Bulleid, A. & H. St. G. Gray (1911) *The Glastonbury Lake Village*, vol.I.
—— (1917) *The Glastonbury Lake Village*, vol.II.
Burgess, C. (1980) *The Age of Stonehenge*.
Case, H. J. (1977) The Beaker culture in Britain and Ireland, in *Beakers in Britain and Europe* (ed R. J. Mercer) 71-101. Brit. Arch. Reps. Suppl. Series 26.
Caulfield, S. (1978) Neolithic fields: the Irish evidence, in *Early Land Allotment* (eds H. C. Bowen & P. J. Fowler) 137-43. Brit. Arch. Reps. 48.
Clarke, D. V. (1976a) Excavations at Skara Brae – A summary account, in *Settlement and Economy in the Third and Second Millennia BC* (eds C. Burgess & R. Miket) 233-50. Brit. Arch. Reps. 33.
—— (1976b) The Neolithic village at Skara Brae, Orkney. 1972-73 Excavations – An Interim Report. HMSO.
Coles, J. M. & F. A. Hibbert (1968) Prehistoric Roads and Tracks in Somerset, England. 1 Neolithic. *Proc. Prehist. Soc. XXXIV*, 238-58.
Coles, J. M., F. A. Hibbert & B. J. Orme (1973) Prehistoric Roads and Tracks in Somerset. 3 The Sweet Track. *Proc. Prehist. Soc. XXXIX*, 256-93.
Collis, J. (1978) 'Fields and settlements on Shaugh Moor, Dartmoor, in *Early Land Allotment* (eds H. C. Bowen & P. J. Fowler) 23-8. Brit. Arch. Reps. 48.
Cornwall, I. W. (1953) Soil science and archaeology with illustrations from some British Bronze Age monuments. *Proc. Prehist. Soc. XIX*, 129-47.
Cunliffe, B. W. (1968) Excavations at Eldon's Seat, Encombe, Dorset. *Proc. Prehist. Soc. XXXIV*, 191-237.
Dennell, R. W. (1976) Prehistoric crop cultivation in Southern England: a reconsideration. *Antiq. J. LVI*, 11-23.
Dimbleby, G. W. (1962) *The Development of British Heathlands and their Soils*. Oxford Forestry Man. XXIII.
Dixon, P. W. (1979) A Neolithic and Iron Age site on a hilltop in Southern England. *Scientific American 241*, no.5, 183-90.
Evans, J. G. (1971) Habitat change on the calcareous soils of Britain: the impact of Neolithic man, in *Economy and Settlement in Neolithic and Early Bronze Age Britain and Europe* (ed. D. D. A. Simpson) 27-73.
Fleming, A. (1978) The Dartmoor Reaves, in *Early Land Allotment* (eds H. C. Bowen & P. J. Fowler) 17-21. Brit. Arch. Reps. 48.
Fox, A. (1954) Celtic fields and farms on Dartmoor, in the light of recent excavations at Kestor. *Proc. Prehist. Soc. XX*, 87-102.
Helbaek, H. (1952) Early Crops in Southern England. *Proc. Prehist. Soc. XVIII*, pt.2, 194-233.
Higham, N. J. (1978) Early field survival in North Cumbria, in *Early Land Allotment* (eds H. C. Bowen & P. J. Fowler) 119-26. Brit. Arch. Reps. 48.
Hillman, G. (1981) in *The Environment in British Prehistory* (eds I. G. Simmons & M. Tooley).
Johnson, N. (1978) The location of pre-Mediaeval fields in Caernarvonshire, in *Early Land Allotment* (eds H. C. Bowen & P. J. Fowler) 127-32. Brit. Arch. Reps. 48.

—— (1980) Late Bronze Age settlement in the South-West, in *The British Later Bronze Age* (eds J. Barrett & R. Bradley) 141-80. Brit. Arch. Reps. 83 (i).

Legge, A. J. (1981) in *Excavations at Grimes Graves 1971-72* (ed. R. J. Mercer) vol.I. HMSO.

Manby, T. G. (1963) The excavation of the Willerby Wold long barrow. *Proc. Prehist. Soc. XXIX*, 173-205.

—— (1974) *Grooved ware sites in the North of England. Brit. Arch. Reps. 9.*

—— (1976) The excavation of the Kilham long barrow, East Riding of Yorkshire. *Proc. Prehist. Soc. XLII*, 111-60.

Mercer, R. J. (1970) The excavation of a Bronze Age hut-circle settlement, Stannon Down, St Breward, Cornwall, 1968. *Cornish Archaeol. IX*, 17-46.

—— (1980) Archaeological field survey in the North of Scotland. *Univ. of Edin. Dept. of Archaeol. Occ. Paper* no.4.

—— (forthcoming) Excavation of the Neolithic settlement site at Carn Brea 1970-1973. *Cornish Archaeol. XIX.*

Monk, M. A. & P. J. Fasham (1980) Carbonised plant remains from two Iron Age sites in central Hampshire. *Proc. Prehist. Soc. XLVI*, 321-44.

Parrington, M. (1978) *The Excavation of an Iron Age Settlement, Bronze Age ring-ditches and Roman features at Ashville Trading Estate, Abingdon (Oxfordshire) 1974-76.* Oxfordshire Archaeol. Unit Report 1, CBA Res. Report 28.

Piggott, S. (1972) Excavation of the Dalladies long barrow, Fettercairn, Kincardineshire. *Proc. Soc. Antiq. Scot. CIV* (1971-72), 23-47.

Pryor, F. (1980) *Excavation at Fengate, Peterborough, England. The Third Report.* Northampton Archaeol. Soc. Monograph 1, Roy. Ontario Mus. Arch. Monograph No.6.

Renfrew, A. C., *et al.* (1979) *Investigations in Orkney.* Rep. Res. Comm. Soc. Antiq. London, XXXVIII.

Ritchie, A. (1975) Knap of Howar, Papa Westray, Orkney. *Discovery Excav. Scot.*, 35-7.

Shotton, F. W. (1978) Archaeological inferences from the study of alluvium in the lower Severn-Avon valleys, in *The Effect of Man on the Landscape: the Lowland Zone* (eds S. Limbrey & J. G. Evans) 27-31.

Simpson, D. D. A. (1976) The Later Neolithic and Beaker settlement site at Northton, Isle of Harris, in *Settlement and Economy in the Third and Second Millennia BC* (eds C. Burgess & R. Miket) 221-31. Brit. Arch. Rep. 33.

Sims, R. E. (1973) The anthropogenic factor in East Anglia in vegetational history: an approach using APF techniques, in *Quaternary Plant Ecology* (eds H. J. B. Birks & R. G. West) 223-36. 14th Symposium of Brit. Ecol. Soc., Oxford.

Smith, A. G. (1975) Neolithic and Bronze Age landscape changes in northern Ireland, in *The Effect of Man on the Landscape: the Highland Zone* (eds J. G. Evans, S. Limbrey & H. Cleere) 64-74. CBA Research Report no.11.

Smith, C. (1977) The valleys of the Tame and Middle Trent – their population and ecology during the late first millennium BC, in *The Iron Age in Britain – A review* (ed. J. Collis) 51-61.

Smith, I. F. (1965) *Windmill Hill and Avebury: Excavations by Alexander Keiller 1925-39*.

Wainwright, G. J. (1972) The excavation of a Neolithic settlement on Broome Heath, Ditchingham, Norfolk, England. *Proc. Prehist. Soc. XXXVIII*, 1-97.

Whittington, G. (1978) A sub-peat dyke on Shurton Hill, Mainland, Shetland. *Proc. Soc. Antiq. Scot. CIX*, 30-5.

Whittle, A. (1978) Resources and Population in the British Neolithic. *Antiquity LII*, 34-42.

—— (1979) Scord of Brouster. *Curr. Archaeol. V*, no.6, 167-70.

Williams, J. H. (1974) *Two Iron Age Sites in Northampton*. Northampton Development Corporation Archaeological Monograph no.1.

British Farming Today: a Bird's-Eye View

MICHAEL J. NASH

I will limit the scope of my account to brief statements on three topics relating to the use of land, which may bear on our subject. These topics are: (i) the size of farms, (ii) the land potential for growing crops or keeping stock, and (iii) the main types of farming systems.

SIZE OF HOLDINGS AND LAND TYPES

A low-level flight over Britain would show that much of our farm land, whether it be cropped, stocked, or both, comprises relatively large-scale units as compared with some countries in Continental Europe.

Table 1 shows that, in 1977, nearly one third of the total 261,800 holdings lay in the largest size category (50 or more hectares, or 125 or more acres) and that these accounted for as much as eighty per cent of the total area of agricultural land. Nearly half of these largest size farms in fact possessed areas in excess of 100 hectares (250 acres). In contrast, in 1977 forty-three per cent of the total number of holdings accounted for a mere six per cent of the total area. The table indicates a significant fall in the proportion of smallest size holdings (under 5 ha) – from eighteen per cent in 1970 to fourteen per cent in 1977. Unfortunately, the agricultural statistics do not indicate the reason for this, but it is fair to assume that these small holdings will have been amalgamated with the largest size farms (50 ha and over), because the proportions of the latter have risen from twenty-seven per cent to thirty per cent over the same seven-year period. However, this trend towards amalgamation does not necessarily preclude the possibilities of an increasing interest in part-time 'back to the land' farming, carried out on very small holdings.

Probably nowhere else in the world is there a country of comparable size which supports so many different farming types. The cause of this variability is not only wide variation in climate – rainfall and temperature – but the complex geological structure of Britain with its extreme variations in soil type and topography. The effect of all these variations may be gauged by the proportions of rough grazings, permanent pasture, temporary grass

Table 1. Proportions (%) of farms and of agricultural land for various size groups in the U.K.

Size of holding (ha)	Percentage of total holdings (1970)	Percentage of total holdings (1977)*	Percentage of total agricultural area (1977)
1 – under 5	18	14	1
5 – under 10	13	13	1
10 – under 20	16	16	4
20 – under 50	26	27	13
50 and over	27	30	81
	100	100	100

* Total holdings = 261,800

('cultivated' or 'rotational' grass) and land under tillage, as between England and Wales on the one hand and Scotland on the other. The greatest differences are found between south and north (less so from east to west). Table 2 shows that whereas the proportions of land areas in England and Wales classed as 'rough grazings' and 'arable' are sixteen per cent and forty-nine per cent respectively, the proportions of these same classes of land in Scotland are virtually reversed, seventy-three per cent and twenty per cent.

Table 2. Approximate proportions (%) of major agricultural land types in Great Britain

	England and Wales		Scotland	
Rough grazings	16		73	
Permanent pasture	15		7	
Temporary grass	12	49*	10	20*
Tillage	37		10	
	100		100	

* = arable land

Clearly, many Scottish farmers are at a severe disadvantage compared to their colleagues south of the Border. Of particular importance is the fact that, in Scotland, the area of agricultural land suited to the production of high yields of crops for human consumption is small, the tillage area accounting for only ten per cent of the total agricultural area whereas in England and Wales the comparable figure is nearly four times greater, as shown in table 2 (see Appendix A for five-year average yields of grain crops).

POTENTIALITY OF LAND FOR CROPPING

It is hardly surprising that increasing attention has been given in recent years to matters concerning the conservation of our valuable heritage – land – and to how best it may be used. Indeed, during the past few years the term 'land use' has been given new meaning. Widespread soil surveys have permitted the drawing up of a scheme of land classification. Only the seven major categories of land are given in table 3, but these are more than sufficient to show that the land of Britain varies greatly in terms of its physical potentialities and limitations to crop production. The purpose of the scheme, of course, is to help farmers to choose a particular farming system (bearing in mind that choice of farming system will also be controlled by the farmer's economic circumstances and by his personal preference), and anyone who is interested in the use of land for agriculture, including government planners and advisers.

Table 3. Land capability classes

1. Minor or no physical limitations	Good soils, well drained, fertile, deep loams, usually on level sites.
2. Minor limitations	Reduction in choice of crops; possible interference with cultivations, e.g. imperfect drainage.
3. Moderate limitations	Greater reduction in range of crops and in timing of cultivations.
4. Moderately severe limitations	e.g. shallow/stony soils, poor drainage, steep slopes.
5. Severe limitations	Use restricted to pasture, forestry, recreation. Some mechanised pasture improvement possible.
6. Very severe limitations	Restrictions to rough grazing, forestry, recreation. No mechanisation possible.
7. Extremely severe limitations	Unforested land limited to poor rough grazing which cannot be rectified.

TYPES OF FARMING SYSTEM

Sufficient has been said to indicate that type of land markedly affects the choice of farming system. There are different ways of classifying farming systems, but the latter are commonly grouped according to seven categories of agricultural production, as shown in table 4.

Table 4. Types of British farming

1. Hill farming	Extensive sheep farming with or without some cattle.
2. Stock rearing	Sheep rearing and beef cattle production.
3. Rearing and feeding	Mainly production of fat cattle and fat sheep
4. Dairying	
5. Cropping with livestock	
6. Cropping	Arable cash and feed crops.
7. Horticulture, fruit, pigs, poultry	

1. *Hill sheep (with or without cattle)*. Some seventy per cent of Britain's rough hill grazing is situated in Scotland. There is a further fifteen per cent in Wales, while much of the remainder is found in Cumberland and West Midland and in the Cheviots and Pennines. It is in these areas that the greatest density of sheep farms are to be found. The typical hill farm is far larger than the average size of holding, which is around 40 ha, and it is widely agreed that at least 400 ha of rough grazing are needed to provide a reasonable living, together with a smaller area of what, in Scotland, is called in-bye land, the purpose of which is to grow good grass together with other fodder crops. The hill sheep farm will be stocked with at least 400 breeding ewes or, to be more specific, stocked at a rate of one ewe per 1–2 ha on the better hill, and one ewe per 4–5 ha on the poorer hill.

It is often thought more profitable to combine hill sheep farming with some cattle enterprise, on the basis that cattle have the ability to graze rough pasture which is not suited to sheep, and hence improve the pasture and therefore increase the overall stocking area.

2. *Stockrearing*. Predominantly stockrearing (*not* fattening) farms are widely distributed in upland areas, and are found in the more accessible glens of the Highlands, in the North East of Scotland, in the Border country, on the foothills of the Pennines, and in the Lake District and in Wales. Because they are situated on the lower hills, these farms possess a much higher proportion of arable to hill grazing compared to the true hill farm, and cattle are therefore much more important simply because the arable area is used mainly to produce crops suitable for animals. As regards farm size, stockrearing farms range from the part-time Highland croft which possesses just a few animals (of marginal significance to agricultural output but of importance to the social fabric), to the large farm comprising 1000–2000 sheep together with 200–300 breeding cattle.

3. *Stockrearing and fattening*. The word fattening implies that the animals are both reared and then continued to slaughter weight. Such farms are situated in North East Scotland (Aberdeenshire), South and South East Scotland, Leicestershire, Warwickshire and Northamptonshire, North Devon, and in the Cambrian uplands. Because of the lower elevations involved, soil and climatic conditions are much more favourable to the production of fodder crops, but not to the widespread cultivation of cash crops such as wheat, barley, sugarbeet and potatoes. Livestock production is the prime consideration on these stockrearing and fattening farms, with sheep being often of less importance than with the former types of farming system.

4. *Dairy farming*. The previous systems largely relate to ruminant livestock production on higher ground where grass yields are invariably poor. Grass reaches its peak of production at lower altitudes where the soil is more fertile, and provided there is moderate to heavy rainfall. Such grass is most profitably utilised by the dairy cow for milk production. In Scotland, around two-thirds of the dairy herds are found in the South

West, e.g. Dumfries area. (Incidentally, the Scottish dairy herd size of 70 is the highest in the EEC, England having a dairy herd size of 50.)

Much of the English and Welsh dairying enterprises are also found in the wetter, western side of the country, in Lancashire, Cheshire, Staffordshire, Derbyshire, Gloucestershire, Berkshire, Wiltshire, Somerset, Dorset, Devon, Cornwall and parts of Wales, notably Glamorgan and Pembrokeshire. In other areas the proximity to industry has over-ridden the dictates of climate, notably in North East England (Northumberland and Durham), in East Anglia and to the North and South of London.

5. *Cropping with livestock.* These farming systems may be grouped according to type of stock used, for example, cropping and dairying, cropping and fattening, cropping with both dairying and fattening.

6. *Cropping.* The more important areas involved in this system of farming are some of the most fertile in Britain, i.e. the fens of Lincolnshire and Lancashire, Cambridgeshire, parts of Norfolk and Suffolk, South Yorkshire; and, in Scotland, Fife, Perth and Angus areas. Variations in cropping systems take the form of differences in emphasis on the various crops grown; wheat, potatoes, sugarbeet, beans, peas, certain market garden crops such as cauliflowers, cabbages, broccoli, carrots, onions. Any livestock is quite subsidiary and, if kept, the animals may be partly fed on the by-products of these cash crops, e.g. the by-products of sugar beet, peas, barley and wheat.

7. *Horticulture, pigs, poultry, fruit.* The common difference between all aspects of horticulture and agriculture is one of intensity – the investment per hectare being extremely high in the case of horticultural systems, not only because of the higher outlays of labour, equipment and machines, including the erection of glasshouses, but because of higher costs of land used for such purposes, together with the cost of the fertilisers used to maximise crop production.

Pigs and poultry are essentially different from other agricultural enterprises, since they occupy a tiny area of land, but they may nevertheless form subsidiary enterprises on farms mainly devoted to those systems of farming already mentioned.

CONCLUSION

There is little to conclude from an introductory paper of this kind, but I should perhaps point out the obvious, namely, that our farming systems are never static – they are always changing to a greater or lesser extent according to the intensity of internal and external forces. In this connection it is conceivable that some of our farming systems could markedly change in the near future, perhaps resulting in a fall in meat consumption with a concomitant increase in the production of primary foods for human consumption – cereal grains, leguminous grains, oilseeds, vegetables - and, of utmost potential importance, increase in the storage of these foods. If marked changes in farming systems do take place, then among the more important external forces which might contribute to these changes would be fuel supplies and prices and, not least, political interference from Brussels if the UK is still a member of the EEC.

APPENDIX A

Yields of dry grains harvested in Great Britain
(5-year average, 1972–76, tonnes/hectare)

Type of grain	England & Wales	Scotland
Wheat	4.3	5.2
Barley	3.7	4.6
Oats	3.7	3.7
Rye	3.0	—
Mixed corn	3.6	3.7
Peas	3.1	—

REFERENCES

Bibby, J. S., & D. Mackney (1975) *Land Use Capability Classification. Tech. Monograph No. 1. The Soil Survey.* Rothamsted Exp. Sta., Harpenden, Herts, and the Macaulay Inst. for Soil Research, Aberdeen.

HMSO (1980) *Agricultural Statistics U.K., 1976-77.*

Lord, R. F., *et al.* (1978) Profitability of farming in south-east Scotland, 1976/77. *East of Scot. Coll. Agric., Bull. 22.*

Meiklejohn, A. K. M. (1976) The agriculture of south-east Scotland. *East of Scot. Coll. Agric., Bull. 15.*

Ministry of Agriculture, Fisheries and Food (1978) *E.E.C. Agricultural and Food Statistics, 1974-77.*

Nash, M. J. (1978) *Crop Conservation and Storage in Cool Temperate Climates.* Oxford: Pergamon Press.

Roy, M. G. & M. N. Hough (1978) Effects of weather and climate on modern British farming. *J. Roy. Agric. Soc. Eng. 139*, 43-53.

Shirlaw, D. W. G. (1971) *An Agricultural Geography of Great Britain.* Oxford: Pergamon Press.

Part One
The Land and Crops

Wildscape to Landscape: 'Enclosure' in Prehistoric Britain

PETER FOWLER

DEFINITIONS

My *wildscape* comes, not from Ratty and Toad's 'wild wood', but from Rackham's (1976) 'Wildwood', and from such current American concepts in landscape resource management as 'wilderness areas', or 'wildfire' (USDI 1980). After all, if a wood or forest fire can be conceptually 'wild', why not the whole 'scape'? My *landscape* is pure Hoskins (1955); the *Enclosure Movement* has been enshrined by generations of historians and teachers (e.g. Tate 1967, Parker 1960); and *Prehistoric Britain* comes from Dr Robert Munro whose book of that title was published in 1913. The theme of this essay is an exploration, through the combination of those apparently disparate elements, of the idea that 'Enclosure', in the historical sense, is a process which can usefully be applied to farming practice in prehistoric Britain.

INTRODUCTION

My thoughts stem in part from my contribution to the opening section of the *Agrarian History of England and Wales* (Piggott 1981). Completed in 1976, and added to during the various proof stages over the last four years in an attempt to keep it up to date, that book tries to outline the story of agriculture in the British Isles from the beginnings to the first century AD. It is therefore by definition based upon archaeological evidence and stops when the nature of the beast begins to change with the appearance of the first documentary evidence. From Caesar and then Tacitus we can at least make agrarian inferences – Caesar's Kent, for example, reads very like a description of an enclosed landscape of largish arable fields interspersed with woodlands and settled in a dense but un-nucleated pattern of farmsteads (*DBG* V, 1, 2).

Despite its unavoidable archaeological base, the prehistoric volume of *The Agrarian History*, embracing some five millennia, was conceived and written within an implicit historical model. This had to be so for it is a part of a *History* of which the other seven volumes, dealing with the mere rump of time since 1042, are largely based upon documentary sources, i.e. history. Of course, there are some who persist in believing that a written source is somehow not only more valid as evidence than a stone axe or a sculpture on the West front of Wells Cathedral, but also that archaeological evidence, material culture in the widest sense, is historically inadmissible (e.g. Kerridge 1976). Maybe the opening part of the *Agrarian History* will substantiate their case for, as all prehistorians know, it *is* extremely difficult to force a story, narrative history, from our sticks and stones and cremated bones. Indeed, we are probably being unfair to the nature of our beast, our sacred donkey, in trying to make it look like a historical horse when perhaps the best we can manage is a materialistic mule, capable of carrying cultural history but not appropriate to the burden of historical narrative.

It has been a signal characteristic of British archaeology that we operate, unconsciously or otherwise, within an historical paradigm. That is a truism pointed out by Piggott (1958) over twenty years ago; but it is necessary to have but the briefest of exposures to the way things are done in, say, North America and the Antipodes, to appreciate not only that there are other ways of approaching our unwritten evidence and especially our undocumented past, but also that the very historical framework which we work within, but which our 'new archaeologists' would abjure, actually provides our work with a sinew we should not lightly sever. In this context I would like to try looking at aspects of the manmade landscape of prehistoric Britain within the framework of an overt historical model rather than the implicit 'historicalness' within which *The Agrarian History* I, I was written.

Indeed, I want to press the idea a little further. Rather than trying to make the prehistoric evidence fit an historical model, I want to explore an historical model in relation to the prehistoric evidence. This is not at all novel, for it is but the game we play with ethnographic evidence, such as that effectively used by Fleming (1979) in the first of his major interpretive papers from Dartmoor, where he seeks illumination of the extraordinary field data there in the recent ethnography of Western Britain (see also his historical study, in Fleming 1978a). In a sense, this essay seeks to complement his approach by, equally tentatively, exploring an historical model, that of the 'Enclosure Movement'.

THE ARCHAEOLOGICAL EVIDENCE: AN INFORMATION EXPLOSION

Let us first review, briefly and in broad outline, the nature, range and distribution in time and space of the archaeological evidence – not a word of it written, not a bit of it still operative (but see below, p. 35), all of it dead until we focus our minds upon it. As it is so easy to despair of making it mean anything, let us remind ourselves with some sense of achievement that, to all intents and purposes, our subject matter has been discerned only within this century, indeed over the last sixty years. We are now at the start of only the third generation of study, following what we might well characterise as the 'Crawford/Curwen pioneering phase' (c. 1920–50) and the 'Bowen morphological phase' (c. 1950–80).

Robert Munro's *Scottish Lake-Dwellings* (1882) included a brief section rather optimistically headed 'Agricultural Implements', but his *Prehistoric Britain* (1913) contained nothing on farming. Nineteen centuries after their demise, prehistoric fields had not been conceptualised. This occurred ten years later, springing, Athena-like, independently and simultaneously, from the minds of Crawford (1923) and Curwen (1923). A Munro Symposium on our topic in the late 1930s would have had much Wessex and Sussex material to discuss, and a percipient interloper from the outback could just about have strung together a respectable lecture of odds and particularly sods from other parts of Britain (Barger 1938). In the mid 1950s the Prehistoric Society devoted one of its conferences to early agriculture, with excellent, new field-specific information by then available from, for example, Dartmoor and Bodmin Moor (Fox 1954, Radford 1952). By 1961 the bibliography of Collin Bowen's *Ancient Fields* ran to eleven pages, while by 1970 the subject had attained both the bulk for and the status of a Rhind Lecture series (Steensberg 1970).

During the seventies the almost exponential growth in the amount of relevant data has outstripped our capacity to log it properly, never mind to publish, assess and understand it, despite extra-mural attempts to build temporary dams at Newcastle in 1976 and Bristol in 1977 (Burgess and Miket 1976; Bowen and Fowler 1978). By then, the Bibliography, which by definition could include only published sources, of my own section of *The Agrarian History* from c. 2000 BC onwards had stretched to twenty-five pages of typescript (Fowler 1981), while the published version of the 37-paper Bristol conference contained a further thirteen pages of references (Bowen and Fowler 1978, 187–99). Now following bold attempts in the mid-70s to synthetise nationally this tidal wave of data from the first millennium BC (Cunliffe 1974, Harding 1974) and from the third and fourth millennia BC (Whittle 1977, see also 1978), comes chapter V of Burgess's (1980) highly informed attempt to do likewise for the second millennium BC.

At the start of the 1980s then, we are in a very different position logistically and conceptually from that of our chalkland predecessors even as lately as twenty years ago. In some ways our position is in both respects similar to that of historians and their Enclosure Movement. As with them, and the implications of their original focus, Parliamentary Enclosure, so with us, and the early concentration on the 'Celtic' fields of Wessex: both existed but by no means represent the whole story. Like them, and their short chronology of twenty years ago, so with us, and our early conflation of the field evidence to a bracket between the Roman period (OS 1956) and, daringly, a Late Bronze Age horizon *sensu* c. 750 BC at Itford Hill (Burstow and Holleyman 1957). As with them, and the current perspective on the place of the classic Enclosure landscape in the mosaic of British landscapes of the second millennium AD (below, p.30), so with us, and *our* current perception of the enormous regional variety of man-made landscapes over the last four millennia BC.

The information behind that perception is reasonably accessible and there is no need to review it in detail here. Piggott (1981) is fairly comprehensive with material and bibliography up to 1976, and developments since then are reasonably well-signposted in Burgess and Miket (1976), Bowen and Fowler (1978), Rees (1979), Burgess (1980) and Barrett and Bradley (1980). To its overview of the Highland Zone (Evans *et al.* 1975), the CBA has also added a complementary volume on the Lowland Zone (Limbrey and Evans 1978), both being full of data and discussion relevant to prehistoric landscapes. All these volumes contain original studies of material in localities and regions throughout Britain. To them can be added others, including specific site studies, published elsewhere, e.g. in the South West, on the Isles of Scilly (Fowler and Thomas 1979) and on Dartmoor (Fleming 1978b, Wainwright *et al.* 1979); in Wessex (Bowen and Smith 1977, Richards 1978, Wainwright 1979a and b, RCHM 1979b, Mercer 1980a, Reynolds 1980); on the Cotswolds (Savile 1980); in the Thames Valley (Parrington 1978, Lambrick and Robinson 1979); in Sussex (Drewett 1978); on the Chilterns (Matthews 1976); in East Anglia (Tilley 1979); in the Midlands (Smith 1979, Hawke-Smith 1979, RCHM 1980) and the North (Pierpoint 1980); on the Isle of Man (Davey 1978); in Wales (Taylor 1980) and in Scotland (Shepherd and Tuckwell 1976–77; Whittington 1977–78; SAF 1979, 1980; Mercer 1980b; & below pp.55–65).

AERIAL PHOTOGRAPHY

I will pick out a few aspects from the flood of data and discussion. The nature of 'the flood' can bear explanation once again, at least for those unfamiliar with the archaeological process. Discovery by aerial reconnaissance and recording by photography from the air have undoubtedly made a tremendous contribution, especially in areas where there is little

Plate 1 (*top*). Whitesheet Hill, Wilts. Three varieties of prehistoric enclosure: *centre foreground*, Neolithic causewayed enclosure, its further perimeter overlain by a ditched round barrow and the whole cut by tracks and a turnpike road; *right centre*, the successive ramparts of a hillfort inside which is a nineteenth-century tree-clump enclosure; *near, top and left centre*, four separate lengths of cross-ridge dyke cutting off the spurs and/or demarcating a block of land consisting of the central plateau otherwise defined by the head of the fairly steep slopes all round. (Author)

Plate 2. Bokerly Dyke area, Dorset/Hants. Three varieties of prehistoric linear enclosure: *centre*, the east end of the Dorset cursus, its ditch showing as a soil mark towards which are orientated long barrows, one bottom left, the other, centre, broken into three bits of mound but showing its continuous side ditches; *centre*, soil mark of a length of linear ditch, part of an extensive system of later second-millennium BC land enclosure (RCHM 1975, map opposite p.55); *right centre to top left*, the sinuous bank and scrub-covered ditch of Bokerly Dyke, in part of late-Roman construction but perhaps of earlier origin and in general marking a boundary zone still followed by the county boundary. (Author)

or nothing to see on the ground (Wilson 1975a, Hampton and Palmer 1977). Aerial photography has radically altered our view of the distribution of prehistoric agriculture both nationally and in given localities. It is now impossible (and would be meaningless) to plot over Britain the incidence of pre-Roman agrarian evidence, and even to map the distribution of early fields alone is fraught with danger (Brongers 1976, fig. 1). Prehistoric fields are certainly not ubiquitous, yet are annually coming to light where they were not previously known to exist, e.g. in East Anglia and Northumbria, and the present extremely widespread evidence for human activity often carries agrarian connotations, even if by no means always of enclosed fields. Photographs from the air also provide a further facility: they allow the production of metrically accurate maps of evidence which, being invisible, is either not susceptible to ground survey or covers such large tracts of country that instrumental survey on the ground is not a realistic proposition. Riley's (1980) excellent book graphically demonstrates this.

The theme of 'enclosure', however, cannot be confined to the study of fields alone, for land could have been, and indeed was, enclosed on much more of a landscape scale, without prejudice as to whether or not the area so bounded contained field systems. Pickering (1980), for example, has argued for the existence of considerable prehistoric boundaries in the Midlands, on a regional or 'tribal' scale, rather than on the district or 'estate' scale implied by the 'ranch boundaries' of Wessex (Bowen 1978), or the contour reaves of Dartmoor (Fleming 1979). Causewayed enclosures (plate 1), *cursus* (plate 2), henge monuments, hillforts (plate 1), all denote a wish and an ability to enclose in perhaps a different sense. In summary we can see three strands in our 'enclosure' evidence: that enclosure occurred at different levels of landscape delineation, from the regional scale to the individual plot; that the different levels were synchronous neither inter- nor intra-regionally; and that the physical materials of, and evidence for, enclosure vary both within and between regions. We can also reasonably infer that the enclosing of land was for different purposes, and not necessarily always agrarian.

OTHER DEVELOPMENTS

The contribution of aerial photography in all this is signal but by no means the only factor. Four others have played their part in the process of enlightenment, or at least of data-logging, represented by the bibliographical eruption signposted above. Programmes of fieldwork, and especially field-walking on arable land in increasingly systematic ways, not least by volunteers, have provided much detail in certain parts of the country about the density and chronology of settlement, the context within which prehistoric farming was practised (e.g. Woodward 1978, RCHM 1980, Russell 1980, Shennan 1980 and, generally, Hayfield 1980). Some of that fieldwork, leading on to excavation carried out in direct response to a 'rescue' or 'salvage' situation, has produced new information relevant to this paper, from somewhat unpromising situations in unlikely circumstances, e.g. plough marks on the routes of modern motorways under Roman roads in Hampshire and Surrey, and in Keuper Marl beneath a Roman-period settlement in the County of Avon (Fasham and Hanworth 1978, Everton and Fowler 1978). I have now lost track of all the examples of ard-marks in Britain, observations of them having multiplied exceedingly since Fowler and Evans 1967. Similarly, some 'rescue' work has produced results that have a general relevance to early farming, even though such was neither the intention nor the expectation, e.g. at Mucking, Essex (Jones 1980) and on the M5 motorway (Fowler 1977b).

The other three factors can be briefly identified, though all are interrelated and indeed in part stem from air photography and fieldwork. One is excavation itself. There has been more of it in the 1970s than ever before, much on a larger scale than previously and, critically for present purposes, some of it of a technically much higher standard than before. Of course, a good deal of it is not yet published and it is not proposed here to reference every recent excavation with an agrarian content; but those for example at Durrington Walls and Mount Pleasant (Wainwright and Longworth 1971; Wainwright 1979a), Fengate (Pryor 1974, 1978), Bishopstone (Bell 1977), Danebury (Cunliffe 1971, 1976), Gussage All Saints (Wainwright 1979b) and in the Somerset Levels (Coles 1975–80, Coles and Orme 1980) suffice to make the point.

A second factor, often closely associated with the excavation developments but also standing alone as non-archaeological research, is the growth of palaeo-environmental studies which are increasingly providing not only a site-context but also a well-attested dimension in which to consider the activities of man, and especially of man the farmer, in relation to his habitat (Fowler 1978). From specific archaeo-environmental site studies (e.g. Lambrick and Robinson 1979) to recent syntheses (e.g. Godwin 1975, Dimbleby 1978) this aspect is expanding very fast, with many important results expected in the next few years. Particularly is this so in the study of arable crops where the analyses of the huge amounts of material recently acquired by flotation techniques will not only vastly improve on, but also highlight the poverty of, the data base available just a few years ago (summarised in Fowler 1981).

The last of the four 'flood' factors is epitomised by this book: far more is being published, particularly through channels which did not exist ten years ago. My bibliography accurately reflects this: while long-standing series are tending to speed up, e.g. the Research Reports of the Society of Antiquaries, the Excavation Reports of the Directorate of Ancient Monuments and Historic Buildings, the Research Reports of the Council for British Archaeology, new series are emerging, e.g. from the British Museum (Occasional Publications), DAMHB (Occasional Papers), the Society of Antiquaries (Occasional Papers, New Series), the Royal Commission on Historical/Ancient Monuments (England) Supplementary

Series, (Scotland) *The Archaeological Sites and Monuments of . . .*, from individual projects like that on the Somerset Levels and, above all, from the private enterprise British Archaeological Reports, Oxford. Similarly, new national journals are established almost yearly, e.g. *Journal of Archaeological Science, Landscape History*. From regional down to local organisations, from University Departments of Archaeology and of Extra-Mural Studies / Adult Education across to numerous *ad hoc* bodies, indeed almost anybody with a stake in the past – they are all publishing more and more. And publishers, from respectable University Presses to the newest *arrivé* with an eye on quasi-respectability as well as profits, are also ready to launch new archaeological series and individual books. There is indeed a crisis in archaeological publication, and in part it is how to disseminate the rising tide of data; but equally, important parts of the tension are not only how to fill the media now available while maintaining academic standards but also, for the individual, how to find time to *read* the outpourings (Alcock 1977–78; see also Parsons 1977). And this is in relation only to the *British* situation. All this may seem irrelevant to farming practice in prehistoric Britain, whereas it is in fact fundamental, if not to the reality of what once was, then certainly to the reality of our current study of it.

CLEARANCE AND BOUNDARIES

Selecting some facets of that farming practice from this mass of material, let us look briefly at the archaeological and environmental evidence for the clearing of land and the physical structure of field boundaries, i.e. the early stages of 'enclosure' (stimulatingly discussed in Bradley 1978, 6–20). Vegetational clearance of land is now attested or suggested in numerous studies, both general (e.g. Shotton 1978), and specific (e.g. Evans 1979). In the latter, part of a meticulous report on excavations of three long barrows near Avebury, the environmental evidence is discussed in terms of human activities as well as natural successions. Relating to farming practice, the evidence from the South Street long barrow alone provokes thoughts on the clearance of woodland, perhaps in patches leaving a mainly wooded background (the 'wildwood'?); on the clearance of sarsen stones, perhaps towards the edge of a cultivated area; on the possible use of pigs as the initial clearer of scrub, and breakers-up of soil; on the possible use of fire to clear vegetation or to burn stubble; on cross-ploughing, again perhaps as part of the clearance operation; on the effects of tillage, notably in levelling the surface of the subsoil and in making the surface of the cultivated soil hummocky, perhaps as a result of hoe or spade action; on manuring; on the grassland existing when the barrow mound was built; on subsequent cross-ploughing when the barrow was probably itself brought under cultivation, and on a long period, from a Beaker horizon to Roman times, when all the evidence indicates a continuous grazing regime.

The archaeological evidence best supposed to represent clearance is the

Plate 3. Bodmin Moor, Cornwall. Earthfast boulders and cairns within a system of enclosed prehistoric fields. *Right foreground and centre* are 'cairns' consisting of smaller stones heaped on top of boulders. (Author)

Plate 4. Puhinui, Wiri, South Auckland, New Zealand. Clearance cairns of loose stones heaped up within a 'prehistoric' (non-European) field system of recent date on land subsequently enclosed with drystone walls. (Author)

cairnfield (plate 3), well known in northern England and Scotland (and further discussed by Halliday, Hill and Stevenson below; bibliography in Fowler 1981). Often individually slight in appearance, though collectively numerous, cairns do not readily betray their age, 'old' ones tending to be dated by association with or propinquity to prehistoric features rather than by known prehistoric characteristics (Feachem 1973); and any one might be recent (e.g. Edwards 1977–78). Nor is their function either obvious or archaeologically agreed. Nevertheless the heaping up of stones into piles, in readiness for tillage, and the removal of those brought to the surface during cultivation, is such a natural act (when everything has to be done by hand) that it is difficult not to accept the simple explanation, even if some cairns do cover burials. What we call cairnfields in Britain occur elsewhere in the world in association with land clearance and tillage (plate 4). One can hardly doubt that on Bodmin Moor, where one can actually see how the hand-sized stones were heaped on top of earthfast boulders, one is witnessing the same phenomenon (plate 3). Furthermore, we have perfectly good examples excavated in an arable context: at, for example, Carn Brea, Cornwall (Mercer 1975, fig.2.1, pl.2a) and at Glenree, Co. Mayo, in western Ireland (Herity and Eogan 1977, 50; Herity 1981).

There is truth in the idea that the history of arable farming in the western and northern British Isles is largely concerned with the problem of shifting stone. Clearance is desirable even for pasture (so cairnfields do not necessarily mean arable). Stones certainly have to be cleared before cultivation; they have, too, a disconcerting tendency to keep appearing during cultivation. Though a marked characteristic of the 'Highland Zone', the same problem occurs in some lowland areas, notably that in central southern England where sarsen stones once lay thick on some areas of downland (Bowen and Smith 1977, figs 1 and 2). The continuous emergence of flints on the shallow downland soils under arable has become only less of a handicap to favoured farmers in the south with the development of modern cropping techniques. The constant need to remove flints after ploughing, often in the biting winds of late autumn or early spring, was presumably as great in the enclosed fields of prehistoric farmers as it was until this century: a thankless, mindless task of bitter memory, but one from which cheap labour could derive a few pence (cf. Street 1932).

Cairnfields, both as a product and as a symbol of 'stone-picking', manifest a process basic to arable farming in stony country. There may be a danger of regarding them *functionally* as something special, largely because they can be identified *archaeologically* as a distinct type of site or field monument; but, in practice, in the context of prehistoric farming, are they not in many cases only a version of a field wall? To put the proposition the other way round; although cairnfields and field walls *look* so different, are not the latter in origin but linear versions of cairnfields?

In the sense that stone has to be put somewhere, and the nearer the better consonant with tillage practice, this view has its merits; but of course it begs the question of why the change, why the move to enclose an area with a boundary instead of leaving it open but dotted with heaps of stone? Not that the two phenomena, cairnfield and enclosed field, are mutually exclusive; indeed they often occur together and the recognition of the one can lead to the recognition of the other. Calder (1955–56, fig.6) is a classic example from the formative years of agrarian fieldwork and Feachem (1973) provides more recent examples, with Gates's and Johnson's (1980) surveys, respectively on Cheviot and Bodmin Moor, providing current illustration of the same point. Information from another current project which includes excavation bears on this matter too.

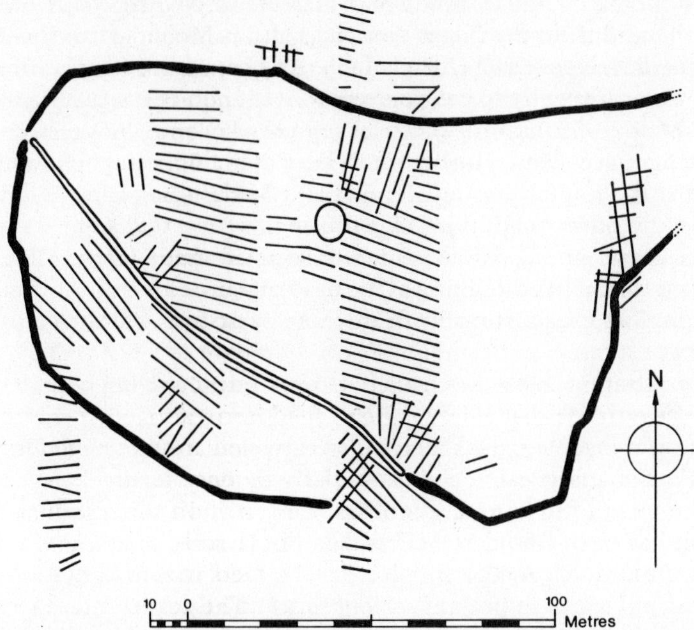

Figure 1. Glenree, Co. Mayo. Plan of later second-millennium BC field walls (earlier outlined, later solid) enclosing and overlying rig, as excavated beneath blanket bog up to 1980 (the areas without rig have not yet been excavated; after Herity 1981.) Scale 1:2,000

At Glenree in Co. Mayo, Herity (1981) reports clearance heaps up to 6.50 by 2.50 m buried beneath blanket bog and related to an area of cultivation which was in part initially bounded by what he describes as a 'series of linear cairns' (figure 1). This irregular line of stones, against which a lynchet developed on the uphill side, was subsequently robbed, its larger stones apparently being used in a double-faced and coursed wall 320 m long around three sides of a field. This enclosure of c. 2.2 ha more than doubled the cultivated area previously at least partly defined, though its construction (visually identical to fields of Parliamentary Enclosure crossing mediaeval ridge-and-furrow in Midland England) cut across earlier ridges from apparently 'unenclosed' cultivation. Having drawn the analogy, let me stress the difference in scale: whereas Midland ridge-and-furrow is characteristically c. 9 m wide and sometimes a metre or more high, the Glenree ridges are on average 1.50 m across and but a few centimetres high. Their origin is thought to be a spade-cultivation of the 'lazy-bed' type, though, as so often with English ridge-and-furrow, they run mainly with the contours for up to 100 m in the area excavated. Some of them form a lattice-pattern, apparently representing successive cultivation of the same area. Pollen analysis indicates wheat-growing, with a suggestion of soil impoverishment perhaps resulting from over-cropping. A stone-based house some 7 m in diameter and with a central hearth lay near the middle of the ridged area and a charcoal sample from beneath the later field wall gave a C14 'date' of 1295 ± 85 bc, supporting the 'Bronze Age' horizon minimally to be expected from the sub-peat situation of the whole complex. The farming practices represented were, however, apparently taking place about a millennium later than the analogous sub-peat evidence at the not far distant Glenulra and Belderg Beg sites (Caulfield 1978). On the other hand, the C14 estimate is within the range of that of layer 5 at Gwithian, Cornwall, where associated spade-marks (Thomas 1970) hinted at the hand-digging of the headland in fields cultivated with a traction implement, presumably an ard (Megaw 1976; Fowler 1981, 195-8).

FIELD SYSTEMS

One generalisation, close to a truism, is worth emphasising here, if only because the attitude that a field is just a field is not altogether extinct, at least among archaeologists. Wherever an early field or adjacent fields have been looked at analytically, and particularly in these relatively few cases where the technique of excavation has been used on them, evidence of sucession has been found as well as detail of farming practice (e.g. Bell 1977, here figure 8). At the simplest level a field system is not just the uninteresting, lesser important *penumbra* around the 'real' sites to which archaeology has tended to devote its attention. Again in simple terms, a field is a unit of production, with the vital qualification *at any one moment of time*. Look at it through time, if possible with its neighbours, and, as with other types of monument, we find that it changes shape and size, its boundaries alter in place and construction, the land it encloses has earlier and later uses, the field itself serves different purposes. Each field is in fact a reservoir of evidence pertinent to its locality and, certainly in our present state of knowledge, often to much wider issues also, as illustrated by projects such as those at Glenree, Fengate (Pryor 1974, 1978) and Mucking (Jones 1980).

From a *plethora* of evidence, the last site, Mucking in Essex, has now produced a plan of fragments of another second-millennium BC landscape (figure 2; Jones and Bond 1980). Two aspects of this recognition are

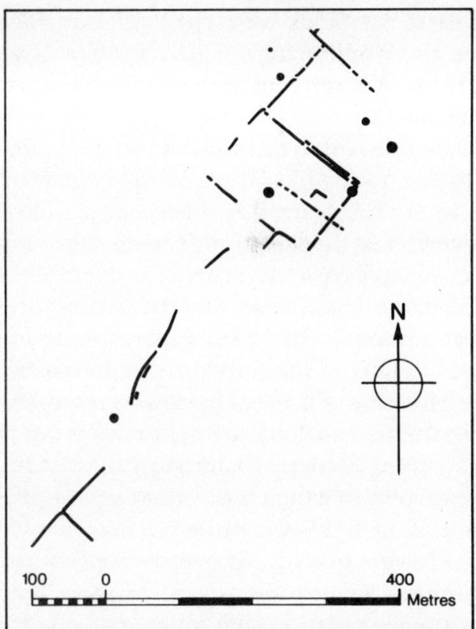

Figure 2. Mucking, Essex. Plan of later second-millennium field ditches and barrow cemetery as excavated (after Jones 1980, fig.1). Scale 1 : 10,000

picked out for present purposes. First, the area is on the 30 m gravel terrace of the Thames. My superficial impression is that, curiously perhaps, not many genuine prehistoric field systems on river gravels have been recognised, let alone planned (cf. RCHM 1960, 12–13; Benson and Miles 1974, fig.11 is an exception; Gates 1975, map 7 is also an exception; Leech 1977). None, for example, have been recognised, so far, in Northamptonshire (RCHM 1980). This is not to say that valley gravels were not cultivated: clearly they were (e.g. Lambrick and Robinson 1979) but apparently not often in contiguous ditched fields. Of course, there are thousands of examples of enclosures recorded on air photographs, but these are often part of or immediately around settlements, suggesting functions as closes, paddocks or even gardens (cf. Lambrick and Robinson 1979, 139). Continuous systems of enclosed fields, as on the chalk downs, are not well-established, and so far certainly not for the second millennium. Fengate and Fisherwick are obvious exceptions, suggesting perhaps that others await recognition (Pryor 1974, 1978; Smith 1979). The Mucking fragments have emerged only from the excavated complexity (Jones 1980, fig.36), not from air photography (Jones 1979). At Mucking, only two contiguous Middle/Late Bronze Age fields have so far been recognised in this complex pattern (though at least one other is implied on the N) but they are perhaps to be related to fragments of a linear ditch system and two further incomplete fields to the SW, all suggestively orientated. The ditches of these SW fields were cut by the ditches of a putative defensive enclosure, the 'South Rings', with C14 'dates' from its mid-ditch silts centering in the mid-ninth century bc (as visible now with hindsight in Jones 1979, pls L, LXIII).

The second aspect of this site relevant to our subject is the relationship of the two northerly fields, each c. 130 by 160 m, to a barrow cemetery with C14 'dates' from ditch silts in the fourteenth–twelfth centuries bc. One barrow is earlier than the easternmost field ditch; this latter being cut into the barrow-ditch for which charcoal gave a C14 'date' of 1150 bc. The field ditch, however, respected the mound, perhaps using it as a marker for the field corner in a way familiar among 'Celtic' field systems on the Chalk downs (e.g. RCHM 1970a, 623). This is the only direct relationship between a field and a barrow at Mucking; the other barrows (ring-ditches as found) were scattered within the area enclosed by field ditches but it was not established whether they were earlier or later than the fields. It is perhaps likely that they were earlier, in which case either they would have been ploughed over or around if the fields were tilled or they would have stood proud in grass if the fields were grazed. Alternatively, of course, the 'fields' could have been funerary enclosures or the barrows built on abandoned fields. Whatever the explanation, the Mucking evidence implies the enclosure of land on gravel in the late second millennium, perhaps for agriculture, perhaps for burial, an apparently clear distinction unlikely to have existed so sharply then (cf. Fleming 1972, Ashbee 1976, Fowler and Thomas 1979).

THE LAWFORD EVIDENCE

Some other valley enclosures located by aerial photographs about forty-four miles to the NE lie N of Lawford on the south bank of the Stour (TM 086327; figure 3, plates 5a and b). They have been illustrated before, though only to make a technical point about the taking of aerial photographs, for which purpose the caption merely drew attention to the crop-marks of ring ditches showing on the two air photographs published (Wilson 1975b, fig. 1). The ring-ditches, which are much more clearly apparent than at Mucking, lie within a ditched enclosure which is part of a larger system of such enclosures, apparently fields. The area could hardly be more low-lying: it is right on the valley floor, dry now by virtue of a system of drains and an embankment along the river's southern edge, and faced on the other side by an area of marshland, as plate 5a illustrates.

The air photographs published here are but two of many of this area now deposited in the National Monuments Record (where all are retrievable by reference to the National Grid). As is usual no one photograph shows exactly the same archaeological data and figure 3 is a composite sketch diagram drawing on all of them, including the two published

---

Figure 3. Lawford, Essex. Diagrammatic sketch plan of second-millennium BC barrow cemetery and fields based on air photographs (cf. plate 3). Scale 1 : 10,000, contours in feet above OD.

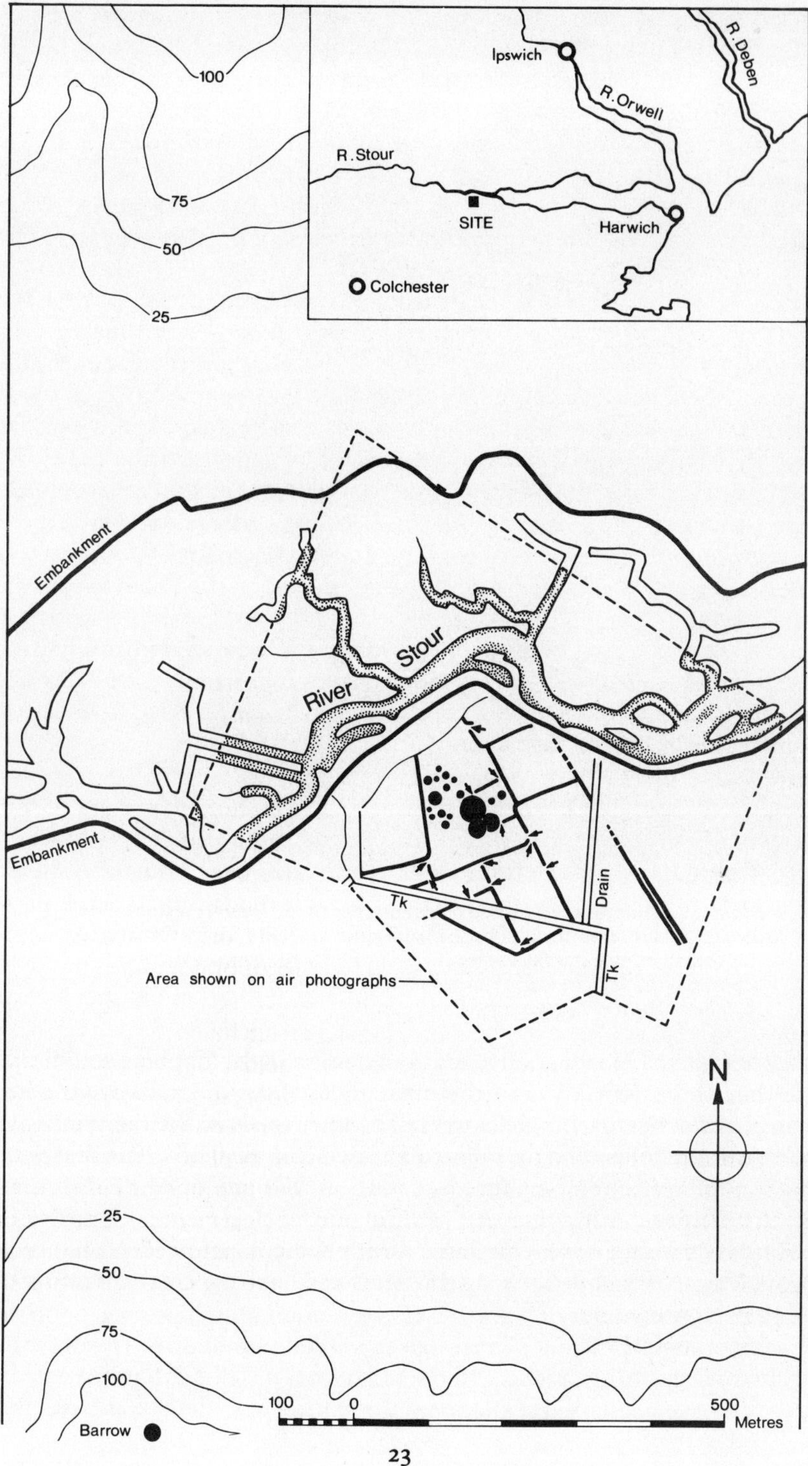
100
75
50
25
Ipswich
R. Orwell
R. Deben
R. Stour
SITE
Harwich
Colchester
Embankment
River Stour
Embankment
Tk
Drain
Tk
Area shown on air photographs
N
25
50
75
100
Barrow
100
0
500
Metres

Plate 5. Lawton, Essex. Ditched fields and a barrow cemetery, presumably of the second millennium BC, on the S bank of the R. Stour. The different crop conditions bring out different features, notably on the barrows and the 'gateways' through the field boundaries cf. figure 3. (*Left* 5a 1974, *right* 5b 1976, NMR, RCHM; Crown copyright.)

photographs. This diagram is highly selective of the air photographic data and has three objectives in the present context: to emphasize the low-lying, almost estuarine, location of the site; to show the relationship of barrows and fields; and to illustrate the detail of the fields. The first point, the topography, is self-evident. Secondly, unlike at Mucking, all eighteen of the barrows are contained within one enclosure; and thirdly, the boundary ditches have entrances through them (arrowed on figure 3), providing access both between the fields and on to the area containing the large barrow cemetery.

Interpretation of this picture raises several points directly relevant to prehistoric farming practice. In the first place, it is difficult to see how the area can have been used at all unless the natural water level was lower than

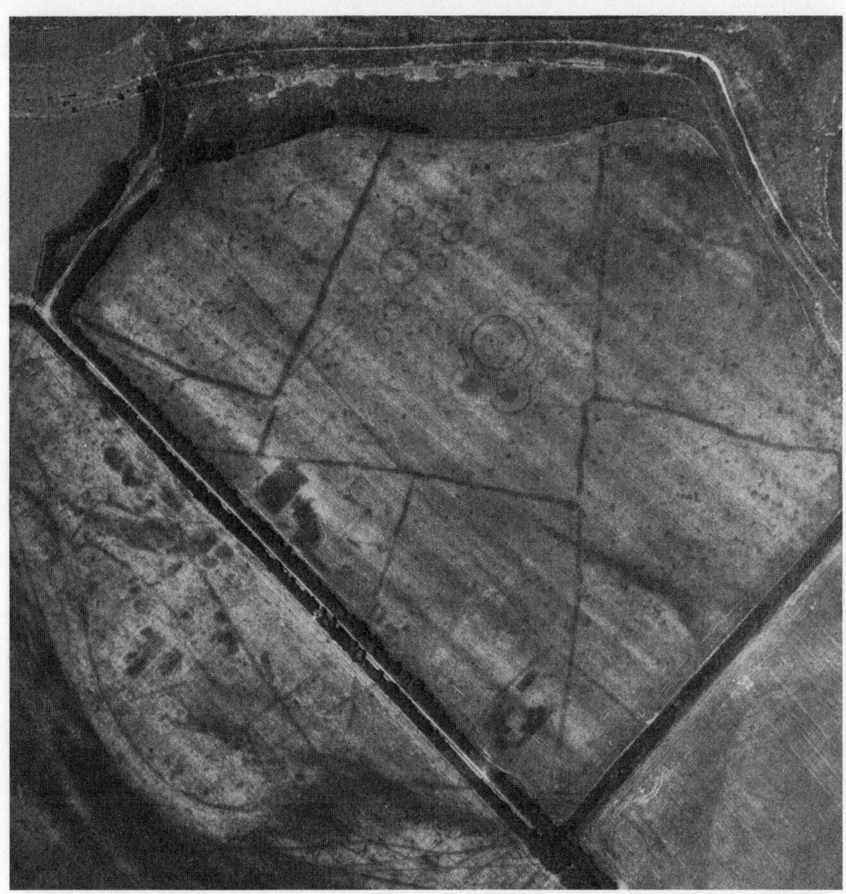

it now is. Either the sea/river level was lower in relation to the land in the second millennium bc or the land was made usable by works – embankments and drainage ditches – of the sort making it agriculturally viable now. The incomplete nature of the fields at the NW and NE corners of the system as plotted implies that the ditches enclosed land now beneath the embankment and perhaps that the river has moved slightly southwards to cut away some of that land since the prehistoric 'enclosure' was established. The barrow cemetery, itself notable in its own right, is part of a known distribution along the valleys of the Stour, Brett, Orewell and Deben and across the Essex/Suffolk coastlands (St Joseph 1966, figs 4, 5, subsequently much added to; this cemetery is not shown, though the single barrow, lower left of figure 3, is). The centrepiece, or focal barrow, appears to be the triple monument of which the largest, double-ditched circle is c. 33 m in overall diameter. While it might at first appear that the cemetery is within a field, closer inspection suggests that the area of land it occupies was defined, negatively as it were, by the encroachment of

Plate 6. Pertwood Down, Wilts. Part of a 'Celtic' field system, partly preserved under sheep-grazed grass, *left*, and under arable, *right*, showing details of lynchets, staggered angles and the sharp prehistoric boundary with unenclosed and formerly uncultivated land to the N. (NMR, RCHM; Crown Copyright)

enclosed fields up to it. In other words, the barrows came to occupy a reserved area, much larger than a single field, in an enclosed, agricultural landscape of contemporary or later date. A specific analogy is provided by the special status apparently accorded to the Snail Down Bronze Age cemetery on Salisbury Plain, as the landscape developed there (Bowen 1975, fig.6; 1978, fig.1). General comparison can be made with the barrow/field relationships in the Stonehenge area (Fleming 1971, RCHM 1979b).

That the fields were formed around the cemetery area at Lawford is suggested by one of the interesting features of their boundaries. The eastern edge of the cemetery is made up of three different though conjoined ditches, one forming the W and N sides of the southernmost field, another forming the W and S sides of the northernmost field, and the third linking the first two. It links them, however, in such a way as to leave a 'staggered angle' at the NW and SW corners respectively of the two fields, between which it bounds a middle field. This arrangement, a familiar characteristic of downland 'Celtic' fields (cf. plate 6), implies that the cemetery is 'outside' the field system. The remarkable feature of these field boundaries is, however, the clear breaks along them: so clear and sys-

Plate 7. Deanshanger, Northants. Pit alignment showing as a line of discrete crop-mark 'blobs' from left to right across the centre of the photograph. Though the distribution of these 'boundaries' as a type now extends over much of Britain with a date range spanning the last few thousand years BC, many seem to relate to land allotment in the later first millennium BC. Curiously, however, not one example is yet known in earthwork form and the phenomenon, known only from air photography and excavation, is little understood. (NMR, RCHM; Crown copyright reserved)

tematic as to justify regarding them as gateways. Ten occur across the ditches around and between fields; three more occur, though not so obviously as 'gateways', at the ends of the narrow ditches (palisades?) running out from the eastern edge of the cemetery area towards the great triple barrow. Their presence in conjunction with 'staggered' angles strongly suggests, here anyway, that the explanation of the latter is not as access ways to the fields (*contra* Bowen 1961, 24 on 'Celtic' fields). The contemporaneity of fields and cemetery is also implied by the access to the latter through three 'gateways', from N, E and W, out of the former. Gaps at the ends of ditches forming enclosures in the second millennium are well-established by excavation at Fengate where they are interpreted as 'entranceways' to fields which 'might well have been used as stock enclosures' (Pryor 1978, 157). While it is perhaps tempting to think of little funerary processions wending their way to the cemetery through the Lawton fields and out through the gateways, the Fengate interpretation reminds us that the gaps in the ditches may actually have been to turn a few cattle out on to a bit of old pasture too bumpy to be ploughed up. At any rate, the riverside at Lawton provides a revealing but enigmatic glimpse of a fragment of a second-millennium landscape in Eastern England, to set beside the better-known *comparanda* on Wessex downland and South Western granite. One 'three-dimensional' difference is that on Dartmoor and Bodmin Moor one can actually see the gateposts (e.g. Fleming 1978b, pl.12 upper).

WHY 'ENCLOSE'?

Many other aspects of prehistoric 'enclosure' must go by default here; for example, a big question mark remains against pit alignments, a major but unexplained type of landscape feature in prehistoric Britain (plate 7; Wilson 1978). Nevertheless, though only a very partial survey, I hope this discussion, backed as it is by Piggott (1981) and other recent work (Bradley 1978b), indicates the sort of evidence now available on farming practice in prehistoric Britain. Obviously we want to know what it means. Why was so much enclosure carried out? Who carried it out? How was it done? And when? We do not have answers to the first two questions, though we can begin to answer the last two. The dating, such as it is, is fairly well-known and need not be rehearsed here (see, for example, Bradley 1978a, Piggott 1981). The method of enclosure was, as later, by digging ditches, building banks and walls, fencing (plate 8) and presumably hedging, for mile after mile often, it seems, within a master landscape plan (figure 4). People did it, but who they were we can but guess, unless the distinction is made between those who caused it to be done, who are anonymous, and those who physically carried out the work, who are also anonymous but would surely have been the prehistoric equivalent of the documented farm labourer of historic times.

Whatever the technology, there is not much alternative in enclosure and whether one is tackling virgin landscape, moving in after grazing livestock, or adjusting an existing landscape, our prehistoric labourers would have had to clear undergrowth, burn or chop down trees, strain and sweat over manhandled boulders, stoop and straighten with hand-sized stones – that scenario is really a non-question at the practical level, though obviously we want to ask different sociological and organisational questions. Was this wall built by work-gangs? Were they slaves, hired labourers or free peasants joyfully singing as they, like the Seven Dwarfs, set about their communal labour of love?

And why was it done? We can never be absolutely certain, and we can probably seldom be certain even in any given instance; but in general agricultural terms we can give some sort of answer, because there is really a very short range of reasons worldwide why a field is built: to keep animals in or out; to protect the crop; to improve the land; to define property (RCHM 1960, 12 defines a field system; Chapman 1969, 96 defines the objects of crop growing). You could add 'for convenience' as another

---

Figure 4. Cheselbourne and Piddletrenthide, Dorset. Diagrammatic interpretation of part of an accurately plotted 'Celtic' field system to emphasize, by using different line thicknesses, the extensive, cohesive, striplike and axial

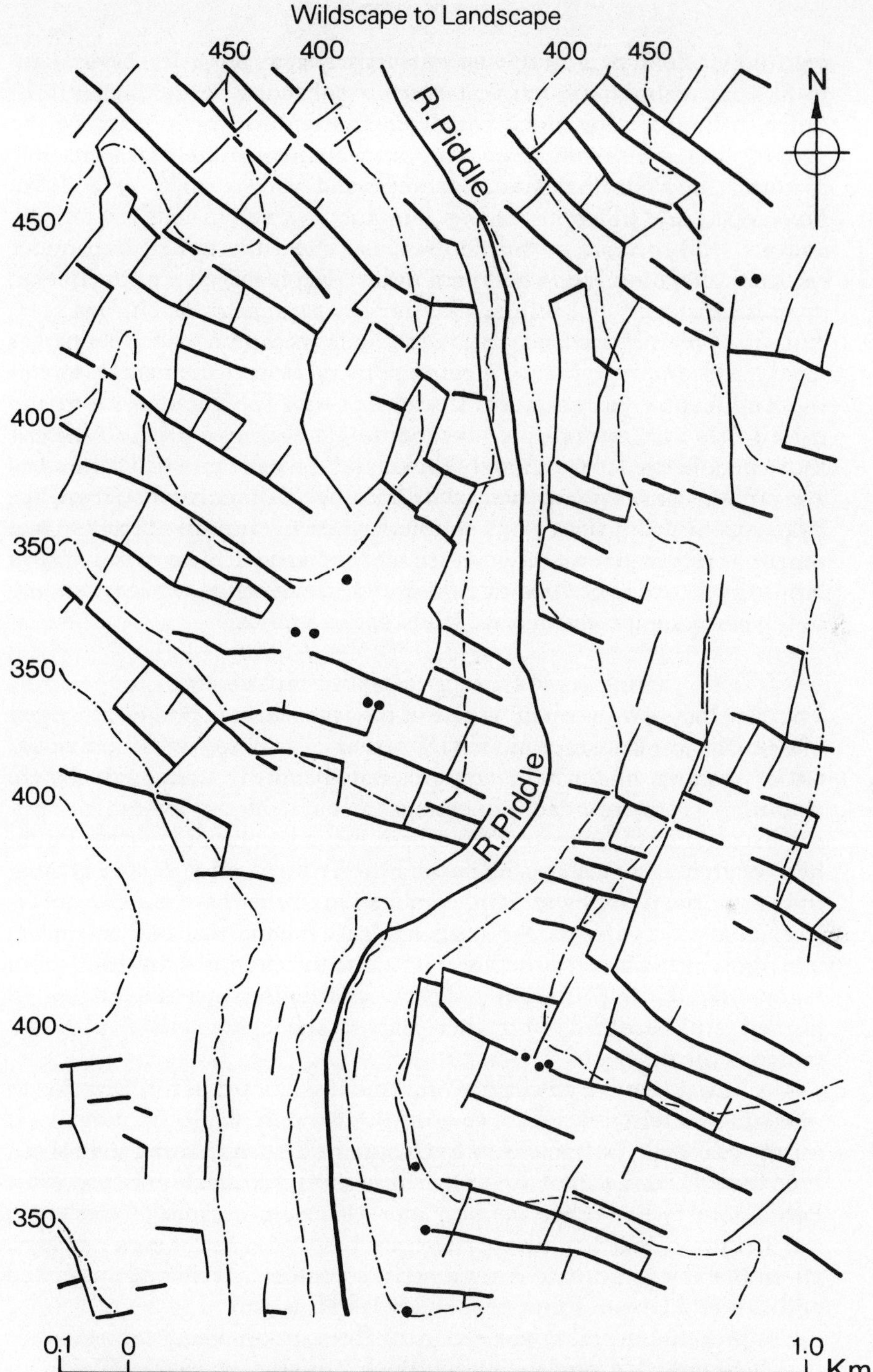

nature of this example of later prehistoric enclosure crossing the valley of the R. Piddle (based on RCHM 1970b, plan in end pocket). Scale 1 : 10,000

reason for a field, by arguing that you might shape a piece of enclosed land to fit your technology; but that is really subsumed in the unstated 'in order to improve the yield' which implicitly follows my 'improve the land'. In fact, greater efficiency is the factor common to all the reasons. For historical English Enclosure, Chambers and Mingay (1966, 79–80) give four apparently different reasons – to allow more efficient farming, to convert land to more profitable uses, to extend the area of land under regular cultivation and to get rid of tithes – but in fact all are but facets of greater efficiency. So, in a sense, there is no mystery about our great extents of prehistoric landscape: the people who were using those areas were quite simply trying to be better farmers, as were their successors in the eighteenth and nineteenth centuries AD. The significance of the palaeo-field systems for us is what they might be able to tell us about how those people tried to (or thought they could) be more productive in times and circumstances not of their own choosing. Neither lynchet, reave nor dyke was built for fun or our delectation; each, with kilometres of like remains, represents a conscious attempt at considerable cost to improve farming practice in prehistoric Britain and, incidentally, each charts a step in the permanent conversion of wildscape to landscape.

THE HISTORICAL ENCLOSURE MOVEMENT

The 'Enclosure Movement' is one of the favourite and best-documented of all historical landscape models. Whether it can in any way illumine our understanding of what is now a single-handedly unknowable large amount of prehistoric data is questionable, but it offers at least an interesting exercise in comparison. We cannot just go on heaping up the dung-heap of archaeological data, expecting the Truth to emerge like a glistening slug driven out by internal combustion; rather have our caterpillar-like ideas to crawl over the heap, with us hoping that one will metamorphose into a butterfly to satisfy us with its perfection for a while before it too, like the 'Neolithic Revolution' or the 'Invasion Hypothesis', is pinned, still beautiful but by then inert, in the lepidopterists' collection which is the history of scholarship.

Assuming that the Enclosure Movement is not yet in historians' eyes one such butterfly, how can we quickly anatomise it? Conventionally, it means of course Parliamentary Enclosure in England, dating from about 1760 into the first half of the nineteenth century; though in fact sporadic Parliamentary Enclosure went on later, Grimston in Dorset for example not being enclosed until 1907 (Bettey 1980, 36), and it never became all-embracing as our surviving greens, commons, patches of waste, and oddities like Laxton show, even in lowland England.

For present purposes, we need to ask three groups of questions:

1. Why did it happen? i.e. what is the historical explanation? Was it, for example, motivated by profit or altruism?

2. Who did it? i.e. was it a corporate or individual response? Can a

Plate 8. Butser Ancient Farm Project, Hants. An impressionistic view of the small hurdle-fenced enclosures, one with Soay sheep, around the 'settlement' on Little Butser Hill, with a fenced trackway separating them from an arable field, *right centre,* and becoming a holloway curving up the distant slope. Does this approximate visually to the sort of three-dimensional reality lying behind our field, cropmark and excavated evidence of prehistoric enclosure? (Author)

particular group of people be singled out as instigators? Who benefited and who suffered?

3. What was the effect on the landscape? i.e. what preceded it? What was its geographical extent? Was there variety in its local impact and variation in its physical form? How long did it last? What superseded it?

History gives apparently firm answers to our questions. The landscape was enclosed by Acts of Parliament because, to give a popular view, 'the mushrooming of populous industrial towns coincided with the development of agricultural ideas which would make possible the feeding of a rapidily increasing urban population. Putting them into practice, however, necessitated a drastic reorganisation of the rural economy, in part aided and in part aggravated by the intervention of the Napoleonic Wars' (Whitlock 1965, 37). That is doubtless too simplistic a summary but, to elevate its essential ingredients to the level of abstraction, we can identify reasons for major landscape change in impersonal economic forces, technological development, population growth and war plus the threat of blockade. Without going into detail, other factors included an intellectual excitement reflected in the correspondence and diaries of the time; a successful propagandist campaign pushed harder after 1793 with the intervention of central Government through the medium of the new Board of Agriculture; a series of poor harvests; and a rapid increase in the availability of professional expertise both to put an Act through Parliament and to sort out the details of the Award subsequently (Tate 1967, Turner 1977). Already the model contains so many explanatory ingredients that one begins to doubt its usefulness in illuminating archaeological phenomena at another time. Nevertheless, this provides a useful antidote, particularly by being so recent and so well-documented, to a monocausal explanation of our mute prehistoric evidence.

One basic fact, relevant to the thoughts of archaeologists looking at their spreads of linear ditches and early fields, is that Enclosure required an enormous physical effort and was often expensive and increasingly so. In Warwickshire, for example, the cost was on average 11 shillings per acre before 1760; it rose to 34 shillings in the 1790s and to nearly 62 shillings after 1801 (Martin 1964, cf. Turner 1973). The details do not matter here; the significance surely is the cost by eighteenth-century values and in their fourfold increase in forty years. Yet the 'Enclosure Movement' happened; during the eighteenth and nineteenth centuries at least 5,400 individual enclosures under nearly 4,200 Acts enclosed some seven million acres. Neither the effort, which must have been of the same order as that required in the first if not the second millennium BC, nor the increasing cost, deterred the movers overall or prevented the 'Movement' from taking place. Does this not raise a little query as to whether profit (the undoubted motive documentarily-speaking) was not helped along to some extent by that elusive, undocumented other factor, fashion? And are we not seeing a bit of that today, as farmer after insurance company pointlessly replaces his Enclosure hedges with invisible hedges against inflation (Shoard 1980)? If so, how on earth do we recognise fashion in the prehistoric landscape? If we think we can do so with art-styles and brooches, for example, why should we not do so with what is after all merely a larger artefact? The difficulties are perhaps physical rather than intellectual; it is cold on Cheviot in winter and warm in the Antiquaries' library.

Our second question was 'who did it?'. With the Enclosure Movement, we can answer both in general and, in many cases, with the names of individuals. Each Act was a corporate promotion in that a group of landholders had first to agree between themselves to initiate the promotion of a Bill. We can wonder about the extent of persuasion, even coercion, at local level within a village and community before such documented agreement was reached (cf. Mingay 1968). In general, it was the substantial landholders who wanted Enclosure and who took the initiative; in general, it was the 'small man', with his minor but, to him, all-important tenurial rights, especially in the common grazing, who had little incentive to change but little resistance to offer against the pressure of his farming and social superiors; though there are examples of successful resistance, like that at Berkhamsted (Munby 1977, 187–8). So there are, predictably, shades of response to subsidiary questions such as 'Was Enclosure a corporate or individual response?' and 'Was a particular group the instigator?'. Similarly, there is no simple answer to 'Who benefited and who suffered?'. In general, the principle of 'unto them that hath shall more be given', and its converse 'the lowly shall remain so', can be argued to have applied; but there are many exceptions (e.g. Martin 1967). So much depended on local conditions of, for example, geology, social structure and available capital (cf. Horn 1980).

To elaborate on the last, the whole point of re-arranging land-holding was so that individuals could hold their land in consolidated blocks; but this was only a means to an end. If, after Enclosure, an individual was then unable to invest the capital necessary to improve the productivity of that land – which was the point of the exercise – by drainage, hedge planting, ditching, new machinery, fertilisers, new crops and livestock, then the change would scarcely of itself be profitable either in increased land values or annual cash returns and might prove in the medium to long term a financial embarrassment. Particularly could this be so on poor quality or marginal land. Our uplands are littered with, literally, the field evidence of failed Enclosure; sometimes the failure is not even archaeologically in evidence. On Fyfield Down, Wiltshire, for example, the immaculate cartography of the Award (Wilts CRO, Trowbridge) with its neat, straight lines of what was to be to the benefit of the Duke of Marlborough finds no counterpart upon the ground. The Down, enclosed in the mid-first millennium BC, was in fact never Enclosed, despite the unambiguous late eighteenth-century documentary evidence which in reality is a blueprint of intention and not a statement of achievement (Chapman 1978 discusses other problems of interpretation of Enclosure Awards).

My third question was 'What was the effect on the landscape?'. The simple answer which it would be nice to give would of course refer to that which we can now see around us. Indeed, discounting recent and current ravage by Man and Nature, for parts of England like the East Midlands the generalisation contains much truth. We all know, however, that this major factor in modern English history, the Enclosure Movement, is, geographically-speaking, of limited extent (Hoskins 1955, fig.14). It does not explain in landscape terms that which we have available for study over most of England, let alone the British Isles; and there is marked, and culturally significant, variety even within one county, e.g. Hertfordshire (Munby 1977, chap.7). Seebohm, Maitland, and then, overtly, H.L. Gray ran into this problem, neatly circumvented by many later writers of history books although illuminated for us in the work of Hoskins and many others over the last twenty-five years (bibliography in Fowler 1980).

Nevertheless, the Enclosure Movement in its nuclear area did produce a distinctive landscape classically characterised by regularity and rectangularity in the layout, size, shape and boundaries of its fields, in the nature of its internal access system, and in its settlement pattern of nucleated villages and new, outlying farmsteads and rows of labourers' cottages. Negatively it does not have sunken lanes, and, importantly for us, the standardised landscape does not denote a particular form of agrarian economy. Enclosure was carried out locally to improve pastoral as much as arable farming and often sustained a range of mixed farming in between. In other words, if the physical evidence of Enclosure had been created in the undocumented second millennium BC instead of AD, we would be on the wrong track in trying to infer uniformity of function from similarity of form.

So far I have used the model of the 'Enclosure Movement' as if it were an historical event, clear-cut in time and with unambiguously defined causes and effects, as if it really were a subject existing only on an 'O' level examination syllabus. Since any historians will be wincing at my crude, generalistic summary, may I say that, unfortunately for present purposes, I know full well that modern historical scholarship does not see it that way at all. The modern work of Chambers and Mingay (1966), Mingay (1977), Thirsk (1957, 1967, 1970), E. L. Jones (1967), Baker and Butlin (1973) and Dodgshon (1980), and of many now working at a local level, both demonstrates enormous county and regional variety and poses fundamental questions about the so-called 'Movement' or the 'Agricultural Revolution' itself. The subject is in fact as controversial as the origins of our earliest farming or the nature of Anglo-Saxon field systems (Fowler 1980). In particular, some historians see that the enormous concentration of research effort on the years c. 1760–1830 happened because of the voluminous and easily accessible documentary evidence from that period; and it resulted in a loss of historical perspective. The Parliamentary tail was in danger of growing larger than the Enclosure dog just as, for a phase of earlier historical scholarship, the ready availability of the documents led for a time to an overemphasis on constitutional history at the expense of, say, medieval social history. Similarly, a largely unconscious concentration on the visible evidence of later prehistoric Wessex led archaeological perspective to become warped, especially in the matter of farming and land-use, as it continues to do, because of the 'obviousness' of the evidence, over Roman Britain.

One aspect of the re-appraisal of historical Enclosure seems particularly relevant to whether there was the prehistoric equivalent or equivalents of what has been regarded as the monolithic late-eighteenth/early-nineteenth-century Enclosure Movement. It is relevant conceptually, and it is relevant in offering a possibility of physically relating in the landscape historical Enclosure and prehistoric evidence. It stems from the continuing analysis, in some detail, of the process of *pre*-Parliamentary enclosure. That this occurred has for long been generally recognised, and has been demonstrated in particular places: the interests of historians and archaeologists finding, literally, common ground in medieval villages abandoned through enclosure by, for example, Cistercian community or Tudor landlord (Beresford and Hurst 1971). In other words, the Parliamentary encloser did not start with a clean slate; indeed in many places the Act was merely an official tidying up at the end of a long, complicated and piecemeal process. And as we have noted, for much of Britain there was no local reflection of the Enclosure Movement as popularly understood at all. Stonewalled fields in current use near Porthmeor, Cornwall, for example, owe nothing to Parliament, having been enclosed in the first if not the second millennium BC.

My main point here is that the recognition and acceptance of an Enclosure perspective, of a concept of long-term enclosing of the land to produce the rural landscape of, say 1830, gives us a fundamentally different model to apply, if we so wish, to our prehistory. We can test the short, sharp shock model of the school text book and the *Oxford History of England* (Watson 1960, 34–5, 520–1), or the 'intermediate 200 year model' (Chambers and Mingay 1966) or, to push the organic approach to its present limits, the 'Hoskins/Taylor archaeo-documentary continuum model' (Hoskins 1955; Taylor 1975, 1980). This last would not only see Parliamentary Enclosure as but the then latest phase of a continual process but would insert into that landscape reshuffle elements from all the preceding phases. They would be there as landmarks of one sort and another: obvious and derelict ones like hillforts, settlements and barrows; less obvious ones like boundary lines and access ways; all a sort of cultural debris littered over the landscape, what we now grace with words like Ancient Monument, Historic Building, Cultural Resource and Countryside Treasure. My emphasis would be that not only was this litter there, but that some bits of it acted as constraints upon a later phase of development. I do not want to enter upon 'the continuity problem' here, not least because the thought in my mind could actually be the antithesis of continuity. The avoidance of a barrow by leaving it alone on a gore between furlongs in a medieval open field is not exactly continuity as usually understood (as at Woodford, Northants, RCHM 1975, 111); but it is a minor example of the sort of 'constraint' I have in mind. More significant by far is the evidence accruing now, not least in the heartlands of Enclosure, that just as the Parliamentary landscape was in part constrained, despite its ruthlessness in places, by the framework of the existing landscape including the open fields, so what was there in the eighteenth century had itself been affected by earlier land arrangements (Taylor and Fowler 1978). I am thinking in particular of the air photographic evidence of undated but earlier boundaries underlying and in places compatible with the now well-attested long headlands (figure 5) which themselves provided the skeleton of the open fields which in their

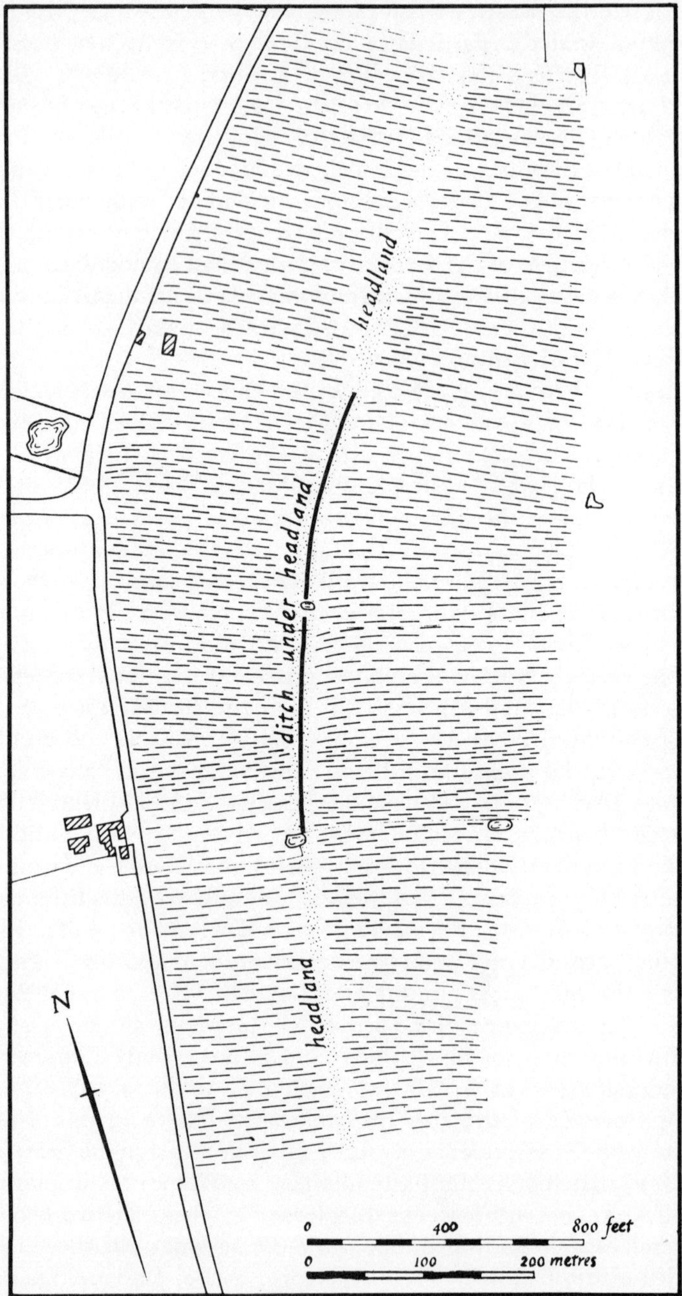

Figure 5. Walgrave, Northants. Plan of a ditch showing as a cropmark beneath a headland between medieval ridge-and-furrow (reproduced from RCHM 1979, fig. 133). Scale approx. 1:6,400

turn conditioned Parliamentary Enclosure (RCHM 1975, xlii–xliv; 1979a, lx–lxiii). In sum, archaeological evidence can add at the more distant end of the time perspective within which Parliamentary Enclosure is now seen by historians; and this can make quite a difference to the model of the Enclosure Movement with which I began.

DISCUSSION

However crude my historical summary, one fact stands out: we sought simplicity and have found complexity. And this for a process which is extraordinarily well-documented, and totally mapped both in the making and subsequently in great detail by the Ordnance Survey at a scale of 1:2500. It is something which has been studied by great scholars, which has left its overwhelming imprint on our daily countryside, and which happened barely 200 years ago. The interpretative implications of that for 2000 and 4000 years ago are plain; but if we ignore the historians' controversies about Enclosure and concentrate on its main elements we can surely identify a baseline usable in looking at our dumb prehistoric evidence. In theory, at a moment in time somewhere in the fifth millennium BC, someone laid out the first British field: the agrarian inroad on the wildscape began, the 'enclosure movement' was under way. We have not yet found that field though, for all we know, its existence is reflected in one of the many pollen diagrams laid before us by our palynological colleagues. Possibly, however, the first enclosures were for livestock rather than crop-production. Despite numerous hints of their existence, fields and more particularly systems of enclosed fields do not actually appear unequivocally in the archaeological record until much later. They must have existed, however, and from an early phase if one reads aright the implications of the subsoil buried beneath the South Street barrow (above, p.16). Reactions of surprise to the mere existence of plausible ard-marks at such an early date, which now, corrected, would be in the middle of the fourth millennium, have perhaps obscured the real significance of that evidence. This surely is that, in looking at the palimpsest of marks, we are looking at evidence for repeated and similar actions over the same area and therefore at the subsoil of a 'field'. This may have been merely a patch of cultivated ground in isolation, conceivably part of an 'outfield' in an infield/outfield system which seems to me much more likely to have been operative then than the much-favoured 'swidden' economy model for which there seems to be no convincing evidence at all (cf. below, pp.85–95). The South Street evidence, though it is *our* earliest, speaks to me of assuredness; its creators knew what they were at; and they possessed the implement for the job (plate 9, cf. Leser 1931, 332. fig.182). They were not leaving us the traces of a tentative experiment; rather were they already operating within a tradition, its roots probably in fifth-millennium south-eastern Europe.

If that patch of preserved ground beneath the South Street long barrow

Plate 9. Possible types of prehistoric ard for breaking up new ground for tillage of a size and strength necessary to create the deep ard-marks beneath the South Street long barrow: (a) an actual example (minus the sawn-off beam) photographed in NW Spain showing the iron bar-share on what is essentially a crook ard formerly used specifically for 'soil-busting'; (b) a remarkably similar but apparently imaginary nineteenth-century reconstruction of the ard type, dressed up with 'Roman' wheels and long stilt. (a, author; b, source unknown)

was once part of an area cultivated in one of a number of contiguous enclosed fields, it will not be too surprising when we find our Middle Neolithic and earlier field systems. They will turn up, perhaps not on the present land surface and probably not in the 'classic' field areas, but buried beneath the erosion deposits in a lowland English valley; or just out of sight below the rim of a bog or marsh (cf. Whittington 1977–78 with a C14 'date' of 2800 bc for a soil beneath a stone dyke); or spread out on a buried surface below a massive sand-dune formation somewhere on coastal western Britain as at Benbecula (Shepherd and Tuckwell 1976–77) and Gwithian (Megaw 1976). We must not expect such discoveries to produce a typologically standard Early/Middle Neolithic field system. Our hypothetical fields of 3000 BC and earlier will be different in different places: we surely should not expect to apply the rigid Parliamentary Enclosure model to them but rather a model of regional variety based on the landscape reality of c. AD 1780. This is indicated in practice as well as theory by the actual Neolithic fields already recorded. Disregarding absolute date for the moment, just take two examples of our culturally Neolithic enclosure patterns. In the far North we can perhaps discern nodes of domestic ritual and agricultural elements in a dispersed settlement pattern (Calder 1955–56), while in the far South-West those same elements appear to be physically integrated into a more systematic land arrangement (figure 6). The Scillonian evidence is of course of the second millennium, and that not always assuredly so, but its absolute lateness should not obscure the fact, on present evidence, that in that particular insular context it is the earliest evidence of any cultural activity at all (Ashbee 1974). The settlers of c. 2000 BC really were able to start with a clean landscape slate, whatever the cultural traditions they brought with them. Of course, that is a very significant qualification but nevertheless they do not appear to have swanned round the islands a-swiddening or outfielding: they enclosed the virgin wildscape and imposed a man-made landscape (Fowler and Thomas 1979). Such a proposition remains tenable even if the megalithic skeleton of that landscape which we can detect today was not, as recent excavation suggests on Scilly as on Dartmoor and in Co. Mayo, everywhere the earliest version of land allotment, i.e. in parts at least stone walls were preceded by wooden fences or ditches.

That it was possible to think of field systems and therefore land allotment in Wessex at a date conventionally in the early second millennium I suggested ten years ago, though not to everyone's satisfaction (Fowler 1971). When, however, 'Wessex-Culture'-type round barrows are recorded on top of well-developed, and therefore old, 'Celtic' field lynchets, it is difficult to resist pointing out at least the chronological implication. Though we are still lacking hard dates in critical places, the work of the last decade has confirmed rather than disproved the suggestion, with the calibration of C14 'dates' pulling the dating for demonstrable field systems back into the middle of the third millennium rather than to c. 2000 BC. For

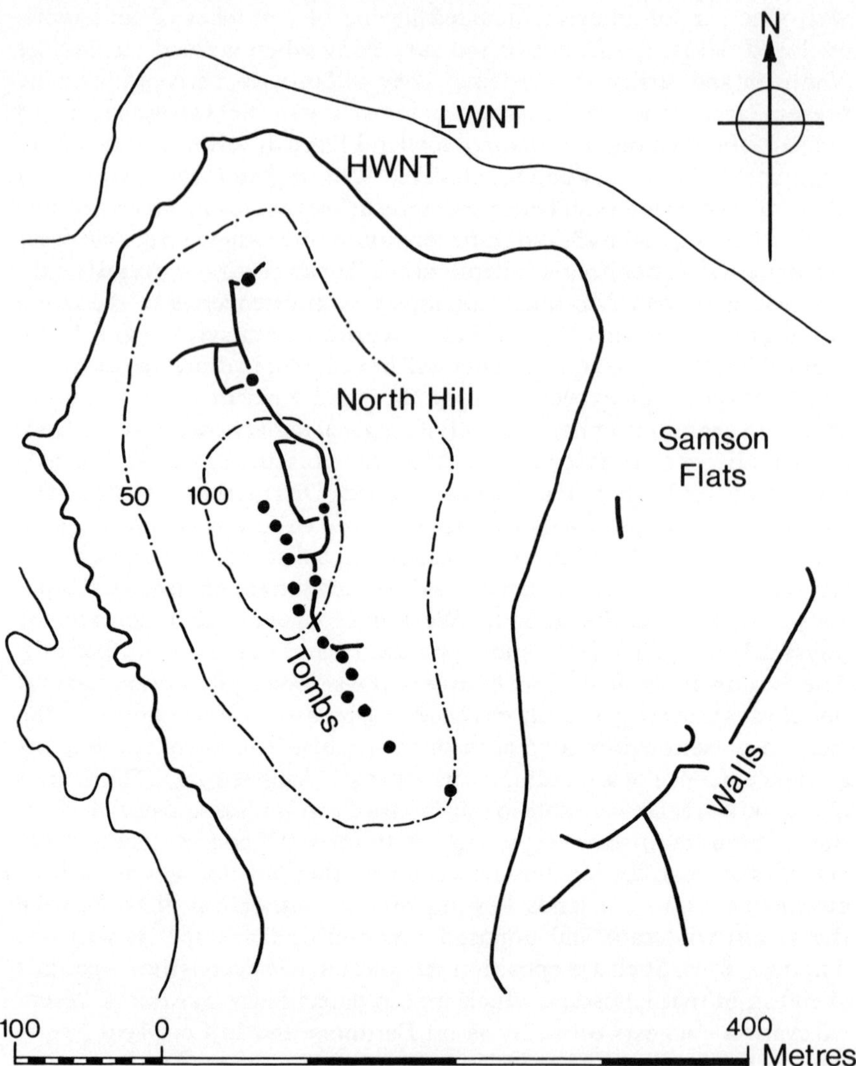

Figure 6. Samson, Isles of Scilly. Second-millennium BC linear cemetery, enclosures and walls on North Hill and the intertidal flats (from original field survey). Scale 1:5,000

a time in the 1970s I tended to believe that it was to a 'Beaker horizon' that we could look for origins of the conscious development of land allotment. I am rather inclined now to look at a 'henge horizon', a culturally late Neolithic context, for that development, as proved in Co. Mayo (Caulfield 1978). Whenever and however it occurred, it is now fairly certain that a considerable proportion of the country was being farmed by the middle of the second millennium, sporadically in places, continually in others, and

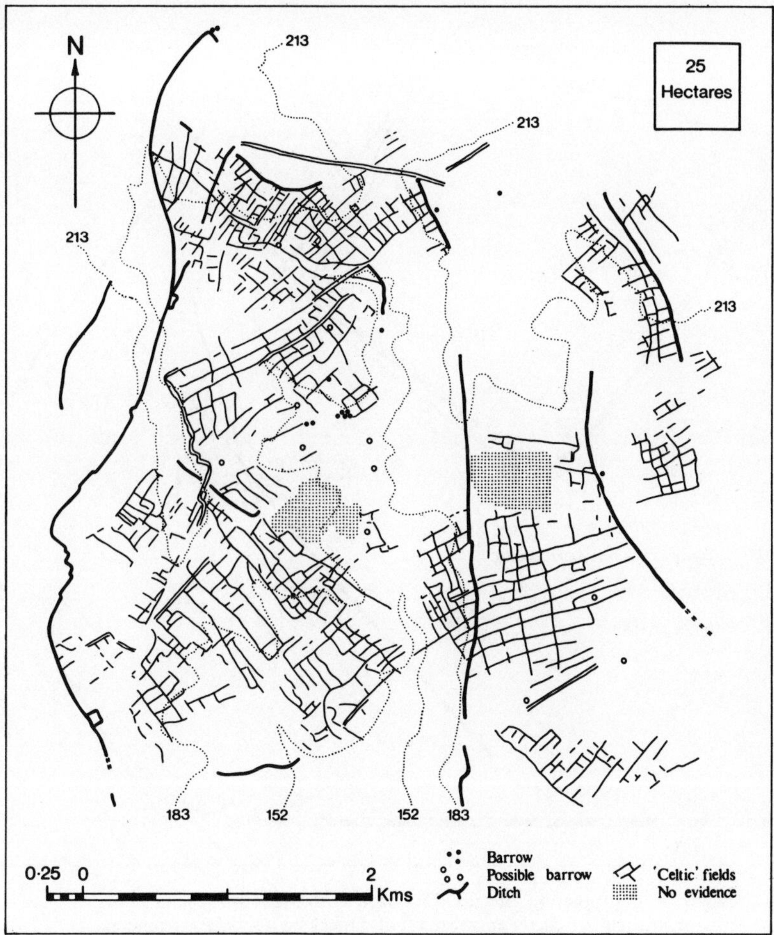

Figure 7. Berkshire Downs, SW of Segsbury hillfort and SE of Uffington Castle. Map largely based on air-photographic evidence showing three sorts of probably successive enclosure in the second millennium BC: into cohesive, striplike 'Celtic' field systems; into less regular systems with smaller fields; and later into large blocks of land defined by linear ditches (after Richards 1978, fig. 11). Scale 1:50,000, contours in feet above OD.

continuously and intensively in at least some areas. It is now at least conceivable that a considerable proportion of the naturally farmable land of pre-Atlantic Britain was or had been in agricultural use by that date, much of it enclosed (figures 7, 9). When one has to look hard for an unused area before being able to define, triumphantly, a genuine blank area among the field systems on Bodmin Moor or when one sees examples of such careful land division between arable fields and, presumably, pasture as on Overton Down, Wilts (plates 10 and 6), then thoughts tend

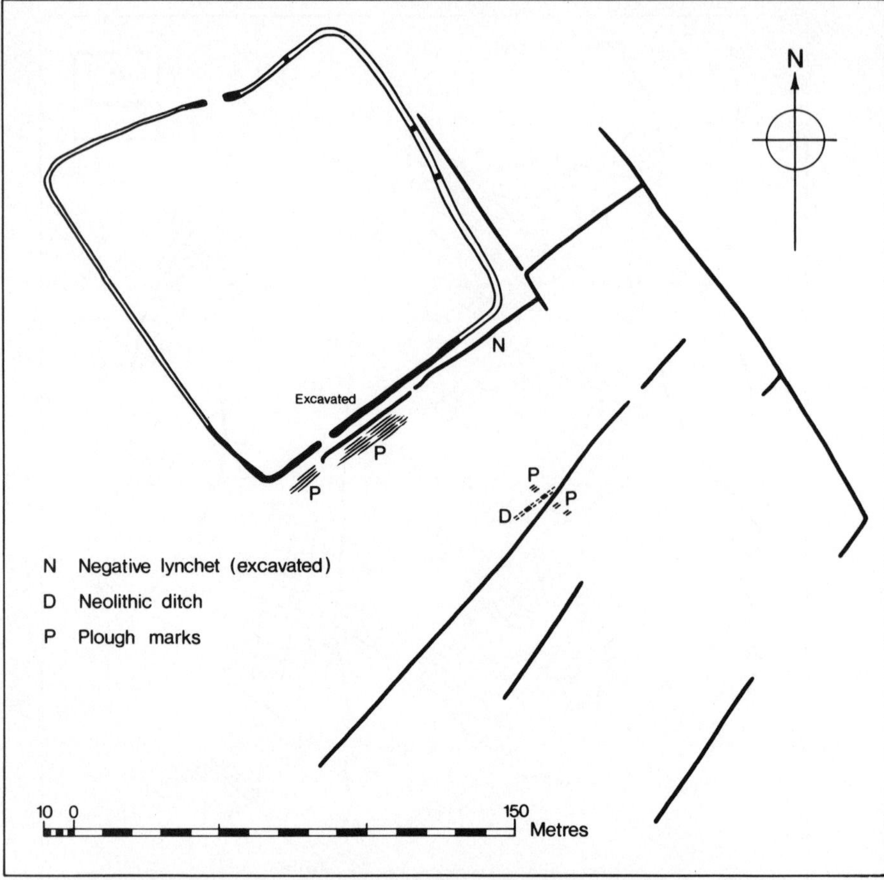

Figure 8. Bishopstone, Sussex. Enclosed settlement of the later first millennium BC as partly excavated (solid black) with a closely related field system. An immediately adjacent field was defined by a negative lynchet (N) parallel to the enclosure ditch and scored by ploughmarks (P); the major surviving field division was a lynchet overlying a Neolithic ditch (D) and further ploughmarks to either side of it (after Bell 1977, various figs). Scale 1:2,500

Figure 9. Field system in West Cornwall. Two examples of very different types of prehistoric field enclosure: *upper*, Trewey-Foage, a nucleated, organic system of fields with scattered huts, large lynchets and clearance mounds; *lower*, Tregonning Hill, a fragment of a system of long, very narrow strip fields, mainly of slight relief but certainly earlier than the two late prehistoric/Romano-British rounds (both plans are plotted from air photographs with detail field-checked; after Johnson 1980, figs 7, 10). Scale 1:5,000

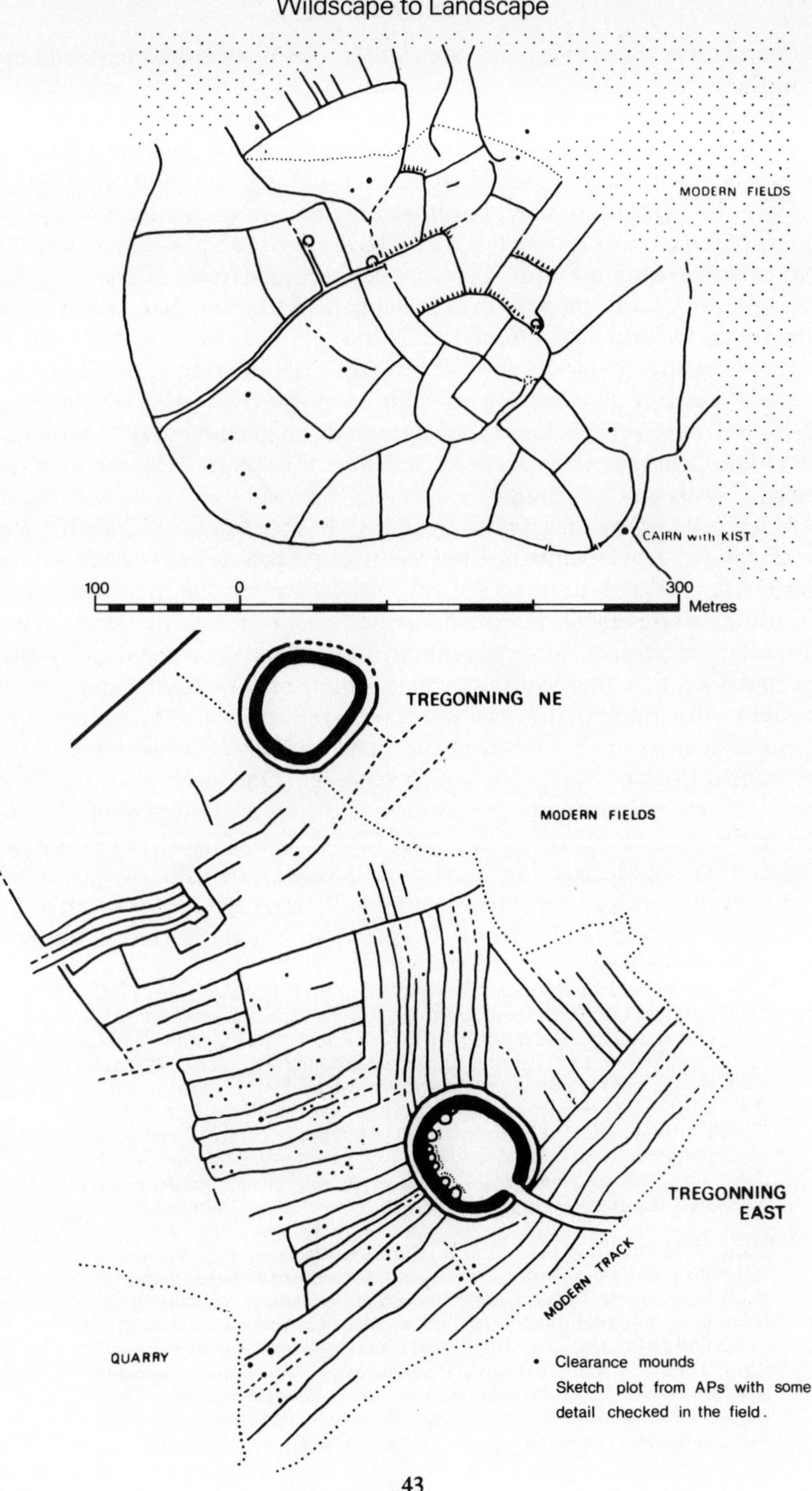
MODERN FIELDS
CAIRN with KIST
100
0
300
Metres
TREGONNING NE
MODERN FIELDS
TREGONNING EAST
MODERN TRACK
QUARRY
• Clearance mounds
Sketch plot from APs with some detail checked in the field.

to wander off towards models of extensive prehistoric land-use and high populations.

The cumulative second-millennium BC evidence from the Scillies in the far South West to Orkney and Shetland allows an assumption of enclosure as a trend if not a Movement. It did not occur ubiquitously, of course, nor synchronously, but it is sufficient attested to infer extensive tracts of it from those stretches which have survived three-dimensionally, *par excellence* in the South-West, or been recorded fragmentarily by aerial camera, or excavation, or both as at Fengate. Accepting that, setting aside detail but recognising regional differences to have existed, and with an uncomfortable suspicion that we are still only looking at the tip of the iceberg, we can then ask the question 'why'? Why were at least parts of Britain extensively enclosed between roughly 2500 and 1500 BC? Are we in fact looking at the evidence for a prehistoric 'Enclosure Movement' in any helpful sense of that phrase?

One could argue that, as in AD 1760, so in 1760 BC: the population was rising, new ideas (manuring) and technology (bronze) were available and 'a drastic reorganisation of the rural economy' (above, p. 31) was both possible and desirable. If we can ascribe a profit-making mentality to our Bronze Age farmers, some of them would see and seize the opportunity. Even with other motivation, farmers' ambitions, or the tensions these created with neighbours, could be seen reflected in the watershed or contour reaves on Dartmoor, in the linear ditches of Wessex and in the basic grid-lines of the Peterborough fen-edge. One might go further and say, taking the independent conventional interpretation of each of those instances, that all represent enclosure for systematised livestock rearing rather than arable farming: such was certainly also the case in much Parliamentary Enclosure. Such a view could be acceptable for much of the actual prehistoric field remains in question, but there is nearly always

---

Plate 10. Fyfield and Overton Downs, Wilts. Prehistoric enclosed fields, here with walls of stone cleared from a naturally sarsen-littered SW-facing slope, separated by a linear ditch (*left to right* across centre), probably of the second millennium BC, from an uncleared, unenclosed (pasture?) area to the NW. The next system of prehistoric enclosed fields is *c.* 1 km distant, off the *top left*. The presence of clay-with-flints over the higher part of the 'blank' area is indicated by the marl-pits showing as 'dimples' in the large nineteenth-century enclosed field next to the contemporary new Totterdown Farm (in trees *top right* – a classic example of late enclosure in 'marginal' farming). (Copyright reserved, University of Cambridge)

Plate 11. Holne Moor, near Venford Reservoir, Dartmoor. Underlying the irregular pattern of modern road (*centre*), sinuous leats (*foreground*) and ridge-and-furrow (*left*), a symmetrical rectilinear layout of second-millennium land allotment divides up the low ridge between two shallow valleys to left and right. The long, roughly parallel strips stretching away from the camera are defined by reaves, their geometry broken in places (as in the *right foreground*) by subdivisions and round, stone-walled houses. The evidence for extensive prehistoric enclosure, for an organised landscape on the grand scale, is hard to deny. (J. White, West Air Photography)

such an intimate relationship between stock-raising and crop-husbandry through the need for fertility that in an apparently pastoral landscape one's instinctive question is always 'where are the cultivated fields?' 'Nowhere' will sometimes be the answer, as in the mid-western cattle ranching country of nineteenth-century America, but it is usually 'Nearby'. The extreme of a pastoral field system, the watermeadows of seventeenth-nineteenth century Wessex, can only be understood in the context of the sheepfolds and the arable on the down slopes above; the neatly enclosed, sheep-grazed New Zealand countryside takes on a new significance as it becomes apparent that much of it blankets hand-cultivated, heavily-fertilised Maori yam-fields immediately below; Fleming (1979) sees patches of arable among the parallel reaves within a system and a landscape organised primarily to regulate grazing (plate 11).

What it is difficult to see on Dartmoor, however, are the 'social superiors' of our Parliamentary Enclosure model. Even if Fleming (1979) is right in interpreting his landscape in terms of communal proprietorship, democracy still tends to throw up a meritocracy and even at Laxton the workings of the agrarian commune produce and indeed depend upon a social hierarchy (Orwin and Orwin 1967). What we conspicuously lack in our second-millennium landscapes of enclosure, but not in the first, are the great buildings – the country houses of the new consolidated landholders and the new farm buildings, especially the large cattle sheds and barns which replaced the tithe barns in adapting to the new way of farming and the new life style that developed from it. We have not found them, but perhaps that is because we have not been ready to find them: have our expectations not been limited by that great obstacle to processual thought, the hut circle? Compare Early Iron Age archaeology and its old 'pit-dwelling' psychosis with modern excavation reality (Cunliffe 1978).

The English Parliamentary Enclosure model is not of course entirely apt for our prehistory; the latter is strained to fit the former. Nevertheless, Caesar describes what is clearly a man-made landscape, so some explanation is needed for the process which created it from the post-Glacial 'wildscape' which, five thousand years earlier, undoubtedly existed. Since most of our direct archaeological evidence on the point consists of variously constructed boundaries forming enclosures of one sort or another, and notably indisputable fields, the idea of a piecemeal, long-drawn out process of Enclosure, punctuated by periods of co-ordinated organisation as c. AD 1780, has its attractions. Parliamentary Enclosure, academically controversial still but at least studyable in terms of its causes and consequences, suggests aspects of interpretation to be looked at and for in the archaeological evidence. Comparing its landscapes, for example, with the less regular enclosures over the immediately preceding centuries, and recalling how its regularity was achieved, does it not at least suggest that there may be weight in the argument for some form of centralised authority – or fashion? – behind the organised landscapes of prehistoric Britain?

We have in turn underestimated the technological, economic and agrarian achievements, and then the size, of early British societies: are we now not in danger of doing likewise with the complexity of those societies themselves?

Any field system, and particularly a system of enclosed fields, represents a capital investment in the land; it represents too a commitment of expenditure to make that capital yield an income, whether of subsistence food or cash from surplus production. Well-farmed land, however, always gives more than income: it gives power. As always, the basic question of farming in prehistoric Britain comes down to 'Who owned the land?' If we knew that, the process of early enclosure, the conversion of wildscape to landscape, and one or two other matters, would be somewhat more intelligible. Were they really all peasants in prehistory? If so, did they own the land they worked? If not, where is the landed gentry of Enclosure in prehistoric Britain?

Postscript. Soon after this lecture had been given, *The British Later Bronze Age* (Barrett and Bradley 1980) was published, making available a great deal more material which would have affected my lecture and airing a lot of speculation which might have. It contains a valuable corpus of plans and a stimulating collection of papers, both of which require time to digest. Rather than attempt to absorb some of its points hurriedly into my text, it seems wiser to draw attention to the fact that the lecture belongs to a pre-Barrett and Bradley (1980) horizon, that this massive new contribution (500 pp.) now exists, and that it is full of data and discussion germane to the above (and much else in this volume). My only comment now would be that its marked editorial theme of questioning the validity of 'landscape archaeology' would be more convincing if the frame of reference for the discussion was that of its practitioners rather than merely that of some socio-economic puzzles in the later British Bronze Age.

ACKNOWLEDGEMENTS

I am grateful to Tim Gates and Nicholas Johnson for familiarising me with their current fieldwork on Cheviot and in Cornwall respectively, and to the latter for slide illustrations for the lecture, in part reproduced here (figure 9); to Mrs M. U. Jones for permission to publish figure 2 and for helpful discussion about the Mucking evidence; to Michael Herity for permission to publish figure 1 and to use his typescript about Glenree before its publication; to Charles Thomas for partnership in our current fieldwork on Scilly; to the Air Photography Committee, University of Cambridge, for permission to publish Professor J. K. St Joseph's air photograph as plate 10, and to John White for his air photograph published as plate 11; to the Royal Commission on Historical Monuments (England) for permission to publish plates 3, 6 and 7 and to base figure 5 on one of its published plans; and to Nigel Fradgley of the Commission's staff, who prepared the line drawings, and to other colleagues in the Photographic and Air Photographic Sections of the Commission for vital assistance with the illustrations. I would also like to thank Roger Mercer and the Munro Committee, University of Edinburgh, for the invitation to lecture at, and hospitality during, an enjoyable Symposium.

REFERENCES

Alcock, L. (1977-78) Excavation and publication: some comments. *Proc. Soc. Antiq. Scot.* 109, 1-6.

Ashbee, P. (1974) *Ancient Scilly; from the First Farmers to the Early Christians.* Newton Abbot.

—— (1976) Bant's Carn. St Mary's, Isles of Scilly: an entrance grave restored and reconsidered. *Cornish Archaeol.* 15, 11-26.

Ashbee, P., I. F. Smith & J. G. Evans (1979) Excavation of three long barrows near Avebury, Wiltshire. *Proc. Prehist. Soc.* 45, 207-300.

Baker, A. R. H. & R. A. Butlin, eds (1973) *Studies of Field Systems in the British Isles.* Cambridge.

Barger, E. (1938) The present position of studies in English field systems. *Eng. Hist. Rev.* 58, 385-411.

Barrett, J. & R. Bradley, eds (1980) *Settlement and Society in the British Later Bronze Age.* BAR 83, Oxford.

Bell, M. (1977) Excavations at Bishopstone. *Sussex Archaeol. Colls.* 115.

Benson, D. & D. Miles (1974) *The Upper Thames Valley: an Archaeological Survey of the River Gravels.* Oxford.

Beresford, M. W. & J. G. Hurst (1971) *Deserted Medieval Villages.* London.

Bettey, J. H. (1980) *The Landscape of Wessex.* Bradford-on-Avon.

Bowen, H. C. (1961) *Ancient Fields.* London: Brit. Assoc. Adv. Sci.

—— (1975) Air photography and the development of the landscape in central parts of southern England, in Wilson 1975a, 103-18.

—— (1978) 'Celtic' fields and 'ranch' boundaries in Wessex, in Limbrey and Evans 1978, 115-23.

Bowen, H. C. & P. J. Fowler, eds (1978) *Early Land Allotment in the British Isles: a Survey of Recent Work.* BAR 48.

Bowen, H. C. & I. F. Smith (1977) Sarsen stones in Wessex: the Society's first investigations in the Evolution of the Landscape Project. *Antiq. J.* 57, 185-96.

Bradley, R. (1978a) *The Prehistoric Settlement of Britain.* London.

—— (1978b) Prehistoric field systems in Britain and north-west Europe: a review of some recent work. *World Archaeol.* 9, 265-80.

Brongers, J. A. (1976) *Air Photography and Celtic Field Research in the Netherlands.* Amersfoort.

Burgess, C. (1980) *The Age of Stonehenge.* London.

Burgess, C. & R. Miket, eds (1976) *Settlement and Economy in the Third and Second Millennia B.C.* BAR 33.

Burstow, G. P. & G. A. Holleyman (1957) Late Bronze Age Settlement on Itford Hill, Sussex. *Proc. Prehist. Soc.* 23, 167-212.

Calder, C. S. T. (1955-56) Report on the discovery of numerous Stone Age house-sites in Shetland. *Proc. Soc. Antiq. Scot.* 89, 34-97.

Caulfield, S. (1978) Neolithic fields: the Irish evidence, in Bowen and Fowler 1978, 137-43.

Chambers, J. D. & G. E. Mingay (1966) *The Agricultural Revolution 1750-1880*. London.

Chapman, D. H., ed. (1969) *Walmsley's Rural Estate Management*, 5th ed. London.

Chapman, J. (1978) Some problems in the interpretation of Enclosure Awards. *Agric. Hist. Rev. 26*, 108-14.

Coles, J. M., ed. (1975-81) *Somerset Levels Papers 1-7*. Dept of Archaeol., Univ. of Cambridge; Dept of History, Univ. of Exeter.

Coles, J. M. & B. J. Orme (1980) *Prehistory of the Somerset Levels*. Somerset Levels Project, Univs of Cambridge and Exeter.

Crawford, O. G. S. (1923) Air survey and archaeology. *Georg. J. 61*, 342-66.

Cunliffe, B. W. (1971, 1976) Danebury, Hampshire: first/second interim report(s) on the excavations, 1969-70/1971-75. *Antiq. J. 51*, 240-52; *56*, 198-216.

—— (1974, 1978) *Iron Age Communities in Britain* (2nd ed. 1978). London.

Curwen, E. & E. C. Curwen (1923) Sussex lynchets and their associated fieldways. *Sussex Archaeol. Colls. 64*, 1-65.

Davey, P. (1978) *Man and Environment in the Isle of Man*. BAR 54.

DBG = Caesar, *De Bello Gallico*.

Dimbleby, G. W. (1978) *Plants and Archaeology*, 2nd ed. London.

Dodgshon, R. A. (1980) *The Origin of British Field Systems: an Interpretation*. London.

Drewett, P. L., ed. (1978) *Archaeology in Sussex to AD 1500*. CBA Res. Rep. 29.

Edwards, K. J. (1977-78) Excavation and environmental archaeology of a small cairn associated with cultivation ridges in Aberdeenshire. *Proc. Soc. Antiq. Scot. 109*, 22-9.

Evans, J. G. (1979) The environment, in Ashbee *et al.* 1979, 275-98.

Evans, J. G., S. Limbrey & H. Cleere, eds (1975) *The Effect of Man on the Landscape: the Highland Zone*. CBA Res. Rpt. 11. London.

Everton, A. & P. Fowler (1978) Pre-Roman ard-marks at Lodge Farm, Alveston, Avon: a method of analysis, in Bowen and Fowler 1978, 179-85.

Fasham, P. & R. Hanworth (1978) Ploughmarks, Roman roads and motorways, in Bowen and Fowler 1978, 175-7.

Feachem, R. W. (1973) Ancient agriculture in the highland of Britain. *Proc. Prehist. Soc. 39*, 332-53.

Fleming, A. (1971) Territorial patterns in Bronze Age Wessex. *Proc. Prehist. Soc. 37*, 138-66.

—— (1972) Vision and design: approaches to ceremonial monument typology. *Man* no.7, 57-73.

—— (1978a) Dartmoor reaves: a nineteenth century fiasco. *Antiquity 52*, 16-20.

—— (1978b) The prehistoric landscape of Dartmoor. Part 1. South Dartmoor. *Proc. Prehist. Soc. 44*, 97-123.

—— (1979) The Dartmoor Reaves: boundary patterns and behaviour patterns in the second millennium bc. *Proc. Devon Archaeol. Soc. 37*, 115-31.

Fowler, P. & C. Thomas (1979) Lyonesse revisited: the early walls of Scilly. *Antiquity 53*, 175-89.

Fowler, P. J. (1971) Early prehistoric agriculture in Western Europe: some archaeological evidence, in *Economy and Settlement in Neolithic and Early Bronze Age Britain and Europe* (ed. D. D. A. Simpson) 153-82. Leicester.

—— (ed.) (1975) *Recent Work in Rural Archaeology.* Bradford-on-Avon.

—— (1977b) Archaeology and the M5 Motorway. Gloucestershire 1969-75: a summary and assessment. *Trans. Bristol Gloucestershire Archaeol. Soc. 95*, 40-6.

—— (1978) Lowland landscapes: culture, time and *Personality*, in Limbrey and Evans 1978, 1-12.

—— (1980) Farming in the Anglo-Saxon landscape: an archaeologist's review. *Anglo-Saxon England* 9, 263-80.

—— (1981) Later Prehistory, in Piggott, S. (ed.) 1981, 61-298.

Fowler, P. J. & J. G. Evans (1967) Plough-marks, lynchets and early fields. *Antiquity 41*, 289-301.

Fox, A. (1954) Celtic Fields and farms on Dartmoor . . . *Proc. Prehist. Soc. 20*, 87-102.

Gailey, A. & A. Fenton, eds (1970) *The Spade in Northern and Atlantic Europe.* Belfast.

Gates, T. (1975) *The Middle Thames Valley: an Archaeological Survey of the River Gravels.* Reading: Berkshire Archaeol. Comm. 1.

Godwin, H. (1975) *The History of the British Flora*, 2nd ed. Cambridge.

Hampton, J. N. & R. Palmer (1977) Implications of aerial photography for archaeology. *Archaeol. J. 134*, 157-93.

Harding, D. W. (1974) *The Iron Age in Lowland Britain.* London.

Hawke-Smith, C. F. (1979) *Man-Land Relations in Prehistoric Britain: the Dove-Derwent Interfluve, Derbyshire; a Study in Human Ecology.* BAR 64.

Hayfield, C., ed. (1980) *Fieldwalking as a Method of Archaeological Research.* Directorate of Ancient Monuments and Historic Buildings, Dept of the Environment, Occas. Paper 2.

Herity, M. (1981) A Bronze Age farmstead at Glenree, County Mayo. *Popular Archaeol. 2*, no. 9 (March), 36-7.

Herity, M. & G. Eogan (1977) *Ireland in Prehistory.* London.

Hinchcliffe, J. & R. T. Schadla-Hall (1980) *The Past under the Plough.* Directorate of Ancient Monuments and Historic Buildings, Dept of the Environment, Occas. Papers 3.

Horn, P. (1980) *The Rural World 1780-1850: Social Change in the English Countryside.* London.

Hoskins, W. G. (1955) *The Making of the English Landscape.* London.

Johnson, N. (1980) Later Bronze Age settlement in the South-West, in Barrett and Bradley 1980, 141-80.

Jones, E. L. (1967) *Agriculture and Economic Growth in England.* London.

Jones, M. U. (1979) Mucking, Essex: the reality beneath the crop-marks. *Aerial Archaeol. 4*, 67-76.

—— (1980) Mucking and the early Saxon rural settlement of Essex, in Buckley 1980, *Archaeology in Essex to AD 1500*, 82-6.

London: CBA Res. Rep. 34. (Quoted here because it provides, p.86, a full bibliography of the site 1967-79.)

Jones, M. U. & D. Bond (1980) Later Bronze Age settlement at Mucking, Essex, in Barrett and Bradley 1980, 471-82.

Kerridge, E. (1976) Review in *Agric. Hist. Rev. 24*, 49.

Lambrick, G. & M. Robinson (1979) *Iron Age and Roman Riverside Settlements at Farmoor, Oxfordshire.* London: CBA Res. Rep. 32.

Leech, R. (1977) *The Upper Thames Valley in Gloucestershire and Wiltshire: an Archaeological Survey of the River Gravels.* Bristol: Comm. Rescue Archaeol. Avon, Gloucestershire, Somerset, 4.

Leser, P. (1931) *Entstehung und Verbreitung des Pfluges.* Munster: reprint, Viborg, 1971.

Limbrey, S. & J. G. Evans, eds (1978) *The Effect of Man on the Landscape: the Lowland Zone.* London: CBA Res. Rep. 21.

Martin, J. M. (1964) The cost of Parliamentary Enclosure in Warwickshire. *Univ. Birmingham Hist. J.* 9, 146-56.

—— (1967) The Parliamentary Enclosure Movement and rural society in Warwickshire. *Agric. Hist. Rev. 15*, 19-39.

Matthews, C. L. (1976) *Occupation Sites on a Chiltern Ridge: Part I: Neolithic, Bronze Age and Early Iron Age.* BAR 29.

Mercer, R. J. (1975) Settlement, farming and environment in South West England to c. 1000 BC, in Fowler 1975, 27-43.

—— (1980a) *Hambledon Hill: a Neolithic Landscape.* Edinburgh.

—— (1980b) *Archaeological Field Survey in Northern Scotland 1976-79.* Dept Archaeol., Univ. Edinburgh, Occas. Paper 4.

Megaw, J. V. S. (1976) Gwithian, Cornwall: some notes on the evidence for Neolithic and Bronze Age settlement, in Burgess and Miket 1976, 51-79.

Mingay, G. E. (1968) *Enclosure and the Small Farmer in the Age of the Industrial Revolution.* London.

—— (1977) *Rural Life in Victorian England.* London.

Munby, L. M. (1977) *The Hertfordshire Landscape.* London.

Munro, R. (1882) *Scottish Lake-Dwellings.* Edinburgh.

—— (1913) *Prehistoric Britain.* London.

Orwin, C. S. & C. S. (1967) *The Open Fields,* 3rd ed. Oxford.

OS (1956) Ordnance Survey, *Map of Roman Britain,* 3rd ed. Chessington.

Parker, R. A. C. (1960) *Enclosures in the Eighteenth Century.* Historical Assoc., Aids for Teachers no. 7.

Parrington, M. (1978) *The Excavation of an Iron Age Settlement ... at Ashville Trading Estate, Abingdon (Oxfordshire) 1974-76.* London: CBA Res. Rep. 28.

Parsons, D. (1977) Editorial Note: the publication of air photographic evidence, in Hampton and Palmer 1977, 183-86.

Pickering, J. (1979) Aerial archaeology and the prehistoric landscape. *Landscape History (J. Soc. Landscape Studies) 1*, 10-15.

Pierpoint, S. (1980) *Social Patterns in Yorkshire Prehistory 3500-750 B.C.* BAR 74.

Piggott, S. (1958) *Approach to Archaeology.* London.

—— ed. (1981) *The Agrarian History of England and Wales,* I.I. Cambridge.

Pryor, F. (1974, 1978) *Excavation at Fengate, Peterborough, England: the First/Second Report(s).* Toronto: Royal Ontario Museum, Arcaheology Monographs 3 and 5.

Rackham, O. (1976) *Trees and Woodlands in the British Landscape.* London.

Radford, C. A. R. (1952) Prehistoric settlements on Dartmoor and the Cornish moors. *Proc. Prehist. Soc. 28,* 55-84.

RCHM (1960) *A Matter of Time: an Archaeological Survey of the River Gravels of England.* London: HMSO.

—— (1970a) *Inventory . . . of Dorset,* II. London: HMSO.

—— (1970b) *Inventory . . . of Dorset,* III. London: HMSO.

—— (1975) *Inventory of Archaeological Sites in North-East Northamptonshire.* London: HMSO.

—— (1979a) *Inventory of Archaeological Sites in Central Northamptonshire.* London: HMSO.

—— (1979b) *Stonehenge and its Environs.* Edinburgh.

—— (1980) *Atlas of Northamptonshire Archaeology.* London.

Rees, S. E. (1979) *Agricultural Implements in Prehistoric and Roman Britain.* BAR 69.

Reynolds, P. J. (1979) *Iron-Age Farm: the Butser Experiment.* London.

Richards, J. C. (1978) *The Archaeology of the Berkshire Downs: an Introductory Survey.* Reading: Berks. Archaeol. Comm. 3.

Riley, D. N. (1980) *Early Landscape from the Air: Studies of Crop Marks in South Yorkshire and North Nottinghamshire.* Dept of Prehistory and Archaeology, Univ. of Sheffield.

Russell, V. (1980) *Isles of Scilly Survey.* Isles of Scilly Museum, St Mary's, and Institute of Cornish Studies, University of Exeter; Cornwall Archaeological Society Parochial Checklist Survey Monograph 2.

SAF (1979) Scottish Archaeological Forum. 9. *Early Man in the Scottish Landscape.* Edinburgh.

—— (1980) 10. *Settlements in Scotland 1000 BC-1000 AD.* Edinburgh.

Saville, A. (1980) *Archaeological Sites in the Avon and Gloucestershire Cotswolds.* CRAAGS 5.

Shennan, S. J. (1980) Meeting the plough-damage problem: a sampling approach to area intensive fieldwork, in Hinchcliffe and Schadla-Hall, 125-33.

Shepherd, I. A. G. & A. N. Tuckwell (1976-77) Traces of Beaker-period cultivation at Rosinish, Benbecula. *Proc. Soc. Antiq. Scot. 108,* 108-13.

Shoard, M. (1980) *The Theft of the Countryside.* London.

Shotton, F. W. (1978) Archaeological inferences from the study of alluvium in the lower Severn-Avon valleys, in Limbrey and Evans 1978, 27-32.

Smith, C. (1979) *Fisherwick: the Reconstruction of an Iron Age Landscape.* BAR 61.

St Joseph, J. K. S. (1966) Air photography and archaeology, in St Joseph 1966, *The Uses of Air Photography,* 113-25. Cambridge.

Steensberg, A. (1970) *Plough and Field Shape from Prehistoric Times to c. 1500 AD.* Rhind Lectures 1970-71, Society of Antiquaries of Scotland. Unpublished.

Street, A. G. (1932) *Farmer's Glory*. London.
Tate, W. E. (1967) *The English Village Community and the Enclosure Movements*. London.
Taylor, C. (1975) *Fields in the English Landscape*. London.
—— (1980) The Making of the English Landscape – 25 years on. *Local Historian 14*, 195-201.
Taylor, C. C. & P. J. Fowler (1978) Roman fields to medieval furlongs?, in Bowen and Fowler 1978, 159-62.
Taylor, J. A., ed. (1980) *Culture and Environment in Prehistoric Wales. Selected Essays*. BAR 76.
Thirsk, J. (1957) *English Peasant Farming*. London.
—— (1967) The Farming Regions of England, in Thirsk 1967, *The Agrarian History of England and Wales*, IV, 1-112. Cambridge.
—— (1970) Seventeenth-century agricultural and social change. *Agric. Hist. Rev. 18* (Supplement), 148-77.
Thomas, C. (1970) Bronze Age spademarks at Gwithian, Cornwall, in Gailey and Fenton 1970, 10-17.
—— (1976) Towards the definition of the term 'field' in the light of prehistory, in Sawyer 1976, *Medieval Settlement: Continuity and Change*, 145-51. London.
Tilley, C. Y. (1979) *Post-Glacial Communities in the Cambridge Region: some Theoretical Approaches to Settlement and Subsistence*. BAR 66.
Turner, M. (1977) Enclosure Commissioners and Buckinghamshire Parliamentary Enclosures. *Agric. Hist. Review 25*, 120-9.
Turner, M. E. (1973) The cost of Parliamentary Enclosure in Buckinghamshire. *Agric. Hist. Rev. 21*, 35-46.
USDI (1980) United States Department of the Interior/Bureau of Land Management, *Promise of the Land* (n.d. but 1980, Washington).
Wainwright, G. J. (1979a) *Mount Pleasant, Dorset: Excavations 1970-1971*. London: Soc. Antiq. Res. Rep. 57.
—— (1979b) *Gussage All Saints: an Iron Age Settlement in Dorset*. London: HMSO.
Wainwright, G. J., A. Fleming & K. Smith (1979) The Shaugh Moor Project: First Report. *Proc. Prehist. Soc. 45*, 1-33.
Wainwright, G. J. & I. H. Longworth (1971) *Durrington Walls: Excavations 1966-1968*. London: Soc. Antiq. Res. Rep. 29.
Watson, J. S. (1960) *The Reign of George III 1760-1815*. Oxford.
Whitlock, R. (1965) *A Short History of Farming in Britain*. London.
Whittington, G. (1977-78) A sub-peat dyke on Shurton Hill, Mainland, Shetland. *Proc. Soc. Antiq. Scot. 109*, 30-5.
Whittle, A. W. R. (1977) *The Earlier Neolithic of S. England and its Continental Background*. BAR S35.
—— (1978) Resources and population in the British Neolithic. *Antiquity 52*, 34-42.
Wilson, D. R., ed. (1975a) *Aerial Reconnaissance for Archaeology*. London: CBA Res. Rep. 12.
—— (1975b) Photographic techniques in the air, in Wilson 1975a, 12-31.
—— (1978) Pit alignments: distribution and function, in Bowen and Fowler, 3-5.

Woodward, P. J. (1978) Flint distribution, Ring Ditches and Bronze Age Settlement Patterns in the Great Ouse Valley: the problem, a field survey technique and some preliminary results. *Archaeol. J.* *135*, 32-56.

Early Agriculture in Scotland

S. P. HALLIDAY P. J. HILL J. B. STEVENSON

In Scotland, as elsewhere in Britain, the rate of recovery of evidence for prehistoric agriculture has accelerated rapidly during the last decade (cf. Childe 1946, Piggott 1958). The authors of this note do not claim to have a comprehensive knowledge of all the recent developments, nor do they consider this a proper time or place to attempt a functional or chronological analysis of the evidence (but see Burgess 1980, Megaw and Simpson 1979). Their aim is, rather, to illustrate the quality and variety of the evidence recovered from recent excavations and surveys, and to provide a guide to the publications within which the archaeological evidence has been reported.

CULTIVATION MARKS

Cultivation marks of various types are now regularly recognized on Scottish prehistoric sites. The majority of these are 'ard' scores identified in the subsoil, although traces of spade cultivation have also been recorded. Of particular interest are the two phases of ard cultivation at Callanish, Lewis (Ashmore 1980), and the remarkable stratified succession of early ploughed surfaces at Sumburgh, Shetland (*DES* 1974, 87–8). Extensive areas of marks have also been exposed at Rosinish, Benbecula (Shepherd and Tuckwell 1977), and here there is a possibility that midden material was being purposely mixed into the tilth by the ard. In the main, however, the information that can be derived from such marks appears to be limited.

Of greater interest and potential are those sites where the contemporary cultivated ground-surfaces have survived. Four Scottish sites have now produced evidence of ridged plots (see also Rudchester, Northumberland (Gillam, Harrison and Newman 1973), and the most securely stratified of these lay beneath the late neolithic barrow at North Mains, Strathallan, Perthshire (Barclay 1980) and consisted of pronounced parallel ridges some 2 m from crest to crest. Two further instances come from Barber's excavations on Arran (*DES* 1979, 34; and *pers. comm.*). In both areas the ridges lay beneath peat but their precise date is uncertain. The fourth group was found during excavations conducted by Burgess at Kilellan Farm, Islay (*DES* 1976, 13), again not securely dated. Here lay steeply-cut, spade-dug furrows surviving in a small area, and the intervening ridges bore the characteristic marks of ard cultivation, although the relationship between spade and ard was obscure. Clearly these surfaces represent a significant addition to the available evidence for early agriculture and, furthermore, promote the possibility that ridged systems need not all be medieval or later in date.

The areas of ard-marks found on machair sites in the West offer a contrast to the field-systems recorded elsewhere in Scotland, as few are associated with enclosures (cf. Gwithian, Cornwall, Thomas 1978, 8–10) suggesting, perhaps, that enclosure may be related as much to soil-type as any other factor. A possible boundary ditch, however, has been recorded at Rosinish, Benbecula (Shepherd and Tuckwell 1977); and at Ardnave, Islay, there is a small stone-walled enclosure (Ritchie, Stevenson and Welfare 1980; RCAMS forthcoming).

FIELD SYSTEMS

Fieldwork, air photography and excavation have shown that the extent of agricultural enclosures and field-systems throughout Scotland is greater than was previously thought. For convenience the country has been divided into two zones – north and west, and south and east – mainly to draw attention to the importance of the cropmark sites in the latter, which add an element not yet located in the former. Major differences in the nature of the remains in the two zones are possibly more apparent than real.

The South and East. Previous discussion of the evidence for early agriculture in southern Scotland has centred on field-systems such as Tamshiel Rig, Roxburgh (RCAMS 1956, 426–7, no.943); Dreva, Peebles (RCAMS 1967, 111–14, no.275); Glenrath Hope, Peebles (RCAMS 1967, 165–7, no.364); Ellershie Hill, Lanark (RCAMS 1978, 110–11, no.246); and Stanshiel Rig, Dumfries (Feachem 1973, 340–2). Groups of small cairns have also been equated with agricultural activity, but the purpose of these cairns remains obscure (RCAMS 1978, 8–10; Graham 1957; Scott-Elliot 1967; Jobey 1968, 46–50); and while some do occur in connection with plots and banks, others do not, and these may be funerary in their initial conception. Amongst these field-systems both strips and small plots have been identified, although these would not appear to be readily comparable with the 'Celtic fields' of southern Britain. Further field-systems comparable to those mentioned above have been recorded on Cockburn Law, Berwick (RCAMS 1980a, 68, no.608) and on Newhall Hill, Dumfries (CUCAP), while attention has also been drawn to traces of cultivation in the vicinity of a few unenclosed platform settlements (Feachem 1973, 340; Jobey 1980, 15–16).

More striking, perhaps, are the pit-defined (Mackay 1980) and ditched boundaries recently revealed as cropmarks; the former often occur close to prehistoric settlements but their apparent relationship should be

Plate 1. Castle O'er Fort, Dumfries. A multi-period fort with an annexe and radiating linear earthworks. (Copyright reserved, University of Cambridge)

treated with caution since documentary references attest the use of pits as boundary markers in the relatively recent past (RCAMS 1980a, 36, no.298). It seems likely, however, that the pitted boundaries around the fort at Drem, East Lothian (RCAMS 1924, 9–10, no.13; NMRS; Harding) are associated with a phase of this site's occupation, and superficial comparison of these enclosures can be made with the Tamshiel Rig field-system, where banks with ditches enclosed an area of 12.75 ha, which had been subdivided into strips and small plots.

Boundaries comparable to those at Drem have been revealed as cropmarks around other forts including Kaeheughs, East Lothian (RCAMS 1924, 48–9, no.74; NMRS; Harding); Blue House and Warlawbank, Berwick (RCAMS 1980a, 36, no.296; 39, nos 321–4; NMRS); and it is fortunate that unploughed examples survive at Milkieston Hill, Peebles (RCAMS

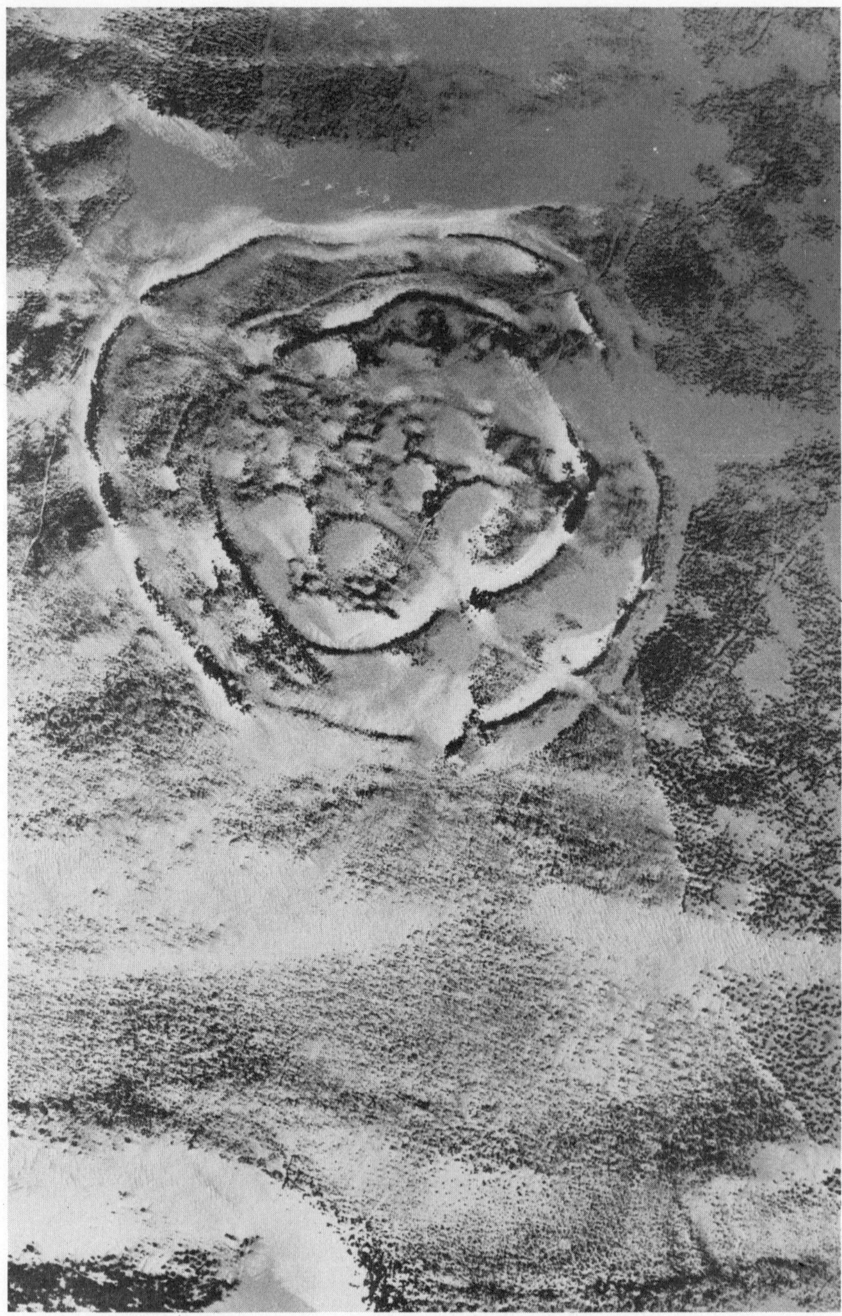

Plate 2. Orchard Rig Settlement, Peebles, with house platforms and concentric annexe, and possible field-banks and traces of cultivation. (Photo M. Brooks, Central Excavation Unit, Scottish Development Department. Crown Copyright)

Plate 3. Rectangular ditched fields, Inveresk, Midlothian.
(Photo J. Dewar, Scottish Development Department. Crown Copyright)

1967, 131–3, no.304) and Marygoldhill Planation, Berwick (RCAMS 1980a, 38, no.316). At both the latter sites the pits are clearly quarries for a flanking bank, and the former presence of banks can be inferred at both Kaeheughs and Drem. Furthermore, the unploughed examples have entrances at which the ends of the banks are staggered on either side of the gap. This feature would seem to have little part to play in an exclusively arable economy, and can be found amongst both the cropmarks and extant remains of many other linear earthworks (e.g. RCAMS 1967, 128–30, no.300). Other hints at stock control may be seen in the annexes that occur at forts such as Castle O'er (plate 1) and Bailiehill, Dumfries (RCAMS 1980c, 8–9, nos.16–17) and the three settlements on Orchard Rig, Peebles (plate 2; RCAMS 1967, 93–5, nos.239–41), and perhaps some of the forts with widely spaced ramparts should also be considered in this context.

While some of these boundary systems may represent discrete units, others, such as those in the area of Ayton, Berwick, and around Castlesteads and Newton, Mid Lothian (NMRS; Harding; Horne 1980) indicate more extensive land divisions, which are possibly elements of a much broader enclosed landscape. Even the apparently discrete unit at Killielaw Knowe, Berwick (RCAMS 1980a, 38, no.313; NMRS) had staggered entrances through its outer boundaries, suggesting that the functioning of the ditch-system required access to the lands beyond.

Cropmarks have also revealed field-systems of a different character close to the Roman forts at Inveresk, Midlothian (plate 3); Carriden, West Lothian; and possibly Camelon, Stirling (NMRS; CUCAP). At these sites there are rectilinear ditched plots that are possibly similar to those excavated at Croy Hill, Dunbarton (*DES* 1976, 28; 1977, 12–13; 1978, 27).

Further evidence for the existence of field-systms, no doubt of widely differing dates, is emerging from the inspection of the aerial photographic cover of Fife and Angus, while the potential of other areas is illustrated by the system of ditches around an enclosure, probably a settlement, at Whinnyrig, Dumfries (MUAP; RCAMS 1981). In the same county an undated system of dykes has come to light around the Castle O'er fort (RCAMS 1980c, 15–16, no.75), and it is worth considering the walling and small enclosures around the fort at Dalmahoy, Midlothian (Stevenson 1949) in terms of the economy of the site rather than as elements of its defences.

The North and West. In the north and west field-systems are widely distributed with particularly interesting concentrations surviving in Perthshire (Feachem 1973), Aberdeen (Ogston 1931), Inverness (Feachem 1973), Easter Ross (RCAMS 1979, 20, no.158), Sutherland (RCAMS 1911a, Fairhurst and Taylor 1971, Mercer 1980), Caithness (RCAMS 1911b, Mercer 1980), Shetland (RCAMS 1946, Calder 1956, Whittle 1979), the Outer Isles (RCAMS 1928, *DES* 1979, 46), Argyll (plate 4; RCAMS forthcoming), and Arran (*DES* 1979, 34). Elsewhere fieldwork has been less intensive, and the difficulties of distinguishing between prehistoric and more recent field-systems should not be underestimated.

Plate 4. **Field-banks and cairns, Oronsay, Argyll.**

Plate 5. Cultivation terraces, Romanno, Peebles. (RCAMS, Crown Copyright)

Feachem (1973) has drawn attention to the small plot systems that are frequently associated with groups of small cairns, and the so-called 'cairn-fields' (Graham 1957) have become synonymous with early agriculture in the north. Small cairns, however, are not *prima facie* evidence for agriculture, and additional evidence in the form of enclosures or terracing should be present before a particular group of small cairns is assigned an agricultural function.

Besides small plots, recent fieldwork has revealed the presence of larger fields and enclosures, some of which may have been tilled and others used as paddocks. The discovery of these larger fields brings the agricultural remains of the north and west more into line with the situation in the south and east, and there is no reason to believe that agriculture in the north was more primitive than in other regions. Achnacree (Barrett, Hill and Stevenson 1976) still remains something of an anomaly in Scotland, its closest parallels existing in the sub-peat wall systems retrieved by Caulfield in Ireland (Caulfield 1978).

Little is known of the agricultural practices which gave rise to these field-systems or of the date ranges involved, especially in view of the uncertainties of the dates of the hut-circles with which such remains frequently occur, but at present it is difficult to associate any fields with settlements of proven Iron Age date. The infield/outfield system, which is so common in later periods, cannot yet be demonstrated archaeologically, but might well account for the combinations of small (infield) and large (outfield) enclosures found at many sites.

CULTIVATION TERRACES

As with rig-and-furrow, cultivation terraces can no longer be assumed to be a phenomenon restricted to the historic period (plate 5), and some types are probably prehistoric in date (cf. Graham 1939). Obvious examples are those that predate the scooped enclosures at Bucht Knowe and Hayhope Knowe, Roxburgh (RCAMS 1956, 356–7, nos 691 and 695); and the relationship between terracing and the settlement at Headshaw Law, the 'hut-circles' at Sourhope Burn, and the scooped enclosures at Burnhead and Mowhaugh (RCAMS 1956, 173–4, no.311; 354, no.684; 355–6, no.689; 458–9, no.1053) would repay closer examination (cf. Stevenson 1947).

OTHER LAND DIVISIONS

As well as boundaries surrounding field-systems there is a further group of earthworks and walls that may be related to agriculture. This group comprises linear earthworks ranging from major boundaries with socio-political status, to more humble works probably related to pasture division. It is not always simple to distinguish earthworks of this type from elements of field-systems, but a selection of sites which illustrates the range covered in this category would include the neolithic wall on Shurton Hill, Shetland (Whittington 1978); the picka or treb dykes of Orkney (Fenton 1978, 13–14; RCAMS 1980b); several of the linear earthworks in the Border counties (RCAMS 1956, 1957, 1967); and on a rather lesser scale, the cross-ridge dykes found in Roxburgh, Peebles and Lanark (RCAMS 1956, 1967, 1978).

CONCLUSION

Although there has been a rapid expansion of the evidence for early agriculture, little is yet known of the farming practices of prehistory. Most of the field-systems are fragmentary, and the evidence of aerial photography and field survey has shown that the landscape must have been managed in ways and with an intensity unsuspected a decade ago. Our understanding of the structure and development of early systems of agriculture, however, awaits more concentrated and co-ordinated programmes of fieldwork, aerial survey and excavation.

REFERENCES

Ashmore, P. J. (1980) *Callanish 1980: Interim Report.* Edinburgh: Scottish Development Department.

Barclay, G. (1980) *North Mains, Strathallan.* The excavation of the barrow, henge and ring-ditches 1978–9: interim report. Edinburgh: Scottish Development Department.

Barrett, J., P. Hill, & J. B. Stevenson (1976) Second Millennium BC banks in the Black Moss of Achnacree; some problems of prehistoric land-use, in *Settlement and Economy in the Third and Second Millennia B.C.* (eds C. Burgess & R. Miket), 283-88.

Burgess, C. (1980) *The Age of Stonehenge.* London.

Calder, C. S. T. (1956) Stone Age house-sites in Shetland. *Proc. Soc. Antiq. Scot. 89*, 340-97.

Caulfield, S. (1978) Neolithic Fields: the Irish Evidence, in *Early Land Allotment* (eds H. C. Bowen & P. J. Fowler), 137-44.

Childe, V. G. (1946) *Scotland Before the Scots.* London.

CUCAP = Cambridge University Committee for Aerial Photography.

DES (Date) = *Discovery and Excavation, Scotland.* Annual Publication of Scottish Group, Council for British Archaeology.

Fairhurst, H. & D. B. Taylor (1971) A hut-circle settlement at Kilphedir, Sutherland. *Proc. Soc. Antiq. Scot. 103*, 65-99.

Feachem, R. W. (1973) Ancient agriculture in the highland of Britain. *Proc. Prehist. Soc. 39*, 332-53.

Fenton, A. (1978) *The Northern Isles: Orkney and Shetland.* Edinburgh.

Gillam, J. P., R. M. Harrison & T. G. Newman (1973) Interim report on excavations at the Roman fort of Rudchester 1972. *Archaeol. Aeliana.* 5 ser., *21*, 81-5.

Graham, A. (1939) Cultivation terraces in south-eastern Scotland. *Proc. Soc. Antiq. Scot. 73*, 289-315.

—— (1957) Cairnfields in Scotland. *Proc. Soc. Antiq. Scot. 90*, 7-23.

Harding = Aerial photographs by Prof. D. W. Harding, University of Edinburgh.

Horne, E. G. (1980) *Aerial Archaeology in the Valley of the Esk, Lothian Region.* MA dissertation, University of Edinburgh.

Jobey, G. (1968) Excavations of cairns at Chatton Sandyford, Northumberland. *Archaeol. Aeliana*. 4 ser., *46*, 5-50.

—— (1980) Unenclosed platforms and settlements of the later second millennium BC in northern Britain. *Scot. Archaeol. Forum 10*, 12-16.

Mackay, G. A. (1980) *A Study of Pit-alignments in Scotland*. MA dissertation, University of Edinburgh.

Megaw, J. V. S. & D. D. A. Simpson (1979) *Introduction to British Prehistory*. Leicester.

Mercer, R. J. (1980) *Archaeological Field Survey in Northern Scotland 1976-9*. Edinburgh University Dept of Archaeol. Occ. Paper No.4.

MUAP = Manchester University Aerial Photographs.

NMRS = National Monuments Record of Scotland.

Ogston, A. (1931) *The Prehistoric Antiquities of the Howe of Cromar*. Third Spalding Club of Aberdeen.

Piggott, S. (1958) Native economies and the Roman occupation of North Britain, in *Roman and Native in North Britain* (ed. I. A. Richmond), 1-27.

RCAMS = Royal Commission on the Ancient and Historical Monuments of Scotland.

—— (1911a) *Inventory of Monuments and Constructions in the County of Sutherland*. Edinburgh.

—— (1911b) *Inventory of Monuments and Constructions in the County of Caithness*. Edinburgh.

—— (1924) *Inventory of Monuments and Constructions in the County of East Lothian*. Edinburgh.

—— (1928) *Inventory of Monuments and Constructions in the Outer Hebrides, Skye and the Small Isles*. Edinburgh.

—— (1946) *Inventory of Shetland*. Edinburgh.

—— (1956) *Inventory of the Ancient and Historical Monuments of Roxburghshire*. Edinburgh.

—— (1957) *Inventory of the Ancient and Historical Monuments of Selkirkshire*. Edinburgh.

—— (1967) *Inventory of the Ancient Monuments of Peeblesshire*. Edinburgh.

—— (1978) *Inventory of the Prehistoric and Roman Monuments of Lanarkshire*. Edinburgh.

—— (1979) *The Archaeological Sites and Monuments of Easter Ross, Ross and Cromarty District, Highland Region*. Edinburgh: Society of Antiquaries of Scotland Field Survey.

—— (1980a) *The Archaeological Sites and Monuments of Berwickshire District, Borders Region*. Edinburgh: Society of Antiquaries of Scotland Field Survey.

—— (1980b) *The Archaeological Sites and Monuments of Sanday and North Ronaldsay, Orkney*. Edinburgh: Orkney Heritage Society: an archaeological survey by R. G. Lamb.

—— (1980c) *The Archaeological Sites and Monuments of Upper Eskdale, Annandale and Eskdale District, Dumfries and Galloway Region*. Edinburgh: Society of Antiquaries of Scotland Field Survey.

—— (1981) *The Archaeological Sites and Monuments of Ewesdale and Lower Eskdale, Annandale and Eskdale District, Dumfries and Galloway Region*. Edinburgh: Society of

Antiquaries of Scotland Field Survey.
—— (forthcoming) *Inventory of Argyll*, vol.5 (Islay, Jura, Colonsay and Oronsay).

Rees, S. E. (1979) *Agricultural Implements in Prehistoric and Roman Britain*. Oxford.

Ritchie, J. N. G., J. B. Stevenson & H. G. Welfare (1980) Recent Excavations in the Southern Inner Hebrides. *Northern Archaeology 1*, pt.1, 25-7.

Scott-Elliot, J. (1967) The Small Cairn Fields of Dumfriesshire. *Trans. Dumfriesshire and Galloway Natur. Hist. and Antiq. Soc.* 3 ser., *44*, 99-116.

Shepherd, I. A. G. & A. Tuckwell (1979) Traces of beaker-period cultivation at Rosinish, Benbecula. *Proc. Soc. Antiq. Scot. 108*, 108-13.

Stevenson, R. B. K. (1947) Farms and Fortifications in the King's Park, Edinburgh. *Proc. Soc. Antiq. Scot. 81*, 158-70.

—— (1949) The Nuclear Fort of Dalmahoy, Midlothian, and other Dark Age Capitals. *Proc. Soc. Antiq. Scot. 83*, 186-98.

Thomas, C. (1978) Types and Distributions of Pre-Norman Fields in Cornwall and Scilly, in *Early Land Allotment* (eds H. C. Bowen & P. J. Fowler), 7-15.

Whittington, G. (1978) A sub-peat dyke on Shurton Hill, Mainland, Shetland. *Proc. Soc. Antiq. Scot. 109*, 30-5.

Whittle, A. (1979) Scord of Brouster. *Current Archaeology 65*, 167-71.

Agricultural Tools: Function and Use

SIAN REES

Any type of information is open to misuse, intentional or unintentional. This truism is particularly apposite to archaeology, where we are forced to stretch limited pieces of evidence further than would be acceptable in many other branches of study. It is also an unfortunate fact that the more often a type of information is scrutinised, the more do possible sources of error come to light. Agricultural implements as a source of evidence have had their fair share of rather naive usage. Often we read in archaeological excavation reports that the presence of an iron sickle or hoe is evidence of arable agriculture having taken place on the site, but if we examine the tools in question, it will often be found that the assumed function was very uncertain or even wrongly attributed. The way in which the tools had been interpreted by the archaeologist to suggest the type of activity that took place on that site was, therefore, misleading. This is the first thing to stress when speaking of the function of tools. Before we can use the evidence of agricultural implements to help to reconstruct a picture of farming activity, we must understand the function of the tools themselves. This is not always simple.

FUNCTION AND DEVELOPMENT

What should we look for when studying agricultural implements? What, ideally, can they tell us? Three main points should be considered. First, we ought to be interested in the tools themselves. The history of the plough, or of harvesting tools, for instance, is in itself interesting, and the more examples of excavated tools we have, the better able are we to understand the development of a tool type in shape, size and material. Are such changes a response to a large scale change, for example in technical knowledge or in climate; or to a small scale change or a regional need for a specialised tool to cope with a specialised problem; or to a need for a labour saving tool in response to a changing socio-economic situation? The understanding of the tools themselves must be foremost, as, from this, the more interpretative points follow.

Secondly, we may use our understanding of the function of a tool to assist us in interpreting the site where it was found. The implements, if used in conjunction with other evidence – environmental evidence for the contemporary landscape, remains of plants and crops grown, animals raised, and the remains of contemporary fields surrounding the site – can help us to appreciate whether the economy was arable or pastoral, specialised or mixed. From such knowledge, we can progress toward an understanding of farming patterns in Britain and Europe and how they relate to different site types at different periods of prehistory. If we find a piece of a plough, it can tell us about the development of the plough, in that area at that date; secondly, if we are sure we know how and why this implement was used, whether for arable agriculture, rather than (for example) to level sites for building, or improving ground for pasture, we can suggest that arable agriculture was practised near the site. If we are happy with that, we can go on to examine that site in relationship to others in the locality, and as part of the larger scale farming pattern in Britain.

Bradley (1978, 44, fig.3:3) attempts to use agricultural implements along with other types of evidence to assess the type of farming practised at sites, and suggests a 'weighting' value as a guide to their reliability as evidence. This is an interesting method, and he wisely gives metal sickles a fairly low rating. If we are to try to use the tools in this way, our interpretation of function is, of course, crucial. What, therefore, do we have to help us with the identification?

Firstly, we have shape and size. Generally, it should be possible to get a reasonable idea of function from the size, shape, direction and length of the cutting edge if it possesses one, any sign it has of the method of hafting, and so on. It is reasonably easy to state that a tool was used for cutting, but more difficult to say what it was used to cut. When attempting to use a tool as evidence for arable agriculture, this is crucial. Take as an example, the group of billhooks shown on figure 1. The billhook is one of those successful tools which has altered little since its introduction in the Iron Age. The illustrations are from a 20th century sales catalogue (Sayce 1936, fig.1), and show regional styles used for different things because used in different environments in different parts of Britain. If three examples, nos 2, 12 and 16, are examined, their very different appearance will be obvious. It would have been easy to attribute quite separate functions to each, for instance harvesting (no.2), hedging (no.12) and butchering (no.16), had we found them on separate archaeological sites. When looking at unfamiliar types of tools it is important to be aware of the contemporary environment of a site, what that locality would produce and require. Yet we do not know what degree of regionalisation and specialisation had occurred by the end of the Iron Age. There is no reason to suppose that regionalisation did not exist, nor that one style of tool was common to all of Britain and used for a variety of tasks. It is virtually inevitable to jump occasionally to dangerous conclusions. Figure 2a

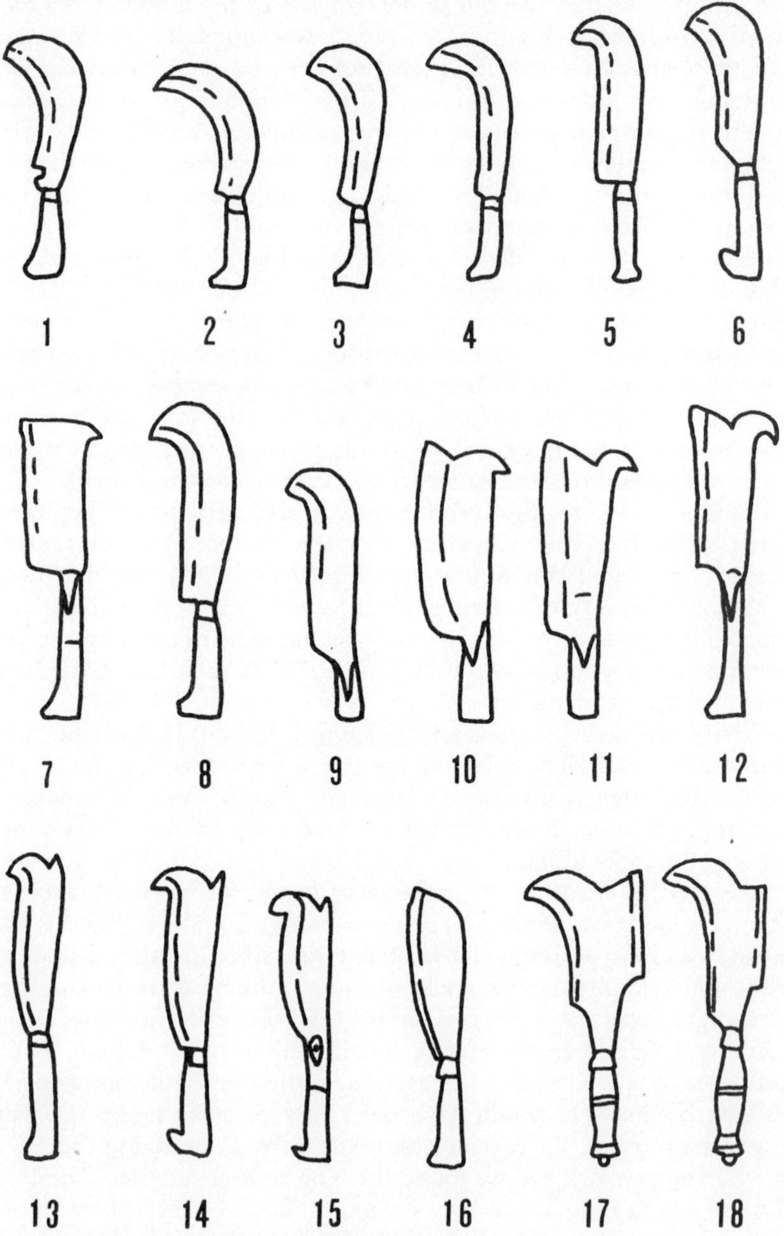

Figure 1. Regional styles of twentieth-century iron billhooks (after Sayce 1936, fig. 1).

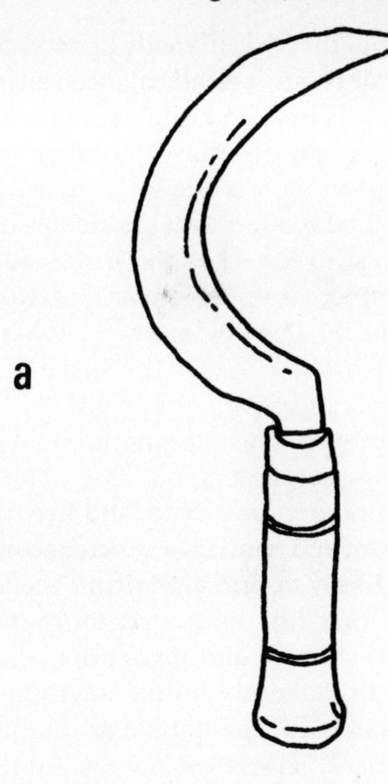

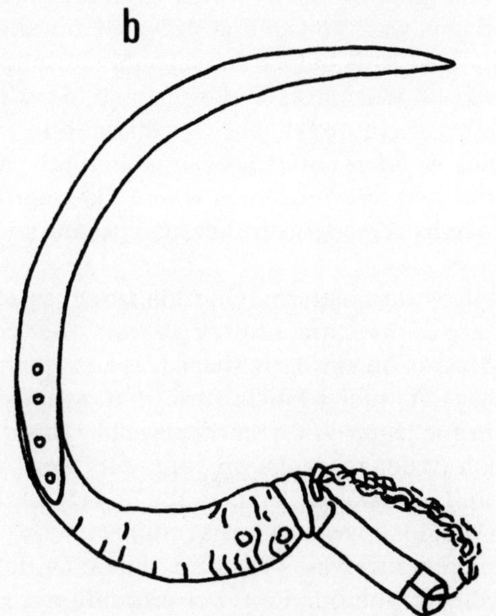

Figure 2. (a) Nineteenth-century iron gorse-cutting knife. Welsh Folk Museum, St Fagans. (b) Modern Iranian sickle with iron blade, horn and wooden handle (after Lerche 1968, fig. 4).

shows a nineteenth-century tool that would easily be accepted as evidence for arable agriculture, so similar is it to a small balanced sickle, had it been excavated on an Iron Age site. It is in fact a knife used for cutting gorse for fodder for animals, i.e. for pastoral economy. Another problem where shape is a factor for assessing function is the variable preservation to be expected on composite tools. The modern Iranian sickle shown on figure 2b has a wooden handle, ram's horn socket and iron blade. If the blade alone were found, in, for example, a founder's hoard, we would have quite the wrong idea of the blade shape. The obvious archaeological analogy is the composite flint sickle – we have no idea of the shape of such a tool, as no wooden settings for the blades survive.

The second factor to take account when attempting to determine function has already been touched upon, that is, our assessment of the needs and limitations of the contemporary landscape, and the inherent probability of a function being required within a given locality. To give a facetious example, one is unlikely to find viticulture knives in the Hebrides at any period, even if one had excavated tools that could have physically performed that task. Shape and probability, however, are of little help when we are faced with tools unlike anything that we have ourselves experienced. An example is the double paddle spades found in prehistoric contexts in Denmark. These tools were studied by Lerche, who came to the conclusion that they were not paddles, as previously thought, but spades. She came to that conclusion primarily because the blades were often unequal in length and heavily worn. What added enormous credence to this hypothesis was the fact that in New Guinea very similar double spades are still used; this helped considerably in suggesting how the spades were used and what tasks they were able to perform (Lerche 1977, Lerche and Steensberg 1973). Such examination of the tools used by different peoples in other countries can be helpful. More relevant still, perhaps, are our own folk museums where older agricultural implements are stored to help us recognise different types and styles.

WEAR PATTERNS

A third method is identification by wear patterns. One dramatic example is the identification by Steensberg of the extraordinary traction spade from Satrup Moor, using the wear marks on similarly shaped stone tools from Hama in Syria (Steensberg 1973). As such a tool is quite unknown to us, a lot of faith had to be placed in the pattern of wear displayed by the stone spades. Wear marks are much easier to detect on some tool types and materials than on others. Iron, for example, tends not to be very good as the surface can corrode and disguise wear patterns; bronze is also not helpful. Wood can be good where it survives. The share from Ashville, for example, shows the mark on the tip where an iron shoe probably protected the end (Fowler 1978), and wear on the tips of the ard-heads from Virdifield shows how the ard had been held asymmetrically in the ground (Rees 1979, fig.43a). Stone ard points often display particularly well preserved wear patterns (Rees 1979, pls 1–3). The similarity between these and that on the wooden foreshare used, in experiments by Hansen (1969, fig.24), on a reconstruction of a bow ard, suggests that the stone tools may have been used in a similar way. Wear marks can therefore be a crucial factor in attributing function. It is not however always easy to identify them. It is all very well when one has some pointer to assist – wear patterns on a similar tool still used today, or on a tool with wear marks produced experimentally to use as a comparison. Studying wear marks 'cold', as it were, can be problematical. The enormous assemblage of stone tools on prehistoric sites from the Northern Isles, such as that produced by the excavations at Scord of Brouster, Shetland, contain many examples of tools with wear marks which are not readily interpretable (Whittle, forthcoming).

Wear can, of course, alter the shape of tools considerably. Stone ard points, when heavily worn, become shorter and blunter; iron tools, as they can be long lived and the material sustain long periods of wear, can become considerably shorter. I know of a scythe in a botanical gardens, where it is used only very infrequently, and is therefore kept on, although over the decades it has become very short and quite altered in shape and hence less effective. Incidentally, had we found this tool on an archaeological excavation, we would possibly have used it as proof of heavy scythe use on that site, rather than almost the reverse – its occasional use over a long period. Important work is being carried out on edge-wear analysis on flint (Keeley 1980), and further work needs to be done on stone tools (for example, the perforated stone 'hoes' and 'axe-hammers') to examine more thoroughly the possibility that these might be agricultural tools. Experiments with such tools are important as a method of testing hypotheses about function, especially, in my opinion, experiments aimed at producing wear patterns on tools to test one's hypothetical identification of wear on archaeological specimens. If a stone tool which looks as though it may have been used as a hoe is copied, and the copy then used as a hoe, to test its efficiency, for long enough to allow wear patterns to be detectable also, this is more useful still.

NEGATIVE EVIDENCE

Another point that the archaeologist should bear in mind while thinking about tools and the farming cycle is the tool that does *not* appear in the archaeological assemblage. Does its non-appearance mean that it was not used, or that it was made of a material that has not survived? To comment on the distribution of iron sickles in the Iron Age and to hypothesise about the different farming patterns that this implies, when what one is really showing is the distribution of the use of iron, is as misleading as conversely to assume that a tool that never appears has merely not survived. Perhaps it never existed at all at that period. We should not forget that uprooting of grain, for example, needs no sickle. Uprooting is a common method of harvesting today in many parts of the world. We do not know to what extent if at all this method was employed in prehistoric Britain, but while we are agonising over flint blades for wear marks compatible with the grain harvest, let us be aware of uprooting as an alternative – though, of course, the use of a knife later in the process for cutting off the heads of the grain is common. Nor should we forget about all the tools used in threshing and winnowing. This can be a very complex process, involving shovels, forks, baskets and sieves. Some – if not all – of these must have been used, though none survive. Presumably the importance of basketry and more especially of wood was paramount in the making of agricultural tools in prehistoric Britain.

CONSERVATISM

From the archaeologist's point of view one helpful feature of agricultural tools is due to the much quoted conservatism of the farmer, once a good, effective tool has been achieved. This has been a source of comment for some years.

> We continue to manufacture the different types, as the traditional demand is still very strong. If we tried to sell a Kent billhook in your part of the world we doubt if we should succeed. It might be an excellent idea to attempt standardisation and undoubtedly we shall have to do this in time but quite frankly there is an inherent danger in trying to force something on people that differs from what they have normally purchased. (Letter quoted in Jenkins 1965)
>
> The backwardness that may be observed and which is so much complained of in some particular districts in respect to the state of their cultivation would seem to depend, in some measure, on an attachment to such implements as they have been in the habit of employing, however imperfect they may be in preference to such as have been recently invented or improved. (Dickson 1807, p.3)
>
> The most ancient farmers determined many of the practices by experiment, their descendants for the most part by imitation. We ought to do both – imitate others and attempt by experiment to do some things in a different way. (Varro, *Re Rustica*)

This tendency, whatever reforming agriculturalists think of it, is helpful to us, as it means that an effective tool like the billhook has survived almost unchanged in Britain for 2,000 years. It also makes it more interesting to speculate about what happened to tools which did disappear, like the Roman harvesting machine, the *vallus*, or the Roman long scythe, like those from Great Chesterford. Both tools, as far as we know, stopped being used when the Roman Empire broke up, although modern experiments with both have shown that they were effective tools. Were they tools that had been invented in response to a social need: lack of labour? Once this social structure had altered perhaps such labour-saving (and probably relatively wasteful) tools disappeared, until a similar need provoked the invention of their modern equivalents in the Industrial Revolution.

THE PRINCIPAL TOOLS

I have, so far, discussed what I see as the main problems and possibilities in assessing the function of agricultural implements in prehistoric Britain, and the directions in which work could be carried out in the future. I have myself catalogued and discussed all the agricultural tools of prehistoric Britain known to me, correct to 1976, so there is at least a data bank as a basis for future work. As this list can be referred to at any time (Rees 1979), there seems little point in doing other now than looking briefly at the tools encountered in prehistoric contexts in Britain, and commenting on any particular features of interest or difficulties arising from them.

PLOUGH AND HARROW

The evidence for the types of ploughs used in Britain in the prehistoric period is largely confined to the shares or working parts of the plough, which tended to be made of the hardest material available, to withstand the strain of the work. Thus shares, or, more correctly, the working points of the ards (a term used to denote a plough which does not possess a mouldboard) survive to us, made of stone (figure 3), hard wood, possibly bone and, during the Iron Age, iron (figure 4). The wooden pieces of ards that survive from early periods – the Lochmaben beam of alder, dated to 80 BC ± 100, the Milton Loch ard-head and stilt dated to 400 BC ± 100, and two undated but very similar ard-head and stilts from Virdifield, Shetland (figure 5) – are all similar to the respective parts of the bow ards found, spectacularly well-preserved, from Hendriksmose, Dostrup and Donnerupland (figure 6). Thus we have tended to assume that the bow ard was the normal type of ard used in prehistoric Britain. It is certainly true that the stone and iron foreshares that we know, are not incompatible with such a use both in their shape and in the wear marks that they display, but I was recently looking at wear marks on a metal share of a modern Bolivian crook ard and, apart from being rather shorter in length, the wear marks were much the same. Experiment may suggest the way in which these shares may have been held, but the truth is that we cannot be completely sure from an ard point what type of ard they were held on. We have no evidence for the types of implements used for harrowing in prehistoric Britain, if indeed specific tools were in existence for this purpose. It might be worth bearing in mind that wear marks on tools used for harrowing would presumably be much the same as on those used for ploughing, and that if only the working parts of those tools are found, it might be difficult to distinguish between them.

A certain amount of evidence survives for the type of traction team commonly employed. The Lochmaben beam is c. 248 cm in length, thus lying between the Hendriksmose beam (c. 2 m) and that of the Dostrup ard (c. 3 m). It is less sophisticated than that of the Hendriksmose beam, which has two notches at the traction end which would have given two alternative positions for adjustment of the height of the beam, which

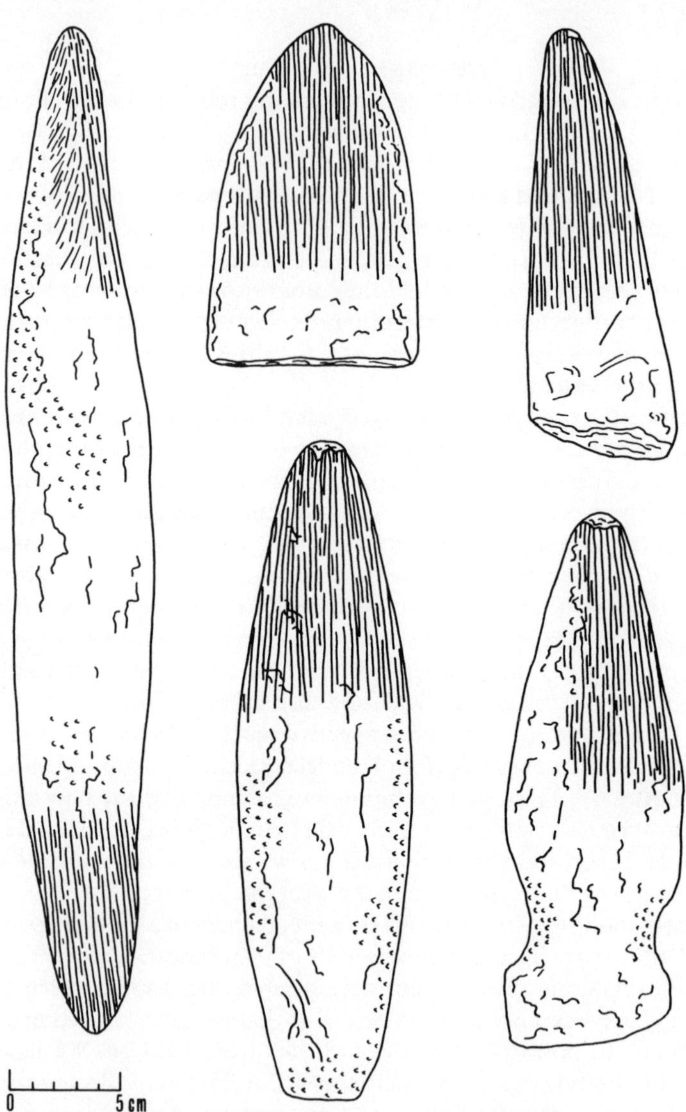

Figure 3. Prehistoric stone ard points from Orkney and Shetland, showing characteristic wear marks.

would affect the depth of penetration of the earth. For the size of the traction team we have to rely on the evidence of the Scandinavian rock engraving scenes of ploughing which probably date to the Bronze Age, and which show that teams of two or four oxen yoked together were normal (Glob 1951, figs 51, 26, 66, 50). Two types of yoke, the head or horn yoke, attached to the horns of the oxen, and the withers yoke, attached to their shoulders, seem to have been used in pre-Medieval Britain. Ex-

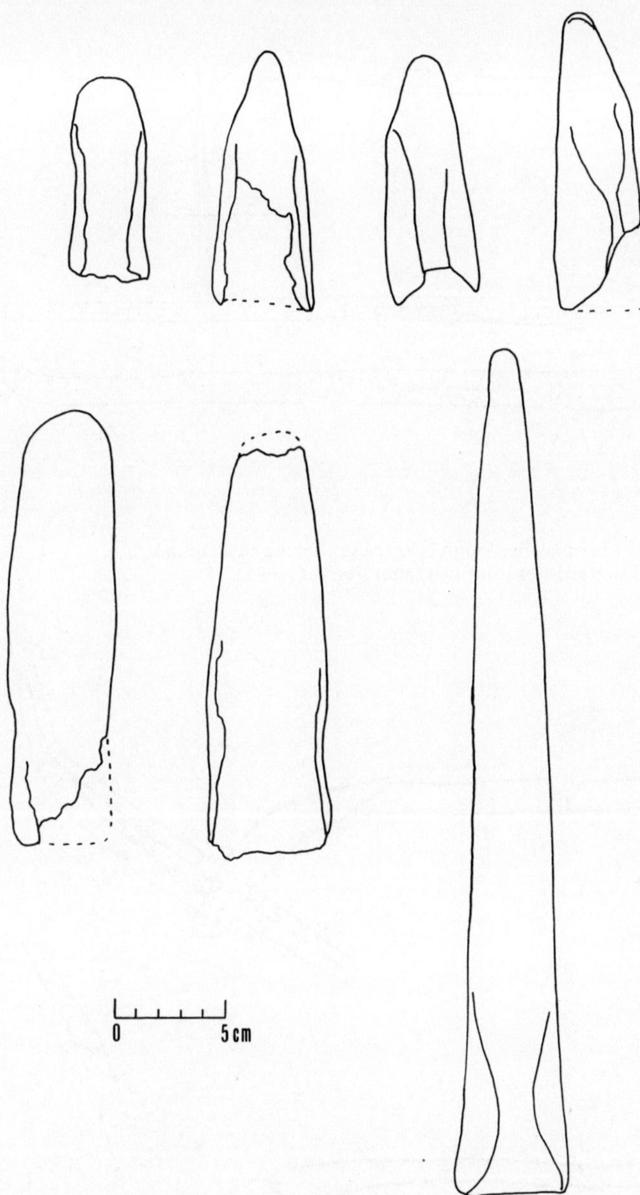

Figure 4. Iron ard points from Iron Age sites in Britain.

amples of both kinds have been found, unfortunately undated, in peat bogs in Scotland and Ireland. The head yokes have lightly curved neck pieces and horizontal central openings for the thongs that attached them to the horns of the animals. The withers yokes have more deeply curved side pieces, central horizontal openings to hold lashings for a beam or

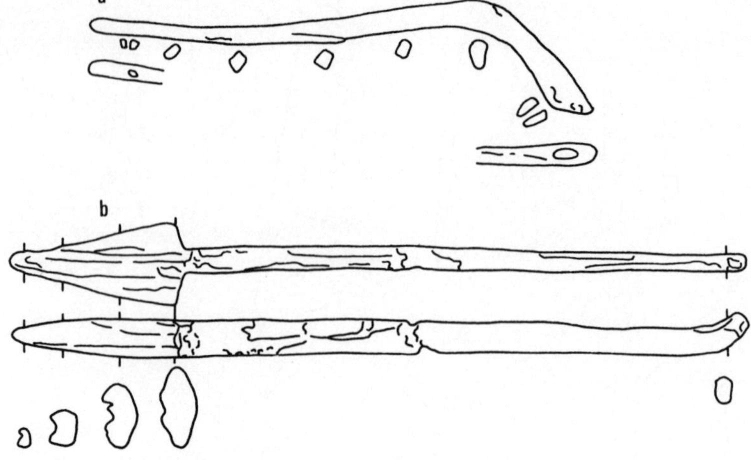

Figure 5. (a) Lochmaben plough beam (after Lerche 1968, fig. 4).
(b) Milton Loch ard-head and stilt (after Fenton 1968).

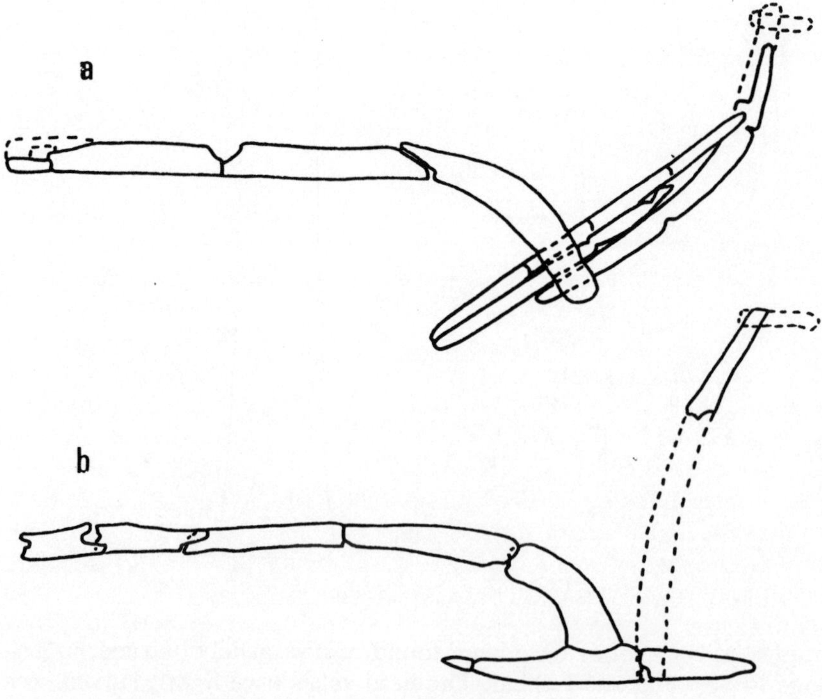

Figure 6. (a) Donneruplund ard (after Glob 1951, fig. 29).
(b) Vebbestrup ard (after Steensberg 1945, fig. 3).

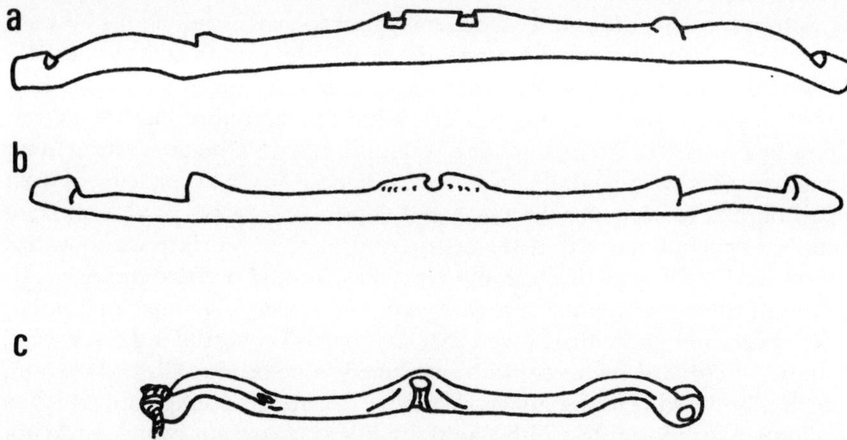

Figure 7. (a, b) Horn yokes; (c) withers yoke.

pole but usually also have vertically bored holes at the side of the neck pieces for thongs which encircled the animals' necks (figure 7). The head yoke, condemned by Columella and Pliny as inefficient and cruel, disappeared in Britain at a fairly early date – it would be interesting to know when. Perhaps a C14 project could be undertaken on the Irish and Scottish material. Until this has happened we must assume that both types coexisted in prehistoric Britain. I was interested to see the horn yoke still being used as the norm in Peru and Bolivia, so – despite Pliny – it cannot be so very inefficient.

Ploughmarks dating from the prehistoric period are being discovered throughout Britain from Shetland to Cornwall. We must therefore assume that the prehistoric ards, of whatever type, were used extensively and could cope with a wide variety of soils. As can be seen from the Danish bog examples, certainly from the end of the Bronze Age and very probably before that, the bow ard was a sophisticated implement which could penetrate the soil to 20 cm. The penetration could often be adjusted by using the different positions on the beam. Ploughmarks are interesting phenomena. If they are examined in conjunction with the actual tools that produced them (as we can do with the spectacular series of marks found at Sumburgh, Shetland and Skaill, Orkney) we can use them to reconstruct the pattern used by the ploughman on a field, and the depth to which he was ploughing (Rees 1979, p.79). An interesting recent hypothesis suggests that the ard could also have been used as a levelling tool to flatten an area before the erection of houses, roads, etc. (Fasham and Hanworth 1978, p.175). The more I look at the irregular, far-spaced ard marks normally found, the more I agree with the theory put forward by Evans (1975, p.118) among others, that the ard was used for some specialised use – levelling, perhaps, or deep ploughing. Steensberg (1973, p.115) made the interesting observation during his experiments with the Satrup Moor implement that, though we frequently find the traces left by the bow ard with its relatively deep penetration, we will find none archaeologically from the traction ard of the Satrup type, nor from the crook ard, as their 5–10 cm deep furrows, more relevant for sowing grain than the deeper bow ard furrows, are just not deep enough. It would be interesting to try experiments with a crook ard, a bow ard and a lazy-bed spade on similar soil depths to compare the types and depths of furrows produced. Hansen's experiments with a reconstruction of the Henriksmose bow ard produced ard traces of the same type that we find archaeologically. Although the experiments were carried out on a specially prepared ground, they certainly show that, given that the top soil covering did not exceed about 15 cm, ard traces could be expected to be produced by ploughing with a bow ard (Hansen 1969). We have normally accepted ard traces as evidence for ploughing with a bow ard, but as far as I am aware, we do not really know what type of traces are left after lazy-bed cultivation with a spade. Again, although we have no direct evidence for the use of the crook ard in Britain, it was certainly used in prehistoric Denmark, as the spectacular find of the Vebbestrup ard shows (figure 6b). We should perhaps keep an open mind about whether the crook ard might have been used in conjunction with the bow ard, perhaps for sowing. More work should perhaps also be done with stone axe hammers. Bradley (1972) has shown interestingly that in a cereal growing area in Cumbria, the disappearance of maceheads, possibly interpretable as weights for digging sticks, coincides with the appearance of the axe-hammer, which he feels may have been used as the working end of a crook ard. It would be worth carrying out a large scale investigation of wear marks on such tools to see if this can be borne out. I have looked at a few specimens and remained unconvinced, but a larger scale search is needed.

SPADES AND HOES

Spades and hoes, in conjunction with the ard (or instead of it in hillier places) would have been important tillage implements. We have little evidence before the Roman period as to the shape of such tools. Spade marks have been found on archaeological excavations, and a few, more or less enigmatic, wooden, bone and stone spade-like tools do survive (Rees 1979, pp.318–22). The perforated stone objects often described as 'hoes' need further study for any surviving wear traces. Hoes are still used for breaking clods after ploughing with an ard, and it was interesting to note, in South America, two or three teams of oxen with crook ards at work together on one field, each followed by a man using a hoe to break up clods. These ards are often used on stony ground in small fields which are now littered with clearance cairns (which could lose a field often as much as one quarter of its cultivable land), among which the ard weaved an irregular and circuitous route. We should not forget how extraordinarily manoeuvrable an implement an ard is, when we are studying, for example, prehistoric field systems in Shetland which are themselves littered with clearance cairns.

SICKLES AND KNIVES

Let us move on to the harvest. Before the Bronze Age, we assume that either flint sickles were used or that uprooting was the norm. Two types of flint sickles were possibly used. One-piece flint sickles, probably hand held, seem, in the archaeological record, to be associated, in southern Britain at least, with the later part of the Neolithic and possibly the earlier part of the Bronze Age. The less definable flint blades would presumably have been housed in a wooden setting fashioned in an unknown shape. Very early balanced composite flint sickles are known from Egypt, and we certainly have no evidence that the balanced sickle was *not* used in Britain from the earliest periods. Bronze sickles (so-called; figure 8) survive, and several forms are known, but none would suggest that the balanced sickle was known in Britain prior to the Iron Age. We do not know how any of these bronze tools were used, whether for cutting corn or not. They are found mainly in the southern part of Britain, though examples have been found in Scotland and Wales. It is probable that, even in the event of their having been harvesting tools, flint sickles continued to be the main instruments for harvesting grain.

Three types of bronze sickles are found in Britain, socketed, riveted, and knobbed. The direction of hafting, at least, is clear on the first two types, though quite how the knobbed type was hafted is open to debate. They were tested, by Steensberg, with a long handle set at right angles to the main blade direction, and proved quite effective. However, they could have been used with short wooden handles set in the same line as the blade, which would make them more of a knife than a reaping implement. It is also interesting to compare later socketed examples, like that from Llyn Fawr, with similarly-shaped iron-socketed tools; a type which continues into the Roman period. They presumably had some specific function which also continued into the Roman period, when the balanced sickle was certainly known. Whatever this function was, it presumably was not used for reaping. The decoration and fine manufacture of other tools suggests that they too were not used for anything heavily utilitarian, and it was Fox himself (1939 and 1941) who suggested that the flint sickle probably remained the main harvesting tool in the Bronze Age.

In the Iron Age, a great variety of curved iron knives were used. Figure 9 shows, I hope, the wide range of shapes and sizes which survive to us. Elsewhere I have attempted (1979, p.450) to classify them in two basic shapes, which I call reaping hooks and pruning hooks. That there are shapes exclusive to each group adds some credence to this classification, but I am not really trying to say anything other than that the tools in these two groups could have been used for reaping and pruning. One has only to examine the great variety of hooks on display in any folk museum, which were used for specialised functions in different parts of the country, to

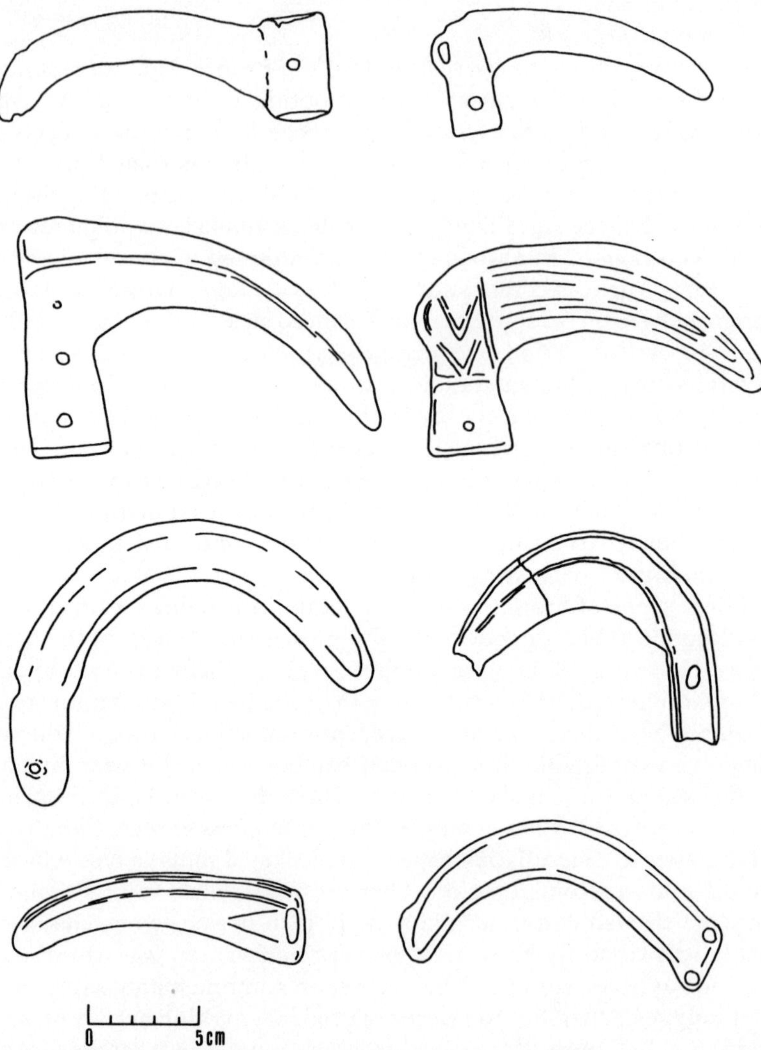

Figure 8. Types of bronze sickles from Britain.

realise the hopelessness of trying to ascribe function too precisely.

Examples of scythes were found at La Tène, but to my knowledge no examples have been found in prehistoric contexts in Britain, and we must assume that it was a Roman, probably a military, introduction into this country. The appearance of the iron billhook (figure 10) in the Iron Age is particularly interesting. Steensberg (1943) associates its arrival with the deterioration of the climate and the subsequent need for winter feed for cattle. This is indeed still an attractive hypothesis although of course we

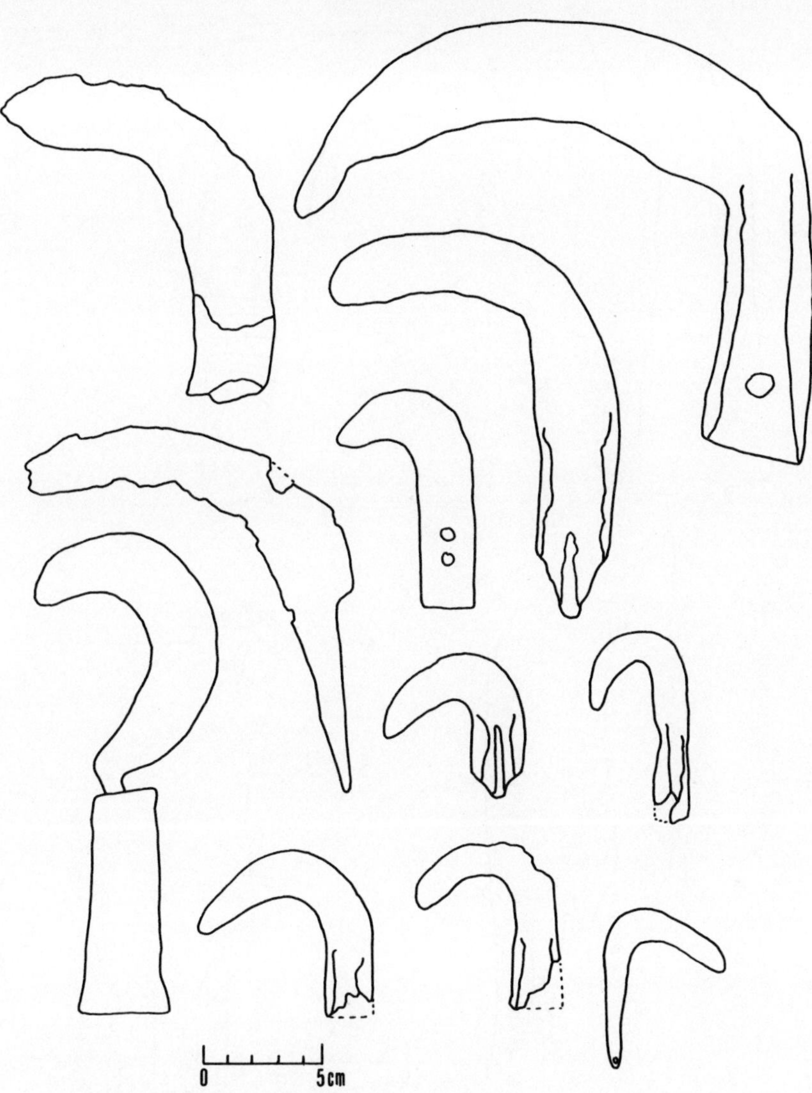

Figure 9. Types of iron reaping and pruning hooks from Iron Age sites in Britain.

do not know if some of the flint or bronze tools had previously been used for this purpose.

FORKS AND RAKES

Other necessary tools of the harvest are pitchforks and rakes, which presumably would all have been of wood. Only one pitchfork (Coles 1978, pp. 114–21) from prehistoric Britain, the Bronze Age in fact, survives. This, found on the Somerset Levels, was possibly used, according to the excavators, for lifting rushes rather than for agricultural purposes. Again,

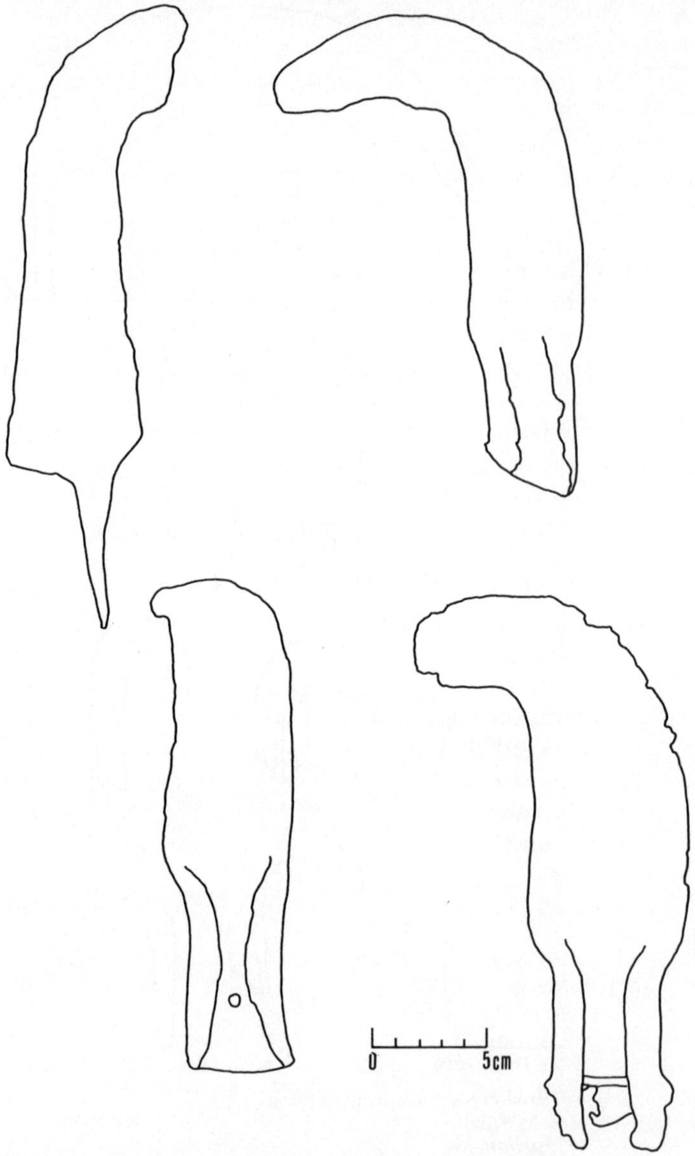

Figure 10. Types of iron billhook from Iron Age sites in Britain.

all the flails, shovels, baskets and sieves which may or may not have been used in the prehistoric period for winnowing and threshing have disappeared. Winnowing and threshing were normally outdoor pursuits on poorer farms in Britain until the eighteenth century, but it is worth remembering that in our climate both are more efficiently performed inside. We should perhaps be looking for archaeological evidence of inside work. The so-called 'working-hollows' can only be very dubiously associated with either process.

It is fairly clear that much of the evidence for agricultural tools and their functions in prehistoric Britain is very incomplete and difficult to interpret. To conclude, therefore, it might be advisable to suggest one or two positive possibilities which face the excavator, even in the short term. One interesting possibility is to try to compare a tool with the environmental work on site. An example of this was at the excavations at Farmoor, Oxon, where a long Romano-British scythe was found (Larnbrick and Robinson 1979). It had been suggested that the scythes were more likely to have been used for the grain harvest than for mowing grass, though experiments had shown that they could be used satisfactorily for either (Anstee 1967). However, the environmental evidence from the site suggested that the farm had had a specialised pastoral economy and no evidence for grain growing was forthcoming. This proves nothing, but we might look again at these scythes as at least dual purpose tools. Another possible way forward is to compare tool types with site types. Many Romano-British agricultural tools are found in towns and forts, many pieces of plough and curved iron hooks at hillforts, and these can be helpful when debating the nature of such sites. We should of course bear in mind other reasons for depositing tools; in smiths' hoards, for example, or possibly for ritual purposes. The longer term should provide a fuller story, as more, careful, excavation work yields better dated implements, more work on ethnographic parallels to open our eyes to the range of possible tools, more experiments to suggest the possible functions of tools, recreate wear patterns experimentally and create furrows with different implements, and, above all, more work on wear patterns on agricultural implements.

REFERENCES

Anstee, J. (1967) Scythe blades of Roman Britain. *The Countryman*, Winter, 365-9.

Bradley, R. (1972) Prehistorians and Pastoralists in Neolithic and Bronze Age England. *World Archaeology 4*, 192-204.

—— (1978) *The Prehistoric Settlement of Britain*. London.

Coles, J. M., ed. (1978) *Somerset Levels Papers* No.4.

Dickson, R. W. (1807) *Practical Agriculture. A Complete System of Modern Husbandry*. London.

Evans, J. G. (1975) *The Environment of Early Man in the British Isles*. London.

Fasham, P. & R. Hanworth (1978) Ploughmarks, Roman roads and motorways, in *Early Land Allotment: a survey of recent work* (eds H. C. Bowen & P. J. Fowler), 175-8. British Archaeological Report series no.48.

Fenton, A. (1968) Plough and Spade in Dumfries and Galloway. *Trans. Dumfriesshire Galloway Nature Hist. Antiq. Soc. 45*, 147-83.

Fowler, P. J. (1978) 'The Abingdon Ard-share' pp.83-8 in Parrington, M. *The Excavation of an Iron Age settlement, Bronze Age ring ditches and Roman features at Ashville Trading Estate, Abingdon (Oxfordshire) 1974-6*. London: CBA Research Report 28.

Fox, C. (1939) The Socketed Bronze Sickles of the British Isles. *Proc. Prehist. Soc.* 5, 222-48.

—— (1941) The Non-Socketed Bronze Sickles of Britain. *Archaeol. Cambrensis* XCVI, 136-62.

Glob, P. V. (1951) *Ard og Plov i Nordens Oltid.* Aarhus.

Hansen, H.-O. (1969) Experimental ploughing with a Dostrup ard replica. *Tools and Tillage 1:2*, 67-92.

Jenkins, J. G. (1965) Traditional design in some modern farm tools. *Man 33*, 43-5.

Keeley, L. H. (1980) *Experimental Determination of Stone Tool Uses*. Chicago and London.

Lambrick, G. & M. Robinson (1979) *Iron Age and Roman Riverside Settlements at Farmoor, Oxfordshire.* Oxford and London: Oxford Archaeological Unit Report 2, CBA Research Report 32.

Lerche, G. (1968) Observations on Harvesting with Sickles in Iran. *Tools and Tillage* I:1, 33-49.

—— (1972) The Radiocarbon Dated Ploughing Implements. *Tools and Tillage* II:1, 64.

—— (1977) Double Paddle-Spades in Prehistoric Contexts in Denmark. *Tools and Tillage* III:2, 111-24.

Lerche, G. & A. Steensberg (1973) Observations on Spade Cultivation in the New Guinea Highlands. *Tools and Tillage* II:2, 87-104.

Rees, S. E. (1979) *Agricultural Implements in Prehistoric and Roman Britain.* BAR British Series 69.

Sayce, R. U. (1936) The Investigation of British agricultural implements. *Man 81*, 63-6.

Steensberg, A. (1945) The Vebbestrup Plough. *Acta Archaeologica 16*, 57-66.

—— (1973) A 6,000 Year Old Ploughing Implement from Satrup Moor. *Tools and Tillage* II:2, 105-18.

Varro, R. R. (1967). *Rerum Rusticarum* (trans. W. D. Hooper & H. B. Ash). Loeb Classical Library.

Slash and Burn in the Temperate European Neolithic

P. ROWLEY-CONWY

The arrival of slash and burn on the European neolithic scene may be said to date from 1941, with the publication of Iversen's 'Land Occupation in Denmark's Stone Age' (Iverson 1941). Iverson's view was that the major decline in the forest curves in the pollen diagrams in the early Sub-boreal was caused by shifting slash and burn agriculture. This view was accepted by ecologically inclined archaeologists – in 1952 J. G. D. Clark wrote:

> Among the earliest European farmers there can at first have been no question of initiating systematic, permanent clearance and the formation of settled fields. Their approach was tentative and their agriculture extensive. Patches of forest would be cleared, sown, cropped and after a season or two allowed to revert to the wild, while the farmers took in a new tract. (1952, 92)

Slash and burn was regarded as primitive and archaic, so that it 'survived longest' (ibid.) in backwaters such as Finland. This whole idea received much support from Boserup (1965), who showed that in Africa slash and burn is the most extensive, least labour intensive type of agriculture, and that the process of intensification involves shortening the fallow period. It is frequently assumed that the same progression can be applied to prehistoric Europe, placing slash and burn at the head of the sequence. Slash and burn is still widely accepted; Iversen's final paper contains a reiteration of the slash and burn arguments (Iversen 1973), and in a recent work Steensberg (1980) suggests parallels between recent tropical and prehistoric European slash and burn systems.

It will be argued here that slash and burn in neolithic temperate Europe is unlikely, because there is no evidence for it, it is ecologically unlikely, and there is evidence pointing in another direction. Support for slash and burn comes from three main areas: the pollen analytical; the analogical; and the experimental, the question of yields. These will be examined in turn.

Much of the pollen work suggesting slash and burn has been done in

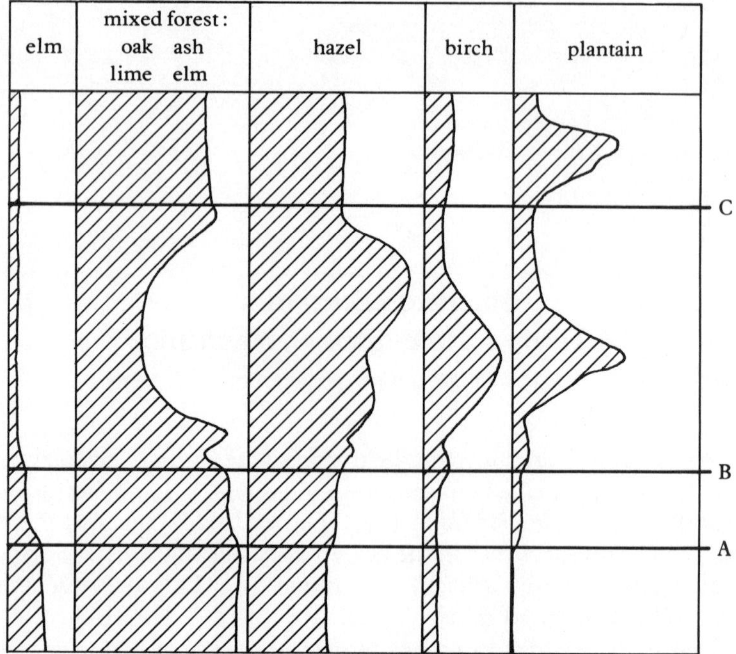

Figure 1. Pollen diagram with clearance phase (after Troels-Smith 1953). A, first farming; B, early Neolithic B; C, Single Grave Culture.

Denmark. Figure 1 shows the well-known diagram published by Troels-Smith (1953), based on the identification of over one million pollen grains. The decline in mixed forest is matched by a peak in plantain, and successive peaks of birch and then hazel before regeneration of the mixed forest. This is the sequence one would expect after burning (Iversen 1941, Troels-Smith 1953). This regeneration succession is thus viewed in terms of the history of a single clearing. Radiocarbon dating of the cultural phases marked in figure 1 makes it clear, however, that the phenomenon stretches over at least 300 (radiocarbon) years, not the sixty or so that regeneration should take (Iversen 1941). In other words, the 'clearance phenomenon' would have to be taken to represent an amalgam of many clearings, a possibility already suggested by Troels-Smith (op. cit., p.52). If this is the case, however, we should not expect so clearly defined a regeneration sequence; with many clearings, at all stages of regeneration, the birch and hazel maxima should be more long drawn out and contemporaneous, not peaked and successive. There seems to be a contradiction within the apparent support that pollen gives to slash and burn.

For a detailed reconsideration of this kind of diagram we may turn to the work of Tauber (1965). He starts by presenting a diagram from the Weier valley, Switzerland, calculated according to standard percentage techniques (figure 2). The diagram starts with the immigration of beech; familiar features include a clearance of beech, a rise in non-arboreal pollen, regeneration by oak, hazel and birch, and finally the re-establishment of beech. The first of three neolithic villages was established in the valley at the same time as the start of the clearance, and would normally be blamed for the whole phenomenon.

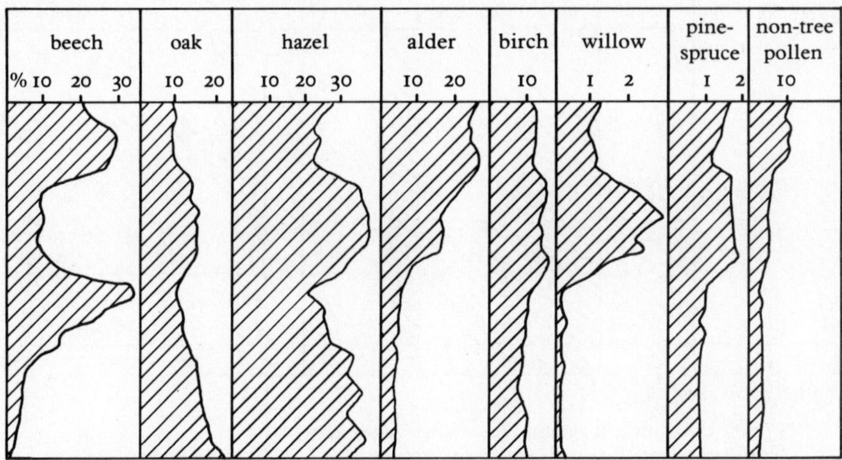

Figure 2. Percentage diagram, Weier (after Tauber 1965).

Tauber states, however, that factors of deposition and filtration should be taken into account before an ecological interpretation of this diagram can be made. The first requisite is an absolute, not a percentage diagram. Pine and spruce probably never grew within the limited confines of the Weier valley; arrival of their pollen was probably roughly constant. Tauber constructs an absolute diagram on this basis, expressing the values of each tree as proportional to the pine–spruce total (figure 3).

In the absolute diagram beech shows much the same curve as before. What is striking, however, is that oak, hazel and to a lesser extent birch all clearly decrease as well. Tauber's absolute diagram thus shows that the regeneration phenomenon is illusory – a product of the percentage method, caused by the greater decrease of beech.

Filtration is important to an understanding of the causes of the curves in the absolute diagram. Much of the pollen would have passed through the trunk space of the forest, and would thus be subject to filtration by the lakeside vegetation before it was deposited in the lake where the pollen core came from. As willow and alder, classic lakeside plants, are the only ones that increase in the absolute diagram, an increase of filtration of other pollen by these two species is a possibility. Basing his work on studies of particle behaviour from such fields as pesticide dispersion, Tauber develops formulae to express what would happen if the willow/

alder belt round the lake widened by ten metres. It is known that the lake level dropped, because the neolithic sites were on the newly-exposed shore; this would have led to a widening of the willow/alder belt as these trees spread onto these newly-exposed areas.

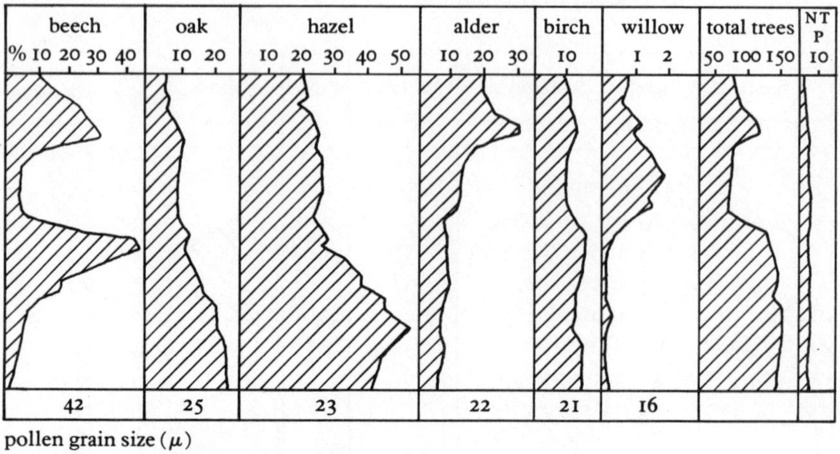

pollen grain size (μ)

Figure 3. Absolute diagram, Weier (after Tauber 1965).
Non-tree pollen does not include Cyperaceae.

The formulae predict that the largest pollen grains would be those most strongly filtered. In figure 3 the species are arranged in order of pollen grain size. Those with the largest grains decrease most, and the curves follow almost exactly the course Tauber's formulae predict. He therefore concludes that the clearance and regeneration phenomenon in the percentage diagram was entirely due to natural and statistical causes. When the effects of filtration are allowed for, no trace can be seen in the pollen frequencies of the activities of the neolithic farmers. 'The curves thus seem to be rather insensitive indicators of such events' (Tauber 1965, 52). Tauber has thus suggested that the pollen evidence need not be taken to support slash and burn.

The second major argument for slash and burn has been the analogical evidence. A review of the European evidence has been given by Steensberg (1955). He quotes a description of the Swedish situation by no lesser an authority than Linnaeus himself:

> What Linnaeus wrote [in 1751] was that slash and burn did exhaust much soil in Smaland; but the woods grew on the very worst soil, which was covered in stones and not suitable for permanent cultivation. From this woodland, otherwise useless, the farmer, by slash and burn, got a year's good cereal production and several years grazing for his animals. (Steensberg 1955, 86, translated from the Danish by the present writer)

This mention of otherwise useless land is a valuable clue. All the descriptions that I have been able to find dealing with recent Scandinavia make plain the fact that slash and burn clearings are not the central feature of the economy: such clearings are always outfields, and permanently cultivated infields always exist in conjunction with them. Even at the present time only some six per cent of the total area of Norway, Sweden and Finland is arable land (Mead 1958). In earlier times the shortage of arable necessitated continuous cereal growing, which in turn required manure to keep up fertility. Because of the limited area of arable, fodder crops could not be grown for the animals. Outfield grazing was thus vital. As S. Montelius writes:

> The forests formed a direct and necessary complement to the arable land. It is by no means certain that the growing of rye was always the greatest incentive to forest clearance. (Montelius 1953, 47–8)

The medieval evidence is similar; in Germany, for example, use was often made of burnt clearings. The main products were often marketable commodities, however, such as timber of uniform development or bark for tanning; grazing and sometimes a single cereal crop were taken as incidental extras (Steensberg 1955).

It looks, therefore, as if burnt outfields have an important role to play in northern Scandinavia because of the shortage of arable. This cannot be used to suggest that neolithic farmers, with all the arable of Europe to choose from, therefore used slash and burn as the central basis of their economy. In fact the Scandinavian slash and burn technique takes its place alongside many other outfield techniques. The burning of turf, for example, was widely used to provide grazing, and thereby infield manure. Fire need not be involved at all. In medieval England, for example:

> Sheep were sacrificed to the land to improve its cropping power through manuring bringing onto the cropped land fertility from the common grazings which were not ploughed. (Thomas 1957, 13)

All this suggests that slash and burn in recent Europe may be viewed as one of a series of tactical solutions to a particular problem – not as a remnant from some once-universal stage of agriculture. Farmers on adequate soils would have no need for the technique. It would not be necessary to go through the roundabout cycle of burning – grazing – infield manuring in order to increase arable production. Newly cleared areas could themselves go straight into cereal production.

Recent experimental evidence and yields must now be examined. The assumption is often made that continually cropped arable loses its fertility; against this, the remarkably high yields sometimes claimed for slash and burn, occasionally even up to a hundred fold (Soininen 1959), seem startlingly high. Montelius (1953) mentions that average production in Sweden in 1732 was under 250 kg of rye per hectare – a very small amount, which appears to conflict with the high yields. Part of the paradox may be resolved by the fact that a special variety of rye was sown in the burnt clearings. This variety was characterized by its high propensity to tiller – up to thirty stalks could be produced from each seed (Soininen 1959). Tillering is encouraged by planting the seeds relatively far apart (Gill and Vear 1966), so that some of the high yield figures might be explicable in terms of low sowing rates and moderate harvests. At all events the high yields of rye in recent Finland can hardly be taken as evidence of massive emmer production in the temperate European neolithic.

Experimental evidence suggests that slash and burn is not likely to produce spectacular yields. The long-awaited publication of the results from the Draved experiments in Denmark show that yields were remarkably low; more often than not the amount produced was less than that sown, and in many cases the plots produced nothing worth harvesting (Steensberg 1979). An experiment at the Butser Hill ancient farm has given somewhat better results – the first year production in the burnt area was the equivalent of 1,600 kg/hectare, but a considerable decline in output occurred in subsequent years (Reynolds 1977).

How might this compare with permanent fields? Both at Draved and at Butser areas were sown which had not been burnt. These areas produced much less even than the burnt areas. However, no ploughing or manuring was carried out in these experiments. We are fortunate to have figures from experimental stations which give an idea of the possibilities.

Figure 4 shows a fifty-year experiment in annual cropping of wheat and barley, with and without manuring, at the Woburn Experimental Station. The manured field produces more than the unmanured one, but both do produce returns over what was planted. The drop in the 1920s was due to a run of bad years, not to final exhaustion of the plots (Russell and Voelcker 1936).

Figure 5 shows annual barley production over 110 years at the Rothamsted Experimental Station, again with and without manuring. The highest decennial average for the manured plot came from the eleventh decade of the experiment (Rothamsted Experimental Station 1970).

Figure 6 shows a cycle of four years wheat and a fallow year, again with and without manuring, at Rothamsted. This experiment took place on plots which had previously grown wheat every year for eighty years, under the same manuring regime in each case. The long term improvement due to the fallow year is notable in the case of the manured plot, as is the peak in the first year after the fallow (Rothamsted Experimental Station 1970).

As Russell and Voelcker conclude:

> Both at Woburn and at Rothamsted the evidence is quite clear: cereal crops can perfectly well be grown in succession for years without risk of injury to yield or soil, provided weeds can be kept down. (1936, 236)

These experiments in long-term crop production all used modern strains of wheat and barley, and it might be argued that emmer, for

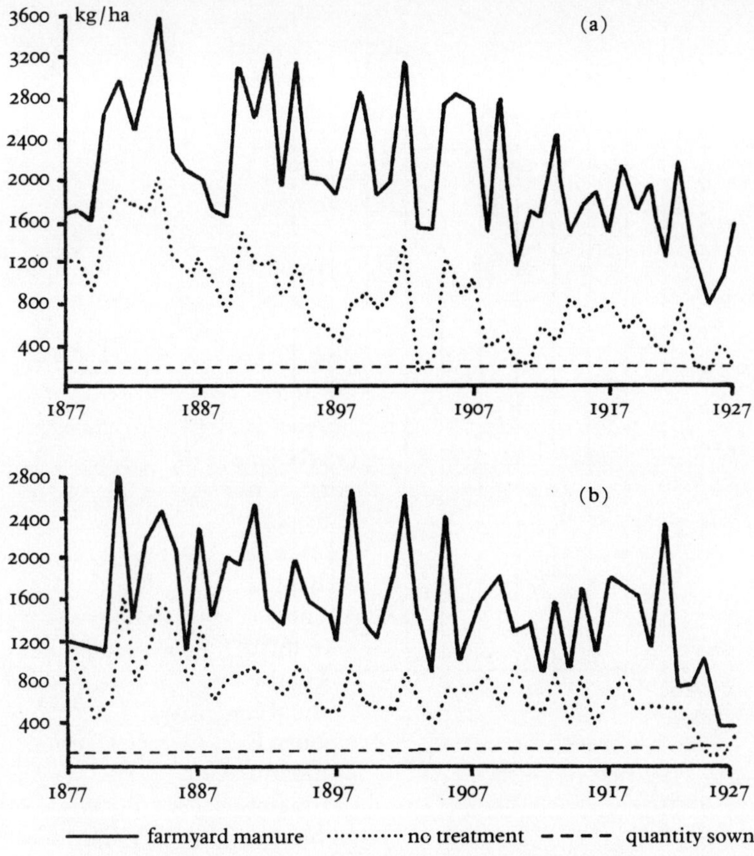

Figure 4. Annual cropping of (a) barley and (b) wheat in kg/ha for fifty years at Woburn (based on figures from Russell and Voelcker 1936).

example, would not respond in the same way. The figures from the first ten years of experiments at Butser (Reynolds, this volume) suggest, however, that emmer might be expected to do as well as, if not better than, modern crops. This experiment has not continued for as long as those using modern crops, and we look forward to the next one hundred years' work at Butser; in the meantime, no decline in emmer yields is visible in the first decade of the experiment.

Slash and burn is therefore not supported by the pollen evidence; the so-called analogies are inappropriate; and consideration of possible production suggests that permanent fields would be a not unlikely alternative to a long fallow system. Two things, however, stand in the way of permanent fields. First, progressive weed infestation could make continual cropping difficult. Secondly, we have no direct evidence that manuring was actually carried out, so it could still be argued that yields might decline in the long term. If we can demonstrate that weed control

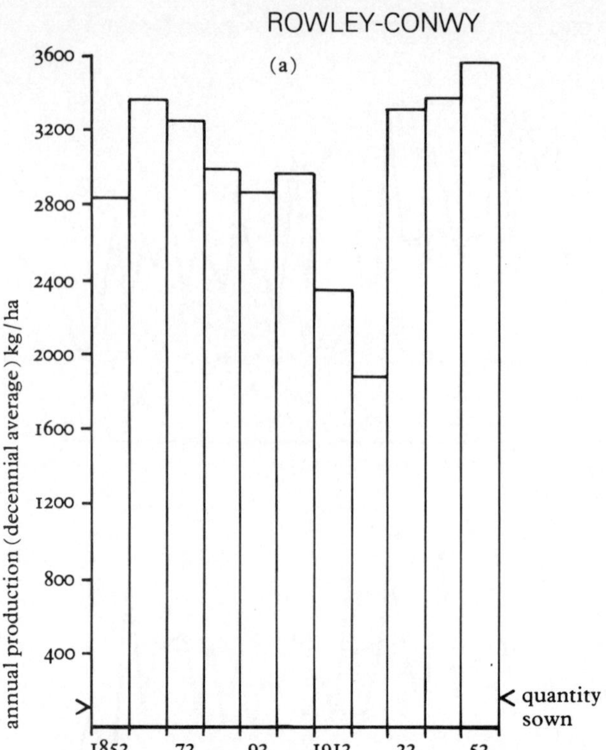

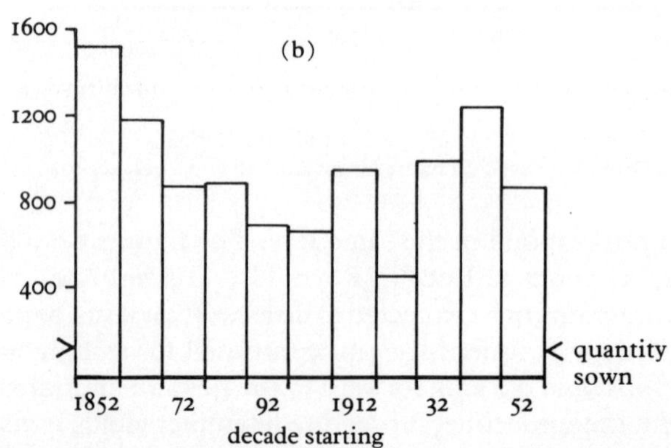

Figure 5. Continuous barley, 110 years, receiving (a) farmyard manure and (b) no treatment (based on figures from Rothamsted Experimental Station 1970).

mechanisms were available, and if the domestic animals can plausibly be linked with the permanent fields, then the case for permanent fields will be considerably supported.

Weeds may be controlled by weeding, by ploughing or by grazing. The first cannot be demonstrated, but there is no reason to regard it as un-

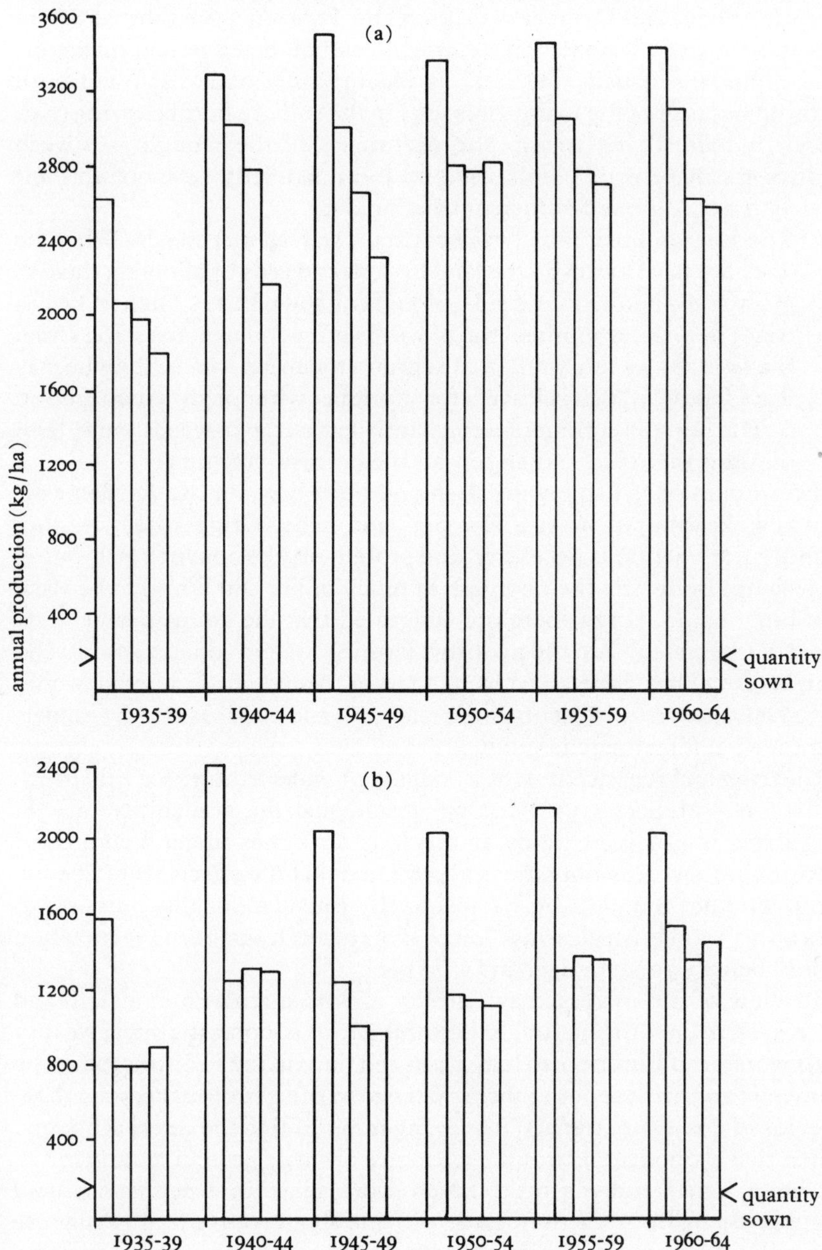

Figure 6. Wheat for four years followed by a fallow year, receiving (a) farmyard manure and (b) no treatment (based on figures from Rothamsted Experimental Station 1970).

likely. The presence of the ard has been documented under megaliths dating from the early third millennium BC in both Britain (Evans and Burleigh 1969) and Denmark (Eriksen and Thorsen 1980); this is before the start of the 'clearance phase' in radiocarbon-dated pollen diagrams. The plough is usually regarded as incompatible with slash and burn farming because of the many roots, etc. in the soil of a burnt clearing (e.g. Boserup 1965, Grigg 1974). The usefulness of the plough as a weed control mechanism is emphasised by John and Sally Seymour in their advice to would-be self-sufficient smallholders:

> The husbandman must wage constant war against weeds. When he does not have a crop on the land he attacks weeds by allowing them to grow and – before they seed – ploughing them in . . . Then, if he has time, he will let another crop of weeds grow and treat them the same. If a field grows too 'foul', that is grows too many weeds, then he may 'bare fallow' it, that is leave it for a summer without growing a crop on it. During this summer he constantly lets a crop of weeds grow, then ploughs them in . . . then repeats the process. (1973, 131)

Economies based solely on slash and burn have no use for domestic animals, keeping at most a few pigs and hens (Grigg 1974). Neither manure nor traction is necessary, and protein may be obtained by hunting or fishing. Believing the neolithic of much of the Old World to be slash and burn based, Grigg therefore suggested that the animals were 'only loosely integrated' into the neolithic farming system (op. cit., p.62); and Harris (1972) has gone so far as to suggest that domestic animals would have had an adverse effect on temperate slash and burn systems by hindering the vital forest regeneration.

Clearing and regeneration of woodland provides grazing for wild mammals too – Mellars (1976) has suggested that the availability of wild ungulates might increase by as much as ten times under a controlled burning policy. It is not always appreciated that the effects would be the same whether the clearing was originally intended for this purpose, or was a slash and burn clearing. Large areas of slash and burn regeneration would be very good for deer and wild pig.

In view of the increased availability of wild ungulates in a slash and burn system, and the neutral or harmful effects of domestic ones, we may well wonder, if Europe is to have slash and burn in the neolithic, what the domestic animals are doing there. Why go to the trouble of keeping three species of domestic animals, irrelevant or harmful to the cereal economy, when that economy ensures the existence of a wild protein mountain?

Sheep, cattle and pig make much more sense in a permanent field system. Apart from traction, cattle provide about twelve tons of manure per animal per year (McConnell 1887). Sheep may be penned on the stubble; apart from fine cleaning, weeding and manuring, their feet tread the soil to a better tilth or soil texture than any machine can produce (Thomas 1957). A special place is reserved for the pig:

> It is the way to bare fallow land. . . . On a small enough area the pigs will destroy every weed, if you leave them there long enough even the horrid perennial weeds like speargrass or twitch. They will bring up valuable elements from the subsoil, they will heavily manure the land, and they will leave it twice as valuable as before. Don't ring them. Let them dig. (Seymour and Seymour 1973, 79)

Each of the domestic animals thus has a definite role in an economy based on permanent fields: cattle are bulk manure providers, sheep detailed cleaners and treaders of arable, and pigs more gross cleaners and breakers of land. It is arguable that these roles might have been as important to the neolithic farmer as the presence of a capital reserve of meat.

The aim of this paper has been to suggest that: the pollen evidence may not be due to slash and burn; the analogical evidence is irrelevant; and the evidence of potential production is indicative of the adequacy of permanent fields. The necessity for a long fallow regime therefore recedes. The archaeologically demonstrated presence of the ard and the domestic animals in fact ties in with a system based on permanent fields, but it is hard to see how they would integrate with a long fallow system. It is therefore suggested that slash and burn would have been an unlikely option in the temperate European neolithic; we certainly have no justification for regarding a long fallow system as a near-universal 'stage' in primitive agriculture.

REQUIRED READING

Much of the pollen evidence discussed above was originally put forward in Denmark. Iversen (1941) was the first to suggest that the curves represented slash and burn, a view later developed by him and others (Iversen 1949, 1973 – and see the useful bibliography given in the latter work; also Troels-Smith 1953). For criticisms, see Tauber (1965).

The fullest range of recent European analogies has been presented by Steensberg (1955), unfortunately in Danish with only a brief English summary. Useful descriptions of tropical slash and burn systems, sometimes compared to the European neolithic, are by Boserup (1965), Grigg (1974) and Steensberg (1980); the article by Harris (1972) contains a good discussion of ecological factors. The drawing of tropical analogies in support for European slash and burn has been effectively criticised by Bay-Petersen (in press – my thanks to her for permission to mention this article).

The important slash and burn experiments are those described by Reynolds (1977) and Steensberg (1979).

REFERENCES

Bay-Petersen, J. L. (in press) Ecological differences in early agriculture in tropical and temperate environments: the ecological implication, in *The Origins of Agriculture and Technology: East or West Asia?* (eds P. Mortensen & P. Sorensen).

Boserup, E. (1965) *The Conditions of Agricultural Growth. Chicago.*

Clark, J. G. D. (1952) Prehistoric Europe. The Economic Basis. London.

Eriksen, P. & S. Thorsen (1980) Begravet Langdysse. *Skalk 2*, 28-30.

Evans, J. G. & R. Burleigh (1969) Radiocarbon dates for the South Street Long Barrow, Wiltshire. *Antiquity* XLII, 144-5.

Gill, N. T. & K. C. Vear (1966) *Agricultural Botany*. 2nd ed. London.

Grigg, D. B. (1974) *The Agricultural Systms of the World. An Evolutionary Approach.* Cambridge.

Harris, D. R. (1972) Swidden systems and Settlement, in *Man, Settlement and Urbanism* (eds P. J. Ucko, R. Tringham & G. W. Dimbleby), 245-62. London.

Iversen, J. (1941) Land Occupation in Denmark's Stone Age. *Danmarks Geologiske Undersogelse* II raekke, *66*, 1-68.

—— (1949) The Influence of Prehistoric Man on the Vegetation. *Danmarks Geologiske Undersogelse* IV raekke, *3*, 6, 6-23.

—— (1973) The Development of Denmark's Nature since the last Glacial. *Danmarks Geologiske Undersogelse* V raekke, *7-C*, 7-126.

Mead, W. R. (1958) *An Economic Geography of the Scandinavian States and Finland.* London.

Mellars, P. (1976) Fire ecology, animal populations and man: a study of some ecological relationships in prehistory. *Proc. Prehist. Soc. 42*, 15-45.

Montelius, S. (1953) The Burning of Forest Land for the Cultivation of Crops. 'Svedjebruk' in central Sweden. *Geografiska Annaler* XXXV, 41-54.

Reynolds, P. J. (1977) Slash and Burn Experiment. *Archaeological Journal 134*, 307-18.

Rothamsted Experimental Station (1970) *Details of the Classical and Long-Term Experiments up to 1967.* Harpenden, Herts.

Russell, E. J. & J. A. Voelcker (1936) *Fifty Years of Field Experiments at the Woburn Experimental Station.* London.

Seymour, J. & S. Seymour (1973) *Self-sufficiency*. London.

Soininen, A. M. (1959) Burn-beating as the Technical Basis of Colonization in Finland in the 16th and 17th Centuries. *Scandinavian Economic History Review* VII, *1*, 150-66.

Steensberg, A. (1955) Med Bragende Flammer. *Kuml*, 65-130.

—— (1979) *Draved. An Experiment in Stone Age Agriculture. Burning, Sowing and Harvesting.* Copenhagen.

—— (1980) *New Guinea Gardens. A Study of Husbandry with Parallels in Prehistoric Europe.* London.

Tauber, H. (1965) Differential Pollen Dispersion and the Interpretation of Pollen Diagrams. *Danmarks Geologiske Undersogelse* II raekke, *89*, 1-69.

Thomas, J. F. H. (1957) *Sheep*. 3rd ed. London.

Troels-Smith, J. (1953) Ertebolle Culture – Farmer Culture. *Aarboger for Nordisk Oldkyndighed og Historie*, 5-62.

Deadstock and Livestock

PETER REYNOLDS

This paper sets out to explore three major hypotheses within the broad theme of prehistoric agriculture. The recherché title of 'Deadstock and Livestock' is intended to imply the balance between archaeological data and present day empirical research, between the inanimate and animate, and to focus attention upon anomalies which have arisen primarily because the balance has not been fully observed, tested or even recognised. The hypotheses themselves are drawn from current research programmes in train at the Butser Ancient Farm Research Project in Hampshire. Details of this project, its purpose and methodology have been published elsewhere (Reynolds 1978, 1979), but in general terms, it is a unique outdoor laboratory devoted primarily to research into prehistoric archaeology and agriculture. The objectives of the research programmes are to invalidate or confirm, by empirical testing, the theories and hypotheses raised from excavated evidence. The main emphasis is firmly placed upon the Iron Age period for climatic reasons discussed below, although investigations into other periods are occasionally carried out (Reynolds 1978, Reynolds and Langley 1980). Of considerable importance is the need to stress that the experiments carried out at the farm and severally reported below are designed to test only those areas that can be subjected to testing within a scientific framework. Similarly it must be emphasised that there is no attempt whatsoever to recreate an Iron Age way of life in the sense of the popular conception of re-enactment. Indeed the major thrust of all the research programmes is to deny as far as possible the inherently variable human factor since the data, if they are to have any validity whatsoever, must be repeatable and not unique. Consequently those experiments which depend upon a developed skill are reported without analyses of time and effort expenditure. Human performance is the reflection of contemporary knowledge and skill and is, therefore, impossible to replicate meaningfully by those of succeeding generations. An expert, burdened by his own knowledge and developed skill, will apply techniques which were probably previously unknown; an amateur, fired only by enthusiasm, denies the skill and knowledge of the past human agency. In effect, empirical tests which seek to impose limitations of time taken upon achievements are virtually impossible to validate and are of very doubtful value. This insistence upon basic objectivity may initially seem to be a rather sterile approach but the results achieved to date from the research programmes, especially the crop yield trials, are such that without objectivity of this nature their credibility would be in question. In this sense, therefore, the Ancient Farm is a laboratory from which will emerge the boundaries of probability rather than an historically true (if such terms do not themselves present a paradox) and proved record.

The ultimate intention, of course, is to be able in the future to construct from all the data achieved over at least two decades all the interactive elements of an agricutural cycle and thus to provide a valid and comprehensible basis for a deeper understanding of the prehistoric economy. It is integral to the overall intention that all of the widely divergent bio-climatic zones as utilised in prehistory should be subjected to the same developed approach as that now in train. At present the *caveat* which must preface any data provided by the Ancient Farm is that those data are relevant to the chalk lands and adjacent soils of central southern England unless otherwise specified.

The three hypotheses outlined below are selected to represent three major elements of agricultural practice as represented by the archaeological evidence. The first considers the problems of cultivation in the sense of ploughing and seed bed preparation. The second offers a selection of results from the crop yield trials carried out at the Ancient Farm, and the third examines the possibility that the archaeological source evidence for prehistoric crops, the carbonised seed, is not necessarily representative of the harvested cereal at all. Within the confines of this paper it is impossible to present overall surveys of the basic range of data upon which the experiments are mounted and consequently those quoted are drawn out only as examples.

ARD MARKS AND ARDS

The primary sources of evidence for cultivation can broadly be placed in four categories. These comprise the marks or scores revealed by excavation and reputed to have been made by prehistoric ards, actual remains of ards and parts of ards, representation of ards and agricultural scenes in rock carvings, and 'Celtic' or more sensibly, ancient fields.

Ard marks have been identified on a large number of widely divergent sites both in the United Kingdom and Europe. That they are prehistoric marks is simply attested by the superimposed layers of identifiable date, or alternatively their association within a site. Generally they comprise interrupted scores in the subsoil occasionally unidirectional, occasionally sets at right angles to each other and more infrequently one or more sets diagonally opposed to others. At the outset it is quite remarkable that such marks have survived at all if they form part of a regular agricultural activity, in that the repeated cultivation of a field with a standard plough would lead to a thorough stirring up of the soil to a consistent depth. The assumption here is simply that a 'standard plough' would have been used. Ard marks have been identified as early as the Neolithic, for example, at the South Street Long Barrow, Avebury where cross ploughing had apparently taken place prior to the creation of the barrow (Ashbee 1979). An early survey of cross plough marks identified to the prehistoric and Roman periods has been published (Fowler and Evans 1967). Subsequent to this early work ard marks have been identified not only on the chalk and sand subsoils but over the full range of soil types including the heavy clays, for example, in Northumberland (Gillam *et al.* 1973) and again near Bristol on the rheatic clay (Everton and Fowler in Bowen and Fowler 1978). The assumption throughout has been that these marks or scores were the product of a prehistoric type ard, the prime evidence for which has come from the peat bogs in Denmark.

There are two fundamental surveys of the prehistoric ard types, the first by Leser (1931) and the second that of Glob (1951). The latter has played a most significant role in studies relating to ard marks and ards and has been the inspiration of several sets of empirical trials to examine the different types of ards (Aberg and Bowen 1960, Hansen 1969, Reynolds 1967, Reynolds forthcoming 1981). In terms of their production of ard marks similar to the prehistoric examples only Hansen has partially demonstrated that such an ard, in this case the Hendriksmose ard, could create such marks in sandy soils. His experiments, however, raised considerable doubts in that the ard could not cope with a root bonded topsoil and would only create scores in the subsoil when a proportion of the topsoil had been removed. Even then the scores were hardly comparable to those archaeologically recovered in the same region.

Recent work at the Ancient Farm has concentrated upon the Donneruplund ard (Glob 1951 and plate 1) which is perhaps the best representative of the class known as beam ards. In contrast to the problems of traction experienced in the earlier experimental works, referred to above, the plough team, a pair of Dexter cattle, the nearest modern equivalent to the Celtic shorthorn (*Bos taurus*), has been fully trained over a long period. The choice of the Donneruplund ard as a type was influenced by the discovery in Scotland of a similar beam in Loch Maben (Fenton 1968) and under share in the Milton Loch Crannog (Piggott 1952–53). It shares the characteristics of the Hendriksmose/Dostrup ard types while differing in specific detail. The results from the experimental work on two sites, the Ancient Farm itself where the soil, a friable redzina averaging c. 0.10 m thick directly on middle chalk, and the Demonstration Area of the Ancient Farm, comprising a hill wash soil c. 0.30 m deep over chalk, indicates that such an ard, while admirable in producing a tilth suitable for planting

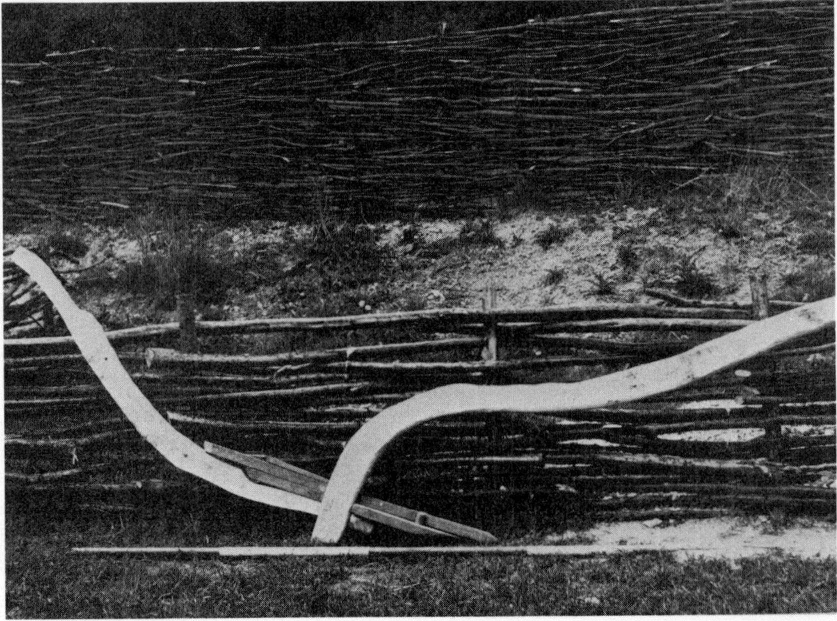

Plate 1. Replica of the Donneruplund ard

crops does not create any kind of mark in the subsoil. In the former case it simply rips up the surface of the chalk rock already subjected to permafrost action and leaves no discernible trace of its passage. In the latter, since its consistent penetration at maximum efficiency is only c. 0.15–0.20 m, it does not penetrate deeply enough to leave any abiding trace. In fact it is virtually impossible, short of breakage of the main beam, for the foreshare to penetrate beyond 0.25 m. The design of the ard is such that the angle of foreshare and undershare to beam is absolutely critical. If the angle is too deep the ard locks forward, forcing the yoke downwards and halting the cattle, too shallow and the share skips ineffectively over the surface.

Further experimentation with a crook ard of the Hvorslev type (Glob 1951) yielded similar results (plate 2). This, perhaps the simplest of the ard types and arguably presaged by the mattock hoe/digging stick or even the rope traction spade ard (Steensberg 1973) is considerably less effective than the Donneruplund ard. Although radiocarbon dating places it earlier than the beam ards allowing some substantiation for a developmental theory to be applied to ard types, it is so ineffective by comparison that an alternative view could be offered. Also both beam and crook ards are represented upon rock carvings of presumed contemporaneity. The function of the ard, of whatever type, is to undercut the soil with the foreshare and to cause it to flow around the foot of the beam. The beam-type ards are

Plate 2. Replica of the Hvorslev ard.

fitted with undershares, which significantly increase the width of the foot of the beam and consequently increase the disturbance inherent in the soil flow. The main purpose of the foreshare, apart from initial penetration, is to hold the foot of the ard in a horizontal attitude just beneath the soil surface. In the experiments with the Hvorslev-type ard, it was discovered that although its functioning, as with the Donneruplund ard, depended upon critical angles, the furrow it produced was only slightly wider than the beam foot and the soil disturbance was minimal in comparison. In the production of a tilth it was signally inferior to either mattock hoes or the beam ard. The alternative view, therefore, suggests that the crook ard is not necessarily designed to create a tilth but rather has the specific function of creating a seed drill. This view is particularly supported by the rock carvings referred to as the Litlesby Ard (Glob 1951).

Since the ard mark as such is regarded as indicative of agricultural practice it is vitally important that an explanation for its production be proffered. There are, therefore, two basic questions involved. First, the fact that ard marks survive at all causes concern in that repeated ploughing would ultimately be self cancelling, the end product being a totally and consistently disturbed soil horizon created by the same implement within its particular depth capacity. However, in the majority of cases the marks, once recognised, are quite clear. In the case of a set of unidirectional marks one could quite properly argue that such a set of marks was the result of the last cultivation pass, although this is rather against the self-cancelling argument being within reach of the standard implement. Yet when there are multidirectional sets remnant in the subsoil, while the self-cancelling argument would possibly aply to a standard ard given the number of cultivation processes required in any one season, one must hypothesise an alternative cause. The experiments carried out with the basic ard types available for study show that they are designed to travel through the soil in the horizontal plane. The protruding share, whether it be in the form of a one-piece crook ard or a bar share of wood or metal in a composite ard, is a device to hold the ard within the body of the soil and has a maximum reach in terms of depth. The tilth is produced by the stirring inherent in the flow pattern of the soil around the heel of the ard.

Figure 1. The Aspeberg ard (after Glob 1951).

Given that the maximum reach of the foreshare of the standard ards is shown to be no more than 0.25 m there would seem to be omitted from the available evidence an implement capable of creating the ard marks. Similarly such an implement, by the definition of the marks themselves, could well be a specialist tool hypothesised here as a 'rip ard'. Its function would be the initial process of creating arable from scrub or woodland and again in the recovery of non-cultivated fallow into arable. The hypothesis is actually supported by the third category of basic evidence, the rock carvings, particularly the rock carving of a ploughing scene as Aspeberg, Sweden (figure 1). The ard is described by Glob (1951) as of the same type as the Donneruplund/Dostrup variety. However, it would seem to differ sharply in that the stilt and share appear as a solid unit and seems more like a hook at a much steeper angle to the ground surface than the other representations. A similar ard appears on a rock carving from the Val Camonica in Northern Italy and in this case the scene is usually complemented by figures following on wielding mattock hoes (Anati 1961). In addition a metal so-called ard tip recovered from an excavation of an Iron Age site at Slonk Hill near Shoreham, Sussex, is very unlike all the other metal objects identified as ard tips (Hartridge 1978). Indeed many of these metal objects are much more likely to be 'spuds', a simple metal flange mounted on a stick and used by a ploughman to clean the soil away from the ard which itself may be entirely of wood (Rees 1979). There is, in fact, very little evidence of metal sheathing for the Danish ards at all. In the Donneruplund/Dostrup types the bar share is adjustable, a facility which would be unnecessary if the share were protected, and experiments with the former variety indicate a wear pattern of c. 2.5 cm over an acre of ploughing on light soil overlying limestone (Reynolds 1967). In the case of the Slonk Hill example, the shape and wear pattern is such that it would fit onto such a hook or rip plough (Reynolds, in Hartridge 1978). Given the following description, it would seem that a metal sheath protection to this type of ard would be much more important than for the previous types.

Within the framework of the present argument it is not unreasonable to refer to a Spanish ard called 'el cambelo' in use today in the mountain region of Lugo province (see Fowler, above, plate 9a). This ard comprises a straight beam from the yoke which is attached to a curved oak bough. The tip of the oak bough is protected by a metal sheath, similar to the example from Slonk Hill referred to above. This ard, in effect a great hook, is used specifically for bringing into arable new ground or old fallow. In practice the tip is dug into the soil and hauled forward by the oxen, commonly a pair of bulls rather than the more usual cows, until it locks under the weight of soil and roots. It is loosened, cleaned and the process is then repeated leaving interrupted tears or heavings of earth, roots and vegetation in the ground surface. Unfortunately it was impossible to excavate the subsoil but to all intents and purposes it penetrated far deeper than any other simple ard, often being buried up to 0.50 m. Inevitably the tip penetrated into the subsoil and must have created a deep narrow score. In total agreement with the rock carvings in the Val Camonica valley, men armed with mattock hoes broke down the soil into a tilth.

Although it is extremely unwise to rely heavily upon ethnographic examples, in this particular case the archaeological evidence itself suggests the parallel rather than the reverse. Also if one is to employ parallels from ethnography at all, the area of example should as far as possible be of the same or similar bio-climatic zone. In this respect the north west of Spain, especially the coastal strip and immediate hinterland, experience a very similar climate to that of southern England.

If one gathers these fragmentary pieces of evidence and allies them to the nature of plough-marks recovered from excavations, an hypothesis emerges which suggests that the ard marks were created by a rip ard rather than a regular prehistoric type ard, given that the soil overburden exceeded 0.25 m. Indeed it has been suggested that the ard marks under the South Street Long Barrow are indicative of the creation of grassland from woodland (Evans 1972), a task completely beyond the physical capabilities of the normal ard group. Certainly the hypothesis above accounts for the depth and definition of the scores and their normally interrupted nature. In the case of unidirectional or criss-cross ard marks one could further hypothesise that such an area was taken into arable once or twice only and thereafter stayed until abandonment as cultivated land. In the case of multidirectional ard marks the theory of regular periods of unploughed fallow could be advanced. Whatever the viability of these hypotheses, it is signal to record that a deliberate investigation by excavation of a group of Ancient fields has yet to be undertaken. Certainly it brings into question the rather facile approach of counting the number of directions of ard marks in an area and equating the result to the number of cultivations. (A detailed report of the experiments carried out at the Butser Ancient Farm with the Donneruplund Ard is to be published in the Proceedings of the Symposium of Woodworking Techniques before 1500 AD held at the National Maritime Museum, Greenwich in September 1980.)

Also inherent in this hypothesis is the consideration, hinted at above, that the development of the ard is not a simplistic one moving steadily forward from the simple to complex in terms of ard construction, with abandonment of one once superseded by another. It would seem more logical, given the functional effects of the different varieties as revealed by practical trials and from re-appraisal of the iconography, that each had a perfectly normal and contemporary role. The conjectured rip ard is the 'sod buster', used on specific and unusual occasions and leaving specific and unusual evidence of its passage. The beam or bow ard of the Donneruplund/Dostrup type is the conventional tilling implement used to disturb the soil prior to creating a seed bed. Trials have clearly demonstrated that the furrows it creates are significantly too deep, some 0.30 m from trough to crest, for seed to be sown directly into them (Reynolds 1981 forthcoming) (plate 3). The final variety, the crook ard is, in practice, used for the drawing of seed drills for which it is admirably suited. It seems a more reasonable approach to allow a farmer a panoply of implements with which to respond to the challenge of agricultural tillage rather than to presume, tacitly or otherwise, a single implement to assume the full range of processes.

PARAMETERS OF CROP YIELD: Some Results from Cropping Trials with the Prehistoric Cereal Types Emmer (*Tr. dicoccum*) and Spelt (*Tr. spelta*).

The second hypothesis is directly involved with the first in that the preparation of the land by whatever means and however many processes is concerned with crop production. The basic economy of the prehistoric period from the Neolithic onwards was indisputably agriculture. Indeed an alternative view of prehistory, rather than determining specific periods by the basic material employed for the manufacture of artefacts, would be to regard it as a straight development of agriculture. The increasing abundance of evidence from archaeological investigations and aerial surveys in the United Kingdom fully support the developmental principle,

Plate 3. The Donneruplund ard under traction.

so much so that by the latter part of the Iron Age, broadly the centuries immediately preceding the Roman invasion of England in 43 AD, the agricultural landscape as we know it today was firmly established (see Fowler above). In fact, there is every reason to believe that even larger areas of arable were in *cultivation,* in that hundreds of hectares of prehistoric field systems evidenced by lynchets and trackways have been and still are under a *pastoral* régime. In this particular case the land is generally of a marginal nature and was once thought to have been exploited by the prehistoric farmers because they lacked the technological ability to deal with the heavier valley soils. Aerial photography and excavation (Everton and Fowler in Bowen and Fowler 1978, Gillam, Harrison and Newman 1973) has now disproved this contention in terms of field evidence, and empirical examination of the available technology has shown it to be sufficiently advanced to cope with all subsoils including the most intractable clays (Reynolds 1980). Indeed the present hypothesis for land use in the prehistoric period and particularly the Iron Age is that those areas of marginal land where prehistoric field systems survive represent the exploitation of marginal land at that time. Their survival today is directly attributable to a change of basic economy from arable to pastoral in the third and fourth centuries AD which has been sustained throughout the millennia. It is only in the last decade that many of these areas are being brought back into arable cultivation with the subsequent loss of archaeological evidence. The implication is clearly one of enormous pressure on available land for arable purposes on the one hand, on the other an extremely successsful and stable agricultural economy.

The classical documentary evidence for this buoyant economy is quite unequivocal. For example, Caesar (*DBG* IV) refers to the export of grain and leather from Britain to the continent. In the same text he describes the densely occupied landscape (*creberrima aedificia*) and further hints at the reason why agriculture was so much more successful here than on the continent when he describes the climate as having less severe frosts (*remissioribus frigoribus*). The Atlantic climate of this country is, indeed, dramatically different to that of the continent and to it can be attributed in part the consistently more advanced agricultural economy throughout the prehistoric and historic periods. This is especially clear in the sixteenth and nineteenth centuries AD (Whyte 1979, Fussell 1959). In any agricultural economy the avoidance of extremes of climate bears directly upon its consistent development and success. It is, of course, the major variable in any consideration of crop husbandry.

The basic source evidence for the crops of prehistoric period comprise the carbonised seeds of cereals and other plants, seed impressions fired into pottery, and pollen grains. The pollen evidence, while of some value, has little relevance to large tracts of the countryside because of minimal preservation and (more importantly) unless actual pollen grain identification is definitely assured, confusion with other *gramineae* species may distort the overall picture.

It is against this background of the basic data that one of the major research programmes at the Butser Ancient Farm Project Trust (Reynolds 1978, 1979) is designed to assess potential yield factors of prehistoric cereal types under different treatments and cultivation techniques. As commented above, the major variable in any attempt to simulate the husbandry of the Iron Age is the climate. In this respect it is argued that the climate of the last three centuries of the first millennium BC and the first two centuries AD are directly comparable to the present day climate (Lamb, *pers. comm.*). Naturally this includes the minor variations and occasional extremes; for example, the drought of 1976 experienced within the modern weather pattern. Thus this variable can be seen as a constant to any empirical study of cereal production. The second variable is the soil itself. In this case the principal land area of the Ancient Farm is particularly suitable. It comprises a spur of middle chalk covered with a thin layer (c. 10 cm) of friable redzina, the typical soil covering the chalk lands of southern England. In addition the land area of the farm has not been cultivated for the past two hundred years and it is doubtful whether it has ever sustained a substantial arable crop of any kind. Certainly there are no archaeological traces of agriculture. There is, however, a prehistoric settlement of Bronze Age/Iron Age date located on the spur and abundant evidence in the immediate vicinity of prehistoric field systems and trackways suggesting that the settlement was, in fact, a farmstead. Thus the soil type, with a consistent pH value of 7.2, is accurate and has been uncontaminated by modern farming techniques. Since the Ancient Farm began in 1972 every care has been taken to avoid any subsequent contamination from modern agrochemicals. The secondary land area of the Ancient Farm comprises the typical hillwash soil of present dry valleys in the chalklands known to have been exploited in the Iron Age. It is composed of a mixture of clay with flints, degraded chalk and redzina with a neutral pH value. For the past hundred years it has been under rough grass cover and is thus unimproved in the modern sense. It was taken under control by the Project in 1976 and the last application of nitrogen to improve the grazing was dated to 1974. Consequently the effects were neutralised by the time of its cultivation.

The varieties of cereals cultivated in the Iron Age are well attested by the analysis of carbonised seed and seed impressions recovered from a large number of excavations of Iron Age sites (Halbaek 1952). As excavation techniques have improved, especially with the introduction of fine mesh wet sieving and flotation systems, so the bulk of carbonised seed evidence has increased proportionally. There is still, however, too little evidence of find location within sites, except in exceptional circumstances, like pits, to determine processes or functions or even crop dominance with any certainty. As discussed below it is preferable at this time simply to regard the evidence of carbonised seed only as statements of presence or absence. Any apparent significance suggested by an abundance of one plant species over another may be an effect of a subsequent process within the settlement and in response to a specific requirement and not reflect the husbandry practice at all. Similarly the very fact that the seed is carbonised at all suggests an unusual event or accident and, therefore, renders it as an atypical element within the artefact assemblage.

Nonetheless the dominant wheat cereals of the Iron Age and Romano-British periods were undoubtedly Emmer wheat (*Tr. dicoccum*) and Spelt wheat (*Tr. spelta*). Consequently, although other cereal types are the subject of cropping trials at the Ancient Farm, Emmer and Spelt wheats are the principal varieties. For this study seed was provided by the Plant Breeding Institute at Cambridge from Asia Minor where it is still cultivated in the remote regions. Careful analysis of the seed proved it to be morphologically the same as the prehistoric seed and, while it can never be proved, it is not unreasonable to believe that its protein characteristics are equally exactly similar. Certainly its characteristics as a stable as opposed to a hybrid plant are beyond question. The development of these cereals is discussed elsewhere (Reynolds 1977).

The cropping trials at the Ancient Farm are both varied and complex. The constant within the trials, the weather pattern and soil structure are subject to continuous recording and analysis with, in the case of the former, a standard meteorological station set on each site. In addition certain fields are monitored for their microclimate. The treatment under which the crops are grown are as far as possible evidenced by either the archaeology or documentary references. The preparation of the fields and rendering of a tilth are always carried out by ard (see below and Reynolds 1981) or by spade and mattock hoe cultivation. Seed is always hand sown in seed drills (Reynolds 1967, 1981) and at a constant rate of 63 kilos per hectare (56 lb per acre). Concomitant arable weed growth is subjected to handweeding and hoeing. In certain trials, because large numbers of arable weeds commonly evidenced in the carbonised seed record are virtually extinct in the British countryside, arable weeds are deliberately introduced to provide specific and accurate competition. In association with the cropping trials, an extensive and complex research programme is devoted to the propagation, germinability and fruiting characteristics and conservation of a large number of arable weed species. Primary focus has been the calcicole species with a secondary focus in the last two years upon the calcifuge species. Throughout the trials the competitive weed flora is monitored and analysed with special reference to potential function indicators (see below). Similarly the crop in the field is monitored as to stand height and tillering and, subsequent to harvest, is further analysed for spikelet length and weight, fruiting capacity and seed:chaff ratio.

The following tables present the results of a selection of the field trials carried out at the Ancient Farm since 1972. The yield data are obtained by sampling the crop in the standard manner of selecting by random metre square avoiding a metre wide perimeter band around the crop where the 'edge effect' can distort results. The figures provided represent gross weight and are presented in kilos per hectare, cwt per acre and seed:yield ratio. This last is the traditional historic system and allows direct comparison with yield figures from the records of the sixteenth century onwards.

Field II	
Location	Ancient Farm Research Site, Little Butser
Soil types	Friable redzina av. 10 cm thick directly overlying middle chalk
pH	7.2
Sowing rate	63 kg/ha (56 lb/acre) in Autumn
Sowing system	Seed drills 0.30 m apart
Cereal varieties	Emmer (*Tr. dicoccum*) and spelt (*Tr. spelta*)
Cultivation	Hand digging and mattock hoes

The objective of this trial is to assess the yield characteristics of the prehistoric type cereals on a typical unimproved soil of a type available in the Iron Age. The crops are grown without any periods of fallow and without any form of added nutrient of any kind. In effect the purpose is to assess the long held and cherished theory of land exhaustion and the need to rotate arable areas. The intention is to continue cropping this field until a non-viable yield is recorded. Non-viability is determined to be a 1:1 or worse seed:yield ratio. Table 1 gives the data yield for sector east of this particular field.

Table 1. Crop yields: Field 11, sector east, Butser Ancient Farm

Winter sown	*Triticum spelta* tonne/ha	*Triticum spelta* cwt/acre	*Triticum spelta* seed/yield	*Triticum dicoccum* tonne/ha	*Triticum dicoccum* cwt/acre	*Triticum dicoccum* seed/yield
1973	2.4	19.0	1:38	2.8	22.8	1:46
1974	2.3	18.3	1:37	3.7	29.8	1:59
1975	1.7	13.7	1:28	1.8	14.1	1:28
1976	0.8	7.2	1:14	0.7	6.4	1:13
1977	2.3	18.4	1:37	1.2	10.0	1:20
1978	2.5	20.1	1:40	2.6	20.8	1:41
1979	0.7	6.2	1:12	0.4	3.3	1:7
1980	1.4	11.4	1:23	1.6	13.0	1:26

Discussion. The relatively large fluctuations can be readily observed over the eight years within the table above but all these fluctuations are directly attributable to the weather patterns rather than any other single factor. For example, the exceptionally low figures for 1979 were caused by continuous heavy frosts on bare ground for six weeks when the ground surface temperature did not exceed 1°C. Similarly the drought of 1976 took an exceedingly heavy toll. What is most significant is the yield when expressed as seed:yield ratio has never fallen below 1:7. Bearing in mind that there are no nutrient additives to this field area at all and the cultivation practice is minimal in modern terms this figure is the more remarkable. Given the validity of the experiments there is an urgent need to determine why, with all the above restraints, this figure should be so much in excess of historical records where seed:yield ratios are significantly lower except in England and the Low Countries (average 1:10 increasing to 1:20). To further point the anomaly, table 2 gives the soil analysis results showing a minimal change in structure and trace element levels over a period of eight consecutive seasons.

Table 2. Soil analysis: Field 11, Butser Ancient Farm.

	% organic matter	Potassium p.p.m.	Potassium index	Phosphorus p.p.m.	Phosphorus index	Copper p.p.m.
1972	24.3	234	2	16.2	3	4.14
1979	20.3	140	2	21.0	4	3.84

(p.p.m. = parts per million)

The levels of organic matter are high and are regarded as indicative of a long period under grass without cultivation. The normal figures for modern arable land is two to five per cent of organic matter. All other levels are regarded as adequate but on the low side. In effect this system of cultivation is not reducing significantly the organic matter in the soil and the cereal varieties in direct contrast to modern hybrids do not require the same high levels of nitrogen input. The further point that must be stressed is the nature of the cereal itself. The spike is naturally significantly larger than that of the typical wheats of the historical period like Rivet wheat and indeed larger than the modern hybrids. There is no real indication, therefore, of soil exhaustion nor yet of deterioration of yield. The last season of 1980 clearly shows that the yield for both Emmer and Spelt has recovered from the disastrously low levels, in terms of the expectation engendered by previous years, of 1979. Similarly although Spelt has been claimed to be a better winter variety than Emmer (Applebaum 1954), with the exception of one season it is outperformed by the latter. Inevitably within the confines of a short paper it is quite impossible to present the total crop yield data achieved within the Ancient Farm research programmes. However, in order to provide a direct contrast to the above table, table 3 shows results drawn from Field VI where the treatments of a hill wash soil described above is subjected to an application of manure at a rate of twenty tonnes per hectare, approximately half the recommended weight distribution of the recent past, once every three years. The first application took place in the winter of 1977 prior to spring sowing of Emmer wheat, in association with other varieties, in 1978.

Table 3. Crop yield: Field VI, Butser Ancient Farm Demonstration Area.

Year	Cereal type Spring sown	t/ha	cwt/acre	seed/yield	Treatment
1978	Emmer	4.65	37.2	1:74	manured + 1
1978	Maris Huntsman	2.91	23.3	1:46	
1980	Emmer	3.19	25.5	1:51	manured + 3
1980	Sicco	1.62	13.0	1:26	

That manuring took place in the Iron Age has been ably demonstrated by Bowen (1961). In this particular field where manuring is applied in simulation of an availability of dung adequate to the area once every three years it can be seen that the reduction in yield is quite significant but that in gross terms the returns are significantly better than those of Field II above. All the results quoted above are statements of the mean and standard deviations are not supplied nor the gross maxima and minima. In simple terms it allows the figures to bear comparison with results from other periods of history provided similarity of conditions *inter alia* is observed. If nothing else these figures support the contention that given the cereal species of the Iron Age the potential for surplus production existed to an extent well capable of sustaining the export industry reported by Strabo.

The figure in the above table referring to modern hybrid varieties point to the problems of comparison. Maris Huntsman in 1978 and Sicco in 1980 were selected as the best standard modern wheats available. Maris Huntsman was particularly disappointing bearing in mind its distinguished role in the development of hybrid varieties and Sicco wheat is generally regarded as one of the best of the present generation in terms of both yield and protein levels. The reasons why these cereals are outperformed seem to lie in two particulars; first, they need a high nitrogen input and, second, their response to weed infestation/competition is poor. By the same token both the prehistoric cereal types require a much reduced nitrogen input and once established are well able to compete most successfully with abundant arable weed infestation. If they are grown within an agrochemical system, lodging becomes an immediate problem although the yield can be commensurate with the best modern varieties.

Comparative cropping of modern cereals in Field II, the autumn sown non-nutrified field, on the main farm site was abandoned by 1975 through purely negative returns. Not only did the cereal variety, again Maris Huntsman, fare badly in growth patterns and maturation, each year all the seed was stripped by bird attack prior to harvest. The awns and the cohesive glumes of Emmer and Spelt serve as extremely effective deterrents to such attack. Indeed it is relatively difficult, given the basic requirements of modern hybrids, to provide comparative data which is meaningful to modern agriculturalists. While the data processing establishing the end figures as quoted are exactly those adopted by the Rothamsted Experimental Station in Harpenden, the real problem is the husbandry techniques. It is, in a sense, quite unfair to expect the modern varieties to be at all viable in such an inimical system. The results simply all point to the performance of the prehistoric types. Of most value, perhaps, is to measure performance against treatment and climate and to value the results accordingly.

In due course the full results of the trials carried out at the Ancient Farm will become available. Reported above are but two sets of data, the first referring to a portion of one field, the second to two seasons results from one further field subjected to a totally different treatment. While it must be appreciated that these are the results from only nine years and four years respectively and that at least twenty years of data are required for clear cut validation, the trends and the problems posed by those trends are undeniable. Should the results be maintained even at the lower and less likely levels, the implications are such that subsistence is an ill-chosen adjective with which to describe the potential agricultural achievements of the Iron Age.

In concluding this second hypothesis devoted to crop yields it is worth recording that one particular species of arable weed has emerged as a potential indicator of agricultural practice. The species, Cleavers (*Galium aparine*) has successfully and quite naturally pervaded the field (II) sown in the autumn while the spring sown field (IV, separated by only a metre-wide strip of turf, is completely innocent of this plant. Table 4 gives the results of the last two seasons survey of this particular species showing the figures from three randomly selected square metres per sector in both fields.

Table 4. Arable weed flora survey: *Galium aparine* (cleavers).

			Sector East	Sector Central	Sector West
1979	Field II	Autumn sown	136	179	85
	Field IV	Spring sown	0	0	0
1980	Field II	Autumn sown	84	109	63
	Field IV	Spring sown	0	0	0

The germination characteristics of this plant show a major peak at the end of March/beginning of April with a minor peak in late October. Normally the spring sown field is cultivated at this time prior to planting early in April and consequently should any plants be about to grow they are eradicated by the cultivation. By contrast the autumn sown field is planted in early October and thus the plant can experience and benefit from both peaks of germination allowing considerable numbers to escape the hoe and hand weeding which is carried out in late April and May. Its total absence from the spring sown field (further surveys substantiated the close search of the randomly selected square metres) is the most significant factor. Its presence in the carbonised seed record (Haelbeck 1952) may well, therefore, be considered as an indicator of autumn or winter planting of cereal crops.

HARVESTING: THE IMPLICATIONS OF IMPURITIES

The third hypothesis is, in fact, a direct result of the cropping trials in that the problem of harvesting was determined to simulate Iron Age practice. The result has become a challenge to the assumed traditional analysis of carbonised seed suggesting that such seed does not necessarily represent the true harvest and consequently, with normal allowance for exceptions, is unlikely to bear evidence of post-harvesting treatments. Precise information of harvesting techniques of the Iron Age, in contrast to the Roman systems (White 1970), is difficult to isolate. We do have the comments by Strabo and Diodoros Siculus that the Celtic practice was to reap the ears or spikes of the crops. Support of these statements can be found in the ubiquitous artists impressions of prehistoric harvesting where the so-called sickle is to be seen neatly cutting off cereal heads. Practice, however, has little in common with imaginative representation. From the observation of some eleven seasons of growing the prehistoric type cereals of Emmer and Spelt wheats, belief in the determination of the typical small 'sickle' has radically waned to the point of offering a specific alternative function: this being the splitting of hazel gads to make into thatching spars, for which the tool is admirably suited and similar in shape and weight to the traditional spar hook. There are further functions like bark stripping, leaf cutting, branch trimming which similarly can be effected with an edged tool of this design. This is not to say that they cannot be used for cutting wheat ears but rather that they are grossly inefficient and far too slow. The problem lies in the nature of the crop itself. Accepting the classical sources as being a reasonable description of the actual harvesting technique, both at Avoncroft Museum and at the Ancient Farm all the crops have been harvested in this way. Each year replica sickles are provided for the purpose, each year they are unanimously rejected by the reapers. The answer is simply that it is much easier to reap the ears by hand picking.

It was realised from the very first season that the prehistoric cereals have two characteristics which are not ordinarily to be found in modern hybrid wheats. The first major difference lies in the disparity of stand heights achieved by the tillers of the same plant. In the case of both Emmer and Spelt wheats this disparity can be as much as a metre from the shortest to the tallest spike, while in a modern hybrid it rarely exceeds 0.40 m. The importance of this characteristic will be developed below. The second characteristic is the 'necking' of the prehistoric types. As the ears ripen so they droop gracefully downwards from the main stalk in the fashion of modern barley. The effect of this not only inhibits water retention within the spike and consequent lodging potential, this being truer of Emmer than Spelt where lodging can be a problem, but also exposes the stalk top to the elements of wind and sun. Once ripe this section of the stalk becomes extremely brittle and is very easy indeed to break off. If allowed to reach maturity the natural result is for the spike to break away from the stalk and seed itself. The skill of farming is, of course, to pre-empt this point by as short a time as possible (plate 4).

Observations of this disparity of stand height have led to the direct recording of each successive crop. Annually a thousand measurements of each crop variety and treatment are made across random transects with sample points 0.30 m apart. The results of just one year are provided to substantiate the present argument. These can be seen represented in histogram form in figure 2. To provide a direct comparison the results from a modern cereal crop grown under exactly the same conditions are included. The selection of examples is further deliberately pointed in that they are drawn from a field which has been continuously cropped for the past eight years without any added nutrient whatsoever. The farm is, of course, free from all modern herbicides, pesticides and fertilizers.

Plate 4. Emmer wheat at harvest.

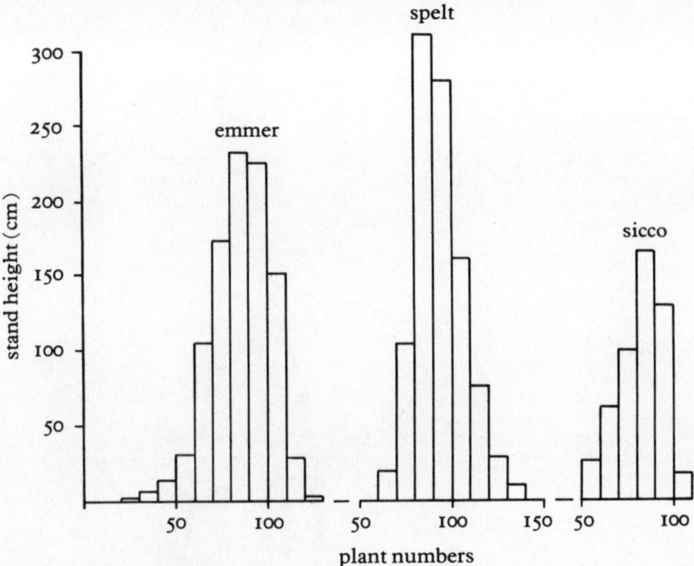

Figure 2. Relative stand heights of Emmer wheat, Spelt wheat and Sicco (modern hybrid) wheat.

The prime archaeological data normally comprise an admixture of cereal and arable weed seeds. Throughout the cropping programme the competitive weed flora has been most carefully monitored. In eleven seasons all the harvests have been effectively pure with but two contaminants. By way of explanation the harvest is taken to be the spikes that can be collected from the crop. The contaminants, in turn, are arable weeds which can be found within the gathered spikes. The harvesting process consistently follows the classical description. However, the crop itself is regularly infested with an abundant weed flora and during the months of June and July particularly is a riot of colour. The primary enemy of farmers of all periods prior to the introduction of herbicides is Charlock (*Sinapis arvensis*; plate 5). It is vitally necessary during the early part of the season to hoe the crop carefully in order to keep at bay this most pernicious of competitors. In this century it was not uncommon to hear of crops being ploughed back into the soil because of Charlock infestation. Farming by definition is the provision of a preferred habitat for a specific plant. However, once the plant is established and can outgrow its competitors, there is no advantage in further hoeing and indeed there can be direct disadvantages in that too much soil disturbance in the secondary stages of crop development can damage the spreading roots of the crop itself. In addition the weed cover actually aids moisture retention in the soil, a matter of some importance with an average depth of 0.10 m. Consequently at harvest time there is an abundance of other plants

Plate 5. Charlock (*Sinapsis arvensis*) is the dominant weed in the spring.

amongst the cereal crops. Careful note has been made of those competitors which reach the reaping height. That is, those plants which head out amongst the majority of spikes and which are likely to be collected by accident during the harvesting process. Such plants are effectively few in number and virtually all of them are sufficiently different in nature and form for avoidance to be a matter of course. The most typical on calcareous soils are the Thistle family (*Cirsia*), Fat Hen (*Chenopodium album*), Poppies (*Papaveraceae*), Charlock (*Sinapis arvensis*) and Hedge Mustard (*Sisymbrium officinale*). On acid soils as well as most of the above Red Shank (*Polygonium persicaria*) and Pale Persicaria (*Polygonum lapathifolium*) are the most common. The two contaminants referred to above are Black Bindweed (*Polygonum convolvulus*) and Sowthistle (*Sonchus arvensis*). The former simply entwines itself up the straw stalks and wraps itself inextricably about the spike. The reaper recognises its presence but can do little about it. In fact, it can be used as a food supply, the seeds being capable of reduction by milling into flour. It hardly detracts from the crop in so far as it is not a poisonous species. The latter is relatively uncommon as a contaminant and only occurs as such since its seed is wind dispersed and occasionally a seed is trapped amongst the awns of the prehistoric type cereals. It too is unlikely to cause any problems in subsequent utilisation of the harvest. It is rare amongst the carbonised seed record as is only to be expected from its nature and it has recently been identified from an Iron Age site along the course of the M3 motorway (P. J. Fasham, pers. comm.). Even though its presence within the harvested spikes is occasional this is not to suggest it is rare amongst the crop. In fact, because of its normal height at fruiting being regularly in excess of one metre it appears as a dominant weed. The presence of but one seed in the carbonised record would suggest that it was similarly a dominant weed in prehistoric crops.

The purity of the harvest is the direct result of the reaping system. Since the abundant weed flora occupies the bases of the crop and while it does not necessarily detract from its overall performance, it does mask from the view of the reapers those spikes which are in the lowest stand height range. It would be counter-productive to hunt about amongst the base of the crop to recover what amounts to less than one per cent of the total yield. Ironically, there is regularly no difference in the overall seed size of these 'lost' spikes to those of the reaped harvest. Consequently they cannot be identified as being distinct in any specific analysis programme. Similarly the observation needs to be made that carbonisation itself does not affect seeds uniformly and thus predictive assessments of original seed size are impossible.

The argument, therefore, is now confused in that to all intents and purposes the norm would have been a pure harvest and yet the carbonised seed samples are normally anything but pure. Returning to the field situation, once the spikes have been harvested there remains still a second and extremely valuable product to be collected, namely the straw. Because of its relatively low gloss factor the straw from the prehistoric cereals is quite palatable for livestock. Similarly it has great value as thatching material, a fact substantiated by the stand heights alone and it would have been required as bedding material for livestock and not improbably for humans. There is always the alternative that then as now the straw could have been burned *in situ* but this does not deny the need for straw within the agricultural economy and it is not unreasonable to assume that it was cut, put into sheaves and carted back into the settlement. In any event the field area would have had to be cleared prior to its recultivation. The straw inevitably contained the mass of weed flora within its bulk. In this way, apart from the harvested cereal the arable weeds could have found their way into the settlement. In order to quantify this exercise, each year several of the straw sheaves from the farm are analysed for the seeds they contain after a winter's storage within a stack. The results from just one

Plate 6. Detail of a typical sheaf of straw showing the level of weed competition (see table 5).

example are given in table 5 (see plate 6). Even this analysis does not give a true reflection of the field state in that the seed release mechanisms of the different species of arable weeds are widely divergent. For example, the thistle population since its seeds are wind dispersed is rarely represented. Similarly the seeds of Charlock (*Sinapis arvensis*), are exploded from a pod at the slightest touch of the trigger element. In fact, just prior to harvest one can actually hear the pods exploding as the wind-blown stalks of wheat brush against the seed pods. Some simple measurements carried out at the Farm have shown that Charlock can deliver its seed up to three metres from the parent plant. Both Thistles and particularly Charlock are dominant weeds of the research crops, a fact which analysis would fail to substantiate. As has been suggested above in reference to Sowthistle (*Sonchus arvensis*) attention needs to be focused upon the characteristics of individual plant species and any analysis needs to take account of these characteristics. An aggressive weed in the field need not necessarily appear in quantity in carbonised material.

Table 5. Sheaf analysis : Field II, Harvest 1979. Remanent seeds.

Harvest 1979. Sheaf II, *Tr. dicoccum*. Gross weight 1.9 kg

Number of straws	980	Arable weeds :	*Sinapsis arvensis*	96
Complete spikes	0		*Papaver rhoeas*	192
Rachis ends	292		*Odontites verna*	380
Seed yield	66		*Galium aparine*	22
			Poa pratensis	476
			Lolium perenne	504
			Other	200

However, there is yet the problem of carbonisation, of which some account should be taken. For carbonisation to occur a fire with a primarily anaerobic atmosphere is required. Undoubtedly some fires are the product of accident, but the following hypothesis seeks to offer a positive alternative to accident. That houses were thatched in the Iron Age is attested by the classical writers and one presumes that straw among other materials was used for this purpose. While it is readily recognised that river reed (*Phragmites*), heather (*Calluna vulgaris*) and even bracken (*Pteridium aquilinum*) could well have been used, the last being a potential explanation of bracken spores identified on calcareous sites, straw undoubtedly was a readily available material product of the agricultural process. The preparation of straw for thatching requires one most critical operation, it must be cleaned of all other materials including its own leaves, any pithy plant stems, all seeds and especially cereal seeds. The reasons are straightforward. Pithy material rots and by so doing would decrease the bulk and cause the ties to loosen. Any seed material attracts the attention of rodents who in turn may well eat the bundle ties in order to reach the food supplies. Traditionally straw cleaning and the preparation of bundles of yealms which form the thatch require the wetting down of the straw to facilitate the drawing of the straw stalks. The possible implications of the process for the disposition of post-holes is discussed elsewhere (Reynolds 1979). The end product of this cleaning process is a pile of damp waste material comprising arable weeds, stems and seeds and waste cereal heads. It is but a small step to hypothesise the disposal of this damp rubbish with a slow-burning bonfire. Such a bonfire inevitably has within it an anaerobic atmosphere which will allow some carbonisation to take place.

The two factors which form the objective of this aspect of cereal investigation are, in effect, the result of two distinct approaches, each relying upon the documentary and archaeological evidence available to us. The first is the pure harvest, the direct result of actually growing prehistoric type cereals in Ancient-sized fields and processing them accordingly. The second, the commonly found admixture of carbonised seeds is questioned as being non-representative of a harvest and an alternative hypothesis is raised. If the first, the pure harvest, is a valid hypothesis then the second is most unlikely to be representative of that harvest. Throughout it must be emphasised that one is dealing with possibilities and at best probabilities and it would be foolish to deny other hypotheses provided that they can be similarly validated. In effect both the above hypotheses are offshoots of the main research purpose, that being to establish probable parameters of yield for the prehistoric cereal types given different soil types, treatments and bio-climatic zones.

In conclusion the second and third hypotheses, the heavy yield potentially experienced in the Iron Age and the argued purity of harvest are to an extent substantiated by a machine. Both classical references by Pliny and relief sculptures at Buzenol in Luxembourg and Arlon in France and Virton in Belgium describe a reaping machine called a *vallus*. That it merits comment from Pliny as a peculiarity of the area and specifically non-Roman is of great importance. It has, naturally enough, received attention from a number of researchers, notably Martens (1958), Fouss (1958), Renard (1959) and de Moule and Coudart (pers. comm.). Its manufacture, apart from the iron bands around the spoked wheels, would seem to be entirely of wood. Its design and operation clearly shown in the illustrations is specifically for the collection of the spikes of the cereals. Trials with a reconstruction (Fouss – personal letter to Mme J-B. Delamarre dated 17 January 1961) describe it to be extremely efficient leaving very few spikes on the ground. To date no trials have been carried out at all with the prehistoric type cereals, which would by nature be most suitable because of the brittle characteristic. (A reconstruction and trial is scheduled for 1981 at the Butser Ancient Farm.) In the present context the most important issue is not so much the efficiency of the machine but rather that its invention actually occurred. Developments in agriculture are traditionally in response to a specific need. A reaping machine, therefore, in a labour-intensive economy would imply surplus production potentially beyond the capabilities of the labour market.

In this paper three hypotheses have been explored, each one of which has resulted from the empirical testing of theories raised upon the archaeological data. Throughout, the methodology has consistently sought to invalidate the hypothesis in the normal tradition of scientific enquiry. The broad results have on the one hand provided negative responses to certain accepted views, on the other have contributed substantiated hypotheses which are essentially positive. It is necessary, however, to draw attention to a major *caveat*. The results quoted here which are statistically valid and achieved under the most rigorous conditions, are relevant to the bio-climatic and geological zone within which they were gained. Specifically they relate to the chalk downs and valleys of Southern England. The sites are, in fact, not the best available in those areas and given more ideal locations the results could well be improved. Given the suitability of the present climate for such simulation studies both in the United Kingdom and on the continent, it is important and urgent that similar research programmes should be mounted in different bio-climatic and geological zones. In addition such research programmes should be designed as parallel and complementary to those described above. In the view of the writer, it is only by this particular research approach that archaeological data can be amplified towards a fuller comprehension of the complex social and commercial structure of the Iron Age period. Not only does it seek to test the basic theories upon which broad generalisations should only be raised, it focuses attention upon the anomalies of the data and indicates those areas in most need of examination. It is signal to conclude with the observation that settlement is the function of farming and not the reverse and that the greatest concentration to date has been indisputably upon settlement. Economy is directly concerned with production.

REFERENCES

Aberg, F. A. & H. C. Bowen (1960) Ploughing experiments with a reconstructed Donneruplund ard. *Antiquity 34,* 144-7.

Anati, E. (1961) *Camonica Valley* (reprint 1965). London: Jonathan Cape.

Applebaum, S. (1954) The agriculture of the British Early Iron Age as exemplified at Figheldean Down, Wiltshire. *Proc. Prehist. Soc. 20,* 103-14.

Ashbee, P., *et al.* (1979) Excavation of the long barrows near Avebury, Wiltshire. *Proc. Prehist. Soc. 45,* 250-300.

Bowen, H. C. (1961) *Ancient Fields.* London: British Assoc. Adv. Science.

Caesar. *De Bello Gallico* IV.

Diodorus Siculus. *History* 5, 21.5.

Evans, J. G. (1972) *Landsnails in Archaeology.* London: Seminar Press.

Everton, A. & P. J. Fowler (1978) Avon – A method of analysis, in *Early Land Allotment* (eds H. C. Bowen & P. J. Fowler), BAR 48, 179-84.

Fenton, A. (1968) Plough and spade in Dumfries & Galloway. *Trans. Dumfriesshire & Galloway Nat. Hist. & Antiq. Soc.* XLV, 147-83.

Fouss, E. P. (1958) Le *vallus* ou la moissoneuse des Trévires. *Le Pays Gaumais,* 124-36.

Fowler, P. J. & J. G. Evans (1967) Plough marks, lynchets & early fields. *Antiquity 41,* 289-301.

Fussell, G. E. (1959) The Low Countries influence on English farming. *Eng. Hist. Rev. 74.*

Gillam, J. P., R. M. Harrison & T. G. Newman (1973) Interim report on excavation at the Roman Fort of Rudchester 1972. *Archaeol. Aeliana* 5th ser., 81-5.

Glob, P. V. (1951) Ard og Plov. *Archus Universitetsforlaget, Jysk Arkaeologisk, Selskabs Skrifter,* Bynd 1.

Hansen, H. O. (1969) *Reports from Experiment in Lejre 1968: 1*. Lejre : Historic-archaeological Centre.

Hartridge, R. (1978) Excavations at the Prehistoric and Romano-British site on Slonk Hill, Shoreham, Sussex. *Sussex Archaeol. Coll. 116*, 69-141.

Helbaek, H. (1952) Early crops in Southern England. *Proc. Prehist. Soc. 18*, pt. 2, 194-233.

Leser, P. (1931) Entstehung und Verbreitung des Pfluges. *Anthropos, B.* III, 3. Munster.

Mertens, J. (1958) Römische Skulpturen von Buzenol, Province Luxemburg. *Germania* XXXVI, 386-92.

Piggott, C. M. (1952-53) Milton Loch Crannog I : a native house of the second century AD in Kirkcudbrightshire. *P.S.A.S.* LXXVII, 134-51.

Pliny. *Natural History* 18.306.

Rees, S. (1979) Agricultural implements in Prehistoric and Roman Britain. Part I. BAR *69(1)*.

Renard, M. (1959) *Techniques et Agriculture en pays trevire et remois*. Paris.

Reynolds, P. J. (1967) Experiment in Iron Age agriculture. *Trans. Bristol & Gloucestershire Archaeol. Soc. 86*, 60-73.

—— (1977) Slash & burn experiment. *Archaeol. J. 134*, 307-18.

—— (1978) *Archaeology by Experiment: A Research Tool for Tomorrow in New Approaches to our Past: An Archaeological Forum*, 39-55. Southampton Univ.

—— (1978) Excavations at the Prehistoric and Romano-British site on Slonk Hill, Shoreham, Sussex. *Sussex Archaeol. Coll. 116*, 99.

—— (1979) *Iron Age Farm: The Butser Experiment*. London : British Museum Publications.

—— (forthcoming 1981) The working agroscape of the Iron Age. Landscape History. *J. of the Soc. for Landscape Studies*, II.

Reynolds, P. J. & J. K. Langley (1980) Romano-British corn drying oven : an experiment. *Archaeol. J. 136*, 27-42.

Steensberg, A. (1973) *Tools & Tillage*, Vol. II.2. Copenhagen : National Museum of Denmark.

Strabo. *Geography* 4,5.5.

White, K. D. (1970) *Roman Farming*. London : Thames & Hudson.

Whyte, P. (1979) *Agriculture and Society in Seventeenth Century Scotland*. Edinburgh : John Donald Publ. Ltd.

Reconstructing Crop Husbandry Practices from Charred Remains of Crops

GORDON HILLMAN

It is a rare habitation site that fails to yield charred remains of food plants once one of the systems of flotation recovery is applied. Furthermore, when the remains include crops, they can provide information not only on the types grown but also on the methods and equipment used to grow them and process their products. The purpose of this paper is to explore the extent to which it is possible to deduce details of farming practice from the composition of samples of crop remains.

Although charred remains are our primary concern, waterlogged 'sub-fossil' remains of crops can yield essentially similar information. These 'sub-fossils' are preserved by anaerobic conditions resulting from uninterrupted waterlogging since the date of deposition. It is however only on rather exceptional sites, such as the 'sunken village' of Feddersen Wierde in Germany, that we find preservation by waterlogging of crop remains on a really large scale in primary habitation deposits (Körber-Grohne 1967). Given the choice, most people quite sensibly founded their domestic buildings where they were unlikely to become permanently waterlogged right up to the deposition surfaces. With the exception of waterlogged gut contents, therefore, what follows will concentrate on the use of crop remains preserved primarily by charring.

The types of crop grown: Different classes of crop require different methods of both husbandry in the field and processing back at the settlement. Any discussion of husbandry practices must therefore be preceded by an outline of which crops were grown, and figure 1 correspondingly attempts a tentative summary of the major temporal changes in Britain's crops during the last five millennia. However, because of the yawning gaps in crop chronologies for any one area, our present picture of temporal changes in British crop assemblages during the past five millennia can be only the crudest generalisation: niches are bound to have existed in which farmers continued cultivating outmoded crops – whether out of agricultural or culinary conservatism. Alternatively, the first wave of

		NEOLITHIC	BRONZE AGE	IRON AGE	ROMAN	DARK AGES	MEDIEVAL
Einkorn wheat	*Triticum monococcum*						
Emmer wheat	*T. dicoccum*						
Spelt wheat	*T. spelta*						
Bread wheat	*T. aestivum* (inc. '*T. compactum*')						
Rye	*Secale cereale*						
6-rowed, hulled barley*	*Hordeum sativum* var. *polystichum*						
6-rowed, naked barley	*H. sativum* var. *polystichum-nudum*						
Cultivated oats	*Avena sativa* + *A. strigosa* (inc. *A. brevis*, etc.)						
Horse ('Celtic') bean	*Vicia faba* agg.						
Field pea	*Pisum sativum*						

* (mostly lax-eared, i.e. '4-rowed')

Figure 1. Crude summary of temporal changes in cultivation of some of Britain's major field crops. For more precise details see the following review articles: *Neolithic to Medieval* Jessen & Helbaek (1949), Hubbard (1980); *Neolithic to Roman* Helbaek (1952); *Neolithic only* Hillman (1981); *Iron Age & Saxon* Murphy (1977); *Iron Age to Saxon* Green (in press), M.K. Jones (in press); *Anglo-Saxon* Monk (1977); *Medieval* Green (1980).
Note of caution: This summary can be no more than provisional as there are more plant remains from British sites currently under study or about to be published than the total of those published to date.

newer crops may have yielded poorly under local climatic or edaphic conditions. It would therefore be wrong to assume that the farmers at any one site in Britain will necessarily have followed the general trend observable in the country as a whole.

I
INTERPRETATION IN TERMS OF FARMING PRACTICE: THE PRINCIPLES

1. INTERPRETATION VIA INTERNAL ANALYSIS AND CONTEXT

Once a sufficiently large number of samples of crop remains from British sites has been analysed, then a pattern of variation in composition can be expected to emerge. Even on its own, such a pattern could immediately provide the basis for suggesting functional relationships for at least a few components. For example, if, in uncontaminated samples of charred remains, a particular type of seed is consistently and almost exclusively associated with remains of a particular crop, and if this pattern is repeated on a number of sites, then it can reasonably be suggested that it was a weed of the crop concerned. It is on this basis, for example, that Heath Grass *Sieglingia decumbens* is thought to have been an important weed of cereal crops at certain Welsh sites, even though today it is rarely (if ever) found as an arable weed (Hillman, forthcoming, i).

Furthermore, *if* the pattern of variation in composition is found to correspond with the distribution of certain classes of site context, and *if* it is possible to assign to each context-type specific activities concerned with crop processing, then, in principle, some progress may be made towards limiting the possible range of agricultural activities likely to have generated crop products of that type. It is the possibilities offered by this sort of approach that were explored and described by Dennell (1972), though the statistical significance of some of the correlations between context and composition cited by Dennell have since been disputed (with some justification) by Hubbard (1976a).

In my experience, it is more common for the composition of samples of plant remains (as interpreted by reference to 'ethnographic models' discussed below) to provide the basis for assigning past functions to the features, structures, or even whole sites from which the samples were recovered than it is for the excavator's identification of context-type to provide the basis for interpreting the composition of samples of plant remains. This observation cannot be stressed too strongly.

An equally practical problem touched on by Dennell is that this approach depends heavily on the remains deposited in any one class of context representing a very narrow range of crop products or by-products. In reality, however, some degree of mixing of different crop products (and by-products) is very widespread and is discussed in detail by Hubbard (1976a, 1976b). But while mixing severely limits interpretation, it would seem that it is not as universal as had at first been expected, as discussed below.

Despite the above limitations, the analysis of context-related variation in sample composition may allow the erection of hypotheses relating to farming practice that, in some cases, may be tested by simple experiment. A good example of this combination is again seen in Dennell's experiments with the laboratory sieving of grain (Dennell 1972), and this experimental approach to a crop-processing practice could doubtless be developed further in cooperation with experimental establishments such as Butser Iron Age Farm (see Reynolds in this volume).

In conclusion, the potential of interpretation based on internal analysis (coupled with context-studies and experiment) can only be judged by the agricultural feasibility of the practices suggested on this basis, for example in Dennell (1974). It is unfortunate, therefore, that all too many of the effects on composition of crop products suggested for specific operations are patently impossible, and precisely the opposite of those observable in practice in, for example, communities where the same primitive crops are grown using techniques similar to those cited. However, this should not dissuade archaeo-botanists from continuing to try to develop and use these techniques, nor, indeed, should it detract from the arguments (e.g. in Dennell 1972) for the need to study context-related variation in composition. But it certainly underlines the need for more detailed studies of traditional agricultural practices still surviving today, before these practices finally disappear altogether; they represent our last chance to observe in action systems likely to have been agriculturally feasible in the past.

2. INTERPRETATION VIA 'ETHNOGRAPHIC MODELS'

In the execution of any one agricultural operation, such as freeing the grain of glume wheats from the enveloping husks, there are relatively few efficient methods available to non-mechanised farmers, whether in terms of the overall sequence of operations that can be applied, or in terms of the execution of any one operation. Certainly in historical times, the types of husbandry and techniques applied to the cultivation and processing of crops such as bread wheat, barley or field peas seem to have shown relatively little variation wherever they were grown (Maurizio 1927, Leser 1931).

On this basis, the use of 'ethnographic models' to interpret assemblages of crop remains, in terms of farming practice, would seem to be feasible in principle. If, however, the crop remains are to be interpreted in terms of practices that make agricultural sense for the particular crop concerned, then the model must obviously be based from the outset on the observed and measured effects of each agricultural operation on the composition of every crop product and by-product. The only alternative is to examine similar sets of relationships under experimental conditions, based in turn upon modern or historical 'ethnographic' parallels, at establishments such as Butser Iron Age Farm (see Reynolds, in this volume).

For each prehistoric crop type, therefore, our interpretive models should, if possible, be based on (a) observations of crop husbandry and processing in areas where entirely traditional methods are still used to produce traditional forms of food; (b) detailed records of the sequence in which these operations are performed and the tool types used; (c) large-scale sampling of the crop products and by-products taken at each step of every processing sequence, each sample to be accompanied by detailed notes on (i) precisely how the crop had been treated – both in the field and after harvesting, and (ii) the classes of village context where each processing stage occurred; (d) detailed analysis of the composition of these samples in terms of (i) the frequency of occurrence of each species of weed seed, (ii) the frequencies of each type of chaff component, (iii) the frequency distributions of grain/seed sizes of both the crop and major weeds, and (iv) the ratios between each of these variables; (e) analysis of these data to measure the correlation between, on the one hand, the types of husbandry and processing methods used and, on the other hand, the composition of the crop products and by-products thereby generated. Any correlation demonstrated to be significant at an acceptable level of confidence can then be built into the interpretive model.

Thus if, in present-day cultivation of prehistoric crop types, a particular feature of the composition of crop products (or by-products) can be demonstrated to result exclusively from the use of a defined operation or sequence of operations then, given a closely similar archaeological sample of plant remains, it can be suggested that these remains were the product of essentially similar operations or sequences of operations that may have been used in the prehistoric context. While precisely this strategy has been applied in the formulation of a model initially intended for interpreting assemblages of plant remains from Near-Eastern sites (see Hillman 1973), no such model appears to have been developed specifically for north-west Europe.

SETTLEMENT CONTEXT IN 'ETHNOGRAPHIC MODELS'

In the formulation of an interpretive 'ethnographic' model as described above, samples of crop products are taken from contexts which are clearly defined in terms of all their associated functions. But such an approach would fail to take into account (a) differential deposition patterns of the various constituents of crop products across present-day settlement surfaces, and (b) differential spatial patterns of preservation of these same materials whether by charring or by waterlogging.

For this extension of an interpretive model it is therefore necessary (a) to recover charred (i.e. potentially persistent) plant remains by large scale flotation from every context in these same present-day settlements in which primitive crops are still grown by traditional methods, (b) to define these contexts both in terms of the full range of their associated functions and in terms of any structural features that would possibly allow them to be identified by excavation, (c) to analyse the composition of the sample, and (d) to measure the correlation between variations in sample and context type as before.

A strategy of this sort formed part of the project at the village of Asvan in Eastern Turkey (see Hillman 1972, 1973). Here the magnitude of the task precluded its completion beyond the sampling of contexts such as ovens, hearths and granaries where flotation was inappropriate or unnecessary. Again, no such study exists for a British or European settlement and, it is unlikely that any suitable, functioning settlements now survive anywhere in northern Europe.

The three components of our idealised 'ethnographic' model can now be represented diagrammatically (figures 2 and 3). As indicated, figure 2 represents two typical archaeological situations and figure 3 represents the relationships that can be observed in the present-day settlements used for the model. While in the *prehistoric* settlement (figure 2) relationships A and B (and sometimes C) are unknown, in the *present-day* settlement, where the same primitive crop types are grown (figure 3), all three relationships can be observed and defined. The results from a sufficiently large number of observations of these relationships in present-day settlements can therefore form the basis of a model to suggest the nature of the relationships (A and B) in the *prehistoric* settlement.

WHERE TO LOOK FOR 'ETHNOGRAPHIC' MODELS

Ideally, our interpretive models must be based on practices observed in areas not too distant from the sites to which the models are to be applied: not only do crop yields and weed floras vary with climatic zone, but so do

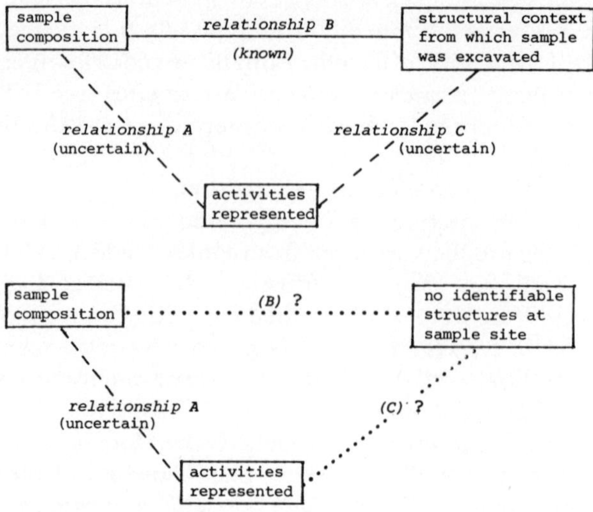

Figure 2. Two sets of relationships encountered on archaeological sites (from Hillman 1973)

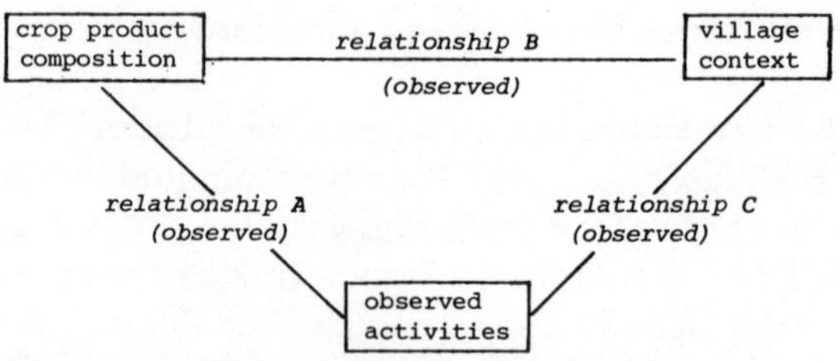

Figure 3. The same relationships on present-day settlements: all are observable and measurable.

agricultural techniques such as threshing.

It is unfortunate, therefore, that no suitable models have been developed in northern Europe and that it is now, alas, too late to find settlements in this area that grow the required prehistoric crop types, or cultivate and process them using traditional methods. Of the crops cultivated in prehistoric Britain (see figure 1), only six-rowed hulled barley is still cultivated and, in the few places where it is still grown for human (rather than animal) consumption, it would appear to be entirely factory-processed. However, traditional methods were still being used at the turn of this century, and although we have inherited no samples of crop products for studying sample composition, a wealth of invaluable information on the tools and methods used in the cultivation and processing of this and other traditional – though probably not strictly prehistoric – crops is available (see Fenton 1978). Books such as Markham (1631) also provide much of the essential agricultural background.

In remote pockets of central and southern Europe, however, the occasional field of prehistoric crop types, such as emmer or even naked barley, is still grown – as they were until recently in parts of Czechoslovakia (see Kühn 1970). However, they now provide little more than animal fodder, and even when, as with spelt and its *Grünkernmehl* in Bavaria, they occasionally find use as human food, it would appear that traditional methods and equipment are no longer used. As in the case of Orkney and Shetland, however, we are fortunate in having detailed accounts of many traditional Central European methods and equipment preserved in works such as Maurizio's *History of Plant Nutrition* (1927) just as we have for Southern Europe – though in less detail – in the works of Classical authors such as Columella, Pliny, and Galen. (For extensive bibliographies and distillations of much of the agricultural detail see White 1970, 1971; and for the final stages of Roman grain processing see Moritz 1957.) However, for interpretive models based on extant practices where crop products can actually be sampled, we are forced to look further afield to south-east Europe and the Near East, the original home of not only our prehistoric cereals, but doubtless many of the associated husbandry and processing techniques that continued to be applied to these crops as their cultivation spread across Europe and into Britain.

A NEAR-EASTERN MODEL

In remote parts of the Near East, it is still possible to find villages where emmer and six-rowed barley are grown for human consumption using methods that, in terms of the types of equipment used, need not have changed for three millennia or more. Indeed, the modern use of flint blades in threshing sledges and even sickles doubtless has even earlier origins. Similarly archaic techniques are – or were recently – also applied to the cultivation and processing of other crops such as einkorn wheat, Vavilov spelt wheat, bread and durum wheats, rye, oats, 'Celtic' bean, field peas, common and bitter vetches, flax and poppy, as well as 'archaic' forms of many other crops. (For crop types, see Zhukovskii 1933.) Wet as well as dry areas exist in the Near East and it is fortunately in some of the wettest areas, where annual precipitation exceeds 750 mm (30 in), that traditional cultivation of crops such as emmer still continues, e.g. in the Black Sea ranges running across the North of Turkey into Soviet Georgia. These figures for annual rainfall actually slightly exceed those for most parts of eastern and central England.

During several years based at the British Institute of Archaeology at Ankara, it was possible to undertake a programme of sampling and recording in order, ultimately, to assemble interpretive models. The programme started in Eastern Turkey in villages where a wide range of primitive races of crops were grown. Several hundreds of samples were taken of all prime products and by-products at every stage of processing from harvesting onwards, this for every type of grain-crop grown. Emmer wheat, however, was not grown in this area and its cultivation and processing were studied and sampled in other parts of Anatolia including areas with high summer rainfall. This, therefore, allowed comparison of methods used in wet and dry areas.

Provisional results show that the broad correlations between crop processing practices and sample composition are sufficiently clear-cut to be definable in respect of the major categories of materials of the sort found in samples of prehistoric charred plant remains. These relationships are summarised in the flow diagram below (figures 5, 6 and 7) and will shortly appear in fuller form in Hillman (forthcoming, ii). The full analysis of all samples is still being prepared however, and further sampling is planned for the near future in order to provide replicate results for the studies of emmer processing. In addition, similar work is now being undertaken by Glynis Jones (in prep. and pers. comm.) on two Aegean islands where equally archaic methods are still used in the processing of a number of indigenous, free-threshing grain crops. Her provisional results appear to confirm the basic relationships described here.

The flow diagrams (figures 5, 6 and 7) will appear somewhat complex. Their essential simplicity, however, becomes apparent when the relationships are viewed in terms of (a) the relatively few by-products that are ever likely to be exposed to fire (see 'F's in diagrams) and, of those few by-products, (b) the relatively narrow range of constituents that are small and dense enough to be preserved by charring (see p. 140 below). (The botanical terms used in the flow diagrams and the ensuing text are explained diagrammatically in figure 4.)

REGIONAL VARIATIONS IN PROCESSING METHODS

In studying traditional agriculture in widely scattered areas of the Near East, the tools and techniques used sometimes appear deceptively dissimilar.

(a) *Threshing:* Particularly striking are the differences in threshing methods between mountainous areas with very wet summers and, on the other hand, villages scattered across the arid plains, plateaus and drier mountain ranges. Thus, in areas with wet summers threshing generally has to be performed under cover either by lashing ('heading') separate sheaves or by using equipment such as sticks or flails appropriate for confined spaces. In areas with consistently dry summers, on the other hand, all the threshing can be done out-of-doors by any convenient method – whether by trampling by animals, pulverising with flint-bladed sledges or – less commonly – by beating with sticks, flails or cudgels (see figure 5).

In the case of threshing, as with winnowing, however, only relatively small differences in composition of crop products result from the use of different methods. Thus, while the effects of threshing can always be recognised in appropriate samples, the different threshing methods can-

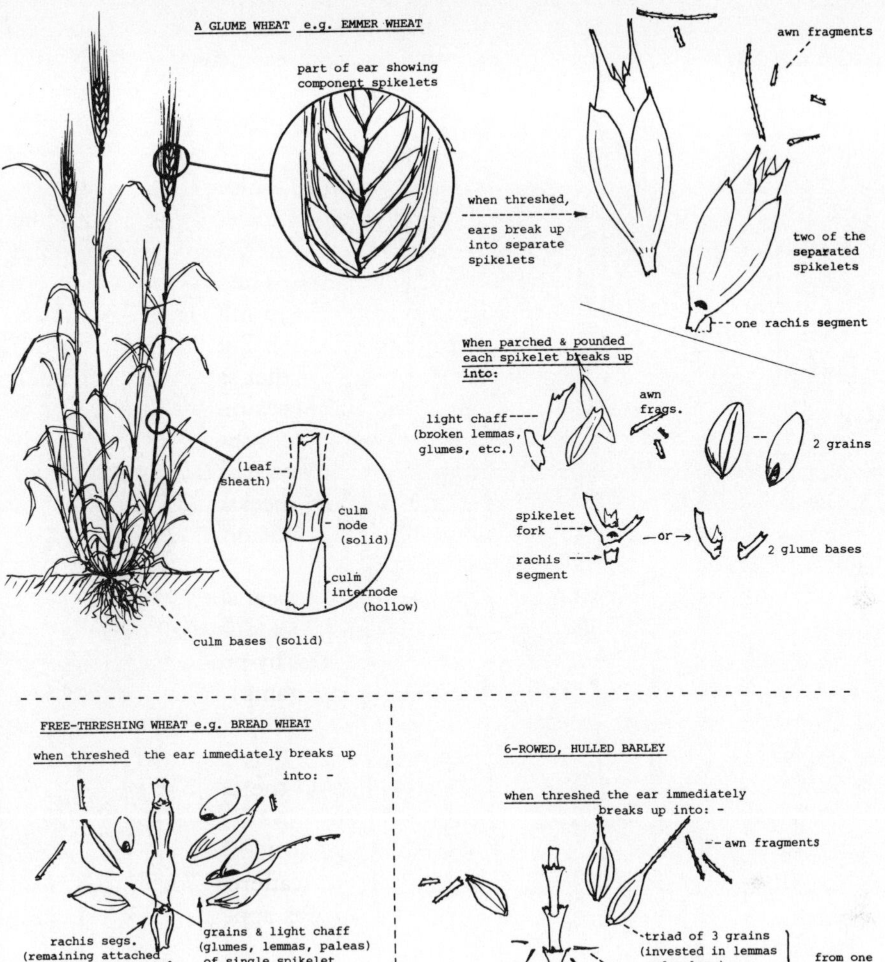

Figure 4. Some of the major components of cereal ears, as an explanation of terms used in the flow diagrams and text.

not be distinguished beyond – at best – two major categories which in this case happen to reflect wet- and arid-zone adaptations. While this represents a limitation on the precision of the model, it clearly has the advantage of allowing a single model for each crop type to be used on settlements representing a wide range of agricultural traditions.

(b) *Variations in storage product:* But perhaps the most fundamental difference in crop products between regions with wet and dry summers lies at the point at which prime products are put into long-term bulk store (whereafter all processing tends to be done in a piecemeal way throughout

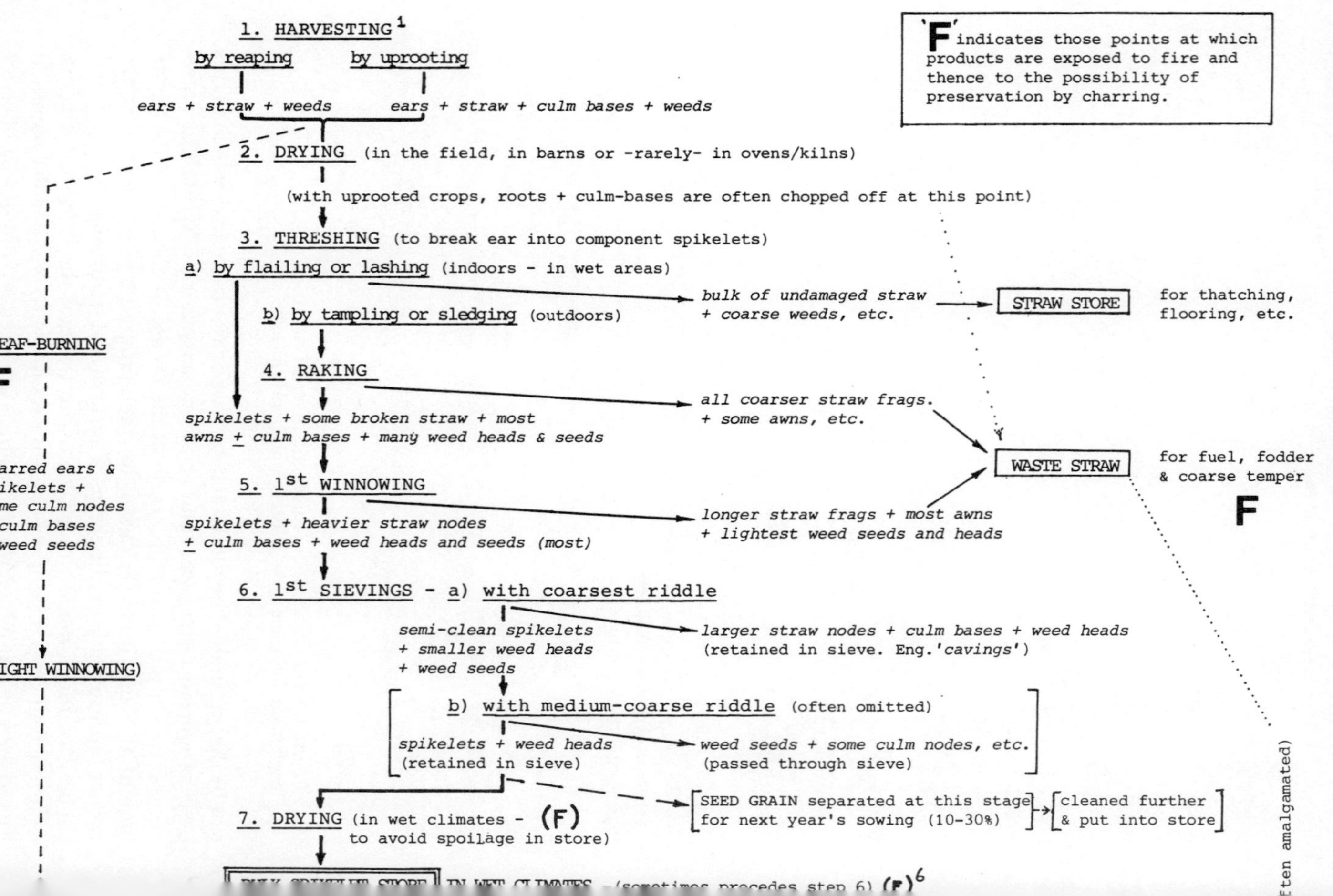

'F' indicates those points at which products are exposed to fire and thence to the possibility of preservation by charring.
1. HARVESTING[1]
by reaping
by uprooting
ears + straw + weeds
ears + straw + culm bases + weeds
2. DRYING (in the field, in barns or -rarely- in ovens/kilns)
(with uprooted crops, roots + culm-bases are often chopped off at this point)
3. THRESHING (to break ear into component spikelets)
a) by flailing or lashing (indoors - in wet areas)
b) by tampling or sledging (outdoors)
bulk of undamaged straw
+ coarse weeds, etc.
STRAW STORE
for thatching, flooring, etc.
4. RAKING
all coarser straw frags.
+ some awns, etc.
spikelets + some broken straw + most awns ± culm bases + many weed heads & seeds
WASTE STRAW
for fuel, fodder & coarse temper
F
5. 1st WINNOWING
longer straw frags + most awns
+ lightest weed seeds and heads
spikelets + heavier straw nodes
± culm bases + weed heads and seeds (most)
6. 1st SIEVINGS - a) with coarsest riddle
larger straw nodes + culm bases + weed heads
(retained in sieve. Eng.'cavings')
semi-clean spikelets
+ smaller weed heads
+ weed seeds
b) with medium-coarse riddle (often omitted)
spikelets + weed heads
(retained in sieve)
weed seeds + some culm nodes, etc.
(passed through sieve)
SEED GRAIN separated at this stage for next year's sowing (10-30%)
cleaned further & put into store
7. DRYING (in wet climates - (F) to avoid spoilage in store)
BULK SPIKELET STORE IN WET CLIMATES -(sometimes procedes step 6) (F)[6]
SHEAF-BURNING
F
charred ears &
spikelets +
some culm nodes
± culm bases
+ weed seeds
(LIGHT WINNOWING)
ften amalgamated)

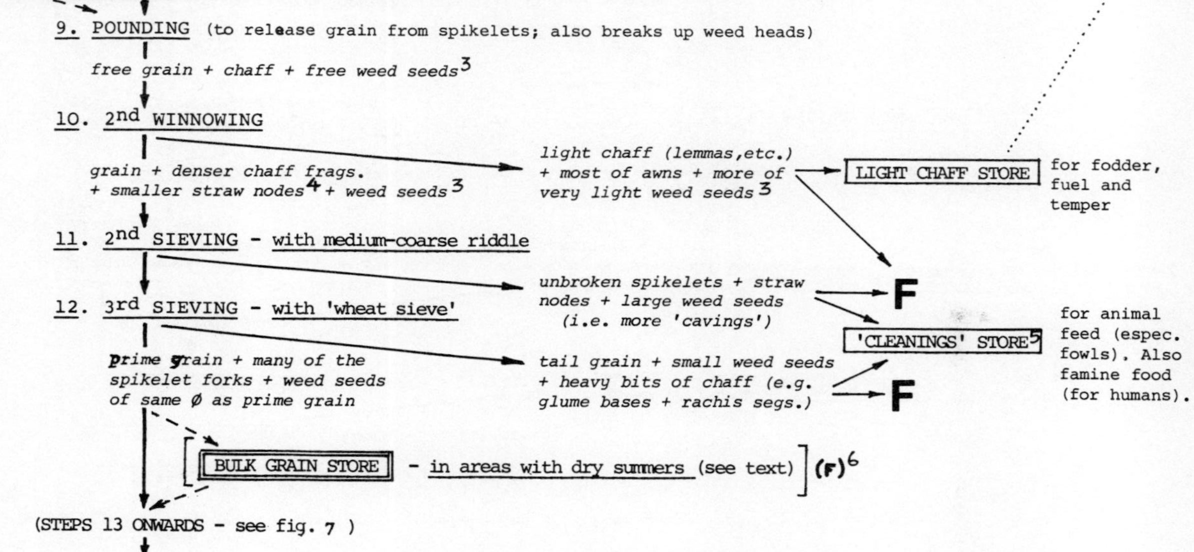

Figure 5. The traditional processing of glume wheats, e.g. emmer, spelt and einkorn and the composition of their products when harvested together with the straw[1]

1 To limit the complexity of this diagram, separate harvesting of ears and straw and its effects on composition have not been incorporated, though they are discussed in the text. 2 Domestic as opposed to manorial. 3 Most of the weed seeds at this stage derive from immature weed heads broken up during pounding (step 9). Many of these seeds are therefore immature to varying degrees. 4 Especially conspicuous are the basal rachis segments left at the top of the straw. 5 The 'cleanings' from steps 11 and 12 are often stored separately (see text), in which case it is the 'cleanings' from step 12 alone that serve as famine food. In wet areas, however, these cleanings are generally thrown straight onto the fire (during the winter months, at least) as they are separated in small quantities day-to-day. 6 See footnote 6 of figure 6.

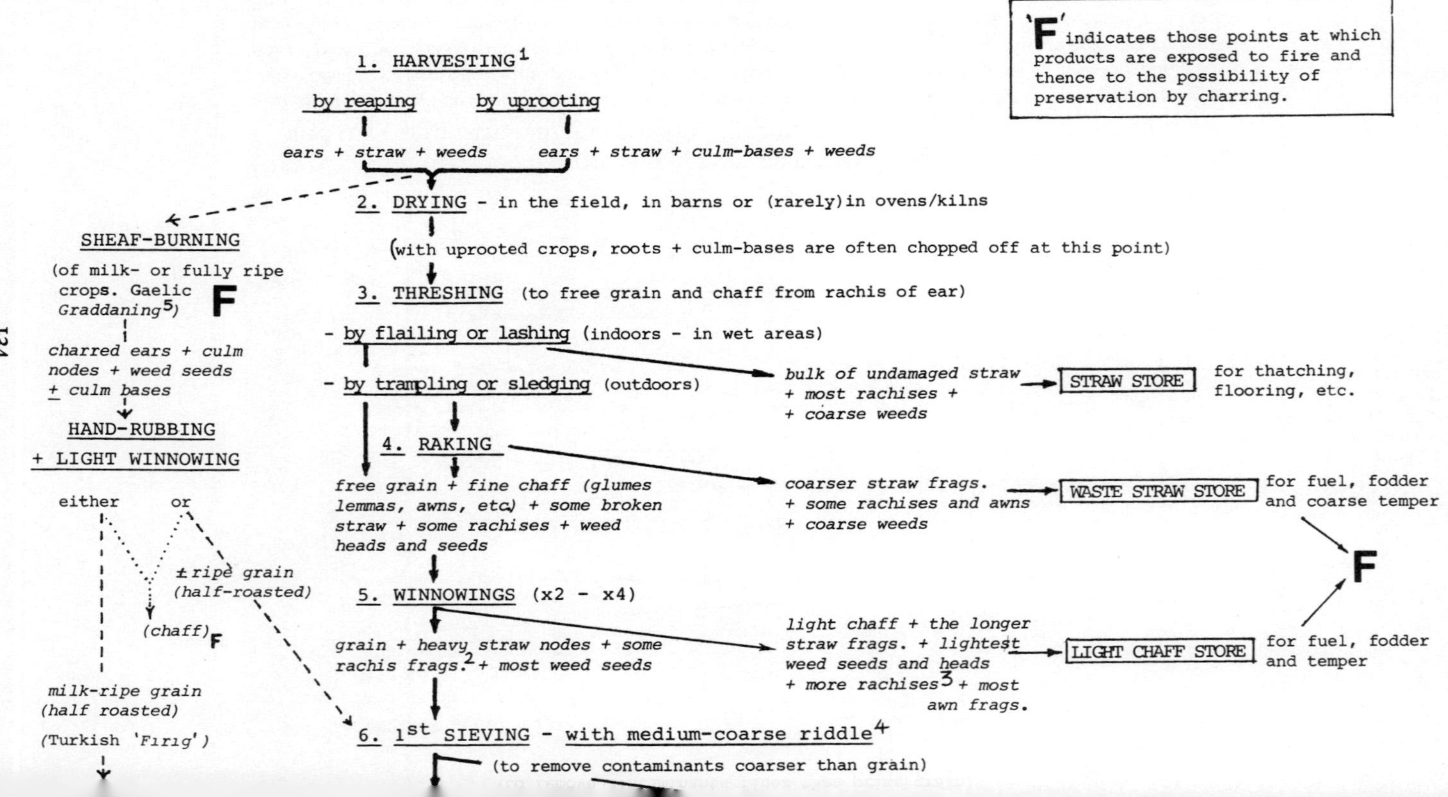
'F' indicates those points at which products are exposed to fire and thence to the possibility of preservation by charring.
1. HARVESTING[1]
by reaping
by uprooting
ears + straw + weeds
ears + straw + culm-bases + weeds
2. DRYING - in the field, in barns or (rarely) in ovens/kilns
(with uprooted crops, roots + culm-bases are often chopped off at this point)
3. THRESHING (to free grain and chaff from rachis of ear)
- by flailing or lashing (indoors - in wet areas)
- by trampling or sledging (outdoors)
bulk of undamaged straw + most rachises + + coarse weeds
STRAW STORE
for thatching, flooring, etc.
4. RAKING
coarser straw frags. + some rachises and awns + coarse weeds
WASTE STRAW STORE
for fuel, fodder and coarse temper
F
free grain + fine chaff (glumes lemmas, awns, etc.) + some broken straw + some rachises + weed heads and seeds
5. WINNOWINGS (x2 - x4)
light chaff + the longer straw frags. + lightest weed seeds and heads + more rachises[3] + most awn frags.
LIGHT CHAFF STORE
for fuel, fodder and temper
grain + heavy straw nodes + some rachis frags.[2] + most weed seeds
6. 1st SIEVING - with medium-coarse riddle[4]
(to remove contaminants coarser than grain)
SHEAF-BURNING
(of milk- or fully ripe crops. Gaelic Graddaning[5])
F
charred ears + culm nodes + weed seeds ± culm bases
HAND-RUBBING + LIGHT WINNOWING
either
or
± ripe grain (half-roasted)
(chaff) F
milk-ripe grain (half roasted)
(Turkish 'Fırıg')

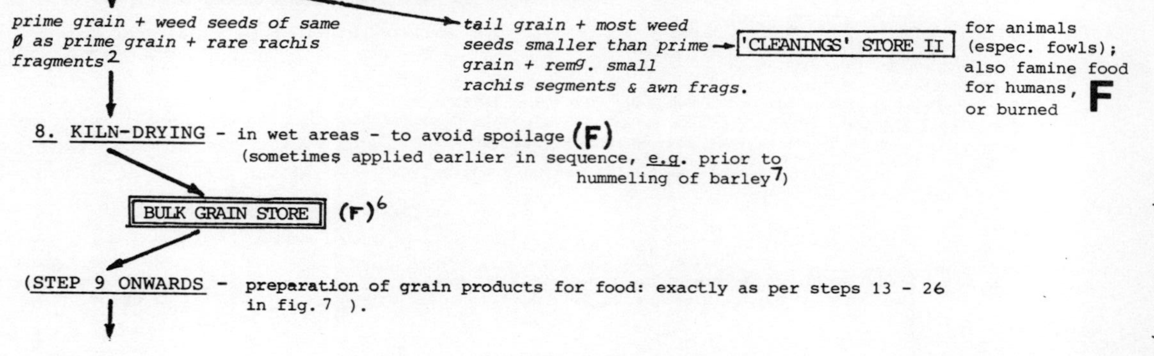

Figure 6. The traditional processing of free-threshing cereals, e.g. bread wheat, rye (and barley[7]) and the composition of their products when harvested together with the straw

(The sequence of operations applied to pulse crops – e.g. horse-beans, field-peas or vetches – is identical in most respects, though the sieve mesh sizes are different and the terminology for chaff fractions is not strictly comparable.)

1 To limit the complexity of the diagram, separate harvesting of ears and straw and its effects on composition have not been incorporated, although they are discussed in the text. 2 The heavy basal rachis segments are disproportionately well represented in the primary products (relative to the lighter upper segments). 3 Many of the lighter upper segments of broken rachises are winnowed out with the fine chaff. 4 These two sets of cleanings are often amalgamated (see text). 5 Fenton (1978), Grant (1961). 6 If prime products are stored in pits, then annual cleansing of these pits by firing will char any grain adhering to the sides (see Reynolds in this volume). 7 The sequence for barley (and oats) differs slightly – in the hulled forms – in that an extra step (hummeling) is applied to remove the remaining basal part of their awns. This is generally done prior to step 5.

Figure 7. Final stages of grain processing (continued from figures 5 and 6)

These final stages are essentially the same for both glume wheats and free-threshing cereals, though they differ in hulled grains (hulled barleys and oats) as against naked grains (wheat, rye and the naked forms of barley and oats)

1 From Fenton (1978). 2 See Moritz (1957). 3 Anatolian Turkish. Interestingly, the equivalent term in NW Iranian Kurdish (an Indo-European language) is *groot*; could this be cognate with English *groats*? If so, it would seem to suggest that this quick and very palatable way of consuming grain products is of some antiquity. 4 Once again, equivalent products can be found in most traditional agricultural societies that still survive; e.g. the Arabic *gerishé*, which is eaten precisely as the Shetland *louts*.

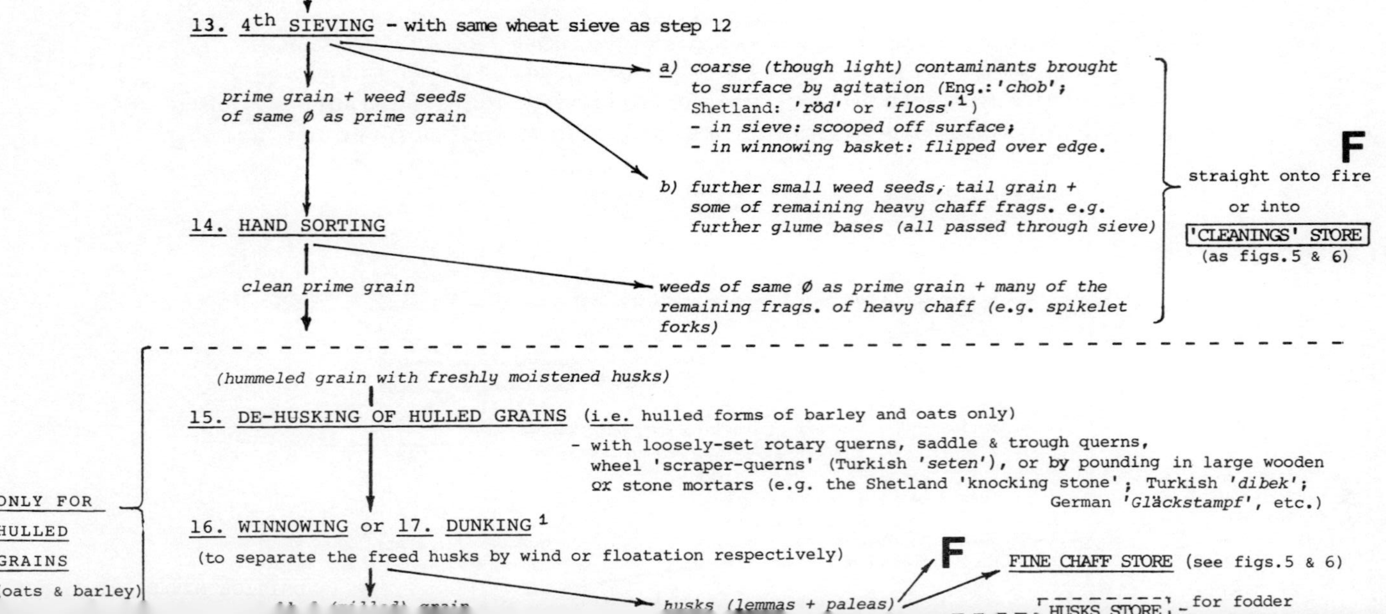

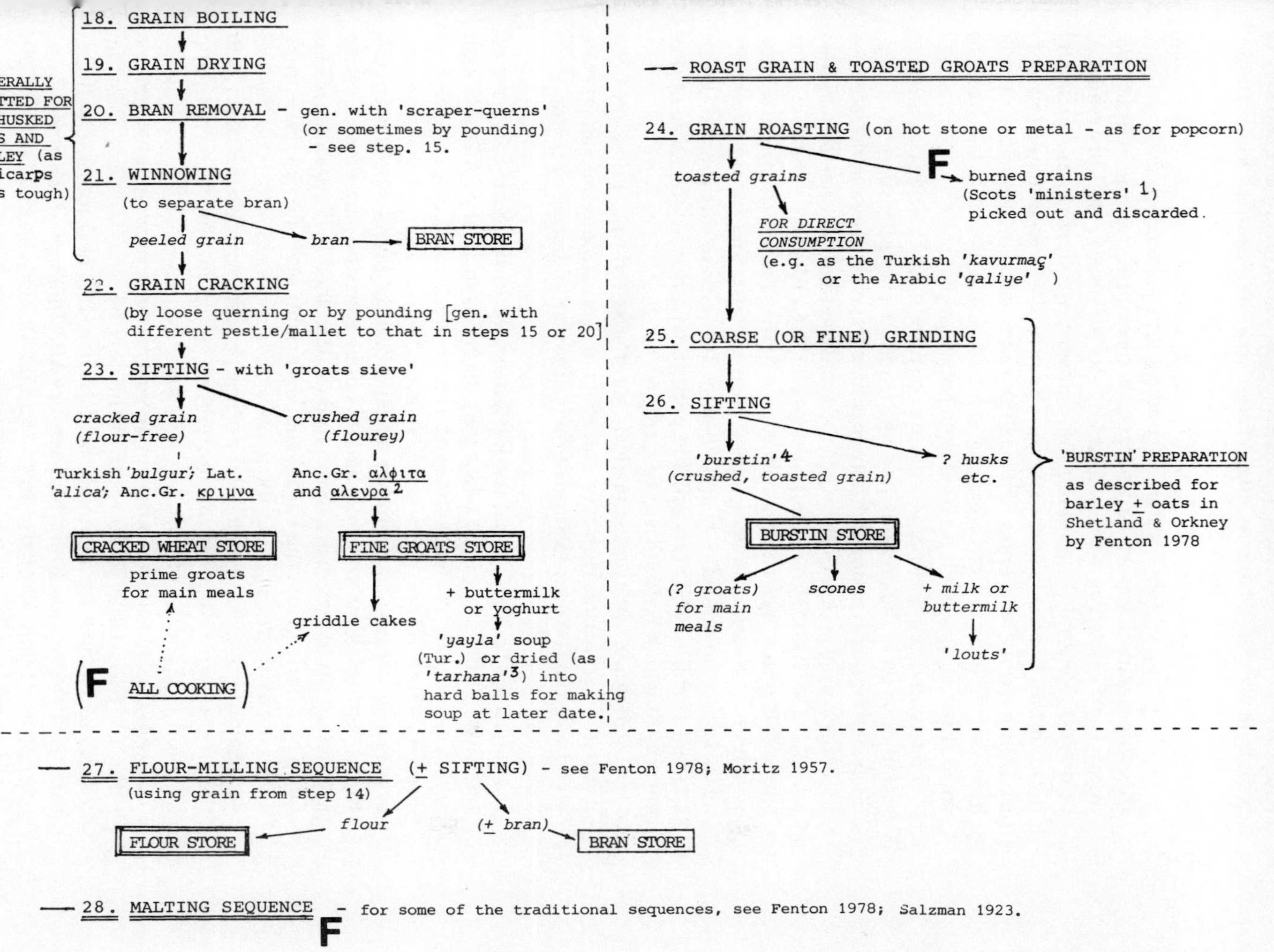
18. GRAIN BOILING
19. GRAIN DRYING
20. BRAN REMOVAL - gen. with 'scraper-querns' (or sometimes by pounding) - see step. 15.
21. WINNOWING
(to separate bran)
peeled grain
bran
BRAN STORE
GENERALLY OMITTED FOR DE-HUSKED OATS AND BARLEY (as pericarps less tough)
22. GRAIN CRACKING
(by loose querning or by pounding [gen. with different pestle/mallet to that in steps 15 or 20]
23. SIFTING - with 'groats sieve'
cracked grain (flour-free)
crushed grain (flourey)
Turkish 'bulgur'; Lat. 'alica'; Anc.Gr. κριμνα
Anc.Gr. αλφιτα and αλευρα 2
CRACKED WHEAT STORE
FINE GROATS STORE
prime groats for main meals
griddle cakes
+ buttermilk or yoghurt
'yayla' soup (Tur.) or dried (as 'tarhana' 3) into hard balls for making soup at later date.
F
ALL COOKING
ROAST GRAIN & TOASTED GROATS PREPARATION
24. GRAIN ROASTING (on hot stone or metal - as for popcorn)
toasted grains
F
burned grains (Scots 'ministers' 1) picked out and discarded.
FOR DIRECT CONSUMPTION (e.g. as the Turkish 'kavurmaç' or the Arabic 'qaliye')
25. COARSE (OR FINE) GRINDING
26. SIFTING
'burstin' 4 (crushed, toasted grain)
? husks etc.
'BURSTIN' PREPARATION as described for barley ± oats in Shetland & Orkney by Fenton 1978
BURSTIN STORE
(? groats) for main meals
scones
+ milk or buttermilk
'louts'
27. FLOUR-MILLING SEQUENCE (± SIFTING) - see Fenton 1978; Moritz 1957.
(using grain from step 14)
flour
(± bran)
FLOUR STORE
BRAN STORE
28. MALTING SEQUENCE
F
- for some of the traditional sequences, see Fenton 1978; Salzman 1923.

the year – as the finished products are required). Thus in wet climates in which most processing is undertaken indoors, emmer, for example, would normally be stored as semi-cleaned spikelets after only minimum large-scale processing (see figure 5) or, in some wet areas, as harvested ears or, even, whole sheaves. Pounding and sometimes even primary threshing will therefore be undertaken piecemeal, as required. On the other hand, in areas with predictably dry summers, the dusty jobs of pounding, second winnowing and subsequent sievings are generally done outdoors as one operation and the primary bulk-storage product is therefore semi-clean grain. These differences also correspond with bulk storage problems: in wet areas, the grain of glume wheats is less likely to spoil if stored as spikelets rather than naked grain.

The overall sequence of processing operations is, however, identical in either area, as is the composition of the products of each sequential step. These climatically adapted differences in storage strategy can therefore be identified only when bulk stores are accidentally or deliberately burned complete with enough of their contents for their function to be clear. This inevitably occurs relatively rarely except perhaps when storage is in pits, in which case, annual cleansing by burning chars any grain or spikelets adhering to the pit wall – as described by Reynolds in this volume. These charred remains will thus provide perfect evidence for the stage of processing at which bulk storage occurred.

(c) *Variations in reaping methods* are just as striking, but seem to be unrelated to climate. However, the effect of these differences can often be recognised in the composition of their products as discussed below.

GENERAL

It could well be argued that models generated in the Near East have no relevance to Britain – even when they derive from areas of Anatolia with summers at least as wet as those of eastern and central England. But, as already stated, there are relatively few effective ways of growing and processing crops such as emmer wheat or 'Celtic' beans when only traditional technology is available, and it is not surprising, therefore, that the methods – and even many of the tools – described by Fenton (1978) for Orkney, Shetland and the Faroes and Marurizio (1927) for Central Europe are essentially the same as those observed in present-day Near Eastern settlements. The ways of using the prime products are also the same, even the roasting of either mature or milk-ripe grain for direct consumption (Fenton 1978, pers. comm.).

However, the validity in Britain of Near Eastern 'ethnographic' models – the only available so far – can ultimately be assessed only from the results when they are applied to British sites. It is perhaps timely, therefore, that the results from third-century AD Wilderspool (Hillman forthcoming, iii) and from the Iron Age and Romano-British site at Cefn Graeanog II (see White *et al.*, forthcoming) are shortly to be published, as they provide an ideal example of some remarkably close correlations between the composition of plant remains recovered from many different features and the composition of specific crop products as defined in the model outlined above.

Until however more samples of crop remains from Neolithic or EBA sites are recovered in quantities sufficient for analysis of composition, the feasibility of using models based on present-day 'Iron-Age' villages for interpreting samples from very early sites clearly cannot be assessed.

3. THE ROLE OF PHYTO-GEOLOGICAL MODELS IN INTERPRETING PLANT REMAINS

In using the presence of particular weed species to suggest, for example, particular sowing practices or soil fertility patterns, precise information is clearly needed on the present-day ecological behaviour of the species concerned. However, studies of the ecology of arable weeds conducted in a country where farming is pervaded by the use of herbicides and weed-destroying mouldboard ploughs are, of course, potentially very misleading and in any case, few of the relevant species have previously been studied in any depth. (Note, for example, the paucity of weed species in entries under the 'Biological Flora of the British Isles' in *J. Ecol.* 1941 onwards.) It has therefore fallen to those researching prehistoric farming to undertake studies of their own on the behaviour of key species such as Charlock, Corncockle and Cleavers under conditions typical of traditional forms of husbandry, in particular, Martin Jones at Oxford and Peter Reynolds at Butser Iron Age Farm (Jones, in press and in preparation; Reynolds, in press and in this volume).

2

PRACTICAL LIMITATIONS ON THE INTERPRETATION OF CHARRED PLANT REMAINS

Before considering the use of 'ethnographic' (and phyto-ecological) models for interpreting plant remains in terms of farming practice, it is first necessary to highlight the two major limiting factors:

1. POOR PRESERVATION OF CHARRED REMAINS ON THE SITE

On most well-drained sites (barring totally dry caves and tombs) plant materials are preserved only by the chance of exposure to fire, and, even then, only when heating is relatively gentle (200–400°C) or, if temperatures are higher, when they are smothered in the ashes (i.e. deprived of oxygen while heated) such that they are preserved intact by charring rather than being burned away altogether to mineral ash. Apart from wood charcoals, then, the bulk of charred remains from British sites represent only those classes of plant products that were likely to end up in hearths, ovens or bonfires, either as (a) a crop product at a stage of *processing* at which it has to be dried or parched in kilns, ovens or over open fires, or (b) a *diseased crop product* such as weed-infested grain in need of sterilisation or destruction by intense heating or burning (see Buckland 1979 and in press); or (c) crop processing 'waste' used as *fuel*; or (d) food products to be rendered palatable by roasting or some other form of *cooking*. (The primary points of exposure to fire are indicated by 'F' in figures 5, 6 and 7.)

Of these four classes, it seems that fuels potentially provide the bulk of the charred crop remains on most British sites. But of the wide range of plant materials usable as fuel, the only components likely to survive at all in charred form are the small, dense items able to drop quickly through the flames and into the ashes without being burned to ash themselves. In the case of chaff and straw used either as the sole fuel or as the tinder to start a wood or peat fire, these small dense components found as charred remains generally include: (a) any *grains* present (e.g. tail grain in the waste from step 12 in figure 5 which has either been amalgamated with light chaff for burning or thrown onto a fire that is already burning); (b) dense *glume bases* and *spikelet forks*; (c) the shorter *rachis* fragments, especially the dense basal segments; (d) occasional short, broken segments of *awn*, especially oat awns; (e) the denser *straw nodes* and *culm bases* in cases where they have become separated from the long internodes; and, lastly, (f) *weed seeds*.

Preservation of crop products *other* than the four groups listed earlier generally occurs, therefore, only in cases of destruction by fire of whole structures such as barns or, better still (for us!), whole sites – whether by accident or design. This, however, would appear to be uncommon on most British sites. The only regular exception here is when storage is in pits that are annually cleansed by burning; in the course of this, any residual grains or spikelets are likely to be charred.

Generally speaking, the charred remains can be expected to represent only specific parts of the overall pattern of activities concerned with the manipulation of plant resources and products. Nevertheless, as we shall see, the charred remains potentially recoverable from many, if not most, of our British sites allow reconstruction of sizeable parts of the overall picture of farming events – at least from reaping onwards.

The preservation of crop remains varies with the extent of their exposure to mechanical damage – whether direct or indirect. In turn, the extent of mechanical damage depends upon (a) the period of exposure; (b) the degree of protection afforded by overlying deposits (most British sites are poor in this respect); and (c) the period of subsequent burial – buried charred remains deteriorate with age.

2. INADEQUATE SAMPLING STRATEGIES AND RECOVERY TECHNIQUES ADOPTED BY THE EXCAVATOR

If the intention is to attempt to reconstruct as complete a picture as possible of agricultural and domestic activities on the site (rather than merely to record presence or apparent absence of major crop species) then the requirements are as follows: (a) to sample from as wide a range of structures and features as possible in order to obtain the products of the widest possible spectrum of activities concerned with the manipulation of plant products, activities that can reasonably be assumed to have been distributed systematically with respect to context type; (b) to replicate this sampling in as many different examples of each structure or feature complex as possible within each occupation phase, so as (i) to improve the chances of embracing the full range of activities associated with each area type at different seasons of the agricultural year, as well as (ii) to try to allow for the multitude of chance factors involved in any particular batch of crop products being preserved; (c) each sample should be sufficiently large to allow the assumption that all the essential features of the composition of the flotation sample are essentially the same as in the parent deposit as a whole. In general, the minimum acceptable sample size varies with the initial rate of deposition of charred remains and their state of preservation which is partially age-dependent – as discussed above. Thus at Tell Abu Hureyra in Syria, with deposits of between 8,000 and 11,000 years old, the average sample size was four barrow-loads of excavated earth (see Moore *et al.* 1975), and at Neolithic Can Hasan III in Central Anatolia, the samples were even larger (French *et al.* 1972). In contrast, at Romano-British Cefn Graeanog II in Wales four buckets of excavated earth per feature or deposit have produced crop and weed remains sufficient for most interpretive needs (see R.B. White *et al.*, forthcoming).

Budgets for excavation and post-excavation work (together with the general backlog of unpublished samples) require, however, that we should operate with samples as few and as small as can be commensurate with recovery of the bulk of the information required. It is hoped, therefore, that having applied the complete, idealised strategy outlined above on five Near Eastern sites during the early seventies, and the same now on two Welsh sites, it will perhaps be possible in the near future to calculate what proportion of these samples and analyses would have been sufficient to produce essentially the same results. These larger projects are therefore providing the basis for formulating minimum-budget strategies for the future.

As for recovery methods, flotation (or better, water flushing) is unavoidable in most cases as the frequency of occurrence of charred crop remains is generally so low that nothing at all will be found unless this form of recovery is applied.

Having identified the charred remains of crops, what are the more obvious questions to be answered?

3
ANSWERING ARCHAEOLOGICAL QUESTIONS VIA 'ETHNOGRAPHIC' MODELS

Precisely how wide a range of farming practices can be deduced from charred crop remains by reference to an 'ethnographic' model? The clearest way of answering this is to pose a series of questions – from the general to the highly specific, and try to identify those areas where the combination of crop remains and ethnographic models can suggest the answers.

1. WAS THE SITE A FARMING SETTLEMENT OR PURELY PASTORALIST?
Pastoralist encampments or settlements, like towns, clearly have to obtain any cultivated plant food that they require from 'primary-producer' settlements. In the case of cereals and pulses, these products are generally exchanged in the same form in which they would normally be put into bulk storage in the 'producer' settlement. From our models (figures 5, 6 and 7), it can therefore be expected that the most commonly traded products would generally be semi-cleaned spikelets in the case of glume wheats (in wet areas, at least) and semi-clean grain in the case of free-threshing cereals and pulses. Products of this sort also offer the advantage of being convenient for transportation when compared, for example, with harvested sheaves.

(a) *Free-threshing cereals:* If the crop type identified is a free-threshing cereal such as bread wheat, then a strictly non-crop-producing site could be expected to be characterised by the presence of prime grain together with weed seeds such as Darnel and Corncockle (which cannot be sieved out) but with relatively few straw nodes or chaff fractions such as rachis. In practice, however, the prime grain itself would not normally be charred on such a site except by accident during operations such as grain roasting (see step 24 of figure 7). All, therefore, that would normally be found surviving in charred form on most such sites is the occasional grain of the crop along with weed seeds of the Darnel/Corncockle category and the occasional rachis fragment. [Weed seeds of this size category (i.e. same diameter as the grain) and any rachis fragments are sorted out by hand as the final stage of cleaning. This stage follows bulk storage and immediately precedes separation of the grain as food (see figure 7, step 14).]

In contrast, at the 'primary producer' settlements where the crop was grown and processed, adequate sampling will generally recover some 'waste' components from operations 3–7 in those cases where they were exposed to fire, e.g. through being used as fuel (see 'F' indications in figure 6).

(b) *Glume wheats:* If the crop is emmer or spelt, however, both 'producer' and 'consumer' settlements will generally contain chaff remains. The reason for this is that, in wet areas, the consumer settlements usually buy-in glume wheat grain in the form of spikelets. In both types of site analysis of charred remains should therefore reveal remains of spikelet chaff released by the processing of spikelets from step 7 onwards (see figure 5) in all cases where the waste was likely to be exposed to fire.

Producer settlements can nevertheless be recognised by having, in addition to this chaff waste, some of the waste fractions from steps 2a to 6 (figure 5). In particular, adequate sampling should recover some of the heavier straw nodes and bases which make up the bulk of the 'cavings' fraction, a proportion of which is commonly preserved in charred form when it is used as fuel (see p.155 below).

It is on the basis of these differences between the plant remains characterising 'producers' and 'consumers' that it has been possible to identify Cefn Graeanog II as a 'producer' settlement (growing spelt wheat as one of its main crops), this despite the fact that its location seems – by modern standards – to be totally unsuitable for growing any form of wheat. This archaeo-botanical conclusion has since been reinforced experimentally by spelt wheat having been grown successfully on land not far from the site (see White *et al.*, forthcoming).

2. WHAT WERE THE FUNCTIONS OF THE EXCAVATED SETTLEMENTS?

The majority of day-to-day activities on rural settlements in prehistoric Britain must have been concerned with food production. Therefore, one of the primary archaeological uses of charred remains of crops and other economic plants in these circumstances is to provide information on the function of structures (and features within those structures) in all cases where the activities involved manipulation of plant materials, whether for food, medicines, fuels, tempering (for adobe or pot-clay), furnishings such as reed matting or building materials such as straw thatch.

This part of the investigation suffers not only from the limitations outlined in the previous section but also from an additional limitation arising out of the inevitable mixing of crop remains that can be expected to have occurred when, for example, the charred results of various minor accidents during spikelet-parching or grain-roasting were dumped on the same midden as the ashes from the burned fuel of hearths and ovens. It could be argued, therefore, that the only unmixed samples will come from those 'primary' contexts where the products were initially charred. If this is true, then, all that can be retrieved is information on the last event in each context prior to its final abandonment.

In practice, however, it seems that mixing of products from different operations was not always so widespread. It is indeed sometimes feasible to use samples recovered from even 'secondary' contexts such as middens where the composition of the remains suggests derivation from a single class of operation. The interpretive models used, however, must be clearly defined so that deductions are testable and repeatable. At third-century AD Wilderspool, for example, the composition of charred spelt remains from a very large midden deposit was precisely that which is today characteristic of the waste fraction from step 12 of similar glume-wheat processing (see figure 5) together with a few straw nodes representing, perhaps, the waste from step 11 which would usually be amalgamated with it, in any case, when they are to be burned as fuel (Hillman, forthcoming, iii). Furthermore, the composition was precisely the same in all samples taken from different parts of the deposit.

Purity and uniformity of this sort should not, perhaps, have surprised us as it did, as accidents during parching or roasting are bound to have been rare relative to the daily accumulation of ashes from the fuel of hearths in which the cereal waste-fraction was probably the same, day by day (see 'sieving' below): primary products could scarcely have been destroyed through carelessness that often. The risk of different crop products being mixed in the same midden is further reduced in cases where the midden contents were regularly cleared out for use as manure. In such cases the accumulation of charred remains derives from a reduced number of events (i.e. from a shorter period hearth use), and the chances of their including an admixture of the charred products of a relatively unusual accident during, say, grain roasting, are correspondingly reduced. This situation seems to apply to the midden cum compost-heaps at Cefn Graeanog II (see R. B. White *et al.*, forthcoming).

Another example comes from Butser Iron Age Farm, where Peter Reynolds has adopted an experimental approach to identifying the function of storage pits from the composition of the charred cereal remains contained in them. From his work, it seems probable that the mass of germinated grain adhering to the pit wall by early summer would generally have been charred in the course of cleansing the pit by fire prior to any new grain being put into storage. Clearly, the ratios between the different chaff components, grain and weed-seeds in the charred debris can yield information not only as to the precise class of product that had been stored, but also – via the ethnographic models or the equivalent experiments – details of how it had been processed prior to storage. On this same basis Martin Jones (forthcoming) has been able to identify grain storage as the function of a pit at Danebury, and on essentially similar lines Monk (1977), at Southampton, was able to use the spectrum of seed remains from pits to suggest their use for storing dung.

A further case study is provided by the Iron Age/Romano-British farmstead of Cefn Graeanog II in Gwynedd, where it has been possible to identify at least some of the functions of a wide range of structures (see R.B. White *et al.*, forthcoming). One example must suffice: ratios between the different classes of charred chaff, grain, straw and weed seeds recovered from various deposits in a building straddling the entrance to the farm and destroyed by fire have provided the basis for interpreting one end as a barn and the other as an animal stall (see Hillman, forthcoming, i). However, while the ratios correspond closely with those to be expected in the remains of sheaves burned complete with ears, it is not entirely impossible that these ratios could also have resulted from the charred remains from incompletely combusted straw thatching having become mixed with a burning spikelet store when the roof collapsed.

Catsgore in Somerset provides a further example where study of the composition of charred remains of cereals has allowed identification of the terminal functions of five 'corn driers'. The final use of four of the five excavated corn-driers was found to have been the roasting of uniformly sprouted grains of spelt – presumably as part of the malting process, while the final use of the fifth kiln was the parching of spelt spikelets prior (presumably) to pounding. In addition, a major component of the fuel used to fire the kilns was identifiable as spelt straw and chaff (Hillman, in press). This example also serves to demonstrate the possibilities offered by studies of composition of crop products of this type.

3. TILLING METHODS?

Charred remains of plants can be expected to yield relatively little information on tilling practice, though the work of Martin Jones and Reynolds on the ecology of arable weeds may well open up new possibilities.

One existing possibility is to distinguish between ard and mouldboard ploughing on the basis of the presence of certain species of weed seed contained in the charred 'waste' fractions of crops (in particular, the waste fraction from step 12, figure 5). Depending on the manner in which they are used, ards disturb the soil sufficiently little to allow the survival of many perennial and biennial weed species that have not now been seen in Britain as arable weeds probably for several centuries. For example, in many parts of Turkey where the ard is still the standard ploughing implement, arable weed floras include (a) perennials such as White Horehound (*Marrubium* spp.), Yellow Cottonweed (*Achillea santolina*), wild roses (*Rosa* spp.) spreading by stolons, Wild Liquorice (*Glycyrrhiza* spp.) and shrublets of Camelthorns (*Alhagi* spp.) and Mesquite (*Prosopis stepaniana*); (b) biennials such as the Hoary Mullein (*Verbascum pulverulentum* and *V. speciosum*), wild artichokes (*Onopordon* spp.) and a wide range of biennial thistles and umbels (members of the Hogweed family). (A number of these plants occur in Britain.)

But as soon as an efficient mouldboard plough is introduced into these areas, most of the perennial and biennial weeds disappear. Thus, while the Mullein's large rosette of leaves formed during the first summer can withstand a certain amount of disturbance by ards, they clearly succumb when inverted and buried by a mouldboard plough. On the other hand, there are a few perennial weeds that actually *increase* under mouldboard ploughing, whether because they can grow from small pieces of their fragmented rhizomes (e.g. Couch (*Agropyron repens*), Bindweed (*Convolvulus arvensis*), Creeping Cinquefoil (*Potentilla reptans*) and Creeping Buttercup (*Ranunculus repens*)) or because they can regenerate from buds produced on fragments of root, e.g. the noxious Field Thistle (*Circium arvense*).

Obviously not all the perennial and biennial weeds characteristic of ard ploughing will be represented in the harvested crop: even when the crop is reaped *low* on the straw, all the largest weeds are easily avoided (see 'harvesting' below). However, at least some seeding heads of these large weeds occasionally get harvested with the crop (see Hillman, in preparation), and their presence in charred remains of the crop can then indicate the absence of efficient mouldboard ploughing.

The primary use of this technique is therefore for Medieval sites where the date of introduction of mouldboard ploughing may be at issue. Even then, however, its use is limited to assemblages in which the plant's status as a weed is clear from the consistent and exclusive association of its seeds with crop remains, particularly with that waste fraction where most weed seeds would normally be expected in any case, namely, the waste from step 12 for glume wheat processing (figure 5) and the equivalent step 7 for free-threshing wheats (figure 6).

Example: Heath grass (*Sieglingia decumbens*) – a tufted perennial – is among the most common of the seed types associated with cereal remains (chaff waste in particular) from both Cefn Graeanog Iron Age/Romano-British Farmstead and the Mediaeval Farmstead nearby. Today, *Sieglingia* is not found in Britain as a weed of arable, but either (in the south-east) as a grass of wetter acid heaths or in the west of Britain as a plant both of limestone heaths (see Etherington 1981) and mountain pastures generally. The explanation for *Sieglingia* having been an important weed at Late Iron Age Cefn Graeanog doubtless lies, therefore, in ploughing having been performed by ard, and in the practice having continued through into the Mediaeval occupation of the later Farmstead. Our present-day view of the ecology of *Sieglingia* in Britain would therefore seem, in part, to be a product of efficient mouldboard ploughing.

4. SOWING TIMES: AUTUMN, SPRING, OR BOTH?

Knowledge of sowing times is important (a) in any evaluation of seasonality of occupation and (b) in assessing overall productivity of the settlement, as most crops yield more heavily when winter sown.

The studies of Martin Jones together with Peter Reynold's experimental work at Butser indicate that the weed flora of a crop sown in autumn differs significantly from that of the same crop sown in spring. They have found, for example, that the noxious weed Cleavers (*Galium aparine*) is confined to autumn sown crops, and have therefore been able to suggest with confidence that its presence in charred remains of spelt wheat from Iron Age and Romano-British sites indicate autumn sowing in all the cases studied so far.

But using the *absence* of Cleavers fruitlets to indicate *spring* sowing is clearly more of a problem. There would appear however to be grounds for suggesting spring sowing if large numbers of samples of charred crop products from a site were found to consistently lack seeds of Cleavers and other autumn-germinating weeds and yet contain high concentrations of weed seeds which were (a) in the same size range as the very variable fruitlets of Cleavers and (b) produced by species of similar height and habit (see 'harvesting methods' below). As for the crops themselves, barley and the pulses would seem to be the most obvious candidates, as they are spring-sown amongst traditional farmers even when they have continued to be important foods, (a) because they can generally produce *some* sort of grain yield even when their vegetative period is drastically curtailed by late sowing, (b) because, in the case of the pulses, they are often too frost-sensitive to be autumn-sown anyway.

Emmer wheat has often been cited in archaeological literature as a consistently spring-sown crop, and some elaborate hypotheses have been erected on the basis of supposedly dramatic shifts to autumn sowing with the arrival of spelt during the Iron Age and thence, ostensibly increased net grain production and land-catchment carrying capacities. However, some caution should perhaps be applied before automatically making this assumption for the following reasons:

(i) Wild emmers – the ancestors of our cultivated emmers – germinate in autumn immediately after the first rains, a fact that is unlikely to have been overlooked by its earliest cultivators. The more primitive our emmer crops, therefore, the more they are likely to have resembled their ancestor in needing autumn germination (i.e. autumn sowing) to produce maximum yields. At the outset, therefore, emmer was probably autumn-sown, and there certainly seems to be nothing in the putative areas of earliest cultivation of Near Eastern cereals that need have prevented this.

(ii) Most crops providing the major part of the diet of traditional farming societies north of latitude 30°N are generally autumn sown whenever working schedules allow and whenever the soil is free of winter water-logging and not subject to sub-zero temperatures for prolonged periods without snow cover, i.e. spring-sown varieties tend to predominate only in areas where these limitations exist.

The reasons for this – in turn – are as follows: (a) Apart from specially selected spring varieties (most of them relatively modern), most wheats yield more grain when sown in autumn than when sown in spring (Watson, Thorne and French 1963; Kirinde 1976). [The number of *tillers*, on the other hand, may sometimes be *increased* by spring sowing, though many (if not most) of these will be sterile or semi-sterile. The table on p.76 of Percival (1920) could therefore be misleading if it is assumed to relate to *grain* yields]. This is due, in part, to the strong vernalisation requirement of many varieties. Assuming, therefore, that a certain weight of grain is required to feed one's household, then to choose to sow one's emmer in spring rather than autumn is to choose to expend more time and energy in producing the required grain, as proportionately more land will have to be tilled, sown and weeded. In the absence of waterlogging or frost problems, therefore, a shift from autumn to spring sowing would generally increase energy expended per unit weight of grain harvested. (b) The desirability of spreading the burden of ploughing and sowing over two seasons clearly favours a system including both sowings whenever soil and climate allow. If, therefore, as appears to be the case for parts of Britain during the Neolithic and Bronze Age, the crops grown were emmer, barley and 'Celtic' beans, and if barley and beans are the crops best adapted to spring-sowing, then it seems unlikely that emmer, too, would have been spring-sown as a matter of choice. (Whenever Turkish farmers were asked why they sowed some of their cereal crops in spring, their answers were always that, although the yields were less, there simply was not time available in autumn to fit in all the ploughing and sowing for both sets of crops.)

(iii) The assumption in British archaeology that emmer was automatically spring-sown seems to date back to Percival (1920), though his comments on the range of emmers he studies are somewhat equivocal (e.g. his 'late' and 'early' refer to time of ripening, not time of sowing which at Reading was autumn throughout, except when stated otherwise). Of the spring-sown emmers that I have seen under cultivation in the present-day, all had been relegated to spring sowing either (a) because the area concerned is at high altitude with winters so severe as to preclude winter-sowing of *any* crop, or (b) because emmer had ceased to be a major contributor to diet and, like any other minor crop where yields are no longer central to survival, its sowing is left to the spring or even omitted altogether if spring arrives late that year. To judge from their areas of origin, several at least, of Percival's emmers were likely to have been in the latter category by the time the samples were obtained.

As regards sowing times, then, recent practice can be somewhat misleading, and ultimately we must rely on evidence from the site itself, e.g. the presence of Cleaver fruitlets as suggested by Jones and Reynolds. But as yet, too few sites (if any) have yielded sufficiently large hoards of emmer remains for the spring-sowing hypothesis to even begin to be tested. If, however, it eventually transpires that emmer was, indeed, always spring-sown in Britain, then experiments with emmer crops will clearly be needed to investigate the reason why.

5. WERE THEY ROGUEING (WEEDING) THEIR CROPS?

Weeding of the standing crop is clearly easier when the crop is sown in drills, and drills are clearly crucial for hoeing. Nevertheless, broadcast-sown crops are sometimes hand-weeded, though in this case weeding is undertaken generally when the crop is still sufficiently green for the intercalary meristems to be capable of returning the tillers to the vertical position following trampling.

The effect of rogueing on the composition of crop products lies in eliminating many of the seeds of at least the taller and more conspicuous weed species that would otherwise be present. However, absence of weed seeds can also result from (a) harvesting the ears separately from the straw or (b) extra zealous cleaning at all the stages indicated in the flow diagrams. But on the other hand, rogueing, unlike (a), does not prevent straw waste from becoming mixed with prime products, and unlike (b), does not eliminate heavy chaff fragments from glume-wheat waste. And even the most thorough weeding will not avoid the seeds of twining weeds such as Black Bindweed (*Polygonum convolvulus*) becoming mixed with crop-products. (Each of these effects are discussed in detail below.)

6. HARVESTING: WHICH METHODS?

(a) *Harvesting of cereals by uprooting* is today used most commonly for barley, especially for the shorter varieties. However, it can also be used for the other cereals wherever the soils are sufficiently damp or friable, e.g. emmer is sometimes uprooted in the wetter parts of Turkey and Leser

(1931) mentions wheat being harvested by this method in China. Certainly, uprooting can be remarkably quick and effective and, in Turkey, is often entrusted to children too young to handle a sickle.

(i) In archaeologically uncontaminated samples of charred primary products, uprooting can first be distinguished by the larger than usual proportion of culm bases present among remains of spikelet chaff, grains and aerial culm nodes. (Clearly, culm bases are rarely present when other forms of harvesting are used unless the sickle is very blunt – indeed deliberately blunted sickles are sometimes used to harvest barley by uprooting in Anatolia today.) But on the other hand, if the crop was threshed by flailing or lashing (see above) performed with unusual care, then relatively few culm bases and nodes should be mixed with the prime products anyway. In practice, however, it is not unusual to find pieces of culm base in grain threshed by flailing. Indeed, small, grain-sized lumps of culm base often stay with the grain through into bulk storage: this is precisely what appears (from preliminary analysis) to be the case with a hoard of naked barley from the Beaker site of Tor More on Arran excavated by John Barber (Hillman and Milles, in preparation).

Uprooting can secondly be recognised by the large numbers of seeds of twining weeds such as Black Bindweed (*Polygonum convolvulus*) and Common Bindweed (*Convolvulvus arvensis*) relative to seeds of non-twining species. The significance of twining weeds here is simply that, while they are inevitably harvested along with the uprooted crop, most other types of weed are conveniently left behind in the field. This effect therefore overlaps with the effect of careful weeding.

(ii) In samples of amalgamated cereal 'waste' fractions (i.e. straw + cavings + chaff + 'cleanings', see figure 5), the effects of harvesting by uprooting whole plants – complete with ears – can be confused only with the effects of separately harvesting the ears prior to uprooting the straw and finally amalgamating the straw waste with the chaff from the ears. Clearly the same mixture of culm-bases, nodes, glume bases or rachises and seeds of twining weeds will result from either strategy, though to be able to reduce the range of possibilities to just two is clearly a step in the right direction.

(iii) In samples of cereal 'waste' where the major fractions are not amalgamated, the composition of each fraction can, again, be confused with the products from a second harvesting method. Thus the burned straw waste left after threshing (by flailing) of uprooted glume wheats will be indistinguishable from the remains of straw uprooted separately after harvesting the ears by plucking – as discussed below: both will contain culm-bases, culm nodes and the very characteristic basal nodes of the ear complete (generally) with one to three diminutive spikelets which are generally sterile. Similar confusion does *not*, however, exist with straw waste from other methods such as the separate *cutting* of the ears (which removes all basal ear-nodes) or straw waste from the normal reaping of straw and ears together.

A further complication here, is that the roots and culm-bases are sometimes cut off prior to threshing, the objective being, as explained by Fenton (1978), to avoid earth and small stones contaminating the grain on the threshing floor. Interpretatively, this poses no problem in identifying the practice of harvesting by uprooting so long as these roots and culm-bases are thereafter amalgamated with the rest of the straw waste. If burned separately, however, the charred remains of the bases would, in isolation, merely indicate that the straw of one of the crops (with or without the ears) had been harvested by uprooting, but with no clue as to precisely which crop was involved.

(b) *Harvesting ears and straw together by sickle-reaping* is today the most familiar method both in Europe and other areas where crops such as wheat, rye, barley and oats are (or were) grown under traditional systems. Reaping fairly low on the straw has the advantage of speed, (a) because both of the major crop products – grain and straw – are harvested in one operation, (b) because each cut of the sickle – whether flint-bladed, bronze or iron – can take twenty or more tillers at a go – and more still if harvesting claws are used. In my experience therefore, this is the fastest of any traditional method of harvesting apart from the scythe and consequently offers particular advantages in areas where the crops have to be harvested during short intervals between bouts of rain.

On the other hand, reaping low on the straw suffers the considerable disadvantage of simultaneously harvesting many of the weeds (depending on cutting height), the seeds of which then become mixed with the grain. Much – if not all – of the time and energy thus saved by harvesting straw and ears in one speedy operation would then seem to be lost in the tedious cleaning operations needed to eliminate these weed seeds and straw nodes from the primary products. However, these cleaning operations can be comfortably spread throughout the rest of the year and, for the glume wheats, are needed in any case for the elimination of fine chaff contaminants such as spikelet forks and rachis internodes, this even when the ears have been harvested separately (see flow diagrams).

Recognition of reaping low on the straw in charred crop remains follows a pattern similar to that outlined for uprooting (and is again subject to the caveats enumerated above, pp. 139–41).

(i) In remains of primary products, then, recognition is based on (a) significantly large numbers of culm nodes relative to grain or spikelets, (b) more generally, the presence of large numbers of seeds of weeds *in addition to* the twining weeds discussed under 'uprooting' above and (c) absence of culm bases.

(ii) In remains of the waste fractions, recognition is based on exactly the same components which, in waste, are present in gratifying higher concentrations. As before, however, the separate harvesting of ears and straw and subsequent amalgamation of waste fractions (before or after burning) can produce a composition identical to that generated by this method. (In this case, however, the confusion lies with *cut* straw rather than uprooted straw.) For a *certain* answer, here, therefore, remains of prime products are again required.

As for precisely how close to the ground the straw was cut, the range of weed species present in both primary products and waste provide the required clues via reference to their present-day heights when growing as weeds of crops in the area of the site today. Thus seeds of *Aphanes arvensis* and *A. microcorpa* – the Parsley Pierts – are useful indicators of low reaping, while reaping high on the straw is characterised by the *absence* of seeds of all low-growing weeds in samples containing ample numbers of seeds of taller weeds such as Corncockle (*Agrostemma*), weed oats (*Avena fatua*) and the docks (*Rumex* spp.). (See, e.g. G. Jones 1979).

(c) *Separate reaping (cutting) of ears and straw* has in recent times been far from the most widely used of traditional harvesting methods, though can still be found in occasional villages in Turkey (Hillman, forthcoming, ii) and Aegean Islands such as Karparthos (Glynis Jones, pers. comm.). Nevertheless, it was this method that was observed in use by at least some Britons by Pytheas who was thereafter quoted by Diodorus Siculus (5.21) through Poseidonius as saying that the Britons 'cut off the ears of grain and store them in houses that are roofed over, and pluck the ears from day to day', while Strabo, apparently quoting from the same source, says of the people of *Thule* that 'as for grain . . . – since they have no pure sunshine – they pound it out in large storehouses, after first gathering in the ears thither . . .' (Jones 1923).

A major disadvantage of this method of harvesting is the need for a second operation to harvest the straw. Ear-harvesting is further slowed-down in many of the more primitive forms of our crops – free-threshing and otherwise – by the uneven height of the ears on any one plant. This often precludes the possibility of cutting more than a few ears at a time unless much of the straw – and therefore some weeds – is cut with each of the taller ears. Indeed, in even a relatively short variety of Anatolian emmer cultivated at Cardiff in summer 1980, ear height ranged from 0.25 m to 1.10 m, many of the lower ears being part of the 'second flush' of smaller ears. Such uneven height (and ripening) is surprisingly common in 'primitive' crops grown today, despite the 10,000 or so years of selection against it.

(i) In charred remains of primary products, separate reaping of the ears can be distinguished from all other methods by the complete absence of contaminants other than chaff derived from the ear itself. But relying on negative evidence is clearly hazardous, and in this case, the absence of weed seeds overlaps with the effects of weeding applied to crops harvested by other methods, though the presence of straw nodes – and often the bases too – still allows these other methods to be recognised in suitable samples. However, any apparent absence of straw nodes should be treated as significant only in samples where the products are still heavily contaminated with those items that are generally eliminated in any operation to remove straw nodes and straw bases. These items include (a) basal nodes of the ears (and sometimes a few awn fragments) in the case of glume wheats, (b) rachis remains (and sometimes own fragments) in the case of free-threshing cereals such as barley.

(ii) In remains of cereal waste fractions, separate reaping of the ears and straw is recognisable *if* the waste from either half of the harvest is stored separately and burned separately (but not if these waste fractions have been amalgamated or become mixed). (a) Remains of the denser chaff 'cleanings' of glume wheats – originating primarily from step 12 (figure 5) – will thus contain spikelet forks, glume bases, rachis internodes and the highly characteristic basal rachis nodes, but no weed seeds or straw nodes. Absence of weed seeds can be treated as significant only in large, archaeologically uncontaminated samples. In these 'cleanings' of heavy chaff, however, their absence is particularly striking because it is in this very fraction that large quantities of all the smaller weed seeds are usually found, even if – as in carefully weeded crops – these seeds come only from twining species. (b) The remains of separately harvested straw is distinguishable from straw remains from normal reaping, in glume wheats by the absence of basal nodes, and in free-threshing cereals by the lack of rachis remains. While the former is a very dubious distinction, the latter is more reliable as rachis remains are otherwise very prominent in charred remains of threshed straw that has been reaped together with the free-threshing ears.

(d) *Plucking of glume-wheat ears* followed by separate reaping or uprooting of the straw is a method experimented with and found to be very effective by Peter Reynolds (in this volume). I have once seen it used in an emmer crop in Turkey, though on only a very small scale by a landless household which had obtained harvesting rights on part of a neighbour's field. Nevertheless, plucking of ears is clearly referred to in the second part of the Diodorus Siculus quotation (above, p. 151), and its 'day to day' application would certainly allow for separate harvesting of each flush of unevenly ripening ears, once – so it seems – the harvesters had 'cut-off' (i.e. reaped) what were perhaps the larger, taller ears that normally characterise the first and major flush of ripening in archaic crops such as emmer and *Triticum macha*. However, this may be reading too much into what was already a third-hand observation originating from Pytheas who Strabo apparently regarded as prone to 'fabrication' (Jones 1923).

The studies of composition of present-day products did not include this harvesting method as no samples could be obtained at the time. It is nevertheless fairly obvious that the one major difference between the primary and waste products of plucking as against the reaping of ears would – as indicated above – lie (a) in the absence of basal rachis nodes and their abortive spikelets in the plucked products and (b) their presence in the remains of the separately harvested straw. The possibility of recognising harvesting by separate plucking of ears of the glume wheats is therefore very poor in charred remains of the primary products, and in uncontaminated straw residues its effects could further be confused with the composition of straw harvested together with the ears and separated from them by threshing and raking.

7. WHEAT THRESHING METHODS?

The wide range of available methods and equipment for threshing have already been mentioned. But from charred remains of crop products only two major groups can be identified, and even then, only in primary products and only when the crop has been harvested by uprooting or reaping low on the straw.

(i) In most areas with wet summers the usual methods involve separating the spikelets (glume wheats) or grain and chaff (free-threshing cereals) from the straw *without* the straw being fragmented. The most familiar of these methods is (a) beating with flails, sticks or clubs. A less familiar method is (b) lashing the heads of small sheaves of corn against a stationary object: Fenton (1978) illustrates purpose-built frames and special lashing stones – projecting from the walls into the threshing area – which were used until recent times in Orkney and Shetland. Similarly, in wet areas of present-day Turkey, the sheaves are sometimes 'headed' against the edges of heavy wooden troughs in which the spikelets (or else grain and chaff) collect, ready for primary winnowing.

(ii) In areas with dry summers, however, the methods most widely used involve fragmentation of both ears and straw, thereby producing a mixture of either spikelets and broken straw in the glume wheats, or grain, chaff and broken straw in the free-threshing cereals and pulses. The two main methods here are trampling with animal hooves and pulverising with threshing sledges. For prehistoric Britain threshing sledges can be dismissed, though it is not impossible that trampling was used in some areas.

In group (i), primary products in the earlier stages of processing will contain relatively few straw nodes but plenty of weed seeds. Even in crops that have been rigorously weeded or harvested by uprooting, the seeds of twining weeds are generally present. The weed seeds therefore distinguish these effects from those of separate harvesting of ears in which the prime products also lack straw nodes right from the outset. In group (ii) on the other hand, large numbers of culm nodes remain mixed with the primary products until stage 6 of both processing sequences (figures 5 and 6), and as bulk storage of the spikelets of glume wheats in wet climates generally precedes processing stage 6, there are reasonable prospects of recovering samples of this sort, if, indeed, threshing by trampling was ever practised in prehistoric Britain at all.

8. PARCHING?

In areas with wet summers, the threshed spikelets of glume wheats are generally parched to render the hulls sufficiently brittle to then be pounded off the grain. However, unequivocal evidence of parching comes only from spikelets found *in situ* in ovens that were being used for this purpose at the point of abandonment. Several such finds exist for the Roman period, but their absence, so far, on earlier sites poses the possibility that, in prehistoric Britain, the spikelets may have been parched on open hearths in some sort of vessel or on hot stones, the equivalent, therefore, of the 'pot-drying' of grain described by Fenton (1978) in which vessels called 'burstins' were used or else clay-rimmed stones called *hellio* as in the Orkneys. Yet another possibility is raised by Fenton's description of grain-drying on St Kilda in which hot stones were rolled amongst the grain, and Fenton's account of the archaeological significance of these stones should certainly be noted by all excavators. Whether any part of Britain is dry enough for parching to have been omitted altogether (as in parts of Anatolia) is uncertain.

9. POUNDING?

To release the grains from the investing hulls, the parched spikelets of glume wheats are pounded in some sort of pestle and mortar. In the process, the lemmas, paleas, rachis internodes and upper parts of glumes are broken off, leaving the hard rachis node with two glume-stubs attached. This is the 'spikelet fork' (see figure 4) which is itself often broken into two 'glume bases'. The presence, then, of charred spikelet forks, glume bases and broken rachis internodes in waste fractions preserved separately from the bulk of the free grain is itself evidence of some sort of pounding operation having been applied to the spikelets, and such finds are common on most sites where glume wheats are present at all, especially on Late Iron Age and Romano-British sites where spelt was grown.

The wood or stone mortars in use today vary in diameter from 15 cm to almost a metre, while the pestles may either be rod-shaped or in the form of long-nosed wooden mallets. Many of the stone bowls or round hollows carved in rocks on our British sites may therefore have been concerned with this operation which, in wet climates, is performed on a day-to-day basis – as the grain is required – using spikelets taken from bulk storage. A British version of an essentially similar technique practised until recent times is the use of the 'knocking stone' and wooden mallet for dehusking barley grain, as described by Fenton (1978) for Orkney and Shetland. Maurizio (1927) similarly describes dehusking and groats manufacture with massive wooden mallets and mortars in central Europe. Whether or not these techniques are direct descendants of those previously applied to dehusking glume wheats (as well as barley) remains uncertain.

Querns of various types are, however, also used occasionally for small-scale freeing of grain, but this method gives the impression of being less efficient. As for whether the products of either method differ in such a way that their charred remains could be distinguished is as yet uncertain as I have never succeeded in obtaining samples of the products of this second method. It is not impossible that the state of fragmentation of spikelet forks bears some relation to the method used. Some experimentation is clearly required here.

10. WINNOWING?

A wide range of forks, shovels, ladles, baskets and fans are used in winnowing (see Hillman, forthcoming, ii). The operation is unavoidable in that it provides the only convenient means of eliminating the light chaff (lemmas, awns, paleas, glumes, straw internode fragments and some light seeds) from the grain, but it can nevertheless rarely be positively identified from charred plant remains simply because these components invariably burn to fine ash on exposure to fire. Thus when, as fuel, it is burned together with denser waste fractions separated by sieving, it is only these latter that remain.

11. SIEVING?

The primary products are cleaned with sieves at several points in the processing sequence (see figures 5, 6 and 7), each stage requiring a sieve (or sieves) with a different mesh diameter which will have been carefully pre-determined by the sieve-makers (see Hillman, forthcoming, ii). Even in Anatolia, however, making sieves of this sort is a rapidly dying craft, as is the intinerant life style that goes with it.

The use of sieves for cleaning grain is doubtless a practice of considerable antiquity and is likely to have involved sieves with meshes made of a wide variety of different materials – gut, leather, spun wool, linen, cane or reed – depending on local traditions and the resources available. Certainly, the regular use of sieves by surviving (or historically recorded) non-agricultural peoples in all cases where they regularly gather the seed of large-flowered wild grasses suggests that the pre-agricultural groups of the Near East who utilised grain gathered from the wild ancestors of our European crops were probably already familiar with the use of sieves before they ever started cultivating. Certainly, cleaning the grain of the heavy chaff fractions *without* sieves would have been difficult. I know of no published archaeological reports of sieves, though what has been described as a *Tasche* from Early Neolithic Egolzwil in Switzerland looks – from the published photograph – as close to being an agricultural sieve as anybody could wish (see Wyss 1971, item 44416 in Museum catalogue).

In present-day Anatolia the major waste fractions from sieving are stored separately in most cases, especially when the crop products are sieved in bulk, i.e. prior to bulk storage. However, amalgamation into two major 'waste' stores – straw-chaff waste and 'cleanings' – is not uncommon in some villages (see figures 5, 6 and 7). But when – as in wet climates – cleaning with sieves is undertaken in small batches, especially in winter when fires are burning in the hearths, it is usual for the waste from the later sievings (steps 11 and 12 in glume wheats, or steps 6 and 7 in free-threshing cereals) to be tossed straight into the fire. Here, many of the denser items will trickle down into the ashes and char. It is not surprising, therefore, that the type of charred remains most commonly recovered from sites where wide-ranging sampling strategies have been applied consists – in the case of Iron Age and Roman sites at least – of smaller weed seeds, tail grains, glume bases and the occasional straw node, i.e. precisely those components generally separated from the prime grain in step 12 (figure 5) together with occasional items from the waste of step 11 (step 7 ± 6 in the free-threshing cereals). Examples here include the plant remains from third-century AD Wilderspool (Hillman, forthcoming, iii) and Iron Age Meare in Somerset where Glynis Jones (1981a) has identified both semi-clean grain containing some grain-sized weed seeds as well as samples of sieved-out waste consisting largely of spikelet forks, glume bases and small weed seeds.

It could perhaps be argued that these items could equally well have been separated from the prime grain by hand-sorting, though anyone who has tried it themselves or seen the women of the households – and sometimes the men, too – sorting the grain for just the last few classes of contaminant left after successive sievings will appreciate the impracticability of this alternative. Basically, then, finding charred remains of these waste fractions inevitably means that the household concerned was cleaning its grain by use of sieves.

12. LATER STAGES OF PROCESSING

For the purpose of this paper the last stages of processing and food preparation must be omitted. They will, however, be published in detail elsewhere (Hillman, forthcoming, ii). Suffice it to say that hoards of sprouted grain charred during malting are not uncommon on British sites – albeit all Roman or later, so far, and evidence is now accumulating for roasting of prime grain – presumably for direct consumption – at the Iron Age site at Pembrey Mountain in Dyfed (Hillman, forthcoming, iv).

GUT CONTENTS AS A SOURCE OF INFORMATION ON FARMING PRACTICES

Helbaek's remarkably thorough analyses of the stomach contents of executed men preserved in peat and dated to the Danish Iron Age revealed seeds of a wide range of plant species including crops such as emmer, spelt and both hulled and naked six-rowed barleys (see Helbaek 1950, 1951, 1958, 1960). It was suggested in these publications that the seeds of all plants other than crops had been specially gathered to prepare meals for the condemned men, and that some of these gathered plants may have been used as food in Iron Age society generally. It certainly seems probable that many wild plants were, indeed, gathered for food, flavouring or medicine at that time, as many still were until two or three generations ago (see Pierpoint-Johnson 1862).

But for the assemblages of wild and cultivated species in these particular 'samples', a simpler and more reasonable explanation would seem to be that the mixtures of what are predominantly arable weeds together with some grains and chaff of crops represent no more than waste separated from the later stages of grain-cleaning (with or without extra grain added to make up a tolerable meal). While these particular 'waste' fractions are, today, commonly retained as animal feed, they have often been used in the recent past as famine-food for humans (see Maurizio 1927). Such low-grade fare might not therefore have been deemed inappropriate for men who were perhaps condemned criminals.

The composition of the stomach contents of at least the men from Tollund and Grauballe is thus closely similar to the composition of present-day waste from both stage 7 of the processing of free-threshing wheats and the equivalent stage 12 for glume wheats – with the possible inclusion of waste from the preceding steps in either case (6 and 11 respectively) (see figures 5 and 6). Thus, apart from the fragmented remains of grain – which may or may not have been tail grain – the cereals were represented by heavy chaff components: spikelet forks, glume bases and rachis internodes of emmer, glume bases and just one spikelet of spelt and, in the Tollund sample, abundant rachis segments of the two barleys. As for the other remains, apart from seeds of cultivated flax, almost all the other seeds recorded as 'abundant' or 'common' in the samples are today either typical weeds of crops or else commonly occur in that role, e.g. Corn Spurrey, Fat-Hen, Pale Persicaria, Black Bindweed, Sheep's Sorrel, Common Hemp Nettle, Ribwort Plantain, Great Plantain, Brome, Yorkshire Fog and Cockspur. It may also be significant that the Tollund sample in which *Camelina lincola* (syn. *C. alyssum* (Mill.) Thell.) – an archetypal weed of flax crops – is present, is also the one sample in which flax seeds are particularly abundant. As a later publication will show (Hillman, in preparation), this sort of assemblage is quite remarkably close to the composition of those waste fractions cited above, especially when some allowance is made for minor variations in weed species with soil type and moisture.

As for those species not generally regarded as ever being arable weeds, none are recorded as 'abundant' and only one – *Deschampsia caespitosa* is 'common' (though only in the Grauballe sample), and it would have needed only a single plant of *D. caespitosa* – growing perhaps at a damp field margin – to contaminate the crop products with many hundreds of its tiny seeds. Heath grass *Sieglingia decumbens* is another of the plants cited as having 'been collected from outside the cultivated area' (Helbaek 1958), but, as indicated above (p. 146), this grass was most probably a weed of arable crops for as long as ards were used for tilling, and the same may apply to some of the other species cited as non-arable.

If, as therefore seems probable, most of the identifiable components represent waste from the last stages of grain cleaning, then they neatly demonstrate the use at the settlements concerned of grain sieves for eliminating the bulk of the contaminants smaller than the prime grain itself. It is appropriate, therefore, that not a single species in the long list of weeds and other plants present produces seed with diameters greater than prime grain of spelt or barley (though the larger seeds of Common Hemp-nettle can often equal it). In addition, from the presence of seeds of fairly short weeds such as Parsley Piert (*Aphanes arvensis*), Chickweed (*Stellaria media*) and Corn spurrey (*Spergula arvensis*), it would also seem that the crops concerned were reaped fairly low on the straw, this at all three sites.

Whether, for the last meals of these three men, these waste fractions were mixed with some prime grain cannot be deduced from the information available. Certainly, the cleanings would have provided a cheap and possibly flavoursome (albeit gritty) way of 'filling-out' meals based on a bare minimum of the prime products. Whether, in addition, the 'many sclerotia of Ergot' would have been sufficient to induce a state of stupor or hallucination in the condemned men prior to their apparent execution also remains uncertain.

CONCLUSIONS

Crop remains represent the primary products of an activity that necessarily preoccupied much of Britain's prehistoric population from the Neolithic onwards. Not only can these remains provide information on which crops were grown but, in many cases, individual samples can yield information on the methods used in their cultivation and processing.

Some of this information can be deduced from internal analysis, but ultimately interpretation in terms of farming practices relies on observations of precisely how such practices affect the composition of crop products in traditional systems of farming functioning in the present-day. In the absence of any of Britain's prehistoric crops still being cultivated and processed by traditional methods anywhere in northwest Europe, a Near Eastern model has been outlined which defines the composition of products generated by each step in the processing of these crops.

By reference both to this 'ethnographic' model and to studies of weed ecology, it is suggested that the composition of most major crop products can yield information on, for example, the methods used in reaping and cleaning the grain, as well as providing clues to other husbandry practices such as ploughing. Similar evidence allows the settlement as a whole to be identified as either agricultural or pastoral, as well as allowing identification of the function of certain site structures where the activities concerned manipulation of plant products.

In combination with historical accounts of recent traditional farming practices in northern Europe, the Near-Eastern model provides not only a means of interpreting assemblages of charred remains, but also provides an overall picture of *one* of systems for growing and processing Britain's prehistoric crops that is agriculturally feasible with archaic technology today and that may therefore have been feasible in prehistoric times.

ACKNOWLEDGEMENTS

I wish to express my gratitude to Mavis Saunders, not only for typing the manuscript but for her forbearance in deciphering the first handwritten draft. I am also very grateful to Glynis Jones for checking the manuscript in detail and for providing a host of valuable suggestions, and likewise to Annie Milles and Lisa Moffat.

REFERENCES

Aksoy, B. & S. Diamant (1973) Çayboyu 1970-1. *Anatolian Studies 23*, 97-108.

Buckland, P. C. (1979) Cereal production, storage, and population: a caveat, in *The effect of man on the landscape: the lowland zone (eds S. Limbrey & J. G. Evans)*. CBA Research Report No.21.

—— (in press) The early dispersal of insect pests of stored products as indicated by archaeological records. *J. Stored Products Research 17* (in press).

Dennell, R. W. (1972) The interpretation of plant remains: Bulgaria, in *Papers in Economic Prehistory* (ed. E. S. Higgs). Cambridge University Press.

—— (1974) Botanical evidence for prehistoric crop processing activities. *J. Arch. Sci. 1*, 275-84.

—— (1977) On the problems of studying prehistoric climate and crop agriculture. *Proc. Prehist. Soc. 43*, 361-9.

Etherington, J, R, (1981) Limestone heaths in southwest Britain: their soils and the maintenance of their calcicole-calcifuge mixtures. *J. Ecol. 69* (in-press).

Fasham, P. J. & M. A. Monk (1978) Sampling for plant remains from Iron Age pits: some results and implications, in *Sampling in contemporary British Archaeology* (eds J. F. Cherry *et al.*). BAR British Series 50, 363-71.

Fenton, A. (1978) *The Northern Isles: Orkney and Shetland.* Edinburgh: John Donald.

French, D. H., *et al.* (1972) Excavations at Can Hasan III 1969-1970, in *Papers in Economic Prehistory* (ed. E. S. Higgs). Cambridge University Press.

Grant, I. F. (1961) *Highland Folk Ways.* London: Routledge & Kegan Paul.

Green, F. J. (1979) *Medieval plant remains: methods and results of archaeo-botanical analyses from excavations in southern England with especial reference to Winchester and urban settlements of the 10th-15th centuries.* M.Phil. thesis, Dept of Archaeology, University of Southampton.

—— (in press) Iron Age, Roman and Saxon crops: the archaeological evidence from Wessex, in *The Environment of Man from the Iron Age to the Anglo-Saxon Period* (eds M. K. Jones & G. W. Dimbleby). BAR British Series.

Helbaek, H. (1950) Tollund mandens sidste Maaltid. *Aarbøger f. Nordisk Oldkyndighed og Historie*, 329-41.

—— (1951) Unkrudtsfro som Naeringsmiddel i forromersk Jernalder. *Kuml, Aarbog f. Jysk Ark. Selskab*, Aarhus, 65-74.

Helbaek, H. (1952) Early crops in southern England. *Proc. Prehist. Soc. 18*, 194-233.

—— (1958) Grauballemandens sidste Maaltid. *Kuml Aarbog f. Jysk Ark. Selskab*, Aarhus, 83-116.

—— (1960) Comment on Chenopodium as a food plant in Prehistory. *Ber. d. geobot. Forschungsinst. Rubel*, Zürich, *31*, 16-19.

Hillman, G. C. (1972) Archaeo-botanical studies (Aşvan 1971), under Recent Archaeological Research in Turkey. *Anatolian Studies 22*, 17-19.

—— (1973) Crop husbandry and food production: modern models for the interpretation of plant remains. *Anatolian Studies 23*, 241-4.

—— (1978) On the origins of domestic rye – Secale cereale: the finds from aceramic Can Hasan III in Turkey. *Anatolian Studies 28*, 157-74.

—— (1981) Crop husbandry: evidence from macroscopic remains, in 'The Neolithic' (A. G. Smith), in *The Environment in British Prehistory* (eds I. G. Simmonds & M. J. Tooley) 183-91. London: Duckworth.

—— (in press) Evidence for Spelt kilning at Catsgore in Somerset, in *Excavations at Catsgore* (ed. R. H. Leech). Bristol: CRAAGS.

—— (forthcoming, i) Crop husbandry at Cefn Graeanog, in R. B. White *et al.* (*op. cit.*).

—— (forthcoming, ii) Traditional processing of grain crops in Anatolia: models for interpeting plant remains. *J. Arch. Sci.* (probably).

—— (forthcoming, iii) Crop processing at 3rd century AD Wilderspool, in *Excavations at Wilderspool 1966-1968* (eds J. Hinchliffe & J. H. Williams). Cheshire County Council monograph.

—— (forthcoming, iv) Iron Age crops at Court Wood Enclosure, Dyved, in Excavations at Pembrey Hillfort (ed. G. Williams). *The Carmarthenshire Antiquary 16*.

Hillman, G. C. & A. Milles (in preparation) A burnt barley store from Late Neolithic Arran, in *Arran Excavations* (ed. J. Barber). Soc. Antiq. Scotland, Monograph Series (5?).

Hubbard, R. N. L. B. (1975) Assessing the botanical component of human palaeo-economies. *Bull. Inst. Arch. London 12*, 197-205.

—— (1976a) On the strength of the evidence for prehistoric crop processing activities. *J. Arch. Sci. 3*, 257-65.

—— (1976b) Crops and climate in prehistoric Europe. *World Arch. 8*, 159-68.

—— (1980) Development of Agriculture in Europe and the Near East, evidence from quantitative studies. *Econ. Bot. 34*, 51-67.

—— (in preparation) Report on plant remains from Tell Medhur, Iraq.

Jessen, K. & H. Helbaek (1944) Cereals in Great Britain and Ireland in prehistoric and early historic times. *Kongelige Danske Videnskabernes Selskab 3*(2), 1-68.

Jones, G. E. M. (1979) *An analysis of the plant remains from Assiros Toumba.* M.Phil. thesis, Dept of Archaeology, Univ. Cambridge.

—— (1981a) The carbonised plant remains, in *Meare Village West*,

1979 (eds B. J. Orme *et al.*). *Somerset Levels Papers 7* (ed. J. M. Coles).

—— (1981b) Crop processing at Assiros Toumba. *Zeitschrift f. Archäologie.*

—— (forthcoming) A note on some cereal and pulse remains from Geometric Iolkos, Thessaly. *Anthropoloka.*

Jones, H. L. (1923) *The Geography of Strabo* (with an English translation), vol.II. London: Heinemann, Loeb Classical Library.

Jones, M. K. (1978) The plant remains, in *The excavation of an Iron Age settlement, Bronze Age ring ditch and Roman features at Ashville Trading Estate, Abingdon, Oxfordshire, 1974-76* (ed. M. Parrington). CBA Research Report No. 28.

—— (in press, i) The development of crop husbandry, in *The Environment of man from the Iron Age to the Anglo-Saxon period* (eds M. K. Jones & G. W. Dimbleby). BAR British Series.

—— (in press, ii) The plant remains, in *Excavations at Barton Court Farm, Oxon.* (ed. D. Miles). CBA Research Report.

—— (forthcoming) in *Excavations at Danebury* (B. Cunliffe).

—— (in preparation) *The archaeological and ecological implications of selected arable plant assemblages in Britain.* Ph.D. thesis in preparation for the Botany School, Oxford.

Kirinde, S. P. W. (1975) *Sowing date effects on the crop physiology of wheat.* Ph.D. thesis, Department of Agricultural Botany, University of Reading.

Körber-Grohne, U. (1967) *Geobotanische Untersuchungen auf der Feddersen Wierde* (2 vols). Wiesbaden: Steiner. (For Niedersächsisches Landesinstitut für Marschen- und Wurtenforschung in Wilhelmshaven.)

Kelly, R. S. (forthcoming) The excavation of a Medieval farmstead at Cefn Graeanog, Clynnog, Gwynedd. *Bul. Board of Celtic Studies.*

Kühn, F. (1970) Das Ausklingen der Emmerkultur in der Tschechoslowakei. *Acta Univ. Agric. Brno* ser. A, *18*, 587-94.

Leser, P. (1931) *Entstehung und Verbreitung des Pfluges.* Munster: Anthropos-Bibliothek, III, 3.

Markham, G. (1631-38) *A Way to get Wealth.* London: R. Jackson.

—— (1631) *The Whole Art of Husbandry.* London: Jackson.

—— (1636) *The Country Farm.* London: Jackson.

Maurizio, A. (1927) *Die Geschichte unserer Pflanzennahrung von den Urzeiten bis zu Gegenwart.* Berlin: Parey.

Monk, M. A. (1977) *The plant economy and agriculture of the Anglo-Saxons in southern England: with particular reference to the 'Mart' settlements at Southampton and Winchester.* Unpublished M.Phil. thesis, Dept Arch., University of Southampton.

Moritz, L. A. (1957) *Grain mills and flour in classical antiquity.* Oxford Univ. Press.

Murphy, P. L. (1976) *Early agriculture and environment on the Hampshire chalklands: circa 800 B.C.-400 A.D.* M.Phil. thesis, Dept Archaeology, Univ. Southampton.

Payne, S. (1972) On the interpretation of bone samples from archaeological sites, in *Papers in economic prehistory* (ed. E. S. Higgs). Cambridge Univ. Press.

Percival, J. (1921) *The wheat plant: a monograph.* London: Duckworth.

Pierpoint Johnson, C. (1862) *The useful plants of Great Britain.* London: W. Kent.

Reynolds, P. (in press) New approaches to old problems, in *The Environment of man from the Iron Age to Anglo-Saxon period* (eds M. K. Jones & G. W. Dimbleby). BAR British Series.

Rickett, R. J. (1975) *Post-Roman and Medieval Drying Kilns.* Unpublished BA dissertation, University College, Cardiff, Dept of Archaeology.

Salzman, L. F. (1923) *Medieval English Industries*, as cited by Rickett (1975).

Sherrat, A. (1980) Water, soil and seasonality of early cereal cultivation. *World Archaeol. 11*, 313-30.

Watson, D. J., G. N. Thorne & S. A. W. French (1963) Analysis of growth and yield of winter and spring wheats. *Annals of Botany 27*, 1-22.

White, K. D. (1970) *A bibliography of Roman agriculture.* University of Reading publn.

—— (1971) *Roman Farming.*

White, R. B. *et al.* (forthcoming) Cefn Graeanog II – an Iron Age, Roman and post-Roman farmstead in Arvon, Gwynedd, in *Cambrian Monographs and Collections* (ed. G. Boon). Cardiff: Cambrian Arch. Ass.

Wyss, R. (1969) Wirtschaft und Technik, in *Archäologie der Schweiz II – der jungere Steinzeit.*

—— (1971) Die Egolzwiler Kultur, Guide no. 12 of the *Schwizerische Landesmuseum.*

Zhukovskii, P. M. (1933) *Türkiyenin Zirai Bünyesi*, Ankara, Türkiye Şeker Fabrikalari A.Ş., Neşriyati no. 20. (Turkish translation of the Russian original: *Zemledelicheskaya Tutsiya*, Leningrad.)

Discussion

DR NASH raised the matter of the grain yields obtained at the Butser experimental farm. He drew attention to the good yields obtained and indicated his surprise that this should be so, in view of the general impression gained from historial literature of the generally poor crop yields occurring in early times. Would it not be desirable to carry out precisely the same plot experiments, using the same sources of seed, on a number of sites in Britain, to cover differences in both soil and climate? Although he could not speak on behalf of University departments of agriculture or Colleges of agriculture he felt that if approaches were made to a number of these bodies then cooperation might be forthcoming. Dr Nash suggested that his colleague, Graham Russell, who is presently engaged in research into cereal yields, might care to comment on this matter of grain yields (*see* Appendix A to Dr Nash's paper, for five-year average yields of grain crops in Great Britain).

DR RUSSELL also emphasized the desirability of setting up trials on different soil types by referring to the slides presented by a previous speaker, which showed how the yields from unfertilised soils declined with time at Rothamsted and Woburn. Yields from the more nutrient-rich and water-retentive Rothamsted soils had not declined as rapidly as those on the sandy Woburn soil.

Some caution should be exercised in interpreting the results of experiments with small plots. It is well known that yields from such plots can be higher than those from larger fields, not only because plants on the edge can intercept more light and absorb more nutrients but also because greater care can be taken in cultivating, sowing, weeding and harvesting a small plot. The former effect is unlikely to cause an increase in yield of more than ten per cent and should be negligible if the outer rows are omitted from the harvest. If pre-historic fields are of a similar size to the plots, the plot yield should be a good estimate of their yield. However, if the exercise is taken a stage further and the grain produced by a community is calculated, account must be taken of the land between the plots, which presumably produces no cereal yield. Consequently the output per hectare of farmland is less than the output per hectare of plot.

It may be helpful when trying to interpret the results of field trials on early cereals to consider the potential yields of the present day and to think how the early cereals differ from the modern types. Using current varieties and techniques the *potential* yield of wheat in England is calculated to be near twelve tonnes per hectare at fifteen per cent moisture content (Austin 1978) and the not inconsiderable number of farmers achieving in excess of ten tonnes per hectare shows that, with good husbandry, modern varieties and farming systems are well matched. The yields achieved by the average farmer are, however, less than half the potential, for a number of reasons including, late sowing, soil acidity, fungal disease, weed infestation and loss of grain during harvest. Maximum yields of grain are likely to be obtained when the wheat is sown in autumn and matures late, so that the leaf canopy has a long season during which it is actively photosynthesising and producing material to form and fill the grains. The modern farmer looks on late maturity with disfavour, as it can lead to high loss of grain during harvest in the poorer weather of autumn, and disrupt the cultivations and sowing of the ground for the following year's crop.

Compared with modern varieties, earlier types of cereals are likely to have been better adapted to grow in conditions of drought, low fertility and disease (Harlan 1975). Percival (1921) noted that emmer can grow in a warm, dry climate and is more or less immune to rust fungi while spelt is one of the hardiest of cereals and can survive drought and extreme cold as well as being resistant to smut, bunt, rust and bird attack. Although they are probably more sensitive to the nutrient content of the soil, even modern varieties are remarkably tolerant of poor climatic conditions. In the drought year of 1976, for example, wheat yields in England were only about twenty-two per cent less than average (Roy, Hough and Starr 1978). Part of the reason why early cereals were more resistant to environmental stresses is probably that, compared with their modern counterparts, they produced more roots and stored more material in their stems (Evans and Dunstone 1970). The increased rooting enables the plants to take up water and nutrients more effectively, while the material stored in the straw can be re-mobilised and translocated to the ear if photosynthesis is reduced by adverse conditions. In good years, however, yields will be less than those of similar plants with less root and straw. During the present century an increase in harvest index (the weight of grain divided by the weight of straw and grain) from about thirty to fifty per cent has been one of the causes of the dramatic rise in yields of wheat in Britain (Austin *et al.* 1980). We can therefore hypothesise that early types of cereal should have lower (but more consistent) yields of grain than present-day varieties. Percival (1921) gave figures which can be used to calculate that *good* yields of spelt and emmer in Central Europe were in the region of 3.5 tonnes per hectare during the early years of this century. This figure is similar to the typical yield at Butser. The very poor yields sometimes recorded at Butser were no doubt due to drought, exacerbated by the shallow depth of soil overlying the chalk.

REFERENCES

Austin, R. B. (1978) Actual and potential yields of wheat and barley in the United Kingdom. *ADAS Q. Rev. 29*, 76-87.

Austin, R. B., *et al.* (1980) Genetic improvements in winter wheat yields since 1900 and associated physiological changes. *J. Agric. Sci.*, Camb. *94*, 675-89.

Evans, L. T. & R. L. Dunstone (1970) Some physiological aspects of evolution in wheat. *Aust. J. Biol. Sci. 23*, 725-41.

Harlan, J. R. (1975) *Crops and Man.* Madison: American Society of Agronomy.

Percival, J. (1921) *The Wheat Plant.* London: Duckworth.

Roy, G. R., M. N. Hough & J. R. Sarr (1978) Some agricultural effects of the drought of 1975-76 in the United Kingdom. *Weather 33*, 64-74.

PETER REYNOLDS. The remarks of Dr Nash are welcomed in that they indicate the surprise normally evinced by such crop yield figures, but more particularly because he touched upon the pressing need for proliferation of the Butser Ancient Farm research programmes onto different soil types in divergent bioclimatic zones. This indeed is the long-term aim, and any ways of furthering this purpose with financial support and the necessary facilities will be most welcome.

Dr Russell's remarks were more specific in nature and questioned the acquisition of results with cautionary references to 'the edge effect' and the need for comparative modern varieties. Naturally the results are acquired with the accepted statistical designs of cropping trials as advised by research agronomists. Not only is the edge effect eliminated by ignoring the perimeter of the crop for a depth of at least one metre, but also great care is taken not to distort the crop yield by horticultural intensity of attention. Samples are isolated by the use of random number tables and are processed far beyond the normally accepted limits. There is, however, an interesting paradox to be pointed. Modern hybrid wheats have been developed specifically for modern method farming, dependent upon high nitrogen input allied with intensive use of herbicides and pesticides. This end itself is a mark of the great technical skill of plant breeding organisations, but it must be emphasised that the development is interdependent upon the 'given' nature of the system. Remove one element, especially the nitrogen input, and the picture changes quickly and radically. In addition this system is having a particular effect upon the nature of the soil structure. The fibre content is reduced to extremely low levels, which in turn reduces the crumb size of the soil. Provided the system is maintained compaction of soil is achieved by increased machine utilisation and results maintained. The long-term effect is another matter. The basic point of referring to these aspects of modern farming is to question the validity of comparing and contrasting modern hybrid versus stable species. It would seem to be unfair to both, but particularly to the modern hybrid. Results would indicate that the modern hybrid fares less well in a competitive state as opposed to a monocrop, whereas the early varieties are seemingly able to sustain quite massive arable weed infestation and still return, unexpectedly within the terms of reference of modern systems, high yields. Nonetheless, within the trials at the Ancient Farm the best of the modern hybrids available are used as standard elements for direct comparative purposes.

One final reflection upon Dr Russell's valuable and supportive comments needs to be recorded. It is observed that the wheat yield figures have risen dramatically during the past century given the new varieties allowing the harvest index (q.v.) to benefit by decrease in straw and root stock. Perhaps it is important to consider the market for the product in this connection. One rather suspects that in previous centuries, even if the modern higher-yielding varieties were to have been available, their use would have been limited simply because the straw itself was a commercial product and its very length and strength were critical factors in its value. Today thatched roofs are not the norm, although their frequency and basic repair requirement are sufficient to reward the grower of suitable straw stocks a greater cash return than the seed itself.

There is, undoubtedly, a great deal more to be learned from the early varieties, especially in terms of their potential modern value as well as in seeking to establish valid parameters of their productivity for the remote past. The need to proliferate the Butser trials cannot be over-emphasised. The author would welcome any participatory programmes.

Part Two
Animal Husbandry

Aspects of Cattle Husbandry

A. J. LEGGE

The proceedings of this conference showed a feeling among the speakers that early agriculture in Britain had a level of organisation and attainment of a higher order than has commonly been perceived. This view fits very well with my own studies on early animal husbandry, where patterns of efficiency can be detected that may be paralleled in modern practice. A picture of ill-fed and poorly managed beasts sits ill with my own interpretations, and with the data presented elsewhere in this volume. Yet to set against that note of optimism, it must also be said that the material available for study can hardly be described as adequate, in that so little animal bone from the Neolithic and Bronze Ages comes from domestic sites. For the purposes of this paper, a 'domestic' site is taken to be a site at which the commonplace daily tasks of arable and animal husbandry are conducted and adjacent to which would be the fields and pastures used by the people living there. This is not intended to exclude seasonal encampments whether they be of those archaeologically elusive pastoralists or seasonal herding camps of otherwise sedentary groups, but is rather to provide a contrast to sites of a 'ceremonial' nature where gatherings might have been periodic for a social or ritual purpose.

For the earlier Neolithic, most of the available animal bone comes from Windmill Hill (Grigson 1965) or Hambledon Hill (Legge, in progress). When complete, the identified animal bones from the Hambledon Hill/Stepleton Complex (Mercer 1980) should number some 8,000–10,000. In the later Neolithic, a substantial fauna is available from Durrington Walls (Harcourt 1971), and a smaller number from Mount Pleasant (Harcourt 1979). From both early and late Neolithic, the samples available number about 12,000; other sites of these periods (some of which may be domestic) have small samples due either to poor preservation or poor recovery in early excavations. For the Bronze Age the picture is hardly less bleak. Recent excavations at Grimes Graves by the Department of the Environment (Mercer 1981) and the British Museum (Longworth and Sieveking, forthcoming) have produced substantial domestic animal remains of the Middle Bronze Age (Legge 1981; Legge, Kyllo and Stevens forthcoming). From this, it is evident that the larger Neolithic faunas represent a few sites within a few square miles of South-West Britain, and it is likely that Grimes Graves (c. 1000 BC) represents the *earliest* domestic site in Britain with good data relating to the subsistence economy.

Yet recent discoveries have increased the number of known causewayed camps to over thirty (Palmer 1976) which argues for both a substantial human presence and a high degree of social organisation. The interpretation of function for causewayed camps has been varied; my first interpretations of the Hambledon/Stepleton data does not support the 'functional' arguments for these sites being cattle enclosures. However, I will begin by summarising my findings from the plant and animal remains from Grimes Graves, and then provide some inferences about practices in the Neolithic period. This has the advantage of beginning with a domestic asemblage, and using that as a point from which to discuss the animal remains at sites which are probably of a social purpose.

The two middens excavated at Grimes Graves do not appear to be connected with the earlier flint mining at this site. The bones and seeds recovered from the DoE excavations have been described (Legge 1981); the reader is referred to that source for detail beyond this short account. Material from the British Museum excavations has been identified, and the findings tabulated. This will be published as part of the British Museum series of fascicles concerned with that site. Sufficient work has been done to confirm that the two midden samples are very similar in the husbandry patterns that they show. Grimes Graves in the Bronze Age has every appearance of a farming settlement, not connected with flint mining. Barley, wheat and peas occur as carbonised seeds in the midden; the sheep bones indicate that settlement was year-round, and not seasonal in nature.

The good bone preservation in the middens allow quite detailed studies of some important aspects of the assemblage. The fauna is made up of cattle (52.5%), sheep and goat (31.9%), pig (5.7%), red deer (4.1%), horse (3.3%), and roe deer (2.5%). Dogs, and some other smaller mammal and bird species were present. The cattle were represented by a high proportion of mandibles, and a rather low proportion of limb-bones. The study showed that nearly half the cattle were killed at only a few weeks or months of age, and about seventy per cent by the age of roughly one year. This means that little of the bone was 'fused' (that is with the articulation and shaft joined by solid bone, after growth is complete) when discarded into the midden and appears then to have been enthusiastically consumed by dogs. Yet while dogs ate much of the juvenile bone (small coprolites of crushed bone were found on the site) the mandibles were little chewed. Most show some gnawing on the ramus or symphysis, but the dogs seemed to be reluctant to hazard their own teeth by chewing cattle teeth.

The proportions of animals given above are based upon the surviving mandibles.

More detailed attention is now being given to the study of age-classes among animals killed at archaeological sites as shown by the mandibles. Payne (1973) has provided a detailed study of this type based upon the tooth eruption and wear in modern sheep and goats, but we do not yet have data of this quality for cattle. For the Grimes Graves study, I used the system of ageing devised by Higham (1967) which was based upon data assembled by Silver (1963). This method relies most on tooth eruption stages, but does not allow the detailed consideration of ageing by tooth wear in the older cattle. In spite of these limitations, it is obvious that the cattle at Grimes Graves were subject to a very high rate of juvenile culling (figure 1), and relatively few lived on to join the adult herd.

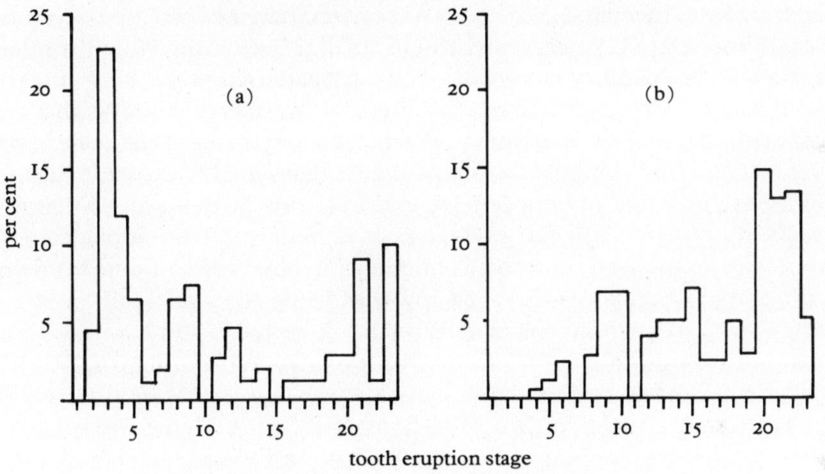

Figure 1. Slaughter patterns in cattle from the sites of (a) Grimes Graves and (b) Troldebjerg (Higham and Message 1969). Stage 5 marks the eruption of the first permanent molar at about six months of age

In his earlier work on animal husbandry, Higham (1967, Higham and Message 1969) emphasized that the age classes shown in the cull should be considered in relation to the proportions of the sexes surviving into the adult herd. A brief reflection on this point will show that the animals culled at early ages will combine 'natural' mortality and killing due to the policy determined by the husbandman. The surviving animals will therefore reflect, in the proportions of males and females, some aspects of this policy. These animals may be most easily 'sexed' from bones such as the pelvis, that seldom survive well in archaeological assemblages. As with most things in archaeology, we must do what we can with the material that survives. Higham and Message (op. cit.) observe two groups in the cattle bones from the site of Troldebjerg in Denmark. One group is of larger animals, and the other of smaller body-size. They consider five ways in which this distribution might occur:

1. Domestic cattle present, with the bison *Bison bonasus*.
2. Domestic cattle present, with *Bos primigenius*.
3. Domestic cattle raised on two planes of nutrition.
4. Males and females of one cattle breed.
5. Two breeds of domestic cattle.

Their detailed discussion of these possibilities need not be repeated here; their conclusions argue for one of the last two possibilities. The data supports number 4 as the most likely; if 5 is preferred, it requires that the two breeds of cattle should lack sexual dimorphism. I have used a similar approach in the study of Grimes Graves and other sites to examine the proportions of the sexes of cattle surviving into the adult herd. For Grimes Graves, figure 2 shows the dimensions of one bone (distal articulation of the metatarsal) plotted as a scatter diagram. Two groups can be seen, one relatively numerous and of smaller body-size, while the other group has few cattle of larger size. The same pattern is present in a range of bones and teeth of cattle from the site, and my interpretation is that the differing degrees of robustness reflects females (smaller) and males (larger). The bone dimensions also suggest that females exceed males in number, in ratios of between 4:1 and 6:1; this further argues that the *majority of those killed at early ages were males*. The economic pattern that may be inferred from this is one in which the main outputs from the cattle herd were calves and aged cows, with the occasional bull or steer. For meat production, this pattern would be unikely, and I would argue that a third output was of interest – that of milk. You could parallel this pattern closely at modern dairy farms, though now the calves are likely to be raised on artificial feeding. The farmers at Grimes Graves did not have that option, and appear to have valued the milk output more highly. Elsewhere (Legge 1981) I have noted that similar patterns occur within Higham's data (1967, 1968) from sites of the Swiss Neolithic, while sites of the Swiss Bronze Age (and Troldebjerg) show patterns more closely related to meat production. Higham (op. cit.) suggested that these were different patterns of meat production. I do not agree with that conclusion, and have suggested that dairy husbandry was characteristic of the earlier Swiss sites, but with more extensive land-use and a 'meat emphasis' in the Swiss Bronze Age. I think it likely that environmental factors underlay the policies followed (Legge, op. cit.).

The lack of Neolithic 'domestic' animal bones in Britain was outlined above. For the causewayed camps and henges such material is important in interpreting the function of these sites. The Hambledon fauna consists of cattle (55%), pig (25%), sheep and goat (15%), and with red deer, roe deer and dog making the remaining five per cent. The Stepleton fauna is very similar (though smaller in number), as is the 'pre-enclosure' fauna from Windmill Hill (Jope 1965). The primary ditch fills from Windmill

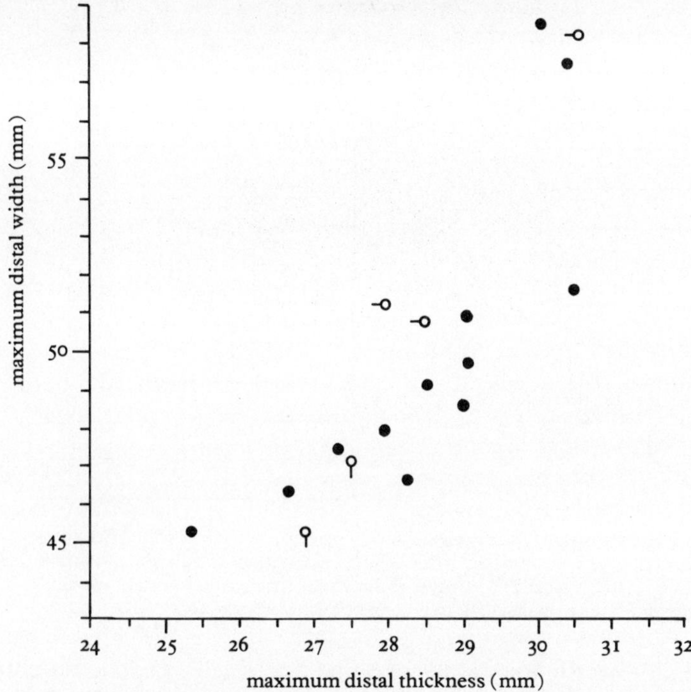

Figure 2. Scatter diagram of distal metatarsal (width of articulation) in cattle from Grimes Graves (Legge 1981). The open circles show bones with slight damage where one dimension is estimated. The known dimension is indicated by short lines.

Hill showed rather higher proportions of sheep, and fewer pigs.

The animal bones from Hambledon Hill do not show the degree of fragmentation commonly seen in 'domestic' faunas, and parts of limbs occur quite commonly in articulation. The lower hind limb of cattle is one such, with the distal tibia, astragalus, calcaneum, navicular-cuboid and proximal metatarsal being found together, and making up the 'heel' joint. This feature has been found in other causewayed camp ditches, such as at Windmill Hill and in the Neolithic ditches of Maiden Castle. Although I cannot yet say how common this is at Hambledon Hill, it further indicates that the 'normal' pattern of bone breaking and dispersal of bones is not common at causewayed camps, and probably not at henges. For Durrington Walls, Harcourt (1971) records an 'astonishingly high number of entire, almost perfect, pig bones' and that 'all members of the skeleton of cattle and pigs were about equally represented with the exception of jaws, teeth and skull'. Harcourt (1979) makes a similar observation for the large mammals of Mount Pleasant, another Dorset henge.

For the Hambledon Hill and Grimes Graves faunas, I have used the method proposed by Brain (1967, 1976) in his investigations of bone

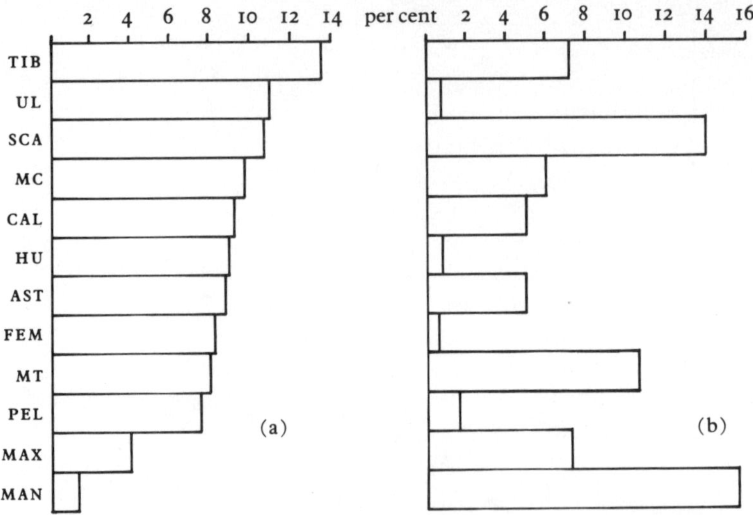

Figure 3. Survival of cattle bones from the sites of (a) Hambledon Hill (Legge, in progress) and (b) Grimes Graves (Legge 1981). The abbreviations indicate, in order, the tibia, ulna, scapula, metacarpal, calcaneum, humerus, astragalus, femur, metatarsal, pelvis, maxilla and mandible.

accumulation in the early caves of South Africa (fig. 3). The Hambledon Hill animal bones are plotted as the percentage that each is of the total, and then placed in descending order of frequency. The Grimes Graves bones are then plotted in the same sequence as the Hambledon material. For Hambledon, the tibia emerges as the most common bone at about fourteen per cent, then the radius and ulna at ten and a half per cent, and so on down to the mandible at less than two per cent. Grimes Graves, by comparison, is deficient in certain bones, especially the ulna, humerus, femur and pelvis, while the mandible and maxilla are well represented. Harcourt (1971) gives for Durrington Walls similar proportions (for a smaller range of bones) to those from Hambledon Hill, with the humerus, radius, tibia and femur all being common. Comparisons between causewayed camps and henges on the one hand, and Grimes Graves as a domestic site on the other, are bound to be oblique at best; the high percentage of juvenile bone destroyed at the latter site will depress the frequencies of limb bones, while juvenile mandibles are well represented. Even so, the different patterns emerging do argue for periods of high meat consumption at the causewayed camps with a lower degree of bone processing in consequence, rather than for a domestic assemblage of bones. Some support for this may be gained from the plant remains from Hambledon Hill and Stepleton. Although this part of the study is at a very preliminary stage, I am struck by the relative frequency of emmer wheat over other species, and the lack of associated weed seeds and spikelet fragments. This looks to me like clean, 'processed' grain being taken to the site, a point with which Gordon Hillman (see this volume) is in agreement.

Turning to a more detailed study of the animal bones from the Neolithic sites, the population structure is of special interest. So far, the age structure cannot be calculated from these bones in any detail. Mandibles at Hambledon Hill are uncommon (figure 2), as they are at Windmill Hill (Jope 1965), Durrington (Harcourt 1971), and Mount Pleasant (Harcourt 1979). We must examine the representation of the sexes to gain insight to this problem. The practice I have used at Grimes Graves is to plot such dimensions on 'scatter diagrams' rather than the more common histograms of a single factor. With histograms, one dimension (commonly the width of an articulation) is plotted in size classes, usually of 1 mm, against the number of occurrences within each size class. Such diagrams can be misleading, not the least in that the chosen intervals of plotting can influence the patterns that emerge. The policy of 'rounding up' or 'rounding down' of fractional measurements to 1 mm classes may create (or eliminate) small gaps or peaks in the distribution. However, this form of representation is the most commonly available, and is used with some reluctance here. Much worse is the common practice of providing only the range of size from largest to smallest measurement with sample number; such data cannot be further investigated, and are of little use. A danger associated with this practice is that 'mean' dimensions for populations of similar age may differ, when *no more than the proportions of the sexes differ* from populations of the same size. For example, the mean dimension for the Troldebjerg sample is 61.18 mm for the width of the distal metacarpal (figure 4b) while that for Windmill Hill (4c) is 56.14 mm, yet the populations represented have the same range of size.

A further problem lies in the fact that sexing by such measurements has been questioned. Uerpmann (1972) regards the work of Higham and Message (1969) as 'an exceptional case', where the apparent success in the sexing of cattle metacarpals is explained by them being an 'isolated island cattle population'. He further notes 'It is known that considerable size reduction of domesticated cattle involves a decrease in sexual dimorphism', and that there is 'no adequate basis for distinguishing between male and female metapodia . . .'. For at least north European cattle, I do not agree with this observation. The distribution of sizes in northern cattle populations (mainly Britain) are shown in figures 4 and 5. In each case there *may* be a mixture of domestic and wild cattle; this possibility is considered below. For Star Carr (fig. 4a) all the cattle are taken as *Bos primigenius* and wild, though the variability of that population has been noted (Frazer and King 1954). In a consideration of this cattle population, Jewell (1963) attributed the smaller cattle to cows, and the larger to bulls. The total range in size represented is slightly ambiguous; Jewell (op. cit.) shows in his figure 18 a range of metacarpal dimensions from 60–86 mm, while his figure 20 gives 63–84 mm. Frazer and King (1954) also give a

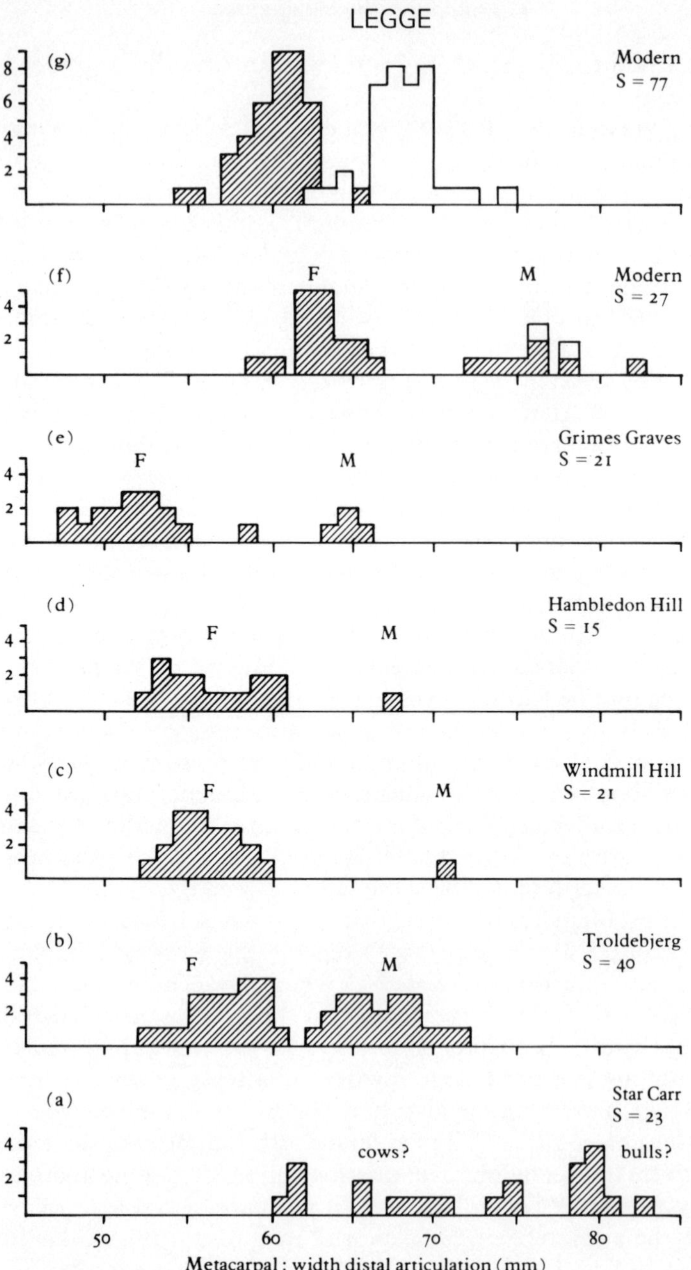

Figure 4. Metacarpal dimensions for cattle from five sites, with two modern samples. Star Carr (a) and modern sample (f) with designations following Jewell 1963; Troldebjerg (b) from Higham and Message 1969; Windmill Hill (c) Grigson 1975; Hambledon Hill (d) Legge in progress; Grimes Graves (e) Legge 1981. Sample (g) of modern Aberdeen Angus redrawn after Higham and Message 1969. In (f) and (g) the open boxes are castrated males. M and F indicate the male and female ends of the range by my interpretation. S = sample size.

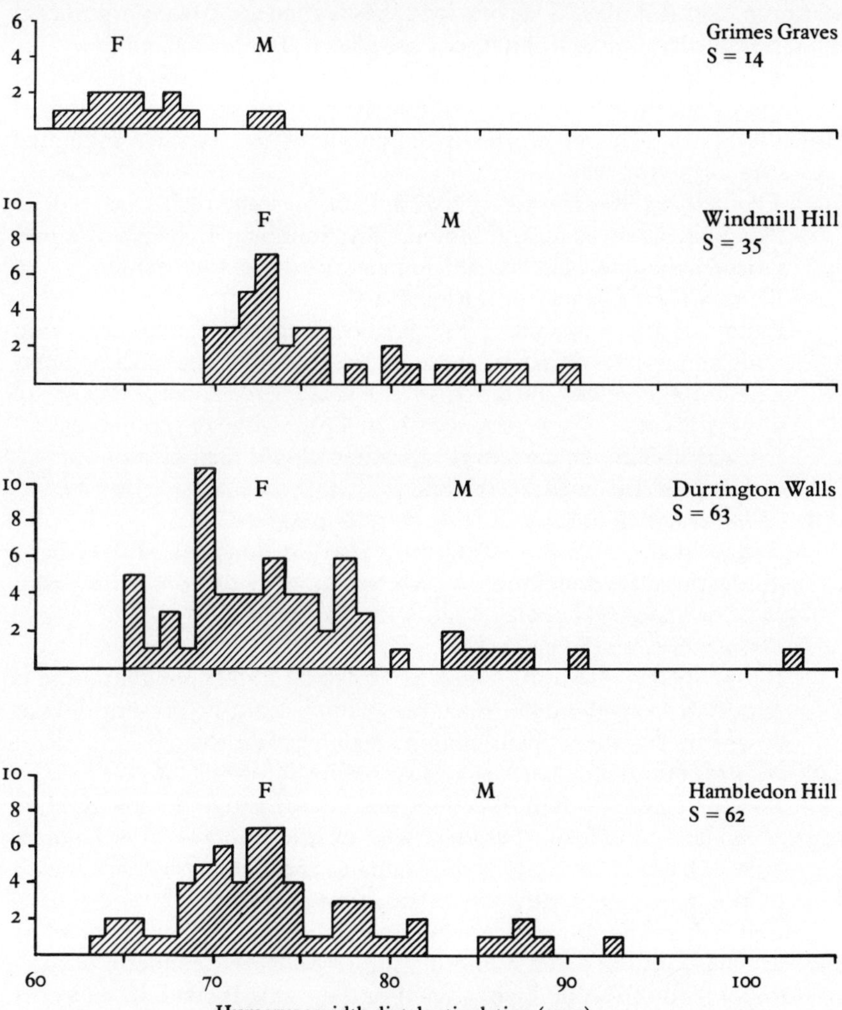

Figure 5. Width of articulation from distal humerus of cattle from four sites. Sources as for figure 4, with also Durrington Walls (Harcourt 1971). The diagram shows dimensions plotted in 1 mm size classes against the number of specimens falling within a class. F = female end of range, M = male end of range, S = sample size.

63–84 mm range in the original Star Carr monograph. This is taken as the correct figure, but as only the range of size and number are given I have used Jewell's data on these animals (figure 4a here), but with the anomalous dimension omitted. The probable range in size for this population is 21 mm. The degree of overlap (if present) of males and females cannot be predicted from the diagram. Size change in *Bos primigenius* from the eighth to the fourth millennium BC cannot easily be determined from the scattered later samples. Grigson (1969) has argued against any significant *reduction* in size in Flandrian Age (Post-glacial) *Bos primigenius.*

The distribution of cattle dimensions in the Neolithic and Bronze Age sites must therefore be considered in relation to the possible presence of large wild cattle. The remaining histograms in figure 4 can be commented on in the following way:

(4b) *Troldebjerg.* Redrawn after Higham and Message 1969.
Range in size = 20 mm. A bimodal distribution; Higham's interpretation is that male and female domestic cattle are represented.

(4c) *Windmill Hill.* Data from Grigson 1965.
Range in size = 19 mm. This may be a bimodal distribution, with male and female domestic cattle, or the isolated large specimen may be *Bos primigenius.* In this case, the smaller animals are one sex of domestic cattle, or two sexes with an 8-mm range of size of metacarpal width. The isolated large specimen would then be a *Bos primigenius* cow; no bulls are evident.

(4d) *Hambledon Hill.* From Legge, work in progress.
Range in size = 16 mm. Observations as for Windmill Hill, either a domestic cattle population with 9 mm range, and a *Bos primigenius* cow, or male and female of one domestic breed.

(4e) *Grimes Graves* (Legge 1981)
Range in size = 19 mm. A smaller body size in this population, as is expected from the date. *Bos primigenius* might be present only as cows; alternatively, male and female domestic cattle.

(4f) *Sample* of modern cattle of known sex from Jewell (1963)
Range in size = 24 mm. White boxes on the histograms are steers.

(4g) *A modern sample* of Aberdeen Angus cattle; redrawn after Higham 1961. The sample contains only females and steers; these are shown by the white areas within the histograms.

The distributions shown by the metacarpal widths can be supported by similar data from the distal humerus (figure 5). Here, samples are larger in number, though from fewer sites. For the original Star Carr data only the range of dimensions is given, which is large, from 70 to 104 mm. Thus the smallest *Bos primigenius* cow falls within Neolithic populations, while the largest male is larger than the entire Neolithic distribution by about 13 mm, except for one large specimen at Durrington Walls, a likely wild male. The humerus diagrams show a very similar pattern to the metacarpals in figure 4, with a numerous group of smaller size, and a less numerous scatter of larger size. These are unlikely to be wild males, but may be wild females *and* domestic males. The alternative view, suggesting that all the domestic cattle fall into my 'female' group would firstly require little sexual dimorphism, and also the proposition that wild females were commonly taken, but males seldom. The small Grimes Graves sample shows a bimodal distribution also, and my interpretation of these diagrams is that they reflect samples in which male and female domestic cattle are represented by the two groups, and in which the females greatly outnumber males. Some further data supports my interpretation; Caroline Grigson (Grigson, in press) has re-examined the horn-cores of cattle from Windmill Hill, comparing these with European *Bos primigenius*. The latter show a marked bimodal distribution in size, with some bias towards males, while horn-cores from Windmill Hill show certainly six (possibly up to 13) males, and 57 (possibly 61) females, a ratio of females to males of between 6:1 and 10:1. Figures 4 and 5 give quite good separation into 'female' and 'male' groups; this might be anticipated where only *selected* bulls survive; in economics where all males survive to 'meat weight' at least, a greater degree of overlap between the two groups is to be expected.

It is possible that the groups of cattle interpreted from the histograms as females might include males that had been castrated (steers). The distal humerus of cattle fuses at an age of 12–18 months in modern cattle (Silver 1963), and animals killed some time after this time will still be 'unfused' on other limb bones. The metacarpal and metatarsal of cattle fuse, respectively, at 2–2½ years and 2¼–3 years (Silver, op. cit.). Yet the histograms of metacarpal size (figure 4) show similar distributions to those of the humerus (figure 5), and this is at a time when greater robustness in steers would be expected. Higham's sample of recent Aberdeen Angus cattle (figure 4g here, redrawn from Higham 1967) shows good discrimination on metacarpal *width*, with slight overlap, and it is likely that these animals did not survive under modern husbandry long beyond that time. For Troldebjerg (Higham 1969) the separation into two groups is good, yet it seems unlikely on practical grounds that the males there survived all as 'entire' bulls. It may well be that the measurement of articular width does not provide an absolute distinction between male and female cattle where castration was practised, though either the histogram or scatter diagram shows that the two sexes are present; the range in size of the modern sample in figure 4g may also be noted.

The histograms for British cattle populations in the Neolithic and Bronze Ages do not indicate the presence of many males, either entire or as steers, and are negatively skewed towards the 'female' end of the range. Additional examples can be seen in Grigson (1965) for the phalanges of cattle, and in Harcourt (1971) for proximal radius, distal radius (among the latest of bones to fuse) and lower third molar.

My argument, therefore, is that the majority of cattle killed at the causewayed camps were female, and that these animals represent the *surplus* available from economics based at lowland (and undiscovered) Neolithic sites. Grimes Graves has a female bias in the adult herd, due to a dairy emphasis in the economy. I would argue that the same female bias at ceremonial sites can be taken to predict a dairy basis to cattle husbandry in the Neolithic of Britain, as in the Swiss Neolithic (Legge 1981). If young males were being carried on to an effective meat weight (as young adults) why do they not appear? I do not think that they are submerged in the female groups, even as castrated males; were this so, a bimodal distribution would be the exception. Is it possible that either calf bones seldom survive, or that the calves were being killed and eaten elsewhere, even in a different season to gatherings at the causewayed camps and henges?

Yet is there already a Neolithic domestic site with a dairy economy in Britain? It seems appropriate, for a Munro symposium held in Edinburgh, to seek a Scottish example. The site of Skara Brae has a rather scanty report on the animal bones (Watson 1931). The few measured cattle bones fall at the 'female' end of expected Neolithic cattle size, and although but 17 mandibles were described, 10 of these are from animals which were very young at death. This was advanced at the time, as 'autumn slaughter' thought to be due to shortages in winter fodder. Yet the killing of calves to take the milk for human use could be likened to autumn slaughtering, in that fodder needs for the animals are reduced while the food output to man will be increased.

This paper has presented an outline of some data from Grimes Graves with good evidence for a specialised form of dairy economy, and an interpretation that similar systems may be found in the Neolithic period. The discussion has entered certain rather technical points in the treatment of animal bone data, because of the recognised problems involved in their interpretation. Future excavations will provide a better test.

ACKNOWLEDGEMENTS

I wish to thank Dr Caroline Grigson for information on her forthcoming study of the Windmill Hill cattle horn cores. While we may have reached similar conclusions on some points discussed here, the responsibility for this article rests with the author.

REFERENCES

Brain, C. K. (1967) Hottentot food remains and their bearing on the interpretation of fossil bone assemblages. *Scientific Papers, Namib Res. Sta. 32*, 1-11.

—— (1976) Some principles in the interpretation of bone accumulations associated with man, in *Human Origins* (eds G. Ll. Isaac & E. R. McCown). Staples Press.

Frazer, F. C. & J. E. King (1954) Faunal remains, in *Excavations at Star Carr* (J. G. D. Clark). Cambridge University Press.

Grigson, C. (1965) Measurements of bones, horncores, antlers and teeth, in *Windmill Hill and Avebury* (ed. I. F. Smith). Oxford University Press.

—— (1969) The uses and limitations of differences in absolute size in the distinction between the bones of Aurochs (*Bos primigenius*) and Domestic Cattle (*Bos taurus*), in *The Domestication and Exploitation of Plants and Animals* (eds P. J. Ucko & G. W. Dimbleby). Duckworth.

Grigson (forthcoming) Sexing Neolithic cattle skulls and horncores, in *Age and Sex Structures of Domestic Animal Populations* (ed. R. Wilson).

Harcourt, R. A. (1971) Animal bones from Durrington Walls, in *Durrington Walls: Excavations 1966-1968* (G. J. Wainwright & I. H. Longworth). London: Rep. Res. Comm. Soc. Ants.

—— (1979) The animal bones, in *Mount Pleasant, Dorset: Excavations 1970-1971* (G. J. Wainwright). London: Rept. Res. Comm. Soc. Ants.

Higham, C. F. W. (1967) Stock rearing as a cultural factor in prehistoric Europe. *Proc. Prehist. Soc. 6*, 84-106.

—— (1968) Patterns of prehistoric economic exploitation on the Alpine Foreland, in *Vierteljarsschrift der Naturforschenden Gesellschaft in Zurich* (ed. A. E. Thomas). Jahrgang 113, Heft 1, 41-92. Zurich.

Higham, C. F. W. & M. Message (1969) An assessment of a prehistoric technique of bovine husbandry, in *Science in Archaeology* (ed. D. R. Bothwell & E. S. Higgs), 2nd ed. Thames and Hudson.

Jewell, P. (1963) Cattle from British archaeological sites, in *Man and Cattle* (eds A. E. Mourant & F. E. Zeuner). Occ. Paper Roy. Anth. Inst. 18.

Jope, M. (1965) Frequencies and age of species (faunal remains), in *Windmill Hill and Avebury* (ed. I. F. Smith). Oxford.

Legge, A. J. (1981) The agricultural economy, in *Excavations at Grimes Graves* (R. Mercer). HMSO.

Mercer, R. (1980) *Hambledon Hill: A Neolithic Landscape.* Edinburgh.

Palmer, R. (1976) Interrupted ditch enclosures in Britain: the use of aerial photography for comparative studies. *Proc. Prehist. Soc. 42*, 161-86.

Payne, S. (1973) Kill-off patterns in sheep and goats: the mandibles from Asvan Kale. *Anatolian Studies* XXIII, 283-303.

Silver, I. A. (1963) The ageing of domestic animals, in *Science in Archaeology* (ed. D. Brothwell & E. S. Higgs). Thames and Hudson.

Uerpmann, H-P. (1972) Animal bone finds and economic archaeology: a critical study of 'osteo-archaeological method'. *World Archaeology 4*, 307-22.

Watson, D. M. (1931) The animal bones, in *Skara Brae, a Pictish Village in Orkney* (V. G. Childe). Kegan Paul, Trench and Trubner.

Livestock Products: Skins and Fleeces

MICHAEL J. RYDER

THE ORIGIN AND HUSBANDRY OF BRITISH SHEEP

Wild sheep died out early in Britain, and so the first domestic sheep were introduced by Neolithic settlers, probably in skin boats (Johnstone 1964). The strictures on colonisation proposed by Case (1969) were not as limiting as he implied. The prior establishment of cultivation before the introduction of livestock would not have been essential since pastoralism can provide all requirements (Ryder 1981a). During the early Neolithic period, owing to possibly dense forest coverage, cattle and pigs were more numerous than sheep and goats, which probably grazed together. The sheep was then probably a 'house' animal enclosed in the settlement at night, which allowed intense selective breeding, e.g. for a finer fleece (Ryder 1981d).

Declining woodland allowed sheep to become predominant by the Bronze Age, and despite increasing evidence for enclosure (Fowler in this volume) their husbandry was probably nomadic, at any rate locally. Ethnographic evidence from recent pastoralists indicates that killing for meat is rare, and that, instead, milk products and blood were developed for food; see below, pp. 194–5. High infant mortality caused castration to be delayed, and coupled with the lack of enclosures led to animal contraception. Rams were fitted with a cloth or leather apron to prevent mating, and antiquity of the custom is suggested by its widespread distribution in Asia, Africa and Europe (Ryder 1981d).

Sheep continued to predominate during the Iron Age, although their smaller size means that they contributed less meat than did cattle. Settled mixed farming was established, and organised wool cloth manufacture appears to have begun. A major advance was the introduction of iron shears to remove the fleece. Previously the only way of obtaining wool was by plucking during the annual spring moult. Shears are common on Iron Age sites on the continent, but Harding (1974) implies that they were introduced into Britain by the Romans.

Ryder (1981a) questioned the assertion that in prehistoric times livestock could not be fed during the winter, so that all but breeding stock had to be killed each autumn, and the animals kept had to be housed. Ethnographic evidence suggests that natural increases are likely to have been too low to allow massive autumn killing, and a high proportion of young among archaeological remains could have come from natural deaths. Much Iron Age evidence, however, indicates the killing of mature animals.

Primitive domestic animals are likely to have been able to withstand winter better, and to have been more efficient at gaining nutriment from a limited diet, than are modern breeds. The feral Soay sheep on St Kilda provides a basis for the interpretation of archaeological remains. Only half of the ewes, and even fewer of the rams survive their first year, which could be interpreted as the preferential killing of young rams.

A lambing rate of eighty per cent and a lifespan of five years was postulated by Ryder (1981a) which means that all the ewe lambs surviving their first year would be required to replace the twenty per cent loss of older animals. Five ram replacements would leave only fifteen ram lambs or nineteen per cent of the lamb crop for 'autumn killing'. This means that the archaeological record would show seventy-three per cent bones from young. If the infant losses were reduced to thirty-three per cent the record would show seventy per cent young, and thirty per cent would be available for killing. But this can be regarded as a cropping process, and not a killing to reduce numbers. Even this small proportion of killing is unlikely before settlement since nomadic peoples kill only on special occasions.

Houses with individual animal stalls go back to the Neolithic on the continent (Waterbolk 1975) but they could have been used only at night, and then mainly with cattle. Housing implies artificial feed – hay or tree branches to which classical authors refer. The initial stimulus to house livestock may have come from the worsening climate of the Iron Age, but later, restricted grazing through increased settlement, and greater stock numbers resulting from improved husbandry became the crucial factors. Evidence supporting this comes from the feral Chillingham cattle which only had to be artificially fed in winter after the size of their park was halved (S. J. G. Hall, pers. comm.). One must not project back too far the evidence from Norse sagas and post-medieval records. The extreme modern situation is seen in Scandinavia where a severe winter, coupled with relatively few lamb losses, necessitates not only complete winter housing, but the cropping of all but replacement lambs during the autumn.

CHANGES IN THE TYPE OF SHEEP KEPT

It will be useful at the outset to say something about wool fibre types, fleeces and sheep breeds. The wild ancestor of domestic sheep has a short, hairy, outer coat composed of bristly fibres known as *kemps* which obscure an even shorter, fine woolly undercoat (figure 1). In the changes since domestication the kemps have been considerably reduced in thickness and number, and a second type of hairy fibre (named hair) has evolved, so that the fleeces of modern breeds contain kemp, hairs and wool in varying proportions.

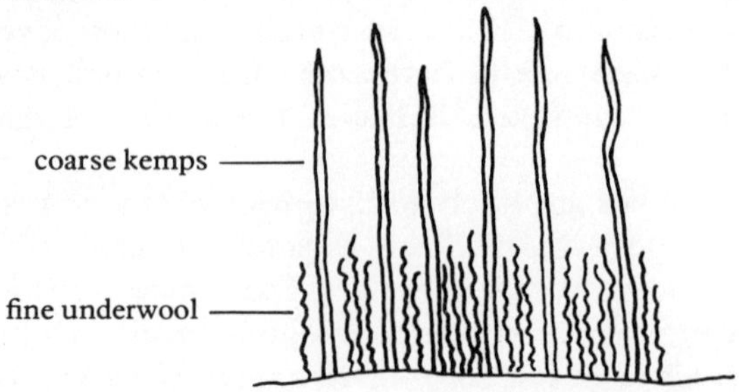

Figure 1. The structure of the coat of the wild sheep (from Ryder 1969a)

The second point to note is that differences between the fleeces of different breeds are almost entirely genetic. It is true that better feed will make a short-woolled fleece grow somewhat longer, but this will not change it into a longwool type.

Neolithic sheep. There is very little evidence to indicate what Neolithic sheep were like. During the nineteenth century it was suggested that they were similar to the small, brown Soay sheep that survives in a feral state on St Kilda. The difficulties of studying changes in the skeleton were discussed by Ryder (1981a, 358) who pointed out that the wild Mouflon has longer legs than the Soay, and suggested that one of the earliest changes following domestication was a shortening of the leg bones. The few measurements of Neolithic bones available support this conclusion. There appear to have been no other major changes in the skeleton until after the Middle Ages.

The coat of the first domesticated sheep must have been the same as that of the wild ancestor, and this is supported by the evidence of skin working, but not of textile manufacture, in Neolithic Britain. The earliest wool remains in Denmark were originally said to contain 'deer hairs' but these are now known to be sheep kemps. In fact the fleece of the Soay is much less hairy than that of the wild sheep, and it is similar to the wool in Bronze Age cloth (Ryder 1969a).

Bronze Age sheep. The Soay therefore appears to be a survival of Bronze Age sheep. The primitive features shared by the Soay with the wild ancestor are a short tail (all modern breeds have a long tail); a coloured fleece in which the belly is white (most modern breeds are completely white) and an annual moult (the wool of virtually all modern breeds grows continuously). To these major and obvious differences between wild sheep and modern domestic breeds can be added the change from a hairy coat to a woolly fleece, and the wool of the Soay is already much less

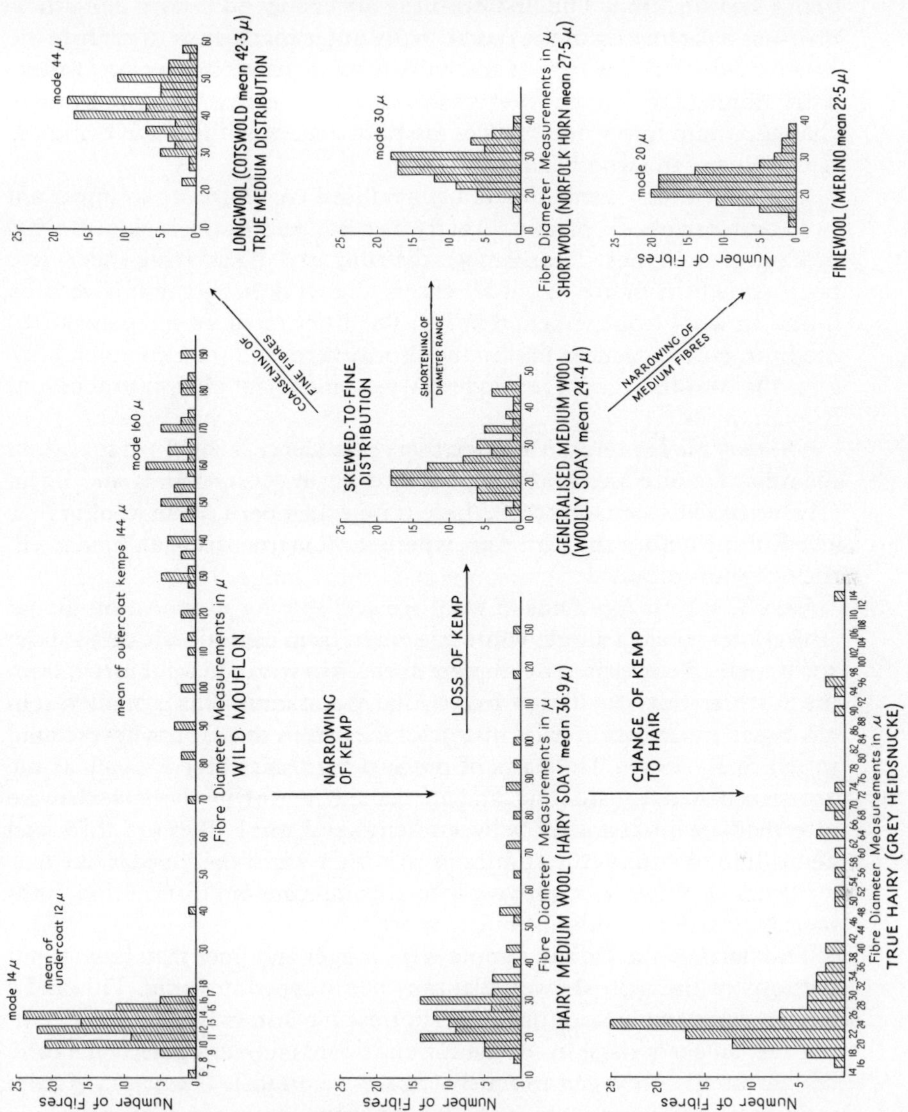

Figure 2. Changes in wool fibre diameter distribution in the fleeces of sheep since domestication (from Ryder 1981d, modified from Ryder 1969a)

hairy than the coat of the wild sheep, but there are hairy and woolly types.

This change is evident in figure 2, from Ryder (1969a), which shows histograms of wool fibre diameter distributions in microns (one micron =0.001 mm). The fibre diameter distribution of the wild sheep is shown at the top, the big difference in diameter between the coarse, hairy outer coat of fibres known as kemps, and the extremely fine woolly undercoat being very striking. The first evolutionary change following domestication was a narrowing of the coarse, hairy outer coat kemps to produce the hairy medium fleece type of the hairy Soay. Further narrowing of these hairy fibres (fine kemps) presumably due to selective breeding by man, changed them into wool fibres of medium diameter, the result being the fleece type of the woolly Soay.

In evolutionary terms this is a generalised type forming an important link between more primitive hairy fleeces, and more highly evolved modern fleece types. The diameter distributions of surviving sheep have been shown in figure 2, but all except the wild distribution have been found in wool from ancient textiles. The hairy medium and generalised medium types appeared first in the Bronze Age, and were common until after the Middle Ages. The modern types on the right began to appear in Roman times.

Sheep of the Iron Age. Although there is evidence from illustrations and records of white sheep as early as 3000 BC in Mesopotamia and Egypt (Ryder and Stephenson 1968), there is no evidence of white wool in Asia and Europe before the Iron Age, where it occurs as part of an increase in the range of colour.

Very few Iron Age finds of wool are available for examination. Ryder (1969a) described a single white specimen from central Asia dated about 400 BC which comprised a complete sheepskin with the wool intact, from the Scythian burial at Pazirik in the Altai Mountains. This is of interest in having an outer coat of hairs instead of the kemps or medium fibres found in the Soay sheep. The hairs of modern true hairy breeds (such as the Scottish Blackface) are long, and are named heterotypes because they are intermediate in character between kemp and wool: they are thick and kemp-like in summer, but thinner in winter when they appear like true wool fibres. Whereas kemps cease to grow preparatory to moulting, hairs merely thin down and continue to grow.

The hairs of the Pazirik sample were longer and finer than kemps, but sections of the skin showed that they had stopped growing. This and a length comparable with only the shortest modern hairy fleeces (12 cm) suggest an early stage in the evolution towards modern heterotype hairs which usually grow continuously (figure 2, bottom). The origin of hairs appears to have been associated with the change from a moulting fleece to one of continuous growth. Moulting is a disadvantage in leading to a loss of wool to the farmer. The normal way of harvesting wool from sheep that moult is by plucking, a method that was in use with the native breed of Shetland until recent times. Selective breeding against moulting is unlikely to have begun until an alternative method of removing the fleece was available, and clipping became possible with the development of iron shears in the Middle East about 1000 BC.

A second Iron Age white fleece sample of somewhat earlier date from Hallstatt in Austria was described by Ryder (1969a) as hairy, although the hairy fibres appeared more like kemps. A third example, again a sheepskin, from a bog dated about 500 BC in northern Germany was also white and hairy (Ryder 1977a). These three samples are of course inadequate to indicate the range of variation in Iron Age wool, and in fact true hairy fleeces of this type are rare until after the Middle Ages. Lacking direct textile evidence, one has to fall back on corroborative evidence from Roman textiles detailed below, and on surviving primitive breeds.

The breeds in question mostly have a short tail, and only the rams are horned, but the skeleton is otherwise similar to that of the Soay. There are still hairy medium as well as woolly fleeces, as in the Soay, and a spring moult, but the breeds are vari-coloured. In addition to the brown of the Soay there are black, white, and grey, as well as piebald, animals. But the wild-pattern white belly is rare, and so this marks the Soay as truly unique among domestic sheep. This vari-coloured type appears to have been common until after the Middle Ages, and widespread throughout Europe, since small pockets of relic breeds survive in isolated areas (Ryder 1981c). Grey animals are a notable feature of the type, which could also be termed 'European grey'.

The main surviving breeds of this type in Britain are the Orkney and Shetland. During the nineteenth century these two breeds formed a single population, but the Shetland has since been selectively bred for white, woolly fleeces, and so only the Orkney retains the full range of colour and fleece type (Ryder 1968a and b). It has already been indicated that the tendency to shed meant that in the past the wool had to be obtained by plucking (Ryder 1966a) but this tendency has largely been bred out today, so that most of the sheep are shorn.

How did this range of colours evolve from the brown Soay with a white belly? White animals are rare among Soay sheep, but wild-pattern (white-bellied) sheep in Iceland have been observed to mutate to all white (Ryder 1980a) so this is one way in which (dominant) white sheep could have originated. White in turn has been observed to mutate to self-colour (all black or all brown animals) and such sheep are found regularly in the Soay. Finally, self-colour has been observed to mutate to grey (which is brought about by a mixture of coloured and white fibres). The sequence therefore appears to have been: white-belly, all white, all coloured, and grey. The gene for grey produces grey in black animals but roan in brown animals, roan, however, is rare in sheep.

Another way of obtaining white, which has been done experimentally with Soay sheep, is to breed piebald animals with greater and greater areas of white (resulting in recessive white animals). Some modern breeds may have become white in one way, and others in the other way, and an entirely new approach to breed origins would be to try to unmask the colour genes that must remain hidden in modern sheep.

Naturally-coloured wools were used until well after the Middle Ages, different colours often being woven together to produce patterns. One might imagine that although white sheep would have been a novelty in themselves, the real stimulus to breed sheep with white wool may have come only after the development of dyes (see textile finishing, below).

Sheep of the Roman period. Although not strictly within the scope of the present paper, it is necessary to consider Roman evidence in order to fully understand the sheep of Iron Age Britain.

Roman textiles from Britain, Europe and the Near East show that the predominant wool type during that period, in addition to being white, was fine to the naked eye. But microscopic examination reveals that the wool contains medium fibres, and so is of generalised medium type. Hairy medium wools were still common, however; at Vindolanda on Hadrian's Wall for instance (Ryder 1977b and table 1). More changes were taking place in fibre diameter distribution and fleece type at that time, and the new types, and how they evolved are summarised in figure 2.

Table 1. The fleece types in Roman wools.

	Vindolanda	all other Roman (incl. Europe)
Hairy	(1)	—
Hairy medium	34% (19)	14% (12)
Generalised medium	34% (19)	15% (13)
Fine, generalised med.	18% (10)	39% (34)
True medium	2% (1)	3.5% (3)
Shortwool	4% (2)	1.5% (1)
Fine	9% (5)	27% (23)

If the medium wool fibres of the generalised medium type had become narrower by selective breeding, then the fibre diameter distribution of the true fine wool seen in the modern Merino would have been produced. The development of the true fine wool began in the Middle East probably soon after 1000 BC (Ryder 1969a). But the emergence of the Merino as a distinct breed occurred in the late Middle Ages in Spain.

In the European breed survey already mentioned (Ryder 1981c) it was expected that remnants of an ancient sheep with a true fine fleece might be found in the Balkans. In the event, the primitive breeds discovered had a fleece of generalised medium type. Thus although true fine wools undoubtedly existed in the Near East about the first century BC–AD (Ryder 1969a) it is of immense interest that the most primitive sheep surviving in south-east Europe have a fleece of the same type as the vari-coloured sheep in northern Europe.

Returning to figure 2, if on the other hand, the finer fibres had become coarser by breeding, then the true medium wool diameter distribution of the modern longwool would have been obtained. Thirdly, if both changes had taken place together, and the range of fibre diameter had become shortened, with a mean between the fine and medium values, the distribution would be comparable with that of the modern shortwool. Textile remains indicate that a few medium wools and shortwools had developed during Roman times, but neither became common in Britain until after the Middle Ages (Ryder 1969a, 1974, 1977b, 1981b).

Using evidence from surviving 'Iron Age' breeds again one should mention that in the primitive Orkney sheep the whole range of fleece types has been observed from hairy medium through generalised medium, to true fine, although the latter is rare (Ryder 1968a, b). In grey sheep of this breed it is usually the coarsest fibres that are black, and such mixtures of pigmented and non-pigmented fibres have been seen in textiles from as early as the Roman period (Ryder 1977b, 1981b).

Although there is virtually no direct evidence, it has always been assumed that the Romans introduced improved livestock into Britain, and this assumption is incorporated in the summary of breed type origin shown in figure 3. Following the Soay type, there are likely to have been vari-coloured sheep in the Iron Age, but to what extent these evolved locally or were introduced is not yet clear. It has been suggested that the Belgae introduced a white, fine-woolled sheep (Wild 1970).

Roman mosaics on the continent illustrate white-faced sheep in which the tail is no longer short, and there are horned as well as polled individuals which could be rams and ewes, as in the Orkney-Shetland type and some modern breeds such as the Merino (Ryder 1981b, 374). Figure 3 assumes the introduction of such a sheep into Britain by the Romans. Crosses of this with the native Soay could have given rise to types that later emerged as breeds such as the white-faced Cheviot and Welsh Mountain in the North and the West. These are horned in the rams only, and any pigment tends to be brown rather than black.

Then the fleece changes outlined above could have produced a primitive longwool on the one hand, and a shortwool on the other. Both types have a white face and lack horns. Most medieval illustrations show white-faced, polled sheep with short wool.

Returning to Vindolanda, this was the first site to yield an adequate sample on which to base conclusions about the range of fleece types. Altogether 56 yarns and one unspun staple were measured. The latter was of interest because of the rarity of unspun wool, and it turned out to be the only true hairy sample from any Roman site. This was 4 cm long and comparable with the hairy Iron Age samples listed above, having a pointed tip not unlike that of staples in the modern Scottish Blackface breed.

The hairy sample has been omitted from the percentages in table 1, which shows the proportion of different fleece types at Vindolanda and compares them with all other Roman wools examined, including samples from the Continent (Ryder 1969a, 1974, and other minor reports). Hairy medium wools and generalised medium wools predominated at Vindolanda, and there was a moderate proportion of a finer type of generalised medium wool. It is of interest that there were more fleeces of the fine type

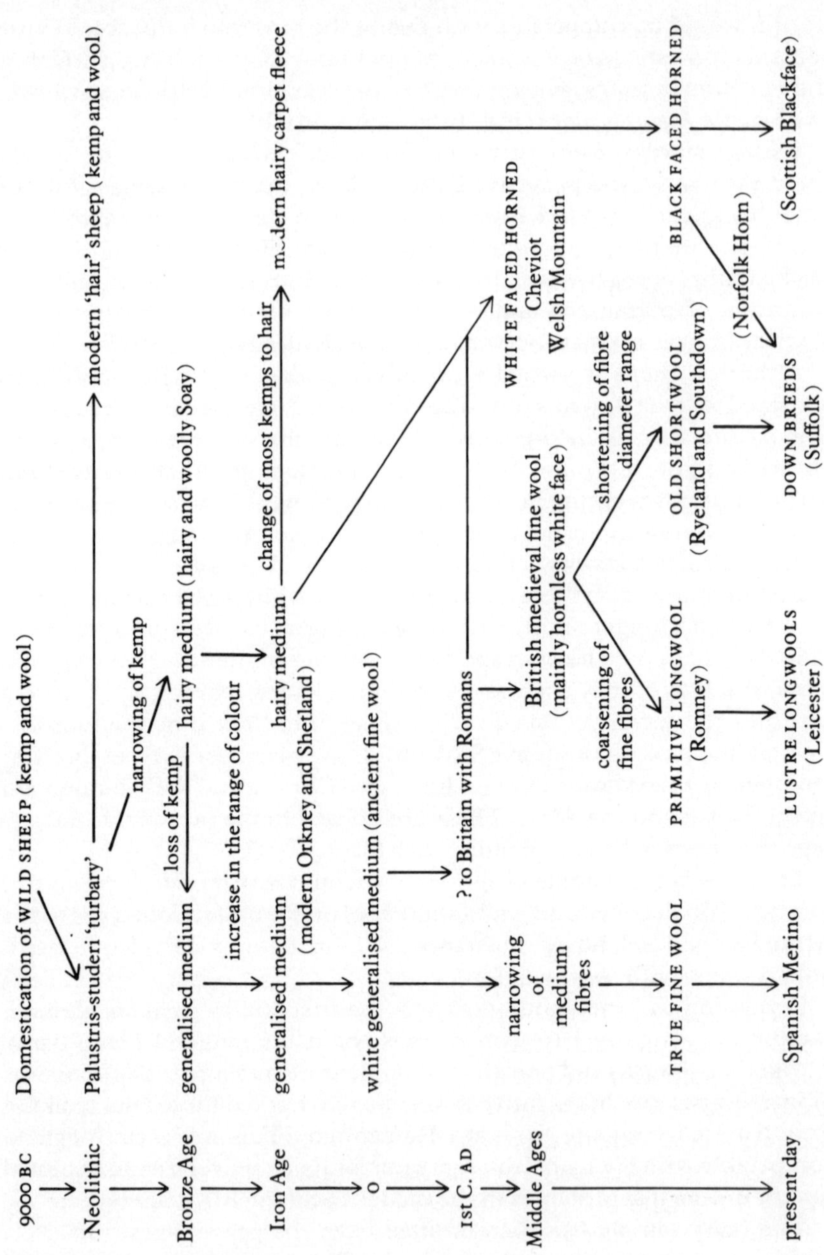

Figure 3. Suggested lines of evolution of fleece types and some main breed types (from Ryder 1981d, modified from Ryder 1969a)

that later emerged on the Continent as the Merino, than there were shortwools and true medium wools, which are thought to have developed in Britain. But these findings indicate evolution as early as Roman times, whereas it was previously thought that they appeared during the Middle Ages. Since Wild (1977; see Ryder 1977b) considers that the Vindolanda wools are unlikely to have been imports, they probably indicate the range of fleece types found in northern Roman Britain in the first century AD. Comparison with the other Roman wools in the table, indicates that these have a greater proportion of finer types (fine, generalised medium and true fine).

The pigment details given in table 2 throw additional light on the breed types. The scarcity of completely pigmented wools indicates a move away from the prehistoric sheep exemplified by the Soay. Of particular interest is the large number of 'grey' wools on this site. This accords with evidence from surviving breeds, that the predominant sheep in Europe from the Iron Age to the Middle Ages had a range of fleece colours (see above).

Table 2. Extent of natural pigmentation in the Vindolanda wools (actual numbers; from Ryder 1981b)

	100% pigmented	mixture ('grey')	no pigment	total
Hairy	–	—	1	1
Hairy medium	3	11	5	19
Gen. medium	1	12	6	19
Fine, gen. medium	1	3	6	10
Fine	–	2	3	5
Shortwool	–	—	2	2
Medium	–	1	–	1

CHANGES IN THE COAT OF CATTLE

The evolution of the coat in domestic cattle presents a more difficult problem than the fleece of sheep (Ryder 1969a). The wild ancestor is extinct, and not only is far less known about variation in the coat of modern cattle, but the relative wealth of material from wool textile remains is lacking. The main source of ancient material is leather, and this has fewer hair remains even than parchment (which is made mostly from sheep skin). It is clear, however, that the coat of modern domestic cattle varies less than do the fleeces of sheep, presumably because there has been little or no selective breeding for different coat types.

The review of knowledge on this subject by Ryder (1969a) has recently been brought up to date from a more recent find by Ryder (1980b). All hairs in cattle are comparable with the outer hairs of sheep; they are also distributed at random, and not in groups as in sheep. The hair remains in Roman and medieval leather indicate a coat similar to that of modern cattle. The first difference from what was obviously cattle hair was found in a fragment of skin from a Neolithic bow from Meare, Somerset, dated 2600 BC. This had hairs, which, although apparently bovine, were much finer than those of modern cattle.

Bronze Age burials have yielded other bovine hairs because human bodies were often buried in a skin, and where this has decayed excavators have sometimes been able to retrieve the hairs. Some of these have been similar to those of modern cattle, whereas another group from Scotland were finer like the Meare specimen.

The identification of these unusual bovine hairs provided a problem. The hair had two characteristics found in the bison (*Bison bonasus*): there was an asymmetric distribution of pigment within the individual hairs, and most of the hairs were fine, giving a skewed hair diameter distribution. The bison, however, is thought to have died out in Britain before the land bridge with the continent was broken. The wild ox (*Bos primigenius*), which can be regarded as a 'cousin' of the bison, on the other hand, is known from skeletal remains to have persisted until the Bronze Age. Since the bison appears to have become extinct in Britain before the wild ox it was suggested that the unidentified bovine hair remains were in fact from the wild ox.

More recently there has been a new hair find at the Neolithic site of Skara Brae. This was found adhering to an ox skull, identified as early domestic *primigenius* type. The new sample had a mean hair diameter within the range 14 to 19 microns found over the previous proposed wild ox samples, whereas the mean hair diameter of most obvious cattle samples (old and recent) was 35 to 50 microns.

Although these more recent measurements of the Skara Brae hair support the previous identification and conclusions, in the island context of Orkney this animal is almost certainly an early domestic type, and indeed one would not expect the coat to have changed by that time. The possibility is therefore raised that the previous samples described above were from domestic and not wild cattle.

From the difference in mean hair diameter between ancient and modern cattle quoted above it appears that the general trend in coat type following domestication has been the opposite of that with sheep, i.e. towards hairiness instead of fineness. Some anomalies might be mentioned; the modern Scottish Galloway breed has a mean of 30 microns, i.e. between the old and recent values, which perhaps indicates a primitive status. The supposedly primitive Scottish Highland breed has a mean within the modern range, and the English Chillingham breed, also thought to be primitive, has a mean of 56 microns, i.e. above the range.

ANIMAL PRODUCTS

Before domestication, and after death, sheep, like other hunted animals provided meat and fat for food, bone and horn for tools, plus skins for clothing and gut for containers. After domestication, animals tended to be more valuable alive than dead, so blood was utilised for food, and a whole range of milk products were developed. It is often claimed that kill-off patterns based on age and sex can indicate whether sheep were kept for meat, milk and wool. I consider this to be a completely false approach since in prehistory all products were used. Although such specialisation began in Roman times, it was uncommon as late as the Middle Ages (Smith 1979).

We now realise that most animals were not domesticated for a particular purpose. The sheep for instance could not have been domesticated for its fleece since this was developed after domestication mainly from the underwool of the wild animal (see above). Although some species tend to have only one function, e.g. pigs supply meat and horses provide transport, originally no species is likely to have had only one use. On the other hand no domestic animal other than the sheep provides so many products, or satisfies so many of man's requirements.

Thus sheep became extremely important to nomadic pastoralists, providing all their needs, including housing (from felt or cloth) and even transport. Sheep still carry packs in the Himalayas. Hard bone objects in museums make it easy to forget that, in addition to food, much of man's equipment comes from what zoologists call the soft parts of animals, and this is rarely preserved. The sheep, however, is virtually unique in the extent to which its fleece and skin have been utilised. Through its wool the sheep has had a major impact on the history of mankind, and subsequent to the period under discussion parchment made from sheepskin was the main writing material of the western world for centuries. Wool and skin will therefore be given detailed treatment in the present account, which is based on the survey of Ryder (1966b) updated in Ryder (1981a) (written in 1970) and in Ryder (1981d).

Since many animal products were in use until the nineteenth century it is difficult to distinguish early uses from later developments. Although some animal products were used before domestication, the major steps forward took place during the Neolithic period, the technology of which lasted until the nineteenth century, even in western Europe. Those products used before domestication will be described first, although the summary in table 3 is based on the usage in a domestic animal. Two or more products are often used together, e.g. black pudding made with blood is enclosed in the gut.

Meat. Man became a meat-eater several million years ago, and only during the Neolithic period, when food began to be produced, did plants again form a major part of the diet. Meat provides more amino acids than do plants, and more minerals, as well as essential vitamins such as B_{12}. Cooking, however, probably began with cereals since these contain repellant substances that need to be neutralised by heat.

After domestication animals tended to be more valuable alive, and so not only would greater efforts have been made to preserve meat, but blood and milk were developed as new foods that avoided the need to kill the

Table 3. Summary of sheep products (modified from Ryder 1981d)

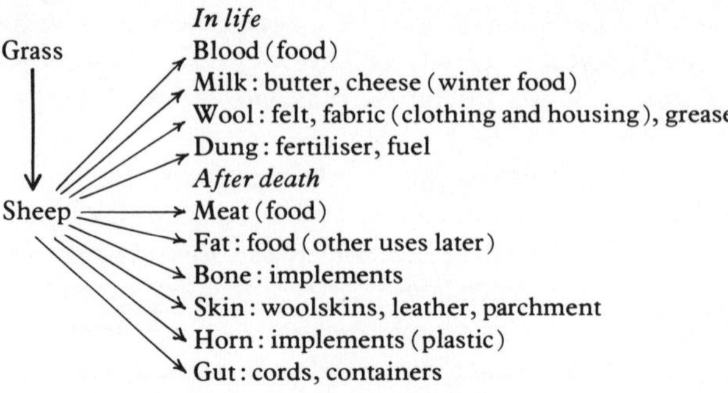

animal. Animals were not always killed to obtain meat. Abyssinians used to cut flesh from cattle and eat it raw, the skin being afterwards pinned over the wound and covered with clay.

The discovery that meat dried in the sun will resist putrefaction was almost certainly made before domestication. The North American Indians used to store dried meat as pemmican, by putting it in a paunch and pouring in molten fat. Cooking over a fire probably led to the discovery of the preservative action of smoke. When salt began to be used in food, and as a preservative, is not clear, but at least twelve coastal sites of salt production are known in Roman Britain. Sheep meat is still cured in Scandinavian countries, and in northern Britain the carcass of a sheep dying of disease used to be cured as 'braxy ham'.

In addition to skeletal muscle, internal organs are eaten as offal (see the haggis under 'gut', below). Other parts of the sheep eaten are the head and the heart, as well as testicles and tails, although tailing may be a fairly recent custom. Unlike pork and beef sheep meat is the only meat that is universally eaten by man – it is not taboo to any race or people.

Fat. Whereas modern sheep tend to put on fat externally, any fat deposited in the leaner Soay is internal, and it is possible that because of its primitive nature the fat is more unsaturated than that of modern breeds. On the whole, however, sheep fat is harder than that of other livestock, so that it was later used to make candles and soap. Some breeds in desert areas have developed a fat tail as a food storage organ.

Blood. The collection of blood from living animals for food is very widespread, and so probably very ancient. Blood must have an even greater energy utilisation than the twenty-seven per cent of milk (see below), but I am not aware that it has ever been measured. It appears to have been more common with cattle than with sheep, presumably because of their larger size. The custom persisted until the eighteenth century in Ireland and Scotland, the blood being eaten mixed with oatmeal. It is still common among African cattle keepers, who drink blood mixed with milk, charcoal, and cattle urine, which provides salt.

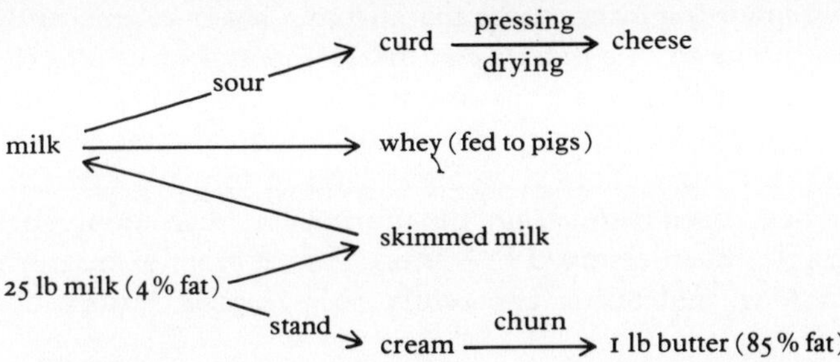

Figure 4. The main changes involved in cheese and butter manufacture (from Ryder 1966b).

Blood was also collected at slaughter and allowed to solidify for storage. That of sheep is still collected to make black puddings, which are probably much more ancient than the description in Homer's *Odyssey*: 'These bellies of she-goats are being cooked on a fire; having filled them with fat and blood . . .', which compares with the modern counterpart. The mention of 'bellies' provides a link with cooking in a paunch (see below). The Roman name for black pudding was *botellus*.

Milk. Along with blood, milk was probably one of the first new products following domestication. It has an energy conversion of twenty-seven per cent compared with only six per cent in meat and that for cheese must be greater. Milking must be much older than the first illustrations in the Middle East of the third millennium BC. It was probably soon noticed that animals let down their milk more readily in the presence of their young (or a replica) and primitive peoples use various stimuli for this purpose. Young need not have been killed early to allow milking. They could have been weaned early, a stick put in the mouth, or the udder of the mother bagged to prevent suckling, which are all customs still in use.

Sheep milk has more fat than that of any other farm animal, and Varro regarded ewes' milk as the most nourishing. It has seven and a half per cent compared with four and a half per cent in the goat, and four per cent in the cow. There is also five per cent of the protein casein compared with two and a half per cent in cows' milk.

The curdling of milk is likely to have been discovered as soon as it began to be used, and so the transformation of the curd into cheese that could be stored for winter food may have begun very early (figure 4). The only prehistoric evidence of cheese making in Europe comes from stone curd strainers, but wicker baskets could have been used before these, as mentioned in Homer's *Odyssey*, and as used in Mediterranean countries today. A cloth strainer is another possibility, but this seems to be a modern development. Cheese is a highly nutritious food containing twenty-five per cent protein compared with twenty per cent in meat, and five per cent in sheep's milk. It has thirty-five per cent fat compared with thirty per cent in meat.

The whey remaining from cheese manufacture has in recent centuries been fed to pigs in an integrated husbandry system, but it, too, can be made into a kind of cheese, a lacto-albumin coagulate. It is possible that the way of speeding up curdling with the use of the enzyme rennet was discovered by carrying milk in a bag made from an animal's stomach. If a skin bag had been used instead, and the journey had been a long one, the milk would have been changed to butter. This appears to have been a discovery of Asia, and butter apparently only reached Europe during historic times.

There is a whole range of other milk products – ghee, kumiss, yoghurt – but since there is no evidence that these were made in prehistoric Europe they will be omitted from the present account.

Bone. The use of bone as a raw material was well-developed before domestication. Man probably soon learnt that bone can be softened by soaking it in water, making it more easily cut with a flint knife. Some tools underwent little preparation, whereas others were intricately carved. Bone scoops forming primitive spoons were in use from Palaeolithic times until the nineteenth century. Sheep cannon bones were used as weaving shuttles at least as early as the Iron Age, and were still used as shuttle bobbins in the Hebrides into the present century.

Other textile uses of bone were in spinning whorls and so-called weaving combs (see, however, section on weaving below). Bones were also used in musical pipes (from the Iron Age) and percussion instruments, but it would be tedious to attempt a complete list of uses (figure 5). In the recent past in Iceland the mineral part of bone was removed with lactic acid made from sheep's blood, and the gristle remaining was eaten as *strjugur*.

Horn. The horn of hooves, and the outer casing of horns, is composed of keratin, the same substance as that of hair and wool, and horn provided the only plastic material until recent times. Although tough and durable, horn can be softened by boiling in water, after which it can be cut, flattened and moulded.

Horn casings were probably first used as containers and drinking cups. The North American Indians carried fire in tinder packed into the horn of a wild Bighorn sheep, which they also made into large bowls. The earliest example of horn shaping I know is in a horn spoon from a Bronze Age beaker found in Aberdeenshire. Other ancient uses were digging hooks, bows and musical horns. By the Middle Ages the horner's craft was well developed, and there was a wide range of uses.

Gut. this is akin to skin in containing much collagen. The alimentary tract of animals provides a source of containers and tubes, and also of fishing lines and bow strings. Its early use is suggested by the cord decoration on Bronze Age pottery being apparently imprinted with twisted gut. Later uses were cords for lathes and spinning wheels, and the strings of musical instruments. There are two associations with Scotland:

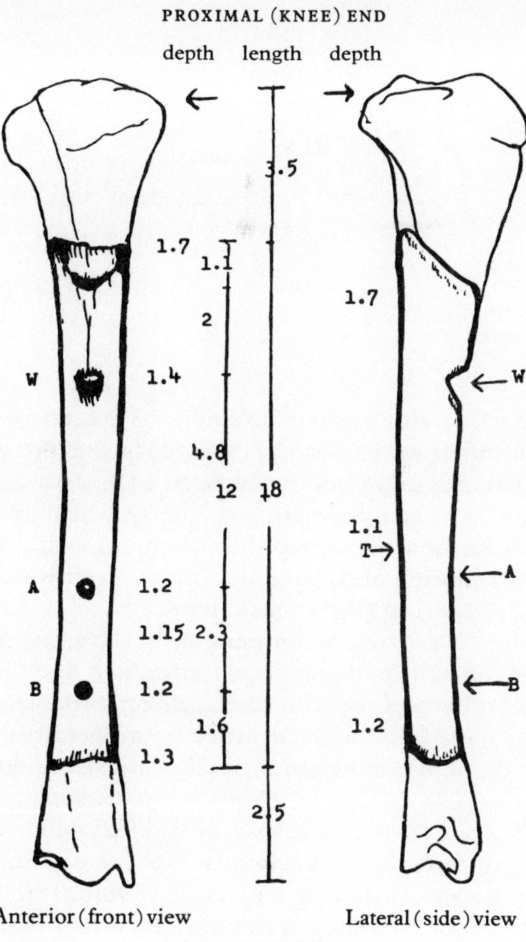

Figure 5. Iron Age musical pipe made from sheep tibia (from Raistrick et al. 1952).

the first bag of bagpipes was probably made from a paunch (it was later made from a complete sheepskin) and the haggis is made in the paunch (rumen) of a sheep's stomach. In addition to liver, haggis contains heart and lungs, i.e. some parts not normally eaten separately. There are references to stuffed paunches in ancient Greek literature, that to black pudding having already been mentioned under 'blood' where cooking directly over a fire was suggested (see cooking in a skin, below, and figure 6).

Apart from sausage skins the only recent use that I will mention concerns the blind caecum (reduced to the appendix in man). This was used as a human contraceptive sheath as early as the sixteenth century.

Dung. Since the initial effect of fresh, concentrated dung is harmful to

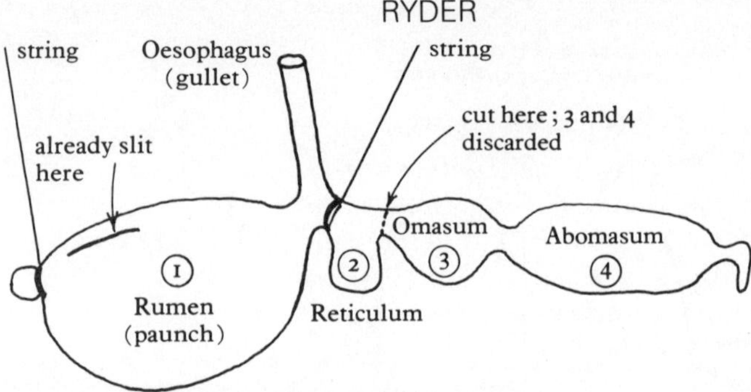

Figure 6. Diagram showing how paunch was removed from sheep's stomach for experimental use as a cooking vessel (from Ryder 1969b).

grass, the observation of its value as a fertilizer must have been made on the periphery of a concentration. This can be observed on St Kilda where the feral Soay sheep shelter at night in stone huts left by the islanders. At the entrance to each hut is a patch of bright green grass, which has been manured by drainage from the accumulated sheep droppings within. The first suggestion of the manuring of crops comes from a manure tank in a Bronze Age cow house at Jarlshof (Trow-Smith 1957).

The collection of dung is one reason for penning sheep at night, and another use is as fuel, after it has been beaten down and dried before removal in sheets. According to those who have made comparisons sheep and goat dung gives out more intense heat than that from other livestock. I believe that the study of ash has indicated the prehistoric use of dung as fuel.

Skin. The first use of skin was probably in fur-skin clothing, which dates back to the Palaeolithic period. Since so far as I am aware there are no skin remains of such great age, evidence for its use in clothing is indirect, coming from remains of bone awls used in the stitching of skins. Sewing is therefore much more ancient than the manufacture of cloth.

The other source of evidence is the skin clothing of primitive peoples who survive in similar cultures today. Tendons are often used to sew skins, but the Kutchin Indians of Alaska used fine strips of untanned skin. These threads are known by the French name *babiche*, and they were also used to make net bags.

A typical eskimo outfit might consist of thin skin (including bird-skin) underwear worn fur inside, with polar fox or reindeer outer clothing worn fur outside. The trousers were of polar-bear skin, the stockings of hare skin, and the boots of depilated seal-skin or caribou skin, which was also used by the Kutchin Indians. The eskimos appreciated the seasonal variation in the length and density of fur when preparing skins, and the Kutchin Indians actually had summer and winter outfits. Before leaving clothing it is worth remembering that until recently oiled skins were worn by North Sea fishermen, their name being perpetuated in what we call oilskins. The desirable fur coat, and fashionable suede jacket are still with us.

Skin, like bone and gut, is composed mainly of collagen, and cattle and sheepskins must have first been used untanned as fur-skins, as well as in the raw-hide of ropes, hurling slings, whips, and later in parchment. Skin, hair and wool decay rapidly in the damp climate of northern Europe, and are destroyed by alkaline soil, but are well preserved in acid water-logged conditions, such as peat bogs, i.e. the conditions that destroy bone (Ryder 1970).

Tanning to produce leather is a chemical process that preserves the skin, tending to make it impervious to water, but allowing the retention of natural pliability. The main tanning methods involve oils, vegetable extracts and minerals. The tanning action of smoke depends on aldehydes. Oil tannage may go back to Palaeolithic times, fish oil being used by the eskimos until recently. Milk, butter and egg yolk were used by Asiatic peoples. Oil-tanned skin was used for clothing in the past, and can be washed, persisting today in chamois leather.

The only ancient mineral process was alum dressing (tawing) which was used in the Near East, and is used today in woolskins, but it is a reversible process since the alum will wash out. In the west vegetable tanning was probably used by the Neolithic period, an extract of oak bark or oak galls being used (Reed 1972). The chemical reaction is different from that of oil, but similar to that of the modern chrome tanning. The alkali used to speed removal of hair (normally occurring with putrefaction) was probably first provided by stale urine (another animal product) and later by ashes, but lime has been used for at least 2000 years.

There is little evidence of the mechanics of pre-historic skin dressing, although the method used by eskimos are well documented, women frequently chewing the skin to soften it by the enzymatic action of saliva before oil or smoke tanning (Waterer 1956). it is important to remove the subcutaneous fat, and any flesh remaining, before treatment, and various bone or flint implement finds have been interpreted as skin scrapers used for this purpose. It has also been thought that bone combs were used to remove hair. But hair removal was probably a later elaboration with the development of vegetable tanning to produce leather, and in any case once the hair or wool roots have putrefied or been attacked by alkali no effort is required to remove the hair. It can be scraped off with a flat bone, or even the back of the hand. The Red Indians of North America used to freeze the hair in ice in order to remove it from a skin.

A skin can be dried in the sun by laying it flat on the ground flesh-side up. An elaboration would be to stretch it on a wooden frame. With no further treatment the result is known as rawhide. The modern application of common salt at this stage to preserve the skin for transport would probably have been too costly in prehistory. Oil and alum tannage can both be carried out with the skin on the ground, and in modern handicraft skin preparation it is usual to 'work' the skin over a bar during the process to maintain flexibility.

For vegetable tanning it is necessary to have pits in which to soak the skin for weeks or months. I know of no evidence of such pits before the Roman period, although simple pits dug into the earth were used until recently in Morocco where simple leather technology reached its highest pre-industrial development. Circular pits were used for liming, but rectangular pits for tanning, the skin being suspended from wooden rods across the pit.

When stretching a skin on a wooden frame it is usual to have this vertical; it is then necessary when scraping to use a curved knife, which will follow the natural contours formed when pressure is applied to a stretched skin. Curved knives for this purpose were made out of jawbones, and the eskimos used one made of slate.

Ryder (1970) showed how the reaction of a routine histological stain for skin tissue, when used with sections of ancient skin threw light on tanning. Fresh skin and oil-tanned skin stain the same, but vegetable-tanned skin stains differently.

Skin, like bone, has a wide range of uses, and we have seen that it probably provided the sole clothing material well into the Neolithic period. Other uses were footwear, bags, fish-net floats, and liquid containers. The first pottery vessels may have imitated a skin bag, a natural source of a small example being the scrotal sac of male animals. It is just possible that cooking was carried out in a suspended skin full of water either by suspending it over a fire, or by dropping hot stones into the water. Ryder (1966c) imitated the depiction in a sixteenth-century Irish hunting scene (which may not have been first hand) of a saucer-shaped skin over a fire, but found it impossible to make the water hot enough for cooking.

Greater success was obtained with paunches (Ryder 1969b) presumably because of their enclosed nature, which suggests that a skin removed as a tube and made into a bag would have been more successful. This might be one way in which stone 'pot boilers' were used. These are often found on aceramic Neolithic sites. I have seen goat and sheep skins removed as a tube in the Balkans and Turkey, and then hung up to dry in the wind. For skinning, the carcass is suspended head downwards. The skin is opened up with a single cut behind the legs under the tail, and then peeled off towards the head as a tube. Sometimes the leg openings are tied with thongs while the skin is still wet. A more elaborate method is to stitch these, along with the original cut, and the neck then becomes the opening of the bag. Again such bags probably go back to Palaeolithic times since the North American Indians made them from the skin of wild animals.

Such bags have been used as containers for liquids and solids, e.g. grain, from ancient times to the present day. In desert water skins the hair is allowed to remain on the outside as a cooling device. But in Turkey I have seen loads of goat skins, hair inside and legs tied, packed tightly with cheese. Other uses of such bags were in the curing of meat, and later in the storage of wine. Homer's *Odyssey* refers to 'wine bottles, bags of leather and well-sewn skins', which indicates the more elaborate construction of bags by stitching. He also wrote of herdsmen sleeping on a sheepskin placed on a cowhide groundsheet.

The use of skins in tents for housing must be as old as their use in clothing. The eskimos lived in tents in summer, and the Red Indian tent was the tepee. The Roman army slept in rectangular tents made of squares of leather sewn together.

Another early use was in boats. The one-man eskimo kayak had a drift-wood and antler frame and was 18 ft long by 2 ft wide (5.5 × 0.61 m). It was covered with sealskin fastened with sinew thongs, the occupant being protected by a skin coat laced to the canoe. There was also a larger boat (for women) named the umiak.

The original river coracles of Wales, and the sea-going curraghs of Ireland, were made from skins stretched over a wooden frame, eight cow skins being traditionally used in a curragh. These presumably therefore perpetuate an ancient design. The words 'coracle' and 'curragh' in fact come from the same root as the Latin *corium* (skin). We have seen that skin boats were almost certainly used to transport the first livestock to the British Isles, and they are in fact very buoyant, actually riding a rough sea better than a planked boat. By Roman times leather was used for sails, and in recent years an imitation medieval leather boat made waterproof with wool grease was sailed from Ireland to Canada (Severin 1979).

Stretched raw-hide in the form of a coarse parchment was used to cover drums as early as 2000 BC in Egypt, and an entire sheepskin replaced the original paunch to make the bag of bagpipes, which were originally very widespread. The manufacture of parchment as a writing material is out of the scope of the present account. It is in fact not tanned, but merely stretched and dried.

The Biblical sling probably dates back to the Neolithic period, but has never survived from antiquity although clay missiles dating from 7000 BC were found in Iraq (Korfmann 1973). The sling comprised a skin or leather pocket for an egg-sized missile, and two thongs about a metre long by which it was swung. It appears that the strings (and perhaps the entire sling) were often made of wool, since Homer in the *Iliad* refers to the defenders of Troy relying on the 'well-twisted wool' used by shepherds. Shepherds used slings to hurl stones at predators, and also to throw earth beyond a straying flock with the object of deflecting the sheep back towards the shepherd. By the Middle Ages this was done with a small scoop at the base of a crook.

Wool. Wool is another important product of domestication, although sheepskins may have been appreciated as clothing before domestication because the hairy outer coat of wild sheep is softer and less coarse than that of deer for instance. The domestic evolution of the fleece has already been covered in section 2 (above) and so the uses of wool will be summarised here. The reduced amount of killing after domestication would have meant fewer skins for clothing, and this could have provided a stimulus to seek alternatives which emerged as felt and cloth.

Wool may first have been used as felt, which is frequently formed naturally during the moult, even in wild sheep (Ryder 1968c). Felting could therefore have been discovered from the natural cotting (matting) of the fleece on the sheep's back. Felt manufacture appears to have originated in Asia, and felt is still used by Asiatic nomads for clothing, boots, mats, and tents.

True felts are non-woven, and are made by the direct felting action of loose wool fibres brought about by repeated compression while wet and warm. In peasant felt manufacture the wool is first fluffed out with a bow, and laid out on a reed mat. The wool is then wetted, and rolled up in the matting, the felting process being carried out by moving the roll back and forth with the feet or the hands.

Burkett (1979) quotes hints that felt might have been made as early as 6500 BC at Çatal Hüyük in Turkey, although the woven cloth I examined from this prehistoric site was linen (Ryder 1965). There are records of felt in China dating back to 2300 BC and perhaps the best known remains of felt are from Pazirik in the Altai Mountains of Siberia dated about 500 BC. The only find of felt I know from Europe was from a Bronze Age grave in Germany dated 1800 BC. Felt certainly reached Europe much later with such peoples as the Magyars, but Burkett (1979) thought that the hooded capes worn by three third-century carved figures at the Roman fort of Housesteads on Hadrian's Wall were of felt. They certainly appear similar to those worn by Turkish shepherds today, but according to Wild (1970 and personal communication) they are neither the *birrus Britannicus* of Roman literature, nor made of felt. He does, however, list a felt helmet lining from Newstead.

Only animal textile fibres have the capacity to felt (which depends on the scaly surface of the fibre), and in no other domestic animal has the use of the coat become so highly developed as it has with the fleeces of sheep. Goat hair is still woven into tent cloth in the Middle East, and there are medieval remains of goat hair cloth in Britain. Most uses of wool or hair involve the prior transformation into felt, cloth, or at least yarn.

Moulting fleeces, which led to the discovery of felting, probably also suggested the spinning of wool, since the shedding wool is often rubbed by the sheep into long strands (Ryder 1968c). Since weaving in basketry was already known before domestication, the idea of spinning threads similar to those formed naturally in fleeces could have led to the great Neolithic invention of cloth manufacture. Flax has usually been thought of as the first fibre to have been spun, but this could be because only flax has survived on the earliest sites. Whereas wool fibres can be spun straight from the fleece, the flex stem requires considerable treatment in order to release the fibres, and this makes it unlikely that flax was the first fibre to be spun (Ryder 1968c).

THE DEVELOPMENT OF WOOL TEXTILE TECHNOLOGY

Textile manufacture involves a wide range of techniques from stitching and net-making, through various types of weaving, which are like basketry, to knitting. The present summary, based on the account of Ryder (1973, 1981d), concentrates on textiles in the narrow sense as fabrics woven from spun (twisted) yarns (threads). We have seen that until shears came into use in the Iron Age, wool was obtained from sheep by pulling. This would have allowed some rejection of coarser, hairy fibres, which tend to stay in the skin and shed later than the wool, and it might explain why some Bronze Age cloth had an unusually high proportion of fine wool fibres, while later cloths (of shorn wool) had the more usual proportion of hairs (Ryder 1969a).

Wool was probably first spun direct from the fleece with little or no preparation. The more primitive (hairy medium or hairy Soay) type of fleece when spun in this way would have given a worsted, in contrast to a woollen, yarn, because of the relatively parallel orientation of the hairy fibres. It is therefore a surprising fact that worsted yarns, which are today regarded as more highly developed than woollen yarns, probably came first. Wool combing to ensure straightness of the fibres, which is today used with mainly the finest wools to make worsted yarns, probably originated before carding, which is now used to prepare mainly coarser wools for spinning into woollen yarns.

Bone combs have survived from prehistoric times, and during the Roman period wool combs were made of sheets of iron with teeth cut into one end. As wool became finer, and possibly shorter (as in the generalised medium type or woolly Soay) it is likely to have matted more readily making it difficult to comb without breakage. This could have led to the development of carding, and in turn to the spinning of woollen yarns.

The name 'card' comes from *carduus* (a thistle) which suggests that carding was originally done with thistle or teasel heads, the latter being also used to raise the nap on cloth. The action of carding opens out the wool and results in a sliver of fibres mixed in all directions. Hand cards are rectangular boards bearing numerous wires set in leather, but there is no evidence of these before the Middle Ages.

When carding originated is not clear since according to Wild (1970) the Roman term *carminare* merely means the preparation of wool for spinning by the teasing out of fibres, and the removal of impurities by hand. We have already seen that a bow was used to do this in the Middle East. The modern British term 'willeying' appears to originate from the earlier practice of beating fleeces with willow branches to remove the dirt. Wool scouring is a factory process; until the nineteenth century sheep were washed in a stream some time before shearing, in a custom going back at

Figure 7. Vertical warp-weighted loom from the Färoe islands (from Loudon's *Encyclopaedia of Agriculture* 1844). To the left stands a long distaff used to hold the unspun wool, which was in use certainly as early as Roman times, and between this and the loom is a spindle and whorl. Note the 'sword' for 'beating up' among the warp threads.

least to Biblical times.

A longer, often forked, stick, the distaff (figure 7), although not essential, is commonly used to hold the prepared wool during the spinning process. Wild (1970) lists several of these from Roman Britain, and I am not aware of any earlier examples.

The advance between the weaving used in basketry in the Palaeolithic period, and the Neolithic weaving of cloth, was the discovery that twist imparts strength to a strand of fibres, i.e. the invention of spinning. Twist does not arise in basketwork because solid rods are used. An untwisted strand of fibres cannot be woven since it lacks cohesion and strength. But the insertion of a few twists (to produce a yarn) gives the strand remarkable strength. It has been indicated above that the idea of spinning may have come from the observation of natural strands in fleeces.

Ryder (1968c) was able to collect twenty such strands up to a metre in length from a single moulting sheep. Some were no thicker than a coarse woollen yarn, and it was possible to weave these together into a rudimentary piece of cloth. Goats have not been observed to form strands during the moult, presumably because the outer hairs are long and therefore less easily bound together by the underwool. This probably excludes goats from the origin of spinning, and may be one reason why the sheep became the main animal developed for different fleece types for textile use.

As skill was gained, the strands would become longer and thinner, and it would be realised that the fibres could be made parallel by drawing them out, resulting on a finer yarn. Drawing (draft) would have originally preceded the twisting, and then drafting and twisting would have been done in one process. Since the extent of draft possible depends on the length of the fibres, the key to successful spinning is a balance between draft and twist, e.g. a strand will break if drawn too much before adequate twist has been inserted to provide strength.

The simplest method of spinning is to rub the fibres between the hands. The spindle may have developed from the use of a stick to wind on the yarn. But it is difficult to spin with an un-weighted stick, and a weight is provided by a disk-like whorl wedged near the base. As well as keeping the spindle vertical, the whorl acts as a flywheel to prolong rotation (figure 7).

Spindles are usually made of wood, and they have a thickening (up to 1 cm across) at one end on which to wedge the whorl. Few are less than 15 cm or more than 30 cm in length. In ancient spindles the yarn was presumably attached to the tip with a half-hitch, whereas many modern ones have a notch or a hook. Whorls have been made from a wide variety of material – stone, wood, shell, bone (frequently the head of an ox femur), antler, ivory, pot, glass and metal. They are, along with loom weights, often the only evidence of textile manufacture found on a site since spindles, looms and fabrics decay.

A common diameter of whorls is 2.5 cm, and Roman whorls were rarely greater than twice this across. It was pointed out by Ryder (1968c) that when recording ancient whorls the weight should be noted along with the dimensions because this can indicate the finest wool that could be spun in a free fall, or that the spindle must have been supported.

The suspended spindle produces a fine, even yarn, but is unsuitable for spinning short, fine fibres unless one uses a light whorl or reduces a draft. A fast-rotating spindle with a heavy whorl causes the fibres to be simultaneously drawn and twisted into a tightly-spun yarn which is suitably strong for the lengthwise (warp) threads of cloth. Strength can also be obtained by twisting two or more yarns together with a spindle (Ryder 1965). The crosswise (weft) yarns need not be so tightly spun, and so for these the spindle was often supported.

When a length of yarn has been spun, the process has to be stopped so that the spun yarn can be wound on the spindle. This occurs when a free-falling spindle reaches the ground. Yarns can be spun in either a clockwise (right-hand) or anti-clockwise (left-hand) direction. The letter Z is used to indicate clockwise twist because on viewing the yarn one can see that the fibres follow the slope of the middle bar of the letter. Anticlockwise yarns are designated S because their fibres have the opposite slope. Most prehistoric yarns in Europe have a Z twist. The whorl was later turned on its side to become the spinning wheel, which did not reach Europe until the Middle Ages and so is out of the scope of the present account.

Weaving involves the interlacing of weft yarns over and under the stronger, lengthwise warp yarns, the device for holding the warp taut being the loom. The development of weaving is less easily traced than the development of spinning since there are many kinds of loom, and whether simple designs are primitive or recent developments is not always clear. The transition from basketry to weaving may have taken place through the vertical warp-weighted loom (figure 7). This has only one cross-beam (at the top) where weaving starts, the warps being held taut in groups by stone or earthenware weights, which are usually shaped like a pyramid, with a hole near the tip. Such loom weights dating about 2500 BC were found at Troy, and depictions on Greek vases show the same design of loom in use about 500 BC. It was later the main type of loom used by the Romans (Wild 1970) and during the European Iron Age. I am not aware of the date of the earliest loom weights in Britain, but they were certainly found at Glastonbury.

In all other looms, the warp yarns are stretched between two cross-beams, the warp beam around which the warps are wound beforehand and the cloth beam for the woven cloth. In the simple horizontal frameless ground loom, the beams are separated by pegs driven into the ground. This type of loom was used in pre-dynastic Egypt, and is still used by nomadic peoples because the parts can easily be transported. One should perhaps be on the look-out for evidence of such looms earlier than the Iron Age in Britain.

The next development was the joining together of the end beams with side beams to form a vertical frame loom. With this loom the cloth was woven from the bottom upwards, and it was used in Egypt as early as the twelfth century BC. It was not until the Middle Ages that the frame loom became horizontal as in modern designs.

The preparatory arrangement of the warps is known as warping. Plain weave is the simplest and oldest pattern, but it is possible to have a plain weave in which more than one weft goes over more than one warp (e.g. in a hopsack). In twills, the wefts pass over more than one warp in a step-wise arrangement, and several heddles (to raise the warps) are required in the weaving. Patterns are produced mainly by weaving together yarns of different colour, and before dyes began to be used, naturally-coloured wools were woven together to produce checks.

In frame looms, each weft thread is 'beaten up' with a comb, and in discussing the concave bone combs from Glastonbury Roth (1950) gave convincing evidence that, because they are usually semi-circular in section, they could not have been used in weaving, particularly with the warp-weighted loom. In recent versions of the latter, a wooden implement named a sword because of its shape was used (figure 7).

Cloth is still in a rough condition when it leaves the loom, and modern factory finishing involves washing, milling (fulling) to shrink the cloth, raising (the 'nap') and cropping it, as well as dyeing and pressing. It is likely that little finishing took place earlier than the ancient civilisations, but by Roman times the fulling of wool cloth was well developed. Fulling was carried out by 'treading' or 'walking' the cloth in a tub of water. The more recent peasant method was to rub the damp cloth with the hands or feet on a flat surface. Fulling in a tub not only shrinks the wool, but loosens dirt, and a common detergent added was stale urine (ammonia).

The cloth was then rinsed in clean water, and while still damp the nap was raised by thistle or teasel heads fixed in a frame to give an implement rather like a hand card. The nap was then trimmed to an even height with cropping shears, which were certainly used by the Romans.

Perhaps the main prehistoric finishing process was dyeing, which must have originated with textile fibres lacking natural pigment (see the section on Iron Age sheep, above). The idea of dyeing may have come from accidental stains of cloth with fruit juice. In northern Europe lichens become caught in fleeces before removal, and these could have caused staining if the fleece had been later washed in alkaline water. Also in northern Europe ancient wool cloth is usually preserved by waterlogging, and peat acids frequently remove or obscure dyes, making their analysis at best difficult.

Lichens may have been one of the first sources of dyes since they can be applied without a mordant, which is needed to attach many dyes to the fibre. Dyeing may also have been originally done in the cold, since Pliny (*Natural History* XXXV, 42) wrote that heating improved the fastness of dyes. In recent times the cloth was boiled with the lichen in an iron cauldron with alkali (again being provided by stale urine). Different species of lichen give different colours, crotal giving the original rich-brown shade of Harris tweed.

Dyes can be applied to raw (clean) wool, i.e. 'dyed in the wool', to yarns, or woven cloth. Dyeing before spinning was the most common method in antiquity, but cloth was also dyed 'in the piece'. A very wide range of natural dyes, mostly of plant origin, was used from prehistoric times until the nineteenth century. No more than a few natural dyes can be listed since they are very varied, and the plant dyes are of local origin. A blue fruit dye comes from the bilberry (*Vaccinium myrtillus*); leaf or stem dyes include blue woad (*Isatis tinctoria*), red madder (*Rubia tinctorum*) and yellow weld or dyer's weed (*Reseda luteola*). The animal dyes cochineal and Tyrian purple are unlikely to have been used in northern Europe in prehistoric time.

Extraction of the dye and its application were often quite complicated, which illustrates the technical achievements of prehistory. Woad, for instance, which probably dates back to the Iron Age, is extracted by first chopping up the plants, fermenting them, making the material into balls and drying them. The dried balls are then milled and the fermentation process repeated. After this the wool to be dyed is put into a colouring bath for two weeks with the fermented woad and some water. This is followed by oxidation in the open air for another two weeks. The dyeing and oxidation steps are repeated a couple of times before dyeing is complete.

Since the theme of this paper has been the inter-disciplinary approach to archaeological interpretation, I will end with the suggestion of G.W. Dimbleby (pers. comm.) that it might be useful to look among pollen analyses for an increase in dye plants during the Iron Age where there is evidence for the appearance of white wool.

REFERENCES

Burkett, M. E. (1979) *The Art of the Felt Maker*. Abbott Hall Art Gallery, Kendal, Cumbria.

Case, H. (1969) Neolithic explanations. *Antiquity 43*, 176-86.

Clark, J. G. D. (1947) Sheep and swine husbandry in prehistoric Europe. *Antiquity 21*, 123-36.

Harding, D. W. (1974) *The Iron Age in Lowland Britain*..

Johnstone, P. (1964) The Bantry boat. *Antiquity 38*, 277-84.

Korfmann, M. (1973) The sling as a weapon. *Sci. Amer. 229* (4), 34-42.

Leach, E. (1973) Concluding remarks, in *The Explanation of Cultural Change* (eds C. Renfrew & D. L. Clarke). London: Duckworth.

Murray, J. (1970) *The First European Agriculture*. Edinburgh: University Press.

Raistrick, A., E. A. Spaul and E. Todd (1952) The Malham Iron Age pipe. *The Galpin Soc. J.* (5), 1–11.

Reed, R. (1972) *Ancient Skins, Parchments and Leathers*. London and New York: Seminar Press.

Roth, H. Ling (1950) *Studies in Primitive Looms*, 3rd edition. Halifax: Bankfield Museum.

Ryder, M. L. (1965) Report on textiles from Çatal Hüyük. *Anatolian Studies 15*, 175-6.

—— (1966a) Shetland sheep and wool. *J. Bradford Textile Soc.* 1965-66, 91-9.

—— (1966b) The exploitation of animals by man. *Advance Sci. 23*, 9-18.

—— (1966c) Can one cook in a skin? *Antiquity 40*, 225-7.

—— (1968a) Fleece structure in some native and unimproved breeds of sheep. *Z. f. Tierzucht u. Zuchtungsbiologie 85*, 143-70.

—— (1968b) The evolution of Scottish breeds of sheep. *Scottish Studies 12*, 127-67.

—— (1968c) The origin of spinning. *Textile History 1*, 73-82.

—— (1969a) Changes in the fleece of sheep following domestication (with a note on the coat of cattle), in *The Domestication and Exploitation of Plants and Animals* (eds. P. J. Ucko & G. W. Dimbleby), pp. 495-521. London: Duckworth.

—— (1969b) Paunch cookery. *Antiquity 43*, 218-20.
—— (1970) Remains derived froom skin, in *Science in Archaeology* (eds D. R. Brothwell & E. S. Higgs), pp. 539-44 (2nd edition). London: Thames and Hudson.
—— (1973) Early textile technology. *J. Bradford Text Soc.* 1972-73, 12-24.
—— (1974) Wools from antiquity. *Textile History* 5, 100-10.
—— (1977a) Some miscellaneous ancient fleece remains. *J. Arch. Sci. 4*, 177-81.
—— (1977b) The Vindolanda wools, in *Vindolanda III The Textiles* (J. P. Wild), pp. 34-41. Hexham: Vindolanda Trust.
—— (1980a) Fleece colour in sheep and its inheritance. *Animal Breeding Abstracts 48*, 305-24.
—— (1980b) Hair remains throw light on British prehistoric cattle. *J. Arch. Sci.* 7, 389-92.
—— (1981a) Livestock, in *The Agrarian History of England & Wales* (ed. S. Piggott), vol. 1, part 1, pp. 301-410. Cambridge University Press.
—— (1981b) Wools from Vindolanda. *J. Arch. Sci. 8*, 99-103.
—— (1981c) The primitive breeds of domestic sheep of Europe. *Proc. 3rd Int. Archaeozoological Conference, Poland 1978* (in press).
—— (1981d) *Sheep and Man*. London: Duckworth (forthcoming).
Ryder, M. L. & S. K. Stephenson (1968) *Wool Growth*. London: Academic Press.
Severin, T. (1979) *The Brendan Voyage*. London: Arrow Books.
Smith, C. D. (1979) *Western Mediterranean Europe – a Historical Geography of Italy, Spain and Southern France since the Neolithic*. London and New York: Academic Press.
Trow-Smith, R. (1957) *A History of British Livestock Husbandry to 1700*. London: Routledge and Kegan Paul.
Waterbolk, H. T. (1975) The evidence for cattle stalling in excavated pre- and protohistoric houses, in *Archaeo-zoological Studies* (ed. A. T. Clason), pp. 383-94. Amsterdam: North Holland.
Waterer, J. W. (1956) Leather, in *History of Technology* (C. Singer & E. J. Holmyard), vol. II. Oxford University Press.
Wild, J. P. (1970) *Textile Manufacture in the Northern Roman Provinces*. Cambridge University Press.

Early Manuring Techniques

ALEXANDER J. FENTON

According to Professor Gudmund Hatt, 'it is in the art of manuring that Eastern agriculture excels, and Chinese farmers are adept at it', with human excreta rather than animal dung as a principal ingredient. The making of compost is also said to be a special Chinese art, using a range of waste materials to provide potassium, phosphorus, lime, magnesium, and nitrogen in the right condition for quick utilisation by the growing plants (Curwen and Hatt 1961). In Europe, archaeologists have been a little coy about getting to grips with this subject, though the realisation of the value of manure and the development of manuring techniques, and with them crop rotations or alternations (including the organisation of grazing), is almost of the same order of importance as the discovery of fire, and may indeed be in part a consequence of it.

A simple system of rotation involving a period of fallow was probably developed quite soon among the early agriculturalists, and the use of some form of manure appreciated (cf. Piggott 1965, 39). By the time of classical writers like Varro, who was 76 years old in 46 BC, manuring techniques were already sophisticated. Which parts of the farm should be manured, how it should be done, and what kind of manure should be preferred, had become part of the planning of the farming year. Roman farmers knew the virtues of cattle dung, pigeon dung, and of bird-droppings from aviaries, which were considered to be of more value than human excreta. The dung of goats, sheep and asses took third place, and that of horses a miserable fourth (Storr-Best 1912, 81–2). Even earlier, in the 2nd century BC, Marcus Cato had spoken of dividing up the manure – of pigeons, goats, sheep and cattle – so that half went on to the grain fields, a quarter around the olive trees, and a quarter on the meadow (Thielscher 1963, 67, 73), which shows that grazing could also be artificially manured.

In assessing relative values here, the Mediterranean climate has to be borne in mind. The Mediterranean imposed a kind of rotation involving a two-year alternation of crop and fallow, and in the fallow year much cleaning and breaking of the soil was done to keep the moisture in. A fine tilth made the best use of the water available (Percival 1976, 107). By the same token, the less moisture-holding the manure the less useful it was, and it should not inhibit the pulverisation of the surface that was necessary to prevent evaporation (cf. Clark 1952, 100) – a purpose, incidentally, to which the ard was well adapted.

In Northern Europe things were otherwise, and in medieval Sweden, for example, horse dung was reckoned a 'hot' manure and therefore good for acid, damp land (Granlund *et al.* 1961, 19). In Scotland, in recent times, horse manure has been ranked as third most valuable after poultry and sheep manure, because of its readiness to ferment and get hot. Pig manure followed, with cattle dung at the end because it contains over three-quarters of its weight in water, is the poorest in soil nutrients and is a cold manure, slow to ferment. It is essential for cattle dung to be mixed with straw, bracken, or some kind of bedding to soak up its moisture and help fermentation (Darling 1945, 33). Farmyard manure can provide only about 10 to 15 lb each of nitrogen and potassium, and 5 lb of phosphorus per ton, and large quantities are required to let growing plants get their essential nutrients (Smith 1958, 31). Questions of quality and quantity have to be borne in mind, therefore, but meantime, these notes concentrate on sources and types of manure that are not so much considered in the text books, but that nevertheless have interpretive value for early manuring and farming techniques in Northern Europe.

A link between the fire and manure is demonstrable at two levels, indoors and out. In North Scotland, houses with central hearths – most of which were long-houses or byre-dwellings – often had hollows in the floor alongside the hearth, towards the end nearest the door. In Shetland this was the *leepie,* in Orkney the *assie-pow,* and in Caithness the *lazy-hole.* To start with, the hollow in the earth floor was caused by the regular scraping of peat-ashes that had been pushed off the hearth. In Orkney practice the hot ash was contained within a circle of wet, sandy peats, which were eventually themselves powdered by the hot ash, and then the ash was used for bedding the cattle in the byre to absorb excess liquid. The Shetland name may be Norse – cf. Norwegian dialectal *løypa,* a mud-hole, heap of pig-swill – but the other names are Scots in origin. In later times the system became more formalised. The Shetland *leepie* could be made as a hole in the floor measuring up to 3 ft deep by 6 ft long by 4 ft wide. A mat of straw or rushes, with handles, and a Norse name, *rudistag,* was put in it, and when it had been filled with ashes and domestic rubbish of all kinds the mat and its contents were lifted out to the midden (Fenton 1978, 195–7). Similar holes for ash have been recorded in farm kitchens in Aberdeenshire and Dunbartonshire. In this way, peat, or turf for fuel were converted into ashes, which then served as bedding in the byre and finally ended up as fertiliser in the fields.

There are three other possibilities relating to the same raw materials:

(1) Turf could be cut from rough grazing areas and composted in middens with byre manure, seaweed, bracken, or any other suitable substances. Such middens were regularly turned, well mixed, and fermented. Composting is at least medieval in date, and is probably older. It involved the cutting of turf with a turf spade, a task well known to our prehistoric forebears. Indeed it has been calculated that an area of 3–4 acres (1.1–1.7 ha) had to be stripped to build a normal Bronze Age tumulus (Lerche 1970, 152) with devastating effects on the grazing. Turf could also be cut for building dykes and the walls and roofs of houses, and when these became tumbledown it could find its way to middens or directly on to the fields.

(2) In several parts of the world, including Scandinavia, the technique of cleaning new land by the burning of tree-covered areas, was of considerable importance. Organic materials – trees, scrub, turf – were reduced to ash which fertilised the following crop (Vilkuna *et al.* 1972, 486–501). There is little or no direct evidence for such slash-and-burn cultivation in this country, but a variant is known that goes back at least to the mid-seventeenth century. About 1662, Gordon of Straloch wrote of North-East Scotland that:

> When, several centuries ago, all places were shaggy with woods to the great hindrance of tillage, as these forest were felled, or were rotting with age, moss grew over them, especially in wet and sunken places. The moss was at first light and spongy, but, increasing every year by new additions, grew hard, and became firm and fertile land, which, no doubt is unfit for the plough unless it is burned, and then the crops luxuriate wonderfully with the ashes. After a year or two new ashes must be had with new fires.
>
> (Gordon (c. 1662) 1907, II, 224, 268)

In this case, burning was on the spot. In other cases turf was cut in one place, carried to another, and there burned. The practice could involve either the spade or the plough. The use of the plough in the technique of 'ribbing and burning' was very much a characteristic of North-East Scotland, though also known in Lanarkshire. It involved cutting furrows of turfy material with unploughed spaces between, drying and heaping the cut turf, and later burning it for the ashes (Fenton 1979, 158–62). The practice is commemorated in the place-name Bruntlands, common in the North East. Curiously enough, the use of the plough for this purpose antedates paring and burning with the paring spade, which reached Scotland from England in the first half of the eighteenth century. The turf, once cut with the paring spade, was treated as for the plough. Paring with the spade and burning became widespread in Scotland, but is a late development that goes with the days of improved farming (Fenton 1970, 162–7). In this it paralleled the situation in Sweden, which owed much to English influence (Bringéus 1970, 89–95). The English evidence goes back to thirteenth and fourteenth-century Devonshire charters and covers mattocks and ploughs as well as paring spades, though the use of paring ploughs appeared only in the eighteenth century (Dodgshon and Jewell 1970, 74). Irish sources show that paring and burning with mattocks and later spades was well established and widespread from the thirteenth century (Lucas 1970, 99–147). Ribbing with the plough, therefore, seems to have been a primarily Scottish practice prior to the eighteenth century. Without going into further detail, the common feature is the use of fire. Whether or not the original inspiration came from observing the effects of ash from the domestic fire on the growth of grass and cereal crops, the fact remains that fire, or the heat of fermentation, help to release chemicals suspended in the soil. However empirical, this was a real discovery.

(3) Manure itself may be used as fuel where other combustibles are scarce. This practice is well enough known in places like India, in parts of which cattle dung is so essential for fuel that it cannot be spared for the fields (Harrison 1954, 229). The same phenomenon was found in Northern Europe – in Iceland, the sandy islands around Denmark, and in this country in Ireland, Northern England, parts of Mainland Scotland and the Hebrides, and in Sanday and North Ronaldsay in Orkney (Fenton 1972, 722–34).

There were at least two ways of handling it and usually it was a job for the women. Cakes of dung gathered in the fields were carried home for drying, or dung from the byre was spread on the grass or against the house walls till dry enough. The Orkney evidence goes back to 1524; that from Northern England to 1499 (Way 1843, I, 63; Fenton 1978, 208–9). The relevance of all this is that the burning of dung was conditioned by the nature of the environment, and that it had to be integrated into a community farming system, in which substitutes like turf and seaweed could be used for manuring the fields. Since the ashes went onto the fields directly or via the byres, the loss was perhaps not so great, except in bulk. From the point of view of terminology, there are signs of a freemasonry in dung-burning in Scandinavian Europe. The northern English expression to *clap cassons* corresponds to the Danish *klap kassen, klappinger*, the Norwegian *klafsa*, to knead a wet, peaty mixture, and the Swedish *klappetorv* (Fenton 1972, 733). There is at least a possibility that the Vikings were familiar with the practice. How much older it is, is hard to say, though vitrified cow-dung ash has been identified at an Iron Age site at Hawk's Hill in Surrey (Evans and Tylecote 1967, 22–3).

It is time to move from the fireside to the byre. The kind of building with living space and byre under one roof had already evolved in Denmark by the Celtic Iron Age (cf. Anderson 1951, 40–64). It is found at sites in the Netherlands dating from the Early Bronze Age, and it has been suggested that the practice of cattle stalling was an innovation which found its origin in the Late Neolithic or Early Bronze Age of continental North-Western Europe (Waterbolk 1975, 393). It appeared in the northern part of Britain during the Viking period. Such byre-dwellings can still be seen, the blackhouse of North-West Scotland being one of its forms. Generally there was a single entrance for man and animals, and as often as not entry to the dwelling space was through the byre. The keeping of cattle in such byres is clear evidence for a developed form of agriculture, involving not only manuring of crops but also a requirement for manure in quantity.

Though partitions of wood or of stone were commonly used to separate animals, in areas like the Northern Isles this was rare. Instead, the animals were tied to dooks of wood or stone ranged along one side of the byre. The Shetland name is *veggle,* and in Orkney *lithie* or *havie,* all three Norse words. In part the device is pre-Viking, to judge by the perforated whale's vertebra found in the wall of a house at the Late Bronze Age settlement at Jarlshof (Hamilton 1956, 19). Such byres were not cleaned out regularly. The normal arrangement was for the dung to be allowed to accumulate throughout the winter, to be taken out in spring for the time of sowing. In byres with stalls it was impracticable to let the dung mound up under the animal's feet, and so it was pulled back and mounded up against the opposite wall, till it reached eaves' height. The dung was being continually intermixed with ashes, sandy peat mould and the like, so that the effect was to produce a compost. If, however, wall dooks were being used, a second row of dooks could be fixed at a higher level in the wall, to take into account the rising level of dung beneath the feet of the animals. This happened with horses too, for the dry nature of their dung made it good for bedding (Firth 1920 (1974), 16).

Under such circumstances, it was all the more necessary to absorb surplus liquid by spreading ash and peat mould, especially in the days before byre drains became fashionable. Evidence from Iceland and Greenland suggests that byre drains were not common until medieval times (Hoffman 1966, XVIII, 121–2). There are no drains in the Viking house at Underhoull in Unst, for example, but only flagstones (Small 1968, 65). This idea is supported by linguistic evidence. An Orkney name for the byre drain is the *sesters,* related to Norwegian *sessetre* and Danish dialectal *saes,* both meaning a plank or flagstone at the rear of the stall, under the animal's hind legs. There therefore appears to be a transference in sense.

The custom of letting the manure build up in the byres during the winter also had an effect on byre architecture, for in some of the nineteenth-century blackhouses of the Hebrides, the byre-end was often built very slackly or even filled in with turf, so that it could readily be opened up to give access for a horse and dung-panniers or a horse and cart. However, this feature, called in Lewis the *toll each,* is relatively late, since the dung was taken out in earlier days, as often as not, in creels on the human back, preferably female.

In the 1790s in Shetland, byre manure was rarely used on its own. It was left in the byre till seed-time, and then frequently mixed with ashes and light mossy earth gathered in the summer and kept in houses for that purpose. In winter, manure was also carried to the outfields, and there made up in small dunghills, composted with earth and seaweed (*OSA* 1973, VII, 586: Aithsting and Sandsting). At the same period in Orkney, middens were being made with cattle dung, ashes and turf, laid in alternate rows. Turf from the moors with a good mixture of peat moss and grit or clay was burned in the houses with a few peats to increase the quantity of ashes, which were obviously important (*OSA* 1975, XIV, 127: Firth and Stenness). And so we return to the elemental fire, with its ability to release appropriate nutrients in a form assimilable by plants.

Another important source was seaweed, which formed part of composts or was applied direct. It could also be burned, producing ash. There is no early evidence for its use as a manure, however, but its virtues were so widely known in later times that the presumption of its early use is strong (Clark 1952, 90; Fenton 1974, III, 147–86).

It can be taken for granted that manure was part of the environment of early farming communities in Britain. The origin of the concept of manuring may lie in part in observation of the effects of ash from domestic fires, and the use of fire in clearing tree and scrub-covered areas – producing, of course, rapid vegetational changes. Each firing of a peaty land surface, too, whether to fertilise a crop or not, led to erosion which could be considerable over the years. Manuring techniques of this and other kinds have had an incalculable effect over the centuries on the land surface and what was grown on it. In discussing prehistoric agriculture in Western Europe, P. J. Fowler has said – to misuse an opening sentence:

> Fertility, an abstract concept involving ideas and urges not only to regenerate but also to increase the bounty of the natural world in which Man finds himself and of which he is, in his own view, one of the important parts, was the major pre-occupation of those early and small populations inhabiting western Europe from c. 5000 onwards. (Fowler 1971, 153)

The same might be said of manure – but manure is far from being abstract.

REFERENCES

Anderson, H. (1951) Et Landsbyhus på Gørding Hede. *Kuml*, 40-64.

Ben, Jo. (1805) Descriptio Insularum Orchadianum, in *The History of the Orkney Islands* (G. Barry).

Bringéus, N. A. (1970) The paring and burning spade in Sweden, in *The Spade in Northern and Atlantic Europe* (A. Gailey & A. Fenton), 88-98. Belfast.

Clark, J. G. D. (1952) *Prehistoric Europe. The Economic Basis.* London.

Curwen, E. C. & G. Hatt (1961) *Plough and Pasture. The Early History of Farming.* New York.

Darling, F. Fraser (1945) *Crofting Agriculture.* Edinburgh and London.

Dodgshon, R. A. & C. A. Jewell (1970) Paring and burning and related practices with particular reference to the south-western counties of England, in op. cit. (A. Gailey & A. Fenton), 74-87.

Evans, R. T. & R. F. Tylcote (1967) Some vitrified products of non-metallurgical significance. *Bulletin of the Historical Metallurgy Group* 1/9.

Fenton, A. (1970) Paring and burning and the cutting of turf and peat in Scotland, in op. cit. (A. Gailey & A. Fenton), 155-93.

—— (1972) A fuel of necessity: animal manure, in *Festschrift Matthias Zender Studien zu Volkskultur, Sprache und Landesgeschichte* (E. Ennen & G. Wiegelmann), II, 722-34.

—— (1974) Seaweed manure in Scotland. *In Memoriam Antonia Jorge Dias* III, 147-86. Lisboa.

—— (1978) *The Northern Isles, Orkney and Shetland*. Edinburgh.

Firth, J. (1974) *Reminiscences of an Orkney Parish* (1920), 16. Stromness.

Fowler, P. J. (1971) Early prehistoric agriculture in Western Europe: some archaeological evidence, in *Economy and Settlement in Neolithic and Early Bronze Age Britain and Europe* (ed. D. D. A. Simpson), 153-82.

Gordon, R., of Straloch (1907) Adnotata ad Descriptionem duarum prefecturam Aberdoniae et Banfiae in Scotia Ultra Montana, in *Geographical Collections relating to Scotland made by Walter Macfarlane (Scottish History Society)* (ed. A. Mitchell), II, 224-68.

Granlund, J., *et al.* (1961) Gödsling. *Kulturhistoriskt Lexikon for nordisk medeltid* VI, 19-24.

Hamilton, J. R. C. (1956) *Excavations at Jarlshof, Shetland*. HMSO.

Harrison, H. S. (1954-58) Fire-making. Fuel and lighting, in *A History of Technology* (eds C. Singer, E. J. Holmyard & A. R. Hall), I, 216-37. Oxford.

Hoffmann, M. (1966) Gamle Fjøstyper belyst ved et Materiale fra Sørvest-Norge. *By og Bygd* XVIII, 115-36.

Lerche, G. (1970) Cutting of sod and heather-turf in Denmark, in op. cit. (A. Gailey & A. Fenton), 148-54.

Lucas, A. T. (1970) Paring and burning in Ireland: a preliminary survey, in op. cit. (A. Gailey & A. Fenton), 99-147.

OSA = *Old (First) Statistical Account*.

Percival, J. (1976) *The Roman Villa – An Historical Introduction*. London.

Piggott, S. (1965) *Ancient Europe from the beginnings of Agriculture to Classical Antiquity*. Edinburgh.

Smith, A. M. (1958) *Manures and Fertilisers*. London.

Small, A. (1968) A Viking longhouse in Unst, Shetland, in *The Fifth Viking Congress, Torshavn, July 1965* ed. B. Niclasen), 62-70. Tørshavn.

Storr-Best, L. (1912) *Varro on Farming. M. Terenti Varronis Rerum Rusticarum Libri Tres*. London.

Thielscher, P. (1963) *Des Marcus Cato Belehrung über die Landwirtschaft*. Berlin.

Vilkuna, K., G. Berg, H. Bjørkvik, S. Thorarinsson, A. Steensberg & K. Hold (1972) Svedjebruk. *Kulturhistorisk Leksikon for nordisk middelalder* XVII, 486-501.

Waterbolk, H. T. (1975) Evidence of cattle stalling in excavated pre- and protohistoric houses, in *Archaeological Studies* (from *Varia Bio-Archaeologica 46*) (ed. A. T. Clason).

Way, A., ed. (1843) *Promptorium Parvulorum sive Clericum*. Camden Society.

Discussion

JULIET CLUTTON-BROCK. The paper by A. J. Legge on animal husbandry in prehistoric Britain raises some interesting points on the origins of dairying and the history of milk as a staple food for adult humans.

All infant mammals feed exclusively on milk until, at the time when the deciduous teeth erupt, they gradually cease to suck and will lose the ability to digest milk, this being directly related to the waning of the enzyme lactase in the digestive system. It is of course an essential adaptive strategy that weaning should occur and that the young mammal should lose its taste for milk. It is only in some humans and some domestic animals, notably the cat, that the desire to drink milk continues into adult life.

The milk of different species of mammal varies in its percentage composition but in general it is composed of water, fat, proteins and lactose with trace elements, vitamins, and other minor constituents. In all land mammals lactose, or milk sugar, provides most of the carbohydrates or milk solids. Lactose is a complicated disaccharide that can only be absorbed after it has been hydrolysed in the small intestine by the enzyme lactase. The amount of lactose varies in different mammals, for example in reindeer there is 2.5 per cent, whilst human milk contains about 7 per cent and cattle about 4.8 per cent (Jelliffe and Jellife 1978).

Within recent years it has been discovered that a very large number of adult humans throughout the world do not produce enough lactase to metabolize the lactose in milk and when they drink it they experience stomach cramps, diarrhoea, and vomiting. Milk products such as cheese and yoghourt do not, however, produce these effects because most of the lactose is removed with the whey, and what remains is hydrolysed to lactic acid. Mature cheese contains no lactose.

Whether lactase is an adaptive enzyme that declines with the withdrawal of milk in the weaned infant or whether its presence or absence in the adult is genetically determined is not fully established. Most investigators, however, believe that lactase production is genetic and that it conforms to a consistent pattern of ethnic differences. Those peoples whose economy today depends on milk production, such as the inhabitants of north-west Europe, north and east Africa and much of Asia, have a low percentage of lactose-deficiency, whilst the peoples of China, south-east Asia, and central Africa, who traditionally do not consume milk, are unable to digest it.

All this implies that lactase-deficiency is the normal condition in human adults as it is in other mammals and the interesting question is when and why did a digestive tolerance of milk evolve. Lactose can be an important source of carbohydrate in the diet and it also enhances calcium absorption so that it may help to prevent rickets in climates where there is inadequate sunshine. It is therefore not hard to postulate that by natural selection the numbers of lactose-tolerant humans would increase in those cultures that for one reason or another could flourish only with the aid of dairy animals. It follows that in northern Europe during the prehistoric period when there was a shortage of food during winter those individuals who were able to metabolize milk would be at an advantage (Simoons 1979).

The regions where milk production developed were rather restricted. For example, there is support for the view that the milking of reindeer has been a relatively late development (Vainshtein 1980) in that the Lapps of Finland have a particularly high proportion of lactase-deficiency amongst the sample of people who were tested (Simoons 1979). The Italians today are not great milk drinkers and it is of interest that Columella, the Roman writer on agriculture had much to say on plough oxen, the breeding of cattle, and the production of sheep's milk cheese, but he made no mention of fresh cow's milk. Varro (c. 47 BC, on agriculture, II, xi, 3) made the following comments on milk, as an afterthought to his section on livestock: 'Of all the liquids which we take for sustenance, milk is the most nourishing – first sheep's milk, and next goat's milk. Mare's milk, however, has the greatest purgative effect, secondly ass's milk, then cow's milk, and last goat's milk.' It is notable that of these animals mare's milk has the highest percentage of lactose (6.2 per cent, Jelliffe and Jelliffe 1978).

Unlike the Romans, the British have by tradition been dairy farmers and it is therefore logical to assume that this way of life has been long established. My question at this symposium is whether it could be so ancient that the Neolithic people of Britain, as exemplified by the pastoralists who killed their calves at Hambledon Hill in c. 3500 BC, had already evolved sufficient tolerance of lactose to be able to flourish on cow's milk.

The killing of calves leads on to my second question which is, whether in a primitive society this really does indicate that the cows were milked. As described in the now classic account of the mechanism of the milk-ejection reflex by Amoroso and Jewell (1963) it is not at all easy to persuade lactating animals to let down their milk in the absence of their young (except with modern 'improved' livestock). The usual way in which this is achieved by most primitive peoples is the 'suckling method' (Vainshtein 1980). The calf is first allowed to suck for a short while and is then removed from the udder and is either tethered or held near the mother while she is milked. If the calf should die or be killed its skin is kept and given to the mother to smell before milking begins. There are other methods of inducing the milk-ejection reflex, such as blowing air into the vagina, but these are more a last resort than a routine.

I should therefore like to suggest that a high proportion of calf remains on a prehistoric site actually argues against an exclusive dairy economy and that at Hambledon Hill cattle were kept for every purpose including perhaps some milk.

REFERENCES

Amoroso, E. C. & P. A. Jewell (1963) The exploitation of the milk-ejection reflex by primitive peoples, in *Man and Cattle* (eds A. E. Mourant & F. E. Zeuner). *Royal Anthropological Institute Occasional Paper 18*, 126-38.

Jelliffe, D. B. & E. F. P. Jelliffe (1978) *Human Milk in the Modern World*. Oxford: Oxford University Press.

McCracken, R. D. (1971) Lactase deficiency: an example of dietary evolution. *Current Anthropology 12*, 479-518.

Simoons, F. J. (1979) Dairying, milk use, and lactose malabsorption in Eurasia: a problem in culture history. *Anthropos 74*, 61-80.

Vainshtein, S. (1980) *Nomads of South Siberia the Pastoral Economies of Tuva* (English translation), 289 pp. Cambridge: Cambridge University Press.

A. J. LEGGE. Dr Clutton-Brock's review of the literature on lactose intolerance confirms the long-standing use of milk as human food in the more northerly European peoples. Just as Roman writers may not have thought much of milk as food, they commonly refer to this as an important part of the diet elsewhere. Caesar's remarks on Britain are well-known '. . . most do not grow corn, but live on milk and meat . . .' (Handford 1960) and for the Germans who '. . . live principally on milk, cheese and meat.' His remarks that the Britons 'do not grow corn' or that the Germans 'are not agriculturalists' gain little support from the archaeological record; it is possible that the description refers to the diet of a ruling group, or that Caesar was 'writing down' the achievements of those subject to imperial expansion, as has been the case with more recent empires. Even so, such observations extend to the edge of the known Roman world, and Solinus, in the third century AD wrote of the Ebudae (Hebrides) that '. . . they lived on fish and milk.' It would seem that milk was a common food in Europe at the time of the Roman Empire.

With regard to the liking for milk, I had imagined that this was quite characteristic of carnivores and omnivores. As well as cats, I have seen pigs, dogs, bears and hedgehogs taking milk with relish; the list might be longer. Whether or not this inheritance in man is genetic is still debated. If the tolerance of lactose is genetic only, it seems a striking example of selection in populations that can have been exposed to domestic stock for only a few thousand years, even assuming a very early date at which milking began.

The question of calf killing and persuading the cow to give milk thereafter, may also have a European characteristic. Many examples of manipulation to induce milk ejection come from African herders in uncertain environments. In such cases, high proportions of young may be 'carried on' to insure against disaster (see Dahl and Hjort for a review) and cows, in consequence, less often surrender their young. They may simply tolerate this less well. On the other hand, early husbandry manuals from Britain find less problem with calf-removal. Walter of Henley in the thirteenth century recommends weaning in two months, with a progressive withdrawal of milk in the second month. While the effect of this rapid process on the calf is not recorded, enough milk remains for its use and value to be the main concern of the instructions in animal husbandry. Fitzherbert, about 1524 AD, is more direct in his approach; 'Yet it is better... to sell those calves than to rear them because of the cost, and also for the profit of the milk to his house . . .'. The same advice is given by Cobbett at a later date (1824) who puts the problem more plainly, and with a certain blunt elegance. 'Sometimes it may be the best way to sell the calf as soon as it is calved; at others to fat it, and at others, if you cannot sell it, which sometimes happens, to knock it on the head as soon as calved . . .'. He goes on to say '. . . and as to the cow and the calf, the one must lose her young, and the other its life . . .'. Altogether this suggests that the toleration of calf loss may not be a feature – at least for Europe – of only 'improved' modern breeds. The main point of my interpretation concerns the proportions of young in the bone assemblages. For Grimes Graves, 30 per cent of the calves were killed by the time that the first traces of wear appear on the deciduous teeth. I am persuaded that this was a deliberate policy, and not natural mortality, by the regularity of the pattern in the two samples from Grimes Graves, and the virtual absence of juvenile mortality at some other sites. Killing such young animals is unlikely to be for meat production; the calves are just too small for this to be economic. Cattle could hardly be kept for the annual production of one little carcass. Of course, there are other sites with a high proportion of 'juvenile' bones – usually judged on bone fusion. Yet many of these animals could be two *years* of age or more; see, for example, Higham (1969), fig. 44; of the bovine radii from Troldebjerg, two-thirds of the male group were 'fusing' at the time of death. If the age for bone fusion is compared with the tooth eruption pattern, it is evident that the majority of cattle killed were 'juvenile' (that is, with unfused bones) though most were *older* than two years.

The contrast lies between 'infantiles' at Grimes Graves, and the more familiar 'juveniles', many of which would have approached adult body size, and would have been more yielding of meat.

At Hambledon Hill, my argument involves the sex-ratios evident (or which I argue to be evident) rather than the proportions of young. There appear to be few of these at the site, where the few jaws will give little tooth eruption data. Dr Clutton-Brock argues that cattle would be multi-purpose in the British Neolithic, a point on which we fully agree. My argument is that Grimes Graves in the Bronze Age, and with some evidence from the British (and some sites in the Swiss) Neolithic, milk was given a priority such that the slaughter policy and herd composition combined to make this the *main* food output from the herd.

REFERENCES

Caesar. *The Conquest of Gaul.* Trans. S. A. Handford, Penguin Books.

Cobbett, W. (1824) *Cottage Economy.* London: Cobbett.

Dahl, G. & A. Hjort (1976) *Having Herds.* Stockholm.

For other references, see Legge above.

A Summing-Up

PETER JEWELL

The past decade has witnessed a remarkable expansion of our knowledge of the ways in which the land of Britain was used in the prehistoric past. The evidence has come from field survey, aerial photography, research excavation and rescue excavation. This new knowledge and the new ideas engendered have begun to be synthetized in a number of publications, of which the Council for British Archaeology volumes on Highland and Lowland Britain are notable examples. The reports from the Butser Ancient Farm experimental project have presented evidence of a complementary kind. In this same period the *Cambridge Agrarian History of England and Wales* has been prepared and several of our speakers have contributed to the volume on prehistoric agriculture. This Munro Symposium has presented a timely up-dating of this process of synthesis, with papers that have fallen into three themes: the occupancy and use of the land; tillage and crop production; livestock and their management.

THE USE OF THE LAND

I greatly valued the setting of the scene by Dr Nash. I cannot escape the fact that if I think about farming in Britain my starting point is the countryside as I know it. That local knowledge is set in perspective by the kinds of maps and statistics that Dr Nash presented. The great diversity of farming systems in Great Britain is an enduring feature and presumably has great relevance to what was possible in prehistoric times. The construction of a land-capability map makes me wonder whether such a construction could be made for prehistoric times. The ingredients are objective – knowledge of climate, rainfall and temperature, soil type, geological formation, topography and drainage, and vegetational cover – and many of these are being quantified by environmental archaeology. The *résumé* of productivity today was equally useful, with arresting facts, as for example the higher yield per hectare of grain crops in Scotland compared with England and Wales.

Whilst our thinking is given a firm basis by knowledge of modern agriculture it should equally be argued, I suspect, that this image is dangerously misleading if used as a guide to the past. We must divest our thinking of the idea that good productivity depends on modern fertilizers and high technology. What could have been achieved by intensive labour? Another obstacle to reconstruction of the past is comprised by the severe deterioration in productive capability of much of upland Britain since prehistoric times. What was its former capability? This is a vital question for Scotland where three quarters of the land is rough grazings. Its carrying capacity today, at one (or fewer) sheep to two hectares may be misleadingly low.

The thought that the Celtic fringe was not so marginal leads naturally to the paper by Halliday, Hill and Stevenson on Early Agriculture in Scotland. The authors presented only a brief review, but one of great significance in showing that Scotland shared with the rest of Britain a previously unsuspected density of human occupation and, necessarily, of food production. They emphasized that there is no longer any reason to suppose that agriculture was more primitive in the north and west than in the south and east. Research in Scotland wholly reinforces the new interpretations that are emerging from the rest of Britain.

To turn now to Peter Fowler's paper, the thesis that he expounded is to me extremely exciting and of cardinal importance to archaeological interpretation. I refer to the concepts of a relatively high population density, of territorial division of the land and of intensive use for agriculture and animal husbandry. I do not expect that the author himself, or other archaeologists, feel the thesis to be instantly exciting because they have been developing these new interpretations for the past decade. I must confess, however, that my own participation in archaeology has had to give way to other work of late and so I have not followed developments closely. The force of new ideas was brought home to me on reading Colin Burgess's 'The Age of Stonehenge', and some of Peter Fowler's own writings, and is now amplified by the present paper and the excellent illustrations we were shown. As a biologist, a supporter of the sociobiological thesis, and an ardent supporter of ideas such as those expressed by Robert Ardry in 'The Territorial Imperative', I am predisposed to embrace ideas of territorial and tribal boundaries, of competition for land and of an occupied landscape. I have thought for a long time that the population size of prehistoric times has been consistently underestimated. I think of human populations as expanding rapidly to occupy available space and – once established – of becoming even more firmly entrenched. I am sorry if we must relinquish idealistic views of Neolithic egalitarianism and primitive communism, but the door is left open for co-operative enterprises and the disruption supposed to have been caused by invasions of successive cultures can be largely dismissed as illusory.

As Fowler showed, then, use of the land was well organized and part of it was intensively farmed by the mid-second millennium BC. Land was enclosed for four reasons – the control of animals, to improve production, to protect crops and to define property. The fourth reason, and perhaps in large part the third, relate to a defensive stance against other men, but, overall, the fields and enclosures reflect the people's adaptation to the realities of their environment. In other words, their ecology is being explored and exposed by modern archaeological research, and to me the prospect of interpretation seems much more manageable. For example, with such great occupancy it is no wonder that the wild horse became extinct in the Neolithic, and wild cattle were becoming exterminated as the enclosures were being defined in the late part of the second millennium. More importantly, the recognition of the intensive occupancy of the land, of widespread settlement and sizeable resident populations removes the mysticism from linear ditches, enclosures, and the multiplicity of boundary earthworks that have now been discovered, and permits them to be seen in their functional role in the economy of the people.

TILLAGE AND CROP PRODUCTION

The papers that fall into this section, by Rees, Reynolds, and Hillman, were notable without exception for their exploration of ethnographic parallels. 'Animal, vegetable, or mineral', evidently continues to be a popular game amongst archaeologists. It suggests to me that rich rewards are still to come from recognizing the curious tools that people use and the further observation and recording of what people with primitive economies do today.

Sian Rees emphasized the need to thoroughly understand the function of a tool before its occurrence can be used to avail in the interpretation of a site. Not surprisingly, she has spent a great deal of time watching people use traditional agricultural implements. She modestly asked us to bear with her in relating her observations on a South American holiday but it seemed to me that this was the very stuff of which discoveries are made. To see the horn yoke in use in Bolivia and Peru translates speculation into knowledge.

Ascribing the correct function to a tool is evidently far more difficult than might be supposed as was tellingly brought home by Dr Rees' illustration of the great variation in modern billhooks. I have used several of these types on farms in southern Britain and thought, as I now see wrongly, that I would recognize this tool anywhere. My consolation is to know that an ancestor held much the same tool in his hand 2000 years ago.

Of the tools of uncertain use my interest was captured by the long Romano-British scythe from Farmoor where the context suggested mowing grass as more appropriate than harvesting grain. More information about making hay in prehistoric times is so important for the interpretation of practices of animal husbandry that I wonder whether grass-cutting would ever be distinguished from corn-cutting by the pattern of wear on a tool?

Peter Reynolds was another speaker who treated us to an illustrated account of his travels, but his particular purpose was to link observations on peasants at work with the experimentation at Butser Ancient Farm. His most striking example was to throw new light on ard marks and evidence for ploughing in prehistory. The known types of ard, when tested experimentally, did not create the deep score in the subsoil that had been expected. This was a disappointing outcome of both the tilling experiments, with trained draft oxen, and of the reconstruction of ards that had been based on British and Danish models. The outcome was puzzling, and the impasse frustrating. To clear his brain Reynolds set off to holiday in Spain (accompanied by our first speaker Peter Fowler). There, in Lugo province, they saw a Spanish ard, 'el cambelo' in use for breaking new ground. As we saw in the photograph it was a massive instrument and I think we could all detect the speaker's delight in its discovery because it appeared capable of producing just such scores as comprise ancient plough marks. I have no doubt that this hypothesis will be put to experimental test.

Another aspect of the work at Butser has been concerned with crop yields. If pre-Roman Britain had a densely occupied landscape and a buoyant economy how was this sustained? The experiments at Butser suggest that one contributory factor was the relatively high yield of emmer wheat and spelt wheat despite lack of fertilizers or other features of modern crop production. In the discussions after this paper some contributors were incredulous of these results, but the techniques of measurement were standard and unexceptionable and these results should indeed occasion genuine surprise. There is an unsuspected productive potential in primitive methods that still requires elucidation. Perhaps it lies in the combination of a robust cereal crop, disease resistance, extra-beneficial effects of intensive labour and, as was suggested, a symbiotic role of 'weeds' whereby they provide low ground cover and promote the retention of water in the soil.

Apart from the planned experiments, a particular delight of the work at Butser has been the unexpected revelations. At harvest, for example, despite the trial of many kinds of tools and 'sickles', the most efficient way of harvesting emmer and spelt proved to be plucking by hand. This fact, together with the reminder given us by Dr Rees and Dr Hillman that many peasants today harvest their cereals by uprooting them, can only cause exasperation for it leaves nothing to be found in the archaeological record. Another bonus was the discovery that the weed called cleavers (*Galicum apraine*) survives and sets seed in autumn sown fields but is destroyed by the cultivations of spring sowing. The presence of these seeds, therefore, may be an indicator of winter wheat. These examples are only the slightest indication of what Butser has to offer to archaeological interpretation.

Butser does not attempt to re-create the living conditions of Iron Age farmers: on the contrary it is a modern open-air laboratory established to test hypotheses about Iron Age agriculture with exacting rigour. Exactly this role was fulfilled in a test of slash and burn clearing in woodland plots at Butser. In the paper given by Rowley-Conwy the results (which gave very poor yields) were used to support his thesis that slash-and-burn is an inappropriate technique in temperate Europe. The sustained yield from permanent fields at Butser helps to support alternative proposals. It seems from the clear evidence that Rowley-Conwy presented that we must be prepared to part company with another cherished concept, and slash-and-burn may have been of little importance in neolithic Britain.

Another traveller in time was Dr Gordon Hillman who showed as fascinating pictures of the way in which peasants in the Near East carry out their agricultural work. In addition to these ethnographic impressions, however, he assembled much comparative botanical material whilst working at the British Institute of Archaeology at Ankara. This material, in turn, has provided the basis for a number of interpretive models. The elements in his interactive ethnographic model are: observation of husbandry practices where traditional food production survives; observations on crop processing; the sequence and types of tools used; the collection of samples of crop and by-products at every stage and analysis of size range and relative numbers of grain, chaff and weed seeds; correlation between processes and the products generated.

The charred remains of crops are the items that must be sought at every archaeological settlement site. To recover these calls for large samples of soil, and separation by flotation. The task is formidable yet must be undertaken if these powerful new techniques, and the models engendered, are to be exploited. Evidence may be sought for the function of excavated structures, times of sowing, methods of coping with weeds, methods of harvesting and threshing, winnowing, pounding and storing. This is botanical detective work of the very highest order.

LIVESTOCK AND THEIR MANAGEMENT

It is a long time ago (1959 to be exact) that I was prompted (and inspired) by Professor F.E.Zenner to review the bone reports then existing on British cattle. In the event the exercise proved useful despite the distressing paucity of data. Bone reports were limited to a few measurements of highly selected and small samples, criteria for determining the age of animals at death were hardly established and sheep could not be distinguished from goats! Concepts have changed and I take it that nowadays all prehistorians wish to extract the last ounce of information from bone assemblages, and other animal remains, yet I fear we cannot be satisfied with the state of our knowledge of the biology of domestic stock, the adequacy of reference material, or the resources available to deal with huge quantities of material.

The talk by Michael Ryder reminded us of all the functions served by animal products and their traces in excavation. He has been prolific in his own contributions in this field, most particularly in the areas where the clues yielded by the remains of skin and fleece might otherwise have remained unexplored. This is a subject that Dr Ryder has made his own and the detail that can be revealed was strikingly illustrated by his reference to his investigations on material from the Roman site of Vindolanda. There preservation was so good that pigmentation of hairs as well as fleece type and 'hairiness' and 'woolliness' could be determined, indicating a great deal about varieties of sheep and the wools available for the production of cloth. Dr Ryder also made good use of ethnographic material based on his own travels amongst stock-keeping people in the Mediterranean region.

On the management practices revealed by bone Dr Ryder again turned to the question of autumn killing and presented further reasons why this is unlikely to have been an established practice. With this I wholly agree. I think the resources of the environment in terms of fodder have not been adequately evaluated. Scrub, foggage, fallow land, haulms and hay would all have made a contribution. Stock can sustain severe loss of condition and yet remain of greater value alive than dead (as meat that would need preservation): the living animal retains a protential for recovery. It would be of great value if we could have a convincing model of how herd structures might have been manipulated in prehistory.

A somewhat neglected aspect of animal remains in archaeological sites – namely their dung – was dealt with by Sandy Fenton. The context was that of manuring and its relevance to crop production, but its importance is to remind us that mixed farming is an integrated system in which plants and animals complement one another. I suspect that the remains of dung are still not forced to reveal the secrets that they could, from pollen, plant spicules, and the egg cases of parasites.

In considering cattle husbandry in pre-Iron Age Britain Tony Legge postulated that herds were managed in pastoral economy for milk production. He based this assertion on cattle remains from two kinds of sites, one the Bronze Age settlement site of Grimes Graves and the other the Neolithic and putatively ceremonial sites of Hambledon Hill and Mount Pleasant. Two features of the assemblages of cattle bones suggested an emphasis on milk production: a preponderance of cows and a high proportion of young animals culled as calves or at under one year old. These young animals were slaughtered, Legge suggests, in order to leave their dam's milk for human consumption. The feature suggesting ceremonial slaughter was the high proportion of articulated lower limbs at Hambledon, apparently not dismembered as would have been necessary to derive the maximum food value. I would need more convincing evidence for a ritual purpose for the intact skeletons of distal limbs but I must agree that this wasteful behaviour needs explanation.

I find the idea that our Neolithic engendered groups of specialized cattle-keeping people, who were in effect pastoralists with milk as the major food, a challenging one that should be seriously explored. Climate, abundant water and abundant fodder would all be conducive to effective production. Were there, however, conditions that would have induced such a specialized economy? What combination of ecological and economic factors would have made pastoralism a preferred way of life over mixed farming and the consumption of meat? Here is a field where ethnographic studies have been neglected. I do not know of accounts of pastoralists in temperate-maritime or Mediterranean environments. My own interests have been in tropical savannas and the pastoralists of semi-arid zones of Africa. I certainly do think there is a great deal of value to be learnt from studying their systems of animal exploitation but it is not easy to apply in a meaningful way to temperate Britain. In this scarcity of information, however, there has been the timely publication in an English translation of Soviet studies on the pastoralists of continental Asia (*Nomads of South Siberia* by S. Vainstein, with an introduction by Caroline Humphrey, CUP 1980). The account is fascinating and has much of relevance to this Symposium. Clan territories are mentioned (although in a reference to hunting); the proportions of stock (sheep, goats, cattle and horses); summer and autumn shearing for wool; the distances covered in seasonal migrations (from 6 km to 30 km being typical), and the use of hay for winter keep are all documented. Interestingly some small scale agriculture with irrigation is practised by these people and it is considered to be an integral part of this nomadic pastoralism and not an outside influence.

To return to aspects of cattle husbandry in prehistoric Britain, puzzles of two kinds persist, the first relate to the necessity for, and adaptiveness of a pastoral economy, and the second to the actual evidence in cattle bones. What conditions would have given rise to a persistent pastoral economy? Our green and pleasant land does not call for the adaptations of nomadism imposed by irregular and erratic rainfall, or by the harsh cold of an inner continental climate. Could the fact that neolithic farmers were intrusive into Britain have been a predisposing factor? The mobility and productivity of domestic stock made them the ideal vehicle for colonization. The 'wildscape' would have presented abundant fodder and a climate more attractive than continental Europe. As 'wildscape' turned to 'landscape' the pastoral way of life would have generated its own traditions and comforts. But, even if possible, what is the actual evidence?

The evidence we have heard rests on the high proportion of the bones of calves and juvenile cattle found among the remains. It emerged in discussion, however, that the meaning of this phenomenon is highly contentious, and several speakers could not accept that it indicated dairying. High natural mortality among young animals, and differential use and survival of bones are objections to be met. I am uneasy with the proposition because the pastoralists that I have come across (in African savannas to be sure) keep the young stock alive, sharing some milk with them, and wean and rear most of them. I can accept that a proportion of bull calves might be killed and eaten but it would seem a more frugal husbandry to keep most on to be killed at greater live weights. In reading about the Siberian nomads I learnt that the age at which they castrate male calves is between one and two years (sheep and goats are castrated at the age of three to four months). I wonder how castration at these ages, instead of a few days after birth (the practice of modern husbandry) would affect skeletal growth, and so the size and appearance of bones after death? More modern comparative material and yet more from excavations should help us to resolve these controversies.

I shall not add to speculation. A clear conclusion from this conference is that ethnographic examples and exacting experimentation can bring great precision to our interpretations. Our speakers have given us ample evidence on which to question the concept of farming only for subsistence and of ill-fed and poorly managed stock. It seems to me that the leads are there to permit a realistic synthesis of farming productivity in prehistoric times and an appraisal of the population density that it sustained.

Appendix

ROGER MERCER

As a tailpiece to this collection of papers on aspects of prehistoric farming practice, some brief indication of the volume of production within likely prehistoric farming systems might be helpful. Until much more of the invaluable experimental work being conducted at the Butser Hill Ancient Farm is available, only the broadest inferences can be drawn, and even these should be regarded with caution. The figures offered may help to give some impression of the scale of enterprise and population implied by much of the present evidence for prehistoric farming in Britain. I have drawn heavily on the information that Butser has already made available, and have also used figures relating to manual farm work, in a nineteenth-century agricultural notebook (McConnell 1885). These figures will hardly reflect prehistoric working rates, but will assuredly represent a more efficient rate of working (in terms of tools and techniques) than prehistoric technique, and will thus provide one limit to the possibilities.

CEREAL CROPS

I have chosen the area of field system, of apparently Middle Bronze Age date, surveyed by Richard Bradley and Julian Richards on downland south-west of Segsbury, Berkshire (Bradley and Richards 1978, fig.7:2) where an area of approximately 9 km^2 of fields is recorded. This area, apparently laid out in five separate but contiguous sections, totals 2250 acres (approx.) and possibly represents five farms of c.400–500 acres. I will now proceed to examine such a unit in terms of cereal production.

Figures published by Reynolds (see above table 1, p.109) for the yields of winter sown emmer wheat (*Triticum dicoccum*) in Field II at Butser, a crop not treated with manure, displays the record of production over an eight year period on a northern facing slope on a chalk subsoil at an elevation of 270 m OD. This record shows production ranging between 3.7 tonnes per hectare and 0.4 tonnes, averaging 1.85 tonnes per annum. Production with dressings of manure would almost certainly enhance this output significantly, and this possibility is indicated by the figures in

Reynolds' table 3 (p.110) for 1978 and 1980. More information is necessary, but for the present exercise I will use the 'unmanured' figures. These figures provide, at least, a reasonable basis for the calculation of prehistoric yields on the chalk lands, although they of course cannot be carried across to other subsoils, crops and environments.

The figures seem to relate quite closely to those of late eighteenth-century British yields given by White (1963), but are well in excess of earlier figures that he presents. The reliability of such earlier figures has often been called into question, compiled as they were for purposes of rental, tithe and tax assessment. Added to such uncertainties is the variation in the local significance of units of measurement prevalent in Britain, and of course elsewhere, until the middle of the last century. This must make any such comparison hazardous. In view of these hazards it would seem reasonable to use the Butser figures *simpliciter* as a unique source which it is not possible to regard in the same light as early documentary accounts. Similarly, early seed/yield figures are difficult to interpret. Again, the Butser figures (see below) closely resemble those in late eighteenth and early nineteenth-century sources.

The average yield in Field II at Butser is 1.85 tonnes per hectare = 0.75 tonnes per acre of emmer wheat, the soil not being dressed with manure.

In the 500-acre parcels apparent at Segsbury, therefore, with two-thirds of the land in production at any one time, and with sufficient population available to work it, the total annual grain product might well approach 250 tonnes. Of this total we can perhaps assume a wastage through spillage, rotting, disease etc., of twenty per cent, leaving 200 tonnes.

In the Butser 1973–80 results, as published in table 1 above, the average seed/yield ratio (again for emmer) for those years (ranging from 1:7 to 1:59) is 1:30. If we can accept this figure as a fair average indication of seed/yield, then of the 200 tonnes, one-thirtieth would have to be stored as seed corn. The figures for 1885 (given in McConnell, 195) are one to three bushels hand sown in broadcast fashion, to thirty-two bushels produce per acre. (Generally, if sown in October, one bushel sown is sufficient – again a seed/yield ratio 1:30.) If, for caution's sake, we assume that one *twentieth* of the produce was put down to store as seed, to compensate for disease, rotting etc., then 10 tonnes of grain would have to be stored per annum for the sowing of an area of this size.

Davies (1971), speaking of Roman military provisioning, states that one tonne of grain is recorded as taking up 1.5 yd^3 in a military granary while McConnell (1885, 18) records that one tonne of wheat will occupy 44 $ft^3 = 1.6\ yd^3 = 1.15\ m^3$, and therefore, in optimum circumstances, the seed corn to sow 330 acres will be stored in $10 \times 1.15\ m^3 = 11.5\ m^3$ of space, however constructed. Two or three 2 m × 2 m 'four post' granaries would be adequate, it would seem, for this purpose. Reynolds (1974) has indicated that beehive and bell storage pits on IA sites tend to observe a standard capacity of $1.2 m^3$ and has calculated that these will hold 1.12 tonnes of modern threshed barley. Reynolds points out that the grain may have been stored in the ear, thus considerably reducing the quantity stored in each pit. At present it is only possible to indicate that, stored in threshed condition, according to the model under consideration, each pit could hold the produce of 1.4 acres, and the seed corn for 42 acres.

The balance of some 190 tonnes of grain would thus remain available for consumption. The total calorific requirement per person per day (recommended in the Report on Public Health and Medical Subjects No.120 HMSO 1969) is

2300–3200 calories Male
2000–2500 calories Female
1200–2000 calories Children

recommended as the daily intake of energy and nutrients for Britain. Perhaps we can accept that an average consumption over the whole population of 2500 calories *per diem* would have been sufficient and that with wastage again taken into account this requirement might be enhanced to 3000 calories *per diem*. Thus the human requirement for one year is generally recognised as about 1 million calories, or 1 SNU (Standard National Unit). One kg of wheat or similar grain will mill down to 900g of meal, which will yield c.3100 calories. Davies (1971) tells us that Roman military rationing (which may well reflect the current 'standard of living' in Barbarian Europe) allowed each soldier ⅓ tonne of corn per annum ≑ 33.3 × 3100 cal = c.1,003,000 cal = c. 1 SNU. Therefore we can perhaps accept that 0.3 tonnes of grain would satisfy a very major proportion of the calorific requirements of one person for one year and that therefore the 190 tonnes available would produce food for a human population approaching 600 persons. It is quite clear from evidence available from northern sites (Rosinish, Benbecula, Shepherd priv. circ. paper 1980; Cnoc Stanger, Caithness, Mercer priv. circ. paper 1981), and from the debris present on southern field systems (Fowler 1981), that manuring was a consistent practice from at least the end of the third millennium bc. The present experiments at Butser may suggest that yields under such a system might be higher by a factor approaching 2 : 1.

On the 500 acre parcel of land, under two-thirds cultivation, would produce sufficient cereal to provide the major element of the diet of 600 people. Any other major source of food, e.g. flesh, milk or game, would of course mean that the cereal would 'stretch' further and be sufficient for a larger population. The need to provide feed for draught animals and for other stock in winter would have been a significant drain upon these resources.

The *minimum* number of the contingent population would be directly related to the number of people required to *harvest* the crop. McConnell, writing in 1885, claims that '¼ acre was cut, tied and set up per reaper daily with the old hook' (1885, 27). Using these figures, 330 acres would require about 1320 man days to harvest by hand billhook in 1885. If we assume the harvest was completed within 40 days this would entail a minimum of 33 men, with, of course, more people to assist with transport and stacking. These latter activities might well imply the existence of draught animals as, of course, might the initial task of ploughing. Threshing could presumably be carried out over a more extended period and so could be done afterwards with no *additional* workforce. At any rate it would appear that, in broad terms, a total workforce of c.50–80 would be required to harvest such an area. It might thus be suggested that a *minimum* population for such an acreage under cultivation might be 100–150, while the *maximum* could be 500–600.

ANIMAL HUSBANDRY

One hundred acres of unimproved grassland will support fifty head of cattle (McConnell 1885, 458) and good average improved grassland will support a hundred. (Both of these figures refer to summer grazing only.)

OTHER DATA

One bull can service forty cows; one young cow will graze one acre of unimproved grass (summer grazing only); one calf will graze a half acre of unimproved grass (summer grazing only); thus a hundred acres of unimproved grass would support one bull, thirty-five cattle and thirty-five calves.

Such a herd at 1885 rates for Dexters (McConnell 1885, 127) is capable of producing 40 lb (18 kg) of milk per cow (or approximately 4 gallons). For prehistoric beasts we perhaps may assume 3 gallons daily per cow.

DAIRY

Five or six female calves retained on their mothers, to maintain six year replacement of the cow population, thus allows for twenty-nine calves to be killed per year. 30 cows × 3 galls *per diem* milk yield = 90 gallons *per diem* (409 kg). As 1 kg milk = 660 calories, therefore product in milk is 270,000 calories *per diem* = calorific intake of c.100 persons *per diem*.

This output of course cannot continue for the whle year and an average *per diem* over a year would most likely be represented by about half this figure. In winter (say five months), 36 cattle and 6 calves will require 24 lb (11 kg) per head *per diem* of hay for cows, and 20 lb (9 kg) per head *per diem* of hay for calves, $=(36\times 11)+(6\times 9)$ kg *per diem*, $=396+54=450$ kg *per diem*; i.e. a total for five months of 67,500 kgs or 67.5 tonnes of hay (assuming grass to be the only fodder).

In good grassland meadow 1.5 tonnes can be cut from each acre, so 67.5 tonnes of hay will require haymaking in 45 acres of good meadow land.

Alternatively, of course, the cattle can feed 'off their backs' through the low growth months, and from what natural feed is available with the supplementation of a little fodder. In these circumstances cows will almost certainly dry out. Reserved grass (fenced off during the growth period) will have died back but might well assist with maintenance during the autumn and early winter (involving, say, an extra 50 acres). Such a scheme will, like hay making, involve 150–200 acres of unimproved grassland for 50 head of cattle *per annum*. Our consistent and, perhaps significant, failure to locate cattle shelters in prehistoric contexts in Britain may well indicate that cattle were left out to fend at least partially for themselves throughout the winter.

Cattle grazing in the field will drop c.57 lbs (26 kg) of solid dung and 21 lb (9.5 kg) of liquid dung daily on summer grazing (in 1885). At half a cow to the acre for summer (6 months grazing) this would represent a total input of c.5130 lb (2332 kg) = 2.3 tonnes of solid dung and 1890 lb (859 kg) = 0.85 tonnes of liquid dung per acre – a very substantial refertilisation of the field. The recommended dressing of manure per acre for wheat in 1885 (McConnell 1885, 78) is 5 tonnes per acre.

BEEF

For beef production with the same number of head of cattle on the same acreage of land, the pattern will of course be somewhat different. By the age of three years a cow will have ceased to be an economic beef producer and will consume more energy in grass than it will build into beef. Perhaps a likely pattern therefore might be: 1 bull, 10 dams, 10 calves, 10 × 1 yr, 10 × 2 yr, 10 × 3 yr old cattle.

Nineteenth-century figures for Dexters would indicate a live weight of a two-year-old at c.800 lb (364 kg) with a 'dead weight' of c.456 lb (edible element by nineteenth-century Smithfield standards) = 207 kg. With poorer feeding in winter it is likely that the live weights might be substantially reduced, let us assume by 20 per cent = 72.8 kg suggesting a live weight of c.290 kg and a consequent dead weight c.166 kg. The average calorific content of meat is 2000 cal. per kg. Thus the product of one beast will be c.333,000 calories and, of the 10 beasts suggested in this model – just over 3 SNU – enough without supplement for a population of 3 (and assuming it possible to retain the meat in edible condition).

These single economy models are set out by the writer for clarity in illustrating the potential of each type. It is naturally endemically likely that mixed economies based on all three or two of the three models would occur. It of course will not have escaped the reader's notice that the dairy/beef model based on an area of 150 acres could be run alongside the cereal economy in the 500 acre model proposed (see above) on the ⅓ of the land left 'fallow' in that model – enhancing the population potential of that model by, in the case of dairying, perhaps some 50 souls.

Even if the figure of population for the 'beef economy' is somewhat conservative it is clear that one nuclear family will require well over 300 acres of land to be able to live by this means alone. Indeed extensive and consistent beef eating is the only possible route to a low population model for any period in British farming prehistory.

As an example here we may select the important site of Fengate, Peterborough (Pryor 1980). Here is situated a series of enclosures covering an area of at least 55 acres and probably much more. This enclosure complex would appear to function between c.1200 and 900 bc. The nature of the enclosure gateways and the droveways that lead to all parts of the system suggested to the excavator the use of the enclosure system as cattle land. It is inconceivable in the writer's view that this system or the known fragment of it could have been for the enjoyment of the kind of population that a beef producing economy would have supported. A dairy economy is endemically more likely (as indeed the scanty bone evidence suggests might be the case) and furthermore the scrupulous control of grazing and repeated access to the animals hinted at in the layout of the system is of less importance to a beef economy. With a dairy economy the known fragment of this system would have supported 30–40 people for at least part of the year and it is indeed significant that occupation evidence on the site is apparently transitory and the excavator suggests might well be subject to seasonal movement.

The labour element in any stock rearing economy is more difficult to assess. Effectively three or four people could have run a dairy system for an enclosure like Fengate for much of the year. Haymaking, if this was part of the farming strategy, and in the circumstances of this site on the Fen edge this might seem less than likely, would have demanded short term concentration of labour and again the demand for traction animals and transport. Anyway it is probably most helpful to look, as the excavator suggests, to Fengate as part of the broader economic system.

The writer is well aware that it will be possible to quarrel in detail with every figure given in this short paper either on specific grounds or on the general basis that a nineteenth-century source is not likely to reflect at all accurately upon prehistoric circumstances. However it would seem unlikely that any of the figures can be so badly awry that they will alter the order of magnitude of the conclusions.

Farming practice in British prehistory had the potential to support massive populations (to be counted, the author would suggest – over the whole of Britain – in millions, from at least the end of the Neolithic). In terms of cereal cultivation alone and on the basis of the figures adopted above one million souls would have required the successful cultivation of 825,000 acres on the chalk downlands of the south (an area equivalent in size to the modern County of Wiltshire and somewhat less than the County of Sussex). In terms of dairy economy the same population would, accepting the above figures (50 people to 150 acres) require upwards of 3,000,000 acres. As soon as we find ourselves in the presence of widespread field system construction (c.2000 bc) it would appear to the writer that these inferences or something of their order are a logical *sequitur*.

However let it not be forgotten that a single year of disease or crop failure (like that recorded at Butser in 1979) would spell appalling hardship heralding widespread disease and death. The volatility of such communities, and the possibility of their decline within the space of perhaps one year must act as a caution to archaeologists adopting too rigid an approach to the record as we have it from the miserably small sample of sites that have been adequately examined. The population hinted at may also serve to bring a sense of proportion to our appreciation of monumental and technological achievements that have perhaps dominated to too great a degree our conception of the period.

BIBLIOGRAPHY

Bradley, R. & J. Richards (1978) Prehistoric fields and boundaries on the Berkshire Downs, in *Early Land Allotment* (eds H. C. Bowen & P. J. Fowler) 53-60. Brit. Arch. Reps. 48.

Davies, R. W. (1971) The Roman military diet. *Britannia II*, 122-42.

McConnell, P. (1883) *Note-book of Agricultural Facts and Figures for Farmers and Farm Students.*

Pryor, F. (1980) *Excavations at Fengate, Peterborough, England: The Third Report.* Northamptonshire Archaeol. Soc. Monograph 1, Royal Ontario Mus. Archaeol. Monograph 6.

White, K. D. (1963) Wheat farming in Roman times. *Antiquity XXXVII*, 207-12.

List of Contributors

J. Clutton-Brock, Department of Zoology, British Museum (Natural History)

A. Fenton, Director, National Museum of Antiquities of Scotland, Edinburgh

P. J. Fowler, Secretary, Royal Commission on Historical Monuments, England

S. P. Halliday, Royal Commission on the Ancient and Historical Monuments of Scotland

P. J. Hill, 2 Haddington Place, Edinburgh

G. Hillman, Department of Plant Science, University College, Cardiff

P. A. Jewell, Professor of the Physiology of Reproduction, University of Cambridge

A. J. Legge, Department of Extra-Mural Studies, University of London

R. J. Mercer, Department of Archaeology, University of Edinburgh

M. J. Nash, Edinburgh School of Agriculture, University of Edinburgh

S. Rees, Welsh Office (Ancient Monuments Branch), Cardiff

P. J. Reynolds, Director, Butser Ancient Farm Project Trust

P. Rowley-Conwy, University of Cambridge

G. Russell, Edinburgh School of Agriculture, University of Edinburgh

M. L. Ryder, Animal Breeding Research Organisation, University of Edinburgh

J. B. Stevenson, Royal Commission on the Ancient and Historical Monuments of Scotland

Index

access ways, xvii, 24, 27, 34, 35, 60
Achnacree, Argyll, xviii, 62
aerial photography, 12-14, 15, 21, 22, 24, 35, 44, 56, 60, 63, 104, 105
agriculture
  Roman, 60, 72, 79, 80, 83, 99, 112, 187, 188, 189, 191, 210
  Anglo-Saxon, 34
  Medieval, 20, 34-5, 56, 89, 145, 146, 184, 186, 187, 188, 189, 191, 193, 196, 201, 202, 203, 206, 211, 212, 214
  representations of, 74, 98, 100, 101, 102, 103, 104, 112, 120, 186, 189, 195, 206
agricultural implements, 11, 66-83, 126, 129, 130, 138
Amoroso, E. C., 220
animal bone, xiii, xix, xx, 169-80, 183, 184, 187, 192, 193, 194, 196, 198, 199, 200, 203, 205, 221
  ageing, 171
  sexing, 171, 175, 178
animal husbandry, xi, xiii, xiv, xv, xvii, xix, xx, xxi, 3, 4, 5, 28, 44, 46, 67, 169-80, 182-208, 213-14, 218-20
  culling/killing, 4, 170, 171, 172, 179, 180, 182, 183, 193, 194, 195, 219, 220, 221, 222
animal products, 192-203
arable, x, xi, xiii, xv, xviii, xix, xx, 2, 3, 4, 9, 14, 15, 18, 34, 41, 44, 46, 60, 66, 67, 70, 89, 95, 102, 103, 104, 105, 106, 108, 109, 110, 111, 112, 115, 117, 118, 119, 124, 139, 145, 146, 156, 157, 169
ard, x, xi, xix, 20, 55-6, 70-1, 73, 77, 78, 94, 95, 98, 99, 100, 101, 102, 103, 104, 108, 145, 146, 157, 211; *see also* shares
  cultivation, 55-6
  Aspeberg, 102
  Donneruplund, 73, 99, 100, 101, 102, 103, 104, 105
  Dostrup, 73, 99, 102, 103, 104
  Hendriksmose, 73, 78, 99
  Hvorslev, 100, 101
  Litlesby, 101
  Lochmaben, 73, 99
  Milton Loch, 73, 99
  Slonk Hill, 102-3
  Vebbestrup, 78
  Virdifield, 70
Ardnave, Islay, Argyll, 56
Ashbee, P., vii, 22, 39, 99
Ashville, Abingdon, Oxfordshire, xx, 70
Aspeberg, Sweden, 102
Asvan, Turkey, 127
Avebury, Wiltshire, 16
Avoncroft Museum, 113
axe-hammer, 71, 78

Ballynagilly, Co. Tyrone, x, xiii
Barber, J., xiv, 55, 60, 149
barley, xi, xvi, xviii, xix, 4, 5, 6, 90, 91, 113, 125, 128, 129, 146, 147, 148, 149, 150, 152, 154, 156, 157, 170
barns, 46, 140, 144
Barrett, J., xiii, 12, 47, 62
barrows, x, xii, xv, xvi, 16, 22, 24, 25, 26, 27, 35, 37, 39, 55, 99
  cemetery, 22, 24, 25, 26, 27
  South Street Long Barrow, Avebury, xv, 16, 37, 94, 99, 103
basket, 72, 82, 155, 195
  basketry, 72, 202, 204, 206
Bay-Petersen, J. L., 95
Beaker Horizon, 16, 40
Beaker pottery, 196
beans, 5
  Celtic bean, xviii, xix, 129, 138, 147
billhook, 67, 72, 80
Bishopstone, Sussex, 15
bison, 192
blood, 182, 192, 193, 194, 195, 196, 197
Bodmin Moor, xvi, 11, 18, 19, 28, 41
bog, xiv, xvi, 19, 39, 75, 99, 187, 199
Boserup, E., 85, 94, 95
boundary systems, xvii, xviii, 14, 16-30, 34, 35, 44, 46, 56-62
  banked, 28, 56, 57, 60
  ditched, xxi, 21, 22, 24, 25, 26, 27, 28, 32, 39, 44, 56, 57, 60
  linear earthworks, xvi, 60, 62

boundary systems—*contd*
pit defined, 28, 56-7, 60
ranch boundaries, xviii, 14
reaves, xvi, xviii, 14, 30, 44, 46
Bowen, C., xi, xix, 11, 12, 14, 18, 26, 27, 99, 105, 110
Bradley, R., xviii, 12, 16, 28, 47, 67, 78
Brain, C. K., 173
Bronze Age, xi, xix, 20, 26, 44, 74, 77, 79, 81, 107, 147, 169, 170, 172, 178, 179, 182, 184, 186, 192, 196, 198, 202, 203, 212, 222
Early Bronze Age, 79, 139, 213
Middle Bronze Age, xviii, 21, 170
Late Bronze Age, xix, 11, 21, 47, 214
Broome Heath, Norfolk, ix, xii
Burgess, C., xvii, 11, 12, 55, 56
burial, x, 22, 156-8, 186, 192, 202, 212
buried cultivated ground surfaces, x, 37, 39, 55-6, 98, 99
Burkett, M. E., 202
burning, xiii, 9, 16, 86, 89, 90, 94, 117, 119, 130, 138, 139, 140, 142, 143, 144, 149, 150, 152, 155, 194, 195, 196, 197, 200, 210, 211, 212, 213, 215
see also carbonised seed, charred remains
Butser, Hampshire, *see* experimentation
byre, 46, 144, 183, 198, 211, 212, 213, 214

cairns
funerary, 18, 56
non-funerary, 18-19, 56, 62, 78-9
see clearance
cairnfields, xiv, 18, 19, 62
see clearnace
Calder, C. S. T., 19, 39, 60
Callanish, Lewis, Outer Hebrides, 55
calves, 172, 180, 219-20, 221
Can Hasan III, Anatolia, 141
carbonised seeds, 98, 106, 107, 108, 112, 117, 119, 170
Carn Brea, Cornwall, xi, 18
Case, H., xvi, 192
castration, 176, 179, 180, 182
Çatal Hüyük, Turkey, 202
Catsgore, Somerset, 144
cattle, ix, x, xiii, xiv, xvi, xviii, xix, xx, xxi, 3, 4, 27, 46, 80, 94, 95, 99, 100, 103, 169-80, 182, 183, 191, 192, 194, 195, 199, 210, 211, 213, 214, 215, 218-20, 221
Aberdeen Angus, 176, 178, 179
Bos longifrons, xvi
Bos primigenius, 172, 175, 177, 178, 179, 192
Bos taurus, 99
Chillingham, 183, 192
Dexter, 99
cattle shed, *see* byres
Caulfield, S., xii, xvi, 20, 40, 62
causewayed enclosures, xi, xii, xx, 14, 170, 172, 173, 174, 179, 180
Cefn Graeanog II, Wales, 138, 141, 143, 144, 146
chaff, 108, 126, 140, 142, 144, 146, 148, 149, 150, 151, 152, 153, 155, 156, 157
chalk/chalklands, x, xi, xii, xiv, 11, 21, 22, 98, 99, 100, 106, 107, 108, 116, 120, 165
Champman, D. H., 28
Chambers, J. D., 30, 34, 35
Charlock, 115, 116, 118, 139
charred remains, 123, 124, 130, 138, 139, 140, 141, 142, 143, 144, 145, 146, 149, 150, 151, 152, 153, 154, 155, 156, 158
charring, 127, 130, 139, 140, 142, 143, 144, 155
cheese, 194-6, 201, 218, 219, 220
Childe, V. G., 55
Clark, J. G. D., 85, 211, 215
Classical sources, ix, 9, 46, 77, 106, 111, 112, 113, 119, 120, 129, 151, 183, 195, 197, 201, 202, 207, 210, 219, 220
Caesar, ix, xxi, 9, 46, 106, 111, 220
Columella, 129, 219
Diodorus Siculus, 112, 151, 152
Galen, 129
Homer, 195, 201
Marcus Cato, 210
Pliny, 77, 120, 129, 207
Poseidonius, 151
Pytheas, 151, 152
Solinus, 220
Strabo, 112, 151, 152
Tacitus, ix, xxi, 9
clay, xii, 99, 105, 215
with flints, 107
clearance, x, xii, xiii, xvi, 16-19, 28, 85-90, 94
stone, xii, xiv, 16-19, 28, 78, 79
woodland, x, xiv, 16, 28, 85-90, 94, 102, 212, 215
climate, ix, xii, xiii, xiv, xvi, xviii, xxi, 1, 4, 5, 66, 80, 82, 97, 98, 103, 106, 108, 111, 120, 121, 124, 127, 130-1, 138, 147, 153, 154, 155, 163, 164, 165, 183, 210, 218
cloth, *see* textile
Coles, J. M., ix, xi, 15, 81
coprolites, 170
Crawford, O. G. S., 11
Crickley Hill, Gloucestershire, xii
crops, ix, xi, xvi, xviii, xx, 2, 3, 4, 5, 15, 33, 67, 89, 90, 91, 94, 98, 104-20, 123-58, 163, 164, 165, 193, 195, 198, 200, 210, 212, 213, 214
cultivation of, xi, xxi, 1, 2, 3, 4, 5, 15, 18, 28, 37, 46, 67, 78, 83, 85, 89, 90, 91, 100, 104, 106, 107, 108, 109, 111, 112, 119, 123-58, 163, 210
processing, 123, 124, 125, 126, 128, 129, 130, 131, 138, 139, 142, 146, 153, 156, 158, 174
products, 124, 125, 126, 127, 128, 129, 130, 131, 138, 139, 140, 141, 143, 144, 145, 148, 149, 150, 151, 152, 153, 155, 157, 158
protection of, 28
crop mark sites, 22, 56, 57, 60
cultivation marks, 55-6
ard, x, xi, xii, 15, 37, 55-6, 77, 78, 98, 99, 101, 102, 103, 104
plough, 15, 77, 99, 103
spade, 20, 55, 78
Cunliffe, B., xx, 11, 15, 46
cursus, 14
Curwen, E. C., 11, 210

dairying, xvii, 3, 4-5, 172, 179, 180, 218-220
Dalladies, Kincardineshire, x
Danebury, Hampshire, 15, 144
Dartmoor, xvi, xviii, xxi, 10, 11, 12, 14, 28, 39, 44, 46
deer, xiv, 94, 170, 172, 201
Dennell, R. W., xi, xvi, xix, 124, 125
digging hooks / sticks, 78, 100, 196
Dimbleby, G. W., xii, xvii, 15, 208
ditching, 28, 33, 39
Dixon, P. W., xi
dog, 170, 172, 220
domestic animals, *see* domestication
domestication, 92, 94, 95, 169, 172, 173, 174, 175, 178, 179, 182, 183, 184, 186, 187, 191, 192, 193, 194, 195, 196, 201, 202, 218, 221
drainage, xviii, 3, 22, 25, 33, 198
dung, 110, 144, 194, 197-8, 210, 211, 213, 214, 215
Durrington Walls, Dorset, 15, 169, 173, 174, 175, 178
dyes, 188, 207-8
  dyeing, 207-8
dykes, *see* field walls

Egolzwil, Switzerland, 155
Eldon's Seat, Dorset, xx
Enclosure, ix, xiii, 9, 11, 14, 16-37, 39, 41, 44, 46, 47, 60, 182
  Movement, 9, 10, 11, 20, 30-5, 37, 39, 44, 46, 47
enclosures, 19-21, 22, 24, 25, 27, 37, 39, 46, 56, 57, 60, 62
  defensive, 22
  funerary, 22
  stock, xvii, xviii, xx, 27, 37, 62, 120
ethnographic comparison, 10, 70, 73, 77, 78, 83, 103, 124, 125, 127-38, 139, 141, 144, 151, 158, 182, 183, 193, 194, 196, 198, 199, 200, 201, 202, 206
Evans, J. G., xiv, 12, 15, 16, 77, 94, 99, 103
ewes, 4, 183, 189
excavation, 14, 15, 19, 20, 21, 44, 46, 55, 56, 63, 83, 98, 105, 127, 141
experimentation, 71, 73, 77, 78, 79, 83, 85, 89, 90, 91, 95, 97-121, 125, 143, 144, 146, 148, 152, 154, 163, 164, 165, 166
  Butser, 90, 91, 97—121, 125, 139, 144, 146, 163, 165, 166
  Draved, 90
  Rothamsted, 90, 111, 163
  Woburn, 90, 91, 163

fallow, 85, 90, 91, 94, 95, 102, 103, 104, 108, 210
farmers, xvi, 2, 3, 15, 18, 30, 44, 72, 85, 88, 89, 95, 123, 124, 125, 146, 147, 164, 172, 186, 210, 219
Farmoor, Oxfordshire, 83
farms, 1, 2, 4, 5, 9, 34, 82, 107, 172, 210
Feachem, R. W., 18, 19, 56, 60, 62
Feddersen Wierde, Germany, 123
fences, 28, 39
Fengate, Cambridgeshire, xvi, xvii, xviii, 15, 20, 21, 27, 44
Fenton, A. J., 62, 99, 129, 138, 150, 153, 154
fertilisers, 5, 33, 107, 108, 109, 110, 111, 113, 165, 194, 198, 211, 212, 215
fields, xi, xii, xv, xvi, xviii, xxi, 9, 11, 14, 18, 19, 20, 21, 22, 24, 25, 26, 27, 28, 30, 32, 34, 35, 37, 39, 41, 44, 46,, 47, 62, 67, 78, 85, 90, 91, 92, 95, 98, 108, 109, 110, 111, 112,, 113, 118, 129, 149, 157, 163, 169, 212, 213
  'Celtic' fields, xviii, 11, 22, 26, 27, 39, 56, 98, 104, 119
field systems, xv, xvi, xx, 14, 20-30, 34, 39, 40, 41, 44, 46, 47, 56-63, 79, 105, 107
  Co. Mayo Field Systems, x, 18-20, 39, 40, 62
  Belderg Beg, xvi, 20
  Glenree, 18, 19, 20
  Glenulra, 20
field walls, xii, xiv, xxi, 18-19, 20, 28, 30, 35, 39, 56, 60, 62, 63, 212
field work, 14, 15, 47, 55, 56, 60, 62, 63
fire, *see* burning
Fisherwick, xxi, 21
fishing, xiv, 94, 220
flail, 82, 130, 153
  flailing, 149
Fleming, A., xvi, xviii, 10, 12, 14, 22, 26, 28, 46
flotation, 15, 107, 123, 127, 141
fodder, 3, 4, 70, 80, 89, 117, 128, 129, 156, 180, 183
forest / forestry, *see* woodland
forks / pitchforks, 72, 81, 155
Fowler, P. J., 70, 99, 103, 105, 182, 215
Fox, C., 79
Frazer, F. C., 175
furrows, 56, 78, 83, 101, 104, 212
Fyfield Down, Wiltshire, 33

Gates, T., 19, 21, 47
geology, 1, 33, 120, 121
Glastonbury, Somerset, xx, 206
Glob, P. V., 74, 99, 100, 101, 102
goat, 170, 171, 172, 182, 195, 198, 200, 201, 202, 204, 210, 219
granary, 127
grass, x, xiii, xv, xviii, 1, 2, 4, 16, 22, 83, 103, 107, 110, 146, 155, 157, 194, 198, 213
Grauballe burial, Denmark, 156-8
grazing, x, xiii, xiii, xvi, xviii, xxi, 1, 2, 3, 4, 16, 22, 28, 33, 46, 88, 89, 92, 94, 107, 182, 183, 210, 212
Grigg, D. B., 94, 95
Grigson, C., 176, 178, 179, 180
Grimes Graves, Norfolk, 169, 170, 171, 172, 173, 174, 175, 176, 178, 179, 180, 221, 222
Gussage All Saints, Dorset, 15
Gwithian, Cornwall, 20, 39, 56

Halstatt, Austria, 186
Hambledon Hill / Stepleton, Dorset, xii, 169, 170, 172, 173, 174, 175, 176, 178, 219, 220, 222
hand digging, xii, 20, 108
Hansen, H-O., 71, 78, 99
Harcourt, R. A., 169, 173, 174, 178, 179
Harding, D. W., 11, 57, 60, 182
Harris, D. R., 94, 95

harrow, 73
harvest, 32, 72, 79, 81, 83, 90, 98, 108, 111, 112, 115, 117, 118, 119, 120, 152, 163, 164, 166
  harvesting, 6, 66, 67, 71, 72, 79-82, 90, 112-16, 117, 126, 129, 138, 142, 145, 146, 147, 148-53, 163
Hatt, G., 210
Hawk's Hill, Surrey, 213
hedges, 28, 32, 33
  hedgeing, 67
Helbaek, H., xi, xvi, xix, 107, 112, 156, 157
Hembury, Devon, ix
henges, xii, 14, 15, 40, 169, 172, 173, 174, 175, 178, 180
Herity, M., 18, 19, 47
Hibbert, F. A., ix
Higham, C. F. W., 171, 172, 175, 176, 178, 179, 221
Highland Zone, xvi, xix, xx, xxi, 12, 18
hillforts, xx, 14, 35, 56, 57, 60, 83
  Chesters, Drem, East Lothian, 57-60
  Danebury, Hants, 15, 144
Hillman, G., xviii, 175
hoards
  grain, 148, 156
  metal, 70, 83
Hockham Mere, East Anglia, xii
hoe, xii, 16, 66, 71, 78
  hoeing, 108, 112, 115, 148
  mattock hoe, 100, 101, 102, 103, 108, 212, 213
horse, 170, 193, 210, 214, 219
Horslip Long Barrow, Wiltshire, x
Hoskins, W. G., 9, 33, 35
Hubbard, R. N. L. B., 124
hunting, xiv, 94, 193, 200
hut circles, 46, 62
  see also Tormore, Arran

infield/outfield system, 37, 39, 62, 89, 215
Invasion Hypothesis, xvi, xviii, 30
Iron Age, xi, xviii, 46, 62, 67, 70, 71, 73, 79, 80, 97, 105, 106, 107, 108, 110, 111, 112, 117, 119, 120, 138, 139, 144, 146, 147, 154, 155, 156, 182, 183, 186, 187, 188, 189, 191, 196, 197, 203, 206, 207, 208, 213
Isles of Scilly, 12, 39, 44, 47
Itford Hill, Sussex, 11
Iversen, J., 85, 86, 95

Jarlshof, Shetland, 198, 214
Jewell, P. A., 175, 176, 177, 178, 220
Johnson, N., xvi, 19, 47
Jones, G., 130, 151, 156
Jones, M., 139, 144, 145, 146, 148
Jones, M. U., 15, 20, 21, 22, 47

Karpathos, Aegean, 151
Kestor, Devon, xxi
Kilellan Farm, Islay, Argyll, 56
Kilham Long Barrow, Yorkshire, x
Kilpatrick, Arran, Argyll, 55, 60
King, J. E., 175
Knap of Howar, Orkney, xiv
knife, 70, 72, 79, 196, 200

lactase, 218-19
lactose, 218-19, 221
lambs, 183
land, ixi, x, xiii, xvi, xviii, xix, 1, 2, 3, 5, 14, 16, 25, 30, 33, 47, 89, 95, 106, 107, 143, 147, 211, 212, 215
  carrying capacity, 147
  exhaustion, xii, xvii, 20, 90, 109
  improvement, 3, 4, 28, 30, 33, 67, 89, 90
  use, xvii, 1-3, 44, 172
land allotment, *see* boundary systems
land division, *see* boundary systems, Field Systems
landscape, xi, xii, xvii, xviii, xix, xxi, 9, 10, 11-12, 14, 20, 26, 28, 30, 31, 33, 34, 35, 39, 46, 47, 60, 63, 66, 70, 105, 106
  'landscape archaeology', 47
  landscape resource management, 9
Lawford, Essex, 22-6
Lawton, Essex, 27-8
Laxton, 30, 46
lazy-bedding, 20, 78
leather, 106, 155, 182, 191, 194, 199-200, 201, 203
Legge, A. J., xi, xii, xvii, xviii, 218
Lerche, G., 70, 212
Leser, P., 37, 99, 125, 148
Linnaeus, 88
livestock, xi, xvii, 1, 3, 4, 5, 28, 33, 37, 44, 46, 60, 97, 117, 182, 183, 189, 194, 198, 201, 219, 220, 221
Lowland Zone, xvi, xix, 12
Llyn Fawr, Wales, 79
lynchet, 19, 30, 39, 105

maceheads, 78
machair, xiv, 56
Maiden Castle, Dorset, 173
manure, 89, 94, 95, 110, 144, 198, 210-15
  manuring, 16, 44, 89, 90, 91, 94, 95, 110, 198, 210-15
marginal land, xii, xvii, 33, 105
Markham, G., 129
Maurizio, A., 125, 129, 138, 154, 156
Meare, Somerset, 156, 191, 192
meat, 172, 174, 182, 192, 193, 194, 195, 201, 220, 221
megalithic architecture, 39, 94
Mellars, P., 94
Mercer, R. J., 12, 18, 48, 60, 169
Merino sheep, 188, 189, 191
Message, M., 171, 175, 176, 178
midden, 55, 143, 144, 170, 211, 212, 215
Miket, R., 11, 12
milk, 4, 172, 180, 182, 193, 194, 195, 196, 199, 218-20, 221, 222
  milking, 195, 219-20, 221
Mingay, G. E., 30, 32, 34, 35
mixed farming, 34, 67, 182
modern farming systems, 1-6, 18
Monk, M. A., 144
Montelius, S., 89
Mouflon sheep, 184
Moulton Park, Northampton, xx
Mount Pleasant, Dorset, 15, 169, 173, 175
Mucking, Essex, 15, 20-2, 24, 47
Munro, R., 9, 11

Neolithic, x, xi, xiii, xvi, xix, 39, 85, 87, 88, 89, 90, 94, 95, 104, 139, 141, 147, 158, 169, 170, 172, 173, 175, 178, 179, 180, 182, 183, 184, 191, 192, 193, 199, 200, 201, 202, 204, 219, 222
Early, xi, xiv, xv, xvi, 39, 155, 169, 182
Middle, x, xi, xiii, xiv, xv, 39
Late, xiii, xvi, xviii, 40, 55, 79, 169, 213
Neolithic Revolution, 30
New Archaeology, 10
North Bersted, Sussex, xx
North Mains, Strathallan, Perthshire, xv, 55
Northton, Harris, xiv

oats, xix, 129, 140, 150
Ogmore, Glamorganshire, xviii
Overton Down, Wiltshire, 41
oxen, x, 74-7, 78, 99-100, 103, 219
see also cattle

palaeo-environmental evidence, xii, 15, 16, 67, 83
Palaeolithic, 196, 198, 199, 200, 204
palynology, x, xii, xiv, 20, 37, 85-8, 91, 94, 95, 106, 208
parching, 153-4
Parrington, M., xxi, 12
pasture, ix, 1, 2, 3, 4, 18, 27, 41, 62, 67, 146, 169
pastoral economy, xiv, xv, xxi, 34, 46, 67, 70, 83, 105, 141, 158, 169, 182, 193, 219
Payne, S., 170
Pazirik, Altai, 186, 202
peas, xiii, xix, 5, 125, 129, 170
peat, x, xiii, xv, xvi, xviii, xxi, 55, 75, 156, 211, 213, 214, 215
Pembrey Mountain, Dyfed, Wales, 156
Percival, J., 147, 148, 164, 211
Pickering, J., 14
pig, x, xiii, xix, xx, 3, 5, 16, 94-5, 170, 172, 173, 182, 193, 196, 211, 220
Piggott, S., x, 9, 10, 12, 28, 55, 210
pits, 107, 138, 140, 144, 200
'pit dwelling', 46
Plant Breeding Institute, Cambridge, 107
plant remains, x, xix, 67, 123, 124, 126, 127, 130, 139, 140, 155, 170, 174
plantain, xiv, 86, 157
plots, 14, 55-6, 57, 60, 62, 90, 163, 164
plough, xi, 66, 67, 73, 83, 94, 99, 103, 139, 145, 212-13
ploughing, 18, 22, 27, 55, 57, 60, 73, 74, 77, 78, 89, 90, 92, 94, 98, 99, 101, 103, 104, 115, 145, 146, 147, 158, 219
cross ploughing, 16, 99
see also traction
plucking
harvest, 113, 139, 151, 152, 153
sheep, 182, 186, 187, 203
population, ix, xiii, xiv, xv, xvii, xviii, xix, xxi, 31, 44, 221
pottery, x, xi, xvi, xix, 200, 205
Beaker pottery, 196
seed impressions in, xvi, 106, 107
poultry, 3, 5, 94, 211
pounding, 154
pruning, 79
Pryor, F., xvii, 15, 20, 21, 27
pulses, 142, 146, 153

Quanterness, Orkney, xiv
quern, xxi, 154

rainfall, ix, xi, xiii, xiv, xvi, xvii, xviii, xx, 1, 4-5, 129, 130, 147, 150
rake, 81
raking, 153
rams, 70, 182, 183, 187, 189
reaping, 79, 112, 113, 116, 117, 138, 140, 149, 150, 151, 152, 153, 158
Rees, S., 12, 103
Reynolds, P. J., 12, 90, 91, 95, 125, 138, 139, 144, 145, 146, 148, 152
rig and furrow, 20, 55-6, 62
Riley, D. N., 14
riverine locations, x, xiv, xvi, xviii, xx, 21-7, 39, 105, 120
Kennet Valley, xviii
Thames Valley, xvi, xxi, 12, 15, 21-2
rogueing, *see* weeding
Roman period, ix, xxi, 11, 15, 16, 34, 72, 78, 79, 105, 107, 138, 141, 144, 146, 154, 155, 156, 182, 186, 189, 191, 193, 194, 195, 200, 201, 203, 204, 205, 206, 207, 219, 220
Roman Forts, 60, 83, 202
Housesteads, 202
Newstead, 202
Vindolanda, 188, 189, 191
roots, 94, 99, 103, 115, 145, 150, 164, 166
Rosinish, Benbecula, Outer Hebrides, 12, 39, 55, 56
Roth, H. L., 206
rye, xix, 6, 89, 90, 129, 150

Salisbury Plain, Wiltshire, xviii, 26
Scord of Brouster, Shetland, xiv, 71
scythes, 71, 72, 80, 83, 150
seed, x, 90, 104, 107, 108, 109, 111, 112, 115, 116, 117, 119, 124, 126, 140, 142, 144, 145, 146, 148, 149, 150, 151, 152, 153, 155, 156, 157, 163, 166, 170, 174, 214
seed bed preparation / seed drills, 98, 101, 104, 108, 148
sieves, 72, 82, 155, 156, 157
sieving, 125, 138, 142, 143, 155, 156
settlement, x, xii, xiv, xvii, xix, xix, xx, 9, 14, 20, 21, 34, 35, 39, 56-7, 60, 62, 87, 88, 106-7, 117, 121, 123, 127, 128, 131, 138, 141, 142, 143, 146, 157, 169, 170, 174, 175, 180, 182, 183
Seymour, J. and S., 94-5
shares, 70, 71, 73, 100, 101, 102, 103
Ashville, Oxfordshire, 70
shears, 182, 186, 203, 207
shearing, 187, 203
sheep, xiv, xvii, xviii, xix, xx, xxi, 3, 4, 89, 94, 95, 170, 171, 172, 173, 182-208, 210, 211, 219
sheepfolds, 46
penning, 198
Shotton, F. W., xix, 16
shovels, 72, 82, 155

Shurton Hill, Shetland, xiv, 62
sickles, 66, 67, 70, 711, 79, 112, 113, 129, 149, 150
Silver, I. A., 171
Sims, R. E., xii
Skaill, Orkney, 77
Skara Brae, Orkney, xiv, 180, 192
slash and burn system, 85-95, 212
Sluggans Moss, Ballylurgan, Co. Antrim, xvi
Smith, A. G., xii, xvi
Smith, C., xx, 12, 21
Smith, I. F., xi, xiii, 18
Soay sheep, 183, 184, 186, 187, 189, 191, 194, 198, 203
soil, ix, x, xi, xii, xv, xvii, xix, xxi, 1, 3, 4, 16, 18, 39, 56, 77, 78, 88, 89, 90, 94, 95, 98, 99, 100, 101, 102, 103, 104, 105, 106, 107, 108, 110, 115, 119, 124, 139, 145, 147, 148, 157, 163, 164, 165, 211, 213
  analysis, 3, 109
  impoverishment, xvii, xix, 20, 88, 110
Somerset Levels, Somerset, ix, xiv, xx, xxi, 15, 16, 81
Sowthistle, 116, 118
sowing, 78, 85, 90, 104, 108, 110, 111, 112, 139, 146, 147, 148, 163, 164, 214
spade, 56, 70, 78, 108, 212, 213
  spade cultivation, xv, 16, 20, 55-6, 78, 100, 108
  Hama traction spade, 70
  Satrup Moor traction spade, 70, 78
spinning, 196, 202-6
  wheel, 206
  spindle whorls, xxi, 196, 205
Stannon Down, Cornwall, xviii
Stanton Harcourt, Oxfordshire, xii
Star Carr, Yorkshire, 175-7, 178
Steensberg, A., 11, 70, 77, 79, 80, 85, 88, 89, 90, 95, 100
St Joseph, J. K., 25, 47
stock, *see* livestock
stomach contents, 123, 156-8
Stonehenge, Wiltshire, 26
storage, 5, 46, 117, 131, 138, 140, 142, 144, 149, 151, 153, 154, 155, 195, 201
straw, 116-19, 140, 142, 144, 145, 148, 149, 150, 151, 152, 153, 155, 158, 164, 166, 211
strips, 56, 57
stubble, 16, 94
sub-peat wall systems, 19, 20, 39, 62
Sumburgh, Shetland, 55, 77
surplus production, 47, 111, 120, 179
swidden system, 37, 39

Tauber, H., 86-8, 95
Taylor, C., 35
Tell Abu Hureyra, Syria, 141
temperature, 1, 109, 147
textile, 182, 184, 186, 187, 188, 189, 191, 193, 195, 196, 198, 202, 203, 204, 205, 206, 207
thatch, 143, 166
  thatching, 113, 117, 119, 144
The Agrarian History of England and Wales, 9, 10, 11
Thomas, C., 12, 20, 22, 39, 47, 56
tillage, 2, 16, 18, 19, 22, 62, 78, 104, 145, 147, 157, 212
threshing, 72, 82, 128, 130, 131, 142, 146, 149, 150, 151, 152, 153, 155, 157
  floor, 150
  sledge, 129, 130, 153
tillers, 113, 147, 148, 150
  tillering, 90, 108
tilth, 55, 94, 99, 101, 102, 103, 108, 211
Tollund burial, Denmark, 156-8
topography, 1, 24
Tormore, Arran, Argyll, 149
trackways, ix, xiv, 105, 107
traction, x, 20, 70, 73-7, 78, 94, 99, 100
  see also ploughing
Troels-Smith, J., 86, 95
Troldebjerg, Denmark, 171, 172, 175, 176, 178, 179, 221
turf, 89, 112, 211, 212, 213, 214, 215

Uerpmann, H-P., 175
Underhoull, Shetland, 214
unenclosed platform settlements, 56
uprooting, 71-2, 79, 148-51, 152, 153

Val Camonica, Italy, 102, 103
vetches, 129

Wainwright, G. J., ix, 12, 15
waterlogging, 123, 127, 147, 207
  waterlogged remains, xii, 123
wear analysis, 70-1, 72, 73, 78, 83, 103
weaving, 187, 196, 202-3, 204, 206
weeds, 90, 91, 92, 94, 95, 108, 111, 112, 115, 117, 118, 119, 124, 126, 127, 139, 140, 141, 142, 144, 145, 146, 148, 149, 150, 151, 152, 153, 155, 156, 157, 158, 164, 174
  weeding, 91, 92, 94, 108, 112, 139, 147, 148, 149, 151, 152, 153, 163
Weier, Switzerland, 86-8
Wessex, xxi, 11, 12, 14, 28, 34, 39, 44, 46
  Wessex Culture, 39
wet sieving, 107
wheat, xi, xvii, xviii, xix, 4, 5, 6, 20, 90, 91, 107, 110, 111, 113, 118, 125, 129, 142, 143, 146, 147, 148, 150, 157, 164, 165, 166, 170
  glume wheats, 125, 138, 142, 143, 148, 149, 150, 152, 153, 155, 157
  einkorn, xi, 129
  emmer, xi, xviii, xix, 90, 91, 104, 107, 108, 109, 110, 111, 113, 129, 130, 138, 142, 146, 147, 148, 151, 152, 154, 156, 157, 164, 174
  spelt, xix, 104, 107, 108, 109, 110, 111, 113, 129, 142, 143, 144, 154, 156, 157, 164
Whittington, G., xiv, 12, 39, 62
Whittle, A., xii, xiv, 60, 71
Wild, J. P., 189, 191, 202, 203, 204, 206
Wilderspool, 138, 143, 156
Willerby Wold Long Barrow, Yorkshire, x
Windmill Hill, Wiltshire, x, xi, xii, 169, 172, 173, 175, 176, 178, 179, 180
winnowing, 72, 82, 130, 131, 153, 155
woodland, ix, x, xi, xii, xiii, 3, 9, 16, 85, 86-9, 94, 102, 103, 182, 212
  regeneration, ix, xii, xiii, xv, xvi, 86-8, 94

wool, xvii, xx, 182, 183, 184, 185, 186, 187, 188, 189, 191, 193, 194, 196, 199, 201-2, 203, 204, 205, 207, 208
fleece, 182, 183, 184, 186, 187, 188, 189, 191, 193, 201, 202, 203, 204, 205
hairy fibre, 184, 185, 186, 187, 188, 189, 191, 201, 203
kemps, 183, 184, 185, 186, 187

yoke, 74-7, 100, 103
yields, xix, 4, 6, 85, 89, 90, 91, 98, 104, 106, 108, 109, 110, 111, 112, 120, 127, 146, 147, 148, 163, 164, 165, 166
improvement in, 30, 90, 163